To St. Louis Community College,
with appreciation for the
supportive atmosphere
allowing me to become an
author in this book. In
hopes that we may someday
make this Country safe,

FV. Powell
r of Psychology

TRANSFORMING A RAPE CULTURE

Transforming A Rape Culture

edited by

Emilie Buchwald
Pamela R. Fletcher
Martha Roth

MILKWEED EDITIONS

Milkweed Editions, 430 First Avenue North, Suite 400, Minneapolis, MN 55401

Printed in the United States of America

Published in 1993 by Milkweed Editions

Designed by Don Leeper. Typeset in Adobe Garamond by Stanton Publication Services.
Printed on Sebago Antique paper by Arcata Graphics.

97 96 95 94 93   5 4 3 2 1

Publication of this book is made possible in part through the generosity of
Penny and Mike Winton and the James R. Thorpe Foundation.

Additional support for Milkweed Editions has been provided by the Elmer and Eleanor Andersen
Foundation; Dayton Hudson Foundation for Dayton's and Target Stores; First Bank System
Foundation; General Mills Foundation; Honeywell Foundation; The McKnight Foundation; Andrew
W. Mellon Foundation; the Minnesota State Arts Board through an appropriation by the Minnesota
State Legislature; the Literature and Challenge Programs of the National Endowment for the Arts;
Northwest Area Foundation; I. A. O'Shaughnessy Foundation; Piper Jaffray Companies;
Beverly J. and John A. Rollwagen Fund of the Minneapolis Foundation; Star Tribune/Cowles Media
Foundation; Surdna Foundation; Lila Wallace-Reader's Digest Literary Publishers Marketing
Development Program, funded through a grant to the Council of Literary Magazines
and Small Presses; and generous individuals.

Library of Congress Cataloging-in-Publication Data

Transforming a rape culture / edited by Emilie Buchwald, Pamela Fletcher, Martha Roth.
    p.   cm.
Includes bibliographical references and index.
ISBN 0-915943-06-9
    1. Sexual harrassment of women.   2. Rape.   3. Women—Crimes against.   I. Buchwald, Emilie.
II. Fletcher, Pamela.   III. Roth, Martha.
HV6556.T73   1993   93-5693
306.7—dc20   CIP

To those who have suffered sexual violence,
and to the not-yet-born
who are entitled to live
in a violence-free society

PREAMBLE

WHAT IS A RAPE CULTURE? It is a complex of beliefs that encourages male sexual aggression and supports violence against women. It is a society where violence is seen as sexy and sexuality as violent. In a rape culture women perceive a continuum of threatened violence that ranges from sexual remarks to sexual touching to rape itself. A rape culture condones physical and emotional terrorism against women *as the norm.*

In a rape culture both men and women assume that sexual violence is a fact of life, inevitable as death or taxes. This violence, however, is neither biologically nor divinely ordained. Much of what we accept as inevitable is in fact the expression of values and attitudes that can change.

More than half of reported rapes are committed by someone the survivor knows. Once we as a society take in the meaning of that fact, we will begin to understand the deeper issues of power, sexuality, and gender relationships surrounding sexual violence.

Most of these essays were written at the editors' invitation to provide models or processes for change. *Transforming a Rape Culture* involves imaginative leaps from our present state of institutionalized violence to a future that is safer and more just. We must summon our imaginations for this task, because history and society have so few precedents for us.

When the editors held focus groups among women and men, white and of color, to help us think our way into this book, we found great depth of concern and a commonality of experience that statistics cannot begin to reflect. Almost everyone has been touched by rape culture.

The result is a sourcebook of visions for a future without rape, strategies to achieve it, and current programs of action that are having some success in changing the climate that encourages sexual violence. A few previously published pieces add perspective. This book is intended to spark private reflection, spur public discussion, and lead to action.

CONTENTS

Contents

Visions & Possibilities

Contents

ACKNOWLEDGEMENTS

AS EDITORS we came together to make a book that would take back the night and the day. A book that would look anew at our rape culture to imagine how to transform it; a book that points the way to a safer world. This book.

Though we faced a heavy task, it became lighter with the assistance of the many individuals who shared our vision to remake a violent society. The board and staff of Milkweed Editions have been committed to the aspirations and goals of this book from its inception several years ago. We thank the members of the board, chaired by Susan Borneman, for their time, expertise, and energies, freely and generously given: Susan Blaser, Robert Chandler, Judith K. Healey, David A. Houghtby, Jane Johnston, Randy Lebedoff, Dustin Macgregor, Dan Odegard, Michael O'Shaughnessy, Edmund J. Phelps, Jr., Lynn Truesdell, and Brenda Wehle. For their dedication to *Transforming a Rape Culture,* and for their significant contributions to the process of getting it out into the world, we gratefully acknowledge the Milkweed staff: Teresa Bonner, Fiona S. Grant, Arlinda Keeley, Diane M. Murphy, Beryl B. Tanis, and Ellen E. Watters.

Kris Hoover ably guided us as we began our study of the literature of sexual assault. For graciously moderating the focus groups that contributed ideas and strategies, we thank Jan Smaby; Dustin Macgregor; Sigurd Hoppe; and Alice Lynch at Black, Indian, Hispanic, and Asian Women in Action (BIHA). For contributing time, insight, and suggestions to the focus groups, we thank each of the participants. For generously hosting our focus groups in their homes and offices, we thank Marion Etzweiler and the Minneapolis Foundation, Sigurd Hoppe, and Randy Lebedoff.

For consulting with us about the movement against sexual violence and other related issues, we thank Nancy Fride Biele, Patricia Faunce, Jane Gilgun, Donna Halvorsen, Alice Lynch, and Naomi Scheman. For pointing us toward others who could assist us with this work, we thank Russ Funk, Kay Leigh Hagen, Michael Kimmel, Myriam Miedzian, Kathleen Ritter, and John Stoltenberg.

For providing us with a year of invaluable assistance while she was a Milkweed intern, we are sincerely indebted to Christina Alburas—for her suggestions in our brainstorming, for her research, and for sharing with us her broad knowledge of gender and multicultural issues. We thank Milkweed interns Julie Buresh, Ellen Hayman, Eliza Herman, Mary Mulcahy, and information-gatherer Dana Buchwald for their work. We appreciate Fiona Grant's organizational abilities in coordinating the bits and pieces of this book as it came together. For their skill and patience with our long process, we thank Don Leeper and the staff of Stanton Publication Services.

Our thanks also go to the Law Enforcement Support Staff at the Bureau of Justice for assistance in checking and updating rape statistics, and to Ronet Bachman of the Bureau of Justice Statistics for her insights about and updates to the rape statistics gathered by the National Crime Victimization Survey.

For their support and love, we thank our families and friends. And for their hope, courage, and belief in change, we thank our readers.

EDITORS' PREFACE

TRANSFORMING A RAPE CULTURE is about changing fundamental attitudes and values. These changes include rethinking the
nurture and education of children, power-sharing between genders,
and revising the demeaning, sexualized images of women presented in
popular media.

Outcries against sexual violence appear in newspapers and on TV
when the details of a particularly brutal sex crime are made known, but
the reality of relentless, everyday sexual violence is ignored. Editorial
responses call for more severe punishments for rapists, for longer prison
sentences, even for the death penalty, as if escalation of punishment
could in and of itself lead to significant change. Incarceration and treatment programs for offenders are merely holding actions to deal with
today's violent men. The rate of recidivism indicates that these measures
have not proven to be successful deterrents or solutions. Until we identify and confront the issues that lead to sexual violence, we will need more
prisons. Protesters against sexual violence seldom address the fact that
underlying attitudes toward women in our culture are causal—a fact that
many of the essays in this book discuss—*and that these attitudes can be
changed.*

As we prepared to work on this book, we spent months reading the
large and growing body of factual literature on sexual violence, beginning with Susan Brownmiller's landmark 1975 work *Against Our Will:
Women, Men, and Rape* . Brownmiller's book established decisively that
rape is a crime of violence rather than passion. Throughout history,
rapes have been treated as pardonable, sometimes even welcome, spasms
of uncontrollable lust—a view that utterly ignores the woman who has
been raped and silences her response. In our century, women's voices at
last are being heard on this subject.

From Brownmiller's book we went on to the stacks of books we
found in library searches and bookstore expeditions: theories of causali-

ty; studies of rapists and of survivors; books on the relationship between pornography and sexual violence (ranging from those who deny any causal connection to those who believe that pornographic materials are practice manuals for rape); works on the intersection of racism and sexual violence; studies of gang rape; books about incest and the sexual abuse of children; articles about sexual harassment; books about how women can avoid rape and books about self-defense; as well as the latest statistical data that show continuing increases every year in reports of sexual violence.

Our reading plunged us deeper and deeper into despair. We began to sink in the morass of hopelessness and frustration such reading inevitably evokes. We knew we needed to change our way of thinking about the issue from one of reaction to a proactive search for possible solutions. At one of several focus groups that we held in our community, women responded with enthusiasm to placing the emphasis on transformation. More than one person told us, "We don't want to live in it as it is anymore. We've got to *change* this culture."

So we shifted our focus from the violent present—which could have filled many volumes—to a vision of possibility. What would it take, we asked, to build a future without rape? We saw with increasing clarity the extent of the problem: on TV programs and ads, in newspapers, novels, poetry, songs, opera, rock, and rap, on every billboard, in every shop window, on every museum wall we found evidence of rape culture. We began to understand the ways girls and boys grow up to be victims and rapists, and we saw how training for this begins early—before nursery school, before birth, in most cases, with our own parental conceptions of the (highly artificial) distinctions between male and female.

We as a society claim to deplore the sexual violence that is so markedly characteristic of our time, yet we rear our sons and daughters in such ignorance of their sexuality that many confuse pleasure with pain and domination. We omit the word *pleasure* from sex education altogether. Sexual arousal is the most undertheorized topic in human psychology. Women who have been attacked feel shame at their victimization, and other women collude by blaming them. We present male and female as polar opposites, instead of close variations of a human model. We could do no worse if we set out deliberately to promote rape.

The transformation of a rape culture demands a revolution of values. Our violence-producing and violence-accepting attitudes must change, because our acquired taste for violence only fosters our adaptation to the culture's terror and dehumanization. In fear, we rear our children as we ourselves have been reared, merely to exist as unwilling participants, seldom questioning the vile conditions of life in a country where rape and fear of rape are a means of social control.

As editors we acknowledge our debt to the writing and activism of the past several decades that opened the eyes of many to the misogyny and gender terrorism that create a rape culture. No book can touch upon every arena, nor does this one claim to. To bring about positive change, the public conversation must become general and ongoing, open to new ideas.

Every man, woman, and child is negatively affected by living in a rape culture in which children, females, and some males are perceived as sexual prey. No one is safe as long as anyone is physically and spiritually violated. Everyone is responsible to her/himself and to society to do what is possible to change the status quo. We must imagine a different world. If we can dream of a safe place, surely we can build one. As editors of *Transforming a Rape Culture*, we challenge our readers to help us make these changes. Please join us in envisioning and building a humane future.

Emilie Buchwald
Pamela R. Fletcher
Martha Roth
1993

LIVING IN A RAPE CULTURE

In addition to the numbers and facts included here, stories of sexual violence, of tragedy and survival, could have filled these pages. Instead, we have chosen voices of resistance. In 1983, Andrea Dworkin called for a day without rape; such a day has not yet dawned. Nor will it ever come to be without ongoing efforts to spur change.

ARE WE REALLY LIVING IN A RAPE CULTURE?

Not a day goes by without a story in the media about sexual violence against women and children. Do rape and sexual assault truly permeate this society, or are we hearing about the sensationalized, isolated cases? Has the rate of sexual violence really increased? Current statistics about the incidence of sexual violence include two programs administered by the U.S. Department of Justice—the Uniform Crime Report and the National Crime Victimization Survey—and other recent studies focused on rape and child sexual abuse. What do these studies and the analyses of their numbers tell us?

The Uniform Crime Report (UCR)[1]**:** The FBI's Uniform Crime Report data is compiled from over 16,000 law enforcement agencies covering 96 percent of the nation's population. Baseless or unfounded complaints are excluded from crime counts. A frequent, recurring criticism of the UCR figures has been that rape is notoriously underreported to the police; thus, the UCR figures represent only a portion of the actual number of rape victimizations.[2]

• In 1991, the UCR recorded 106,593 rapes. That's 292 rapes each day of the year, or 12 rapes every hour, or 1 rape every 5 minutes.

• The UCR reported 1.5 million female survivors of forcible rape or forcible rape attempts in this country, during the twenty year period of 1972 to 1991 alone. These are the most conservative numbers available and should be considered the baseline or minimum rape figure.

• The number of rapes reported to the UCR has risen steadily over most of the past twenty years: From 1972 to 1991, there was a 128 percent increase in the number of reported rapes. During the same time period, the forcible rape rate per 100,000 inhabitants increased 88 percent.

The National Crime Victimization Survey (NCVS)[3], the largest nationally representative, household-interview crime survey in the United States, is administered by the Bureau of the Census for the Bureau of Justice Statistics.

• The NCVS reported 171,420 rapes for 1991. <u>That's 469 rapes each day of the year, or 19 each hour, or 1 rape every 3.5 minutes.</u>

• The NCVS recorded <u>2.3 million rapes</u> of females during the years from 1973 to 1987. Thus, in a fifteen-year period, the NCVS recorded almost 1 million more cases of rape than the twenty-year UCR numbers. For a comparable twenty-year period, the number of female rape survivors in this country would be <u>3 million women for that twenty-year period alone.</u>

• Intimates (husbands, ex-spouses, boy friends, ex-boyfriends) committed 20 percent of rapes, acquaintances 50 percent, and strangers 30 percent of the rapes reported to NCVS between 1987–1991.[4]

Rape in America: A Report to the Nation[5] The National Women's Study (NWS), issued in 1992, was conducted by the Crime Victims Research and Treatment Center. The respondents were women 18 years and older at the time of the initial survey.

• Thirteen percent of women surveyed reported having been victims of at least one completed rape. Thirty-nine percent of this group had been raped more than once. The majority of rape cases occurred during childhood and adolescence, with 29 percent of all forcible rapes occurring when the victim was less than eleven years old, and another 32 percent of rapes occurring between 11 and 17 years of age.

• The NWS found that <u>only 22 percent of rape victims were assaulted by someone they had never seen before or did not know well.</u> Nine percent were raped by husbands or ex-husbands, 11 percent by their fathers or stepfathers, 10 percent by boyfriends or ex-boyfriends, 16 percent by other relatives, and 29 percent by other non-relatives, such as friends and neighbors.

• Only 16 percent, or approximately one out of about six rapes, were ever reported to police. If the Uniform Crime Report numbers represent only one of about six rapes actually committed, the true number of rapes in the United States each year is likely to be in the range of 639,500. <u>At that rate over a twenty-year period, there would be more than 12 million American women rape survivors.</u>

Other Facts about Sexual Abuse and Rape Prosecution and Conviction:

• The National Committee for Prevention of Child Abuse in its 1991 survey of child protective service agencies listed 404,100 reports of child sexual abuse. These reports do not take into account sexual abuse by non-caretakers.[6]

• About 16,000 women a year have abortions as a result of rape or incest.[7]

• One in 100 rapists is sentenced to more than one year in prison.[8]

• Almost one quarter of convicted rapists are not sentenced to prison but instead are released on probation.[8]

Are we really living in a rape culture? Rape is a pervasive fact of American life, and its incidence is growing dramatically. The most conservative figures show an 88 percent increase in the rate of forcible rape per 100,000 inhabitants over the past twenty years. There are, at minimum, 105,000 rapes annually in the United States and perhaps more than 630,000. In the time it took to read these statistics at least one person has been raped. Over a twenty-year period, as many as 12 million women and children—nearly 10 percent of the current female population of the United States—have been raped. Both the victims and their attackers carry the fact of rape through their lives and, one can argue, through their families' lives as well. We will continue to live in a rape culture until our society understands and chooses to eradicate the sources of sexual violence in this culture.

—The Editors

NOTES

1. Federal Bureau of Investigation, United States Department of Justice, *Crime in the United States, 1991,* August 30, 1992, pp. 14, 17, 24, 58, Table 1.—Index of Crimes, United States, 1972–1991.

2. Larry Baron and Murray A. Straus, *Four Theories of Rape in American Society* (New Haven: Yale University Press, 1989), p. 27.

3. A National Crime Victimization Survey Report, *Criminal Victimization in the United States, 1991,* December 1992, NCJ-139563, pp. 72–75, 79, 148–149; United States Department of Justice, Bureau of Justice Statistics, *Female Victims of Violent Crime,* by Caroline Wolf Harlow, January 1991, NCJ-126826, pp. 1–3, 7.

4. Ronet Bachman, "Female Victims of Violence," paper presented at the 1993 Annual Meeting of the American Society of Criminology, November 1993, p. 23, Table 11.

5. National Victim Center and the Crime Victims Research and Treatment Center, *Rape in America. A Report to the Nation,* April 23, 1992, pp. 1–16. A complete Methodology Overview is given on page 15.

6. The National Resource Center on Child Sexual Abuse, brochure, 107 Lincoln Street, Huntsville, Alabama 35801, 1-800-KIDS-006.

7. "Facts in Brief: Abortion in the United States," The Alan Guttmacher Institute, 1993, p. 1.

8. Report of the Majority Staff of the Senate Judiciary Committee, "The Response to Rape: Detours on the Road to Equal Justice," May 1993, pp. 11, 25–60.

I WANT A TWENTY-FOUR-HOUR TRUCE DURING WHICH THERE IS NO RAPE

by Andrea Dworkin

It is astonishing that in all our worlds of feminism and antisexism we never talk seriously about ending rape. Ending it. Stopping it. No more. No more rape.

This was a speech given at the Midwest Regional Conference of the National Organization for Changing Men in the fall of 1983 in St. Paul, Minnesota. One of the organizers kindly sent me a tape and a transcript of my speech. The magazine of the men's movement, M., published it. I was teaching in Minneapolis. This was before Catharine MacKinnon and I had proposed or developed the civil rights approach to pornography as a legislative strategy. Lots of people were in the audience who later became key players in the fight for the civil rights bill. I didn't know them then. It was an audience of about 500 men, with scattered women. I spoke from notes and was actually on my way to Idaho—an eight-hour trip each way (because of bad air connections) to give a one-hour speech on Art—fly out Saturday, come back Sunday, can't talk more than one hour or you'll miss the only plane leaving that day, you have to run from the podium to the car for the two-hour drive to the plane. Why would a militant feminist under this kind of pressure stop off on her way to the airport to say hi to 500 men? In a sense, this was a feminist dream-come-true. What would you say to 500 men if you could? This is what I said, how I used my chance. The men reacted with considerable love and support and also with considerable anger. Both. I hurried out to get my plane, the first hurdle for getting to Idaho. Only one man in the 500 threatened me physically. He was stopped by a woman bodyguard (and friend) who had accompanied me.

I HAVE THOUGHT a great deal about how a feminist, like myself, addresses an audience primarily of political men who say that they are antisexist. And I thought a lot about whether there should be a qualitative difference in the kind of speech I address to you. And then I found myself incapable of pretending that I really believe that that qualitative difference exists. I have watched the men's movement for many years. I am close with some of the people who participate in it. I can't come here as a friend even though I might very much want to. What I would like to do is to scream: and in that scream I would have the screams of the raped, and the sobs of the battered; and even worse, in the center of that scream I would have the deafening sound of women's silence, that silence into which we are born because we are women and in which most of us die.

And if there would be a plea or a question or a human address in that scream, it would be this: why are you so slow? Why are you so slow to understand the simplest things; not the complicated ideological things.

You understand those. *The simple things.* The clichés. Simply that women are human to precisely the degree and quality that you are.

And also: that we do not have time. We women. We don't have forever. Some of us don't have another week or another day to take time for you to discuss whatever it is that will enable you to go out into those streets and do something. We are very close to death. All women are. And we are very close to rape and we are very close to beating. And we are inside a system of humiliation from which there is no escape for us. We use statistics not to try to quantify the injuries, but to convince the world that those injuries even exist. Those statistics are not abstractions. It is easy to say, "Ah, the statistics, somebody writes them up one way and somebody writes them up another way." That's true. But I hear about the rapes one by one by one by one by one, which is also how they happen. Those statistics are not abstract to me. Every three minutes a woman is being raped. Every eighteen seconds a woman is being beaten. There is nothing abstract about it. It is happening right now as I am speaking.

And it is happening for a simple reason. There is nothing complex and difficult about the reason. Men are doing it, because of the kind of power that men have over women. That power is real, concrete, exercised from one body to another body, exercised by someone who feels he has a right to exercise it, exercised in public and exercised in private. It is the sum and substance of women's oppression.

It is not done 5,000 miles away or 3,000 miles away. It is done here and it is done now and it is done by the people in this room as well as by other contemporaries: our friends, our neighbors, people that we know. Women don't have to go to school to learn about power. We just have to be women, walking down the street or trying to get the housework done after having given one's body in marriage and then having no rights over it.

The power exercised by men day to day in life is power that is institutionalized. It is protected by law. It is protected by religion and religious practice. It is protected by universities, which are strongholds of male supremacy. It is protected by a police force. It is protected by those whom Shelley called "the unacknowledged legislators of the world": the poets, the artists. Against that power, we have silence.

It is an extraordinary thing to try to understand and confront why it is that men believe—and men do believe—that they have the right to rape.

Men may not believe it when asked. Everybody raise your hand who believes you have the right to rape. Not too many hands will go up. It's in life that men believe they have the right to force sex, which they don't call rape. And it is an extraordinary thing to try to understand that men really believe that they have the right to hit and to hurt. And it is an equally extraordinary thing to try to understand that men really believe that they have the right to buy a woman's body for the purpose of having sex: that that is a right. And it is very amazing to try to understand that men believe that the seven-billion-dollar-a-year industry that provides men with cunts is something that men have a right to.

That is the way the power of men is manifest in real life. That is what theory about male supremacy means. It means you can rape. It means you can hit. It means you can hurt. It means you can buy and sell women. It means that there is a class of people there to provide you with what you need. You stay richer than they are, so that they have to sell you sex. Not just on street corners, but in the workplace. That's another right that you can presume to have: sexual access to any woman in your environment, when you want.

Now, the men's movement suggests that men don't want the kind of power I have just described. I've actually heard explicit whole sentences to that effect. And yet, everything is a reason not to do something about changing the fact that you do have that power.

Hiding behind guilt, that's my favorite. I love that one. Oh, it's horrible, yes, and I'm so sorry. You have the time to feel guilty. We don't have the time for you to feel guilty. Your guilt is a form of acquiescence in what continues to occur. Your guilt helps keep things the way they are.

I have heard in the last several years a great deal about the suffering of men over sexism. Of course, I have heard a great deal about the suffering of men all my life. Needless to say, I have read *Hamlet*. I have read *King Lear*. I am an educated woman. I know that men suffer. This is a new wrinkle. Implicit in the idea that this is a different kind of suffering is the claim, I think, that in part you are actually suffering because of something that you know happens to someone else. That would indeed be new.

But mostly your guilt, your suffering, reduces to: gee, we really feel so bad. Everything makes men feel so bad: what you do, what you don't do, what you want to do, what you don't want to want to do but are going to do anyway. I think most of your distress is: gee, we really feel so bad. And

I'm sorry that you feel so bad—so uselessly and stupidly bad—because there is a way in which this really is your tragedy. And I don't mean because you can't cry. And I don't mean because there is no real intimacy in your lives. And I don't mean because the armor that you have to live with as men is stultifying: and I don't doubt that it is. But I don't mean any of that.

I mean that there is a relationship between the way that women are raped and your socialization to rape and the war machine that grinds you up and spits you out: the war machine that you go through just like that woman went through Larry Flynt's meat grinder on the cover of *Hustler*. You damn well better believe that you're involved in this tragedy and that it's your tragedy too. Because you're turned into little soldier boys from the day that you are born and everything that you learn about how to avoid the humanity of women becomes part of the militarism of the country in which you live and the world in which you live. It is also part of the economy that you frequently claim to protest.

And the problem is that you think it's out there: and it's not out there. It's in you. The pimps and the warmongers speak for you. Rape and war are not so different. And what the pimps and the warmongers do is that they make you so proud of being men who can get it up and give it hard. And they take that acculturated sexuality and they put you in little uniforms and they send you out to kill and to die. Now, I am not going to suggest to you that I think that's more important than what you do to women, because I don't.

But I think that if you want to look at what this system does to you, then that is where you should start looking: the sexual politics of aggression; the sexual politics of militarism. I think that men are very afraid of other men. That is something that you sometimes try to address in your small groups, as if if you changed your attitudes towards each other, you wouldn't be afraid of each other.

But as long as your sexuality has to do with aggression and your sense of entitlement to humanity has to do with being superior to other people, and there is so much contempt and hostility in your attitudes towards women and children, how could you not be afraid of each other? I think that you rightly perceive—without being willing to face it politically—that men are very dangerous: because you are.

The solution of the men's movement to make men less dangerous to each other by changing the way you touch and feel each other is not a solution. It's a recreational break.

These conferences are also concerned with homophobia. Homophobia is very important: it is very important to the way male supremacy works. In my opinion, the prohibitions against male homosexuality exist in order to protect male power. *Do it to her.* That is to say: as long as men rape, it is very important that men be directed to rape women. As long as sex is full of hostility and expresses both power over and contempt for the other person, it is very important that men not be declassed, stigmatized as female, used similarly. The power of men as a class depends on keeping men sexually inviolate and women sexually used by men. Homophobia helps maintain that class power: it also helps keep you as individuals safe from each other, safe from rape. If you want to do something about homophobia, you are going to have to do something about the fact that men rape, and that forced sex is not incidental to male sexuality but is in practice paradigmatic.

Some of you are very concerned about the rise of the Right in this country, as if that is something separate from the issues of feminism or the men's movement. There is a cartoon I saw that brought it all together nicely. It was a big picture of Ronald Reagan as a cowboy with a big hat and a gun. And it said: "A gun in every holster; a pregnant woman in every home. Make America a man again." Those are the politics of the Right.

If you are afraid of the ascendancy of fascism in this country—and you would be very foolish not to be right now—then you had better understand that the root issue here has to do with male supremacy and the control of women; sexual access to women; women as reproductive slaves; private ownership of women. That is the program of the Right. That is the morality they talk about. That is what they mean. That is what they want. And the only opposition to them that matters is an opposition to men owning women.

What's involved in doing something about all of this? The men's movement seems to stay stuck on two points. The first is that men don't really feel very good about themselves. How could you? The second is that men come to me or to other feminists and say: "What you're saying about men isn't true. It isn't true of me. I don't feel that way. I'm opposed to all of this."

And I say: don't tell me. Tell the pornographers. Tell the pimps. Tell the warmakers. Tell the rape apologists and the rape celebrationists and the pro-rape ideologues. Tell the novelists who think that rape is wonderful. Tell Larry Flynt. Tell Hugh Hefner. There's no point in telling me. I'm only a woman. There's nothing I can do about it. These men presume to speak for you. They are in the public arena saying that they represent you. If they don't, then you had better let them know.

Then there is the private world of misogyny: what you know about each other; what you say in private life; the exploitation that you see in the private sphere; the relationships called love, based on exploitation. It's not enough to find some traveling feminist on the road and go up to her and say: "Gee, I hate it."

Say it to your friends who are doing it. And there are streets out there on which you can say these things loud and clear, so as to affect the actual institutions that maintain these abuses. You don't like pornography? I wish I could believe it's true. I will believe it when I see you on the streets. I will believe it when I see an organized political opposition. I will believe it when pimps go out of business because there are no more male consumers.

You want to organize men. You don't have to search for issues. The issues are part of the fabric of your everyday lives.

I want to talk to you about equality, what equality is and what it means. It isn't just an idea. It's not some insipid word that ends up being bullshit. It doesn't have anything at all to do with all those statements like: "Oh, that happens to men too." I name an abuse and I hear: "Oh, it happens to men too." That is not the equality we are struggling for. We could change our strategy and say: well, okay, we want equality; we'll stick something up the ass of a man every three minutes.

You've never heard that from the feminist movement, because for us equality has real dignity and importance—it's not some dumb word that can be twisted and made to look stupid as if it had no real meaning.

As a way of practicing equality, some vague idea about giving up power is useless. Some men have vague thoughts about a future in which men are going to give up power or an individual man is going to give up some kind of privilege that he has. That is not what equality means either.

Equality is a practice. It is an action. It is a way of life. It is a social practice. It is an economic practice. It is a sexual practice. It can't exist in a vacuum. You can't have it in your home if, when the people leave the home, he is in a world of his supremacy based on the existence of his cock and she is in a world of humiliation and degradation because she is perceived to be inferior and because her sexuality is a curse.

This is not to say that the attempt to practice equality in the home doesn't matter. It matters, but it is not enough. If you love equality, if you believe in it, if it is the way you want to live—not just men and women together in a home, but men and men together in a home and women and women together in a home—if equality is what you want and what you care about, then you have to fight for the institutions that will make it socially real.

It is not just a matter of your attitude. You can't think it and make it exist. You can't try sometimes, when it works to your advantage, and throw it out the rest of the time. Equality is a discipline. It is a way of life. It is a political necessity to create equality in institutions. And another thing about equality is that it cannot coexist with rape. It cannot. And it cannot coexist with pornography or with prostitution or with the economic degradation of women on any level, in any way. It cannot coexist, because implicit in all those things is the inferiority of women.

I want to see this men's movement make a commitment to ending rape because that is the only meaningful commitment to equality. It is astonishing that in all our worlds of feminism and antisexism we never talk seriously about ending rape. Ending it. Stopping it. No more. No more rape. In the back of our minds, are we holding on to its inevitability as the last preserve of the biological? Do we think that it is always going to exist no matter what we do? All of our political actions are lies if we don't make a commitment to ending the practice of rape. This commitment has to be political. It has to be serious. It has to be systematic. It has to be public. It can't be self-indulgent.

The things the men's movement has wanted are things worth having. Intimacy is worth having. Tenderness is worth having. Cooperation is worth having. A real emotional life is worth having. But you can't have them in a world with rape. Ending homophobia is worth doing. But you can't do it in a world with rape. Rape stands in the way of each and every one of those things you say you want. And by rape you know what I mean. A judge does not have to walk into this room and say that according to statute such and such these are the elements of proof. We're talking about any kind of coerced sex, including sex coerced by poverty.

You can't have equality or tenderness or intimacy as long as there is rape, because rape means terror. It means that part of the population lives in a state of terror and pretends—to please and pacify you—that it doesn't. So there is no honesty. How can there be? Can you imagine what it is like to live as a woman day in and day out with the threat of rape? Or what it is like to live with the reality? I want to see you use those legendary bodies and that legendary strength and that legendary courage and the tenderness that you say you have in behalf of women; and that means against the rapists, against the pimps, and against the pornographers. It means something more than a personal renunciation. It means a systematic, political, active, public attack. And there has been very little of that.

I came here today because I don't believe that rape is inevitable or natural. If I did, I would have no reason to be here. If I did, my political practice would be different than it is. Have you ever wondered why we are not just in armed combat against you? It's not because there's a shortage of kitchen knives in this country. It is because we believe in your humanity, against all the evidence.

We do not want to do the work of helping you to believe in your humanity. We cannot do it anymore. We have always tried. We have been repaid with systematic exploitation and systematic abuse. You are going to have to do this yourselves from now on and you know it.

The shame of men in front of women is, I think, an appropriate response both to what men do do and to what men do not do. I think you should be ashamed. But what you do with that shame is to use it as an excuse to keep doing what you want and to keep not doing anything else; and you've got to stop. You've got to stop. Your psychology doesn't matter. How much you hurt doesn't matter in the end any more than how much we hurt matters. If we sat around and only talked about how much rape hurt us, do you think there would have been one of the changes that you have seen in this country in the last fifteen years? There wouldn't have been.

It is true that we had to talk to each other. How else, after all, were we supposed to find out that each of us was not the only woman in the world not asking for it to whom rape or battery had ever happened? We couldn't read it in the newspapers, not then. We couldn't find a book about it. But you do know and now the question is what you are going to do; and so your shame and your guilt are very much beside the point.

They don't matter to us at all, in any way. They're not good enough. They don't do anything.

As a feminist, I carry the rape of all the women I've talked to over the past ten years personally with me. As a woman, I carry my own rape with me. Do you remember pictures that you've seen of European cities during the plague, when there were wheelbarrows that would go along and people would just pick up corpses and throw them in? Well, that is what it is like knowing about rape. Piles and piles and piles of bodies that have whole lives and human names and human faces.

I speak for many feminists, not only myself, when I tell you that I am tired of what I know and sad beyond any words I have about what has already been done to women up to this point, now, up to 2:24 P.M. on this day, here in this place.

And I want one day of respite, one day off, one day in which no new bodies are piled up, one day in which no new agony is added to the old, and I am asking you to give it to me. And how could I ask you for less— it is so little. And how could you offer me less: it is so little. Even in wars, there are days of truce. Go and organize a truce. Stop your side for one day. I want a twenty-four-hour truce during which there is no rape.

I dare you to try it. I demand that you try it. I don't mind begging you to try it. What else could you possibly be here to do? What else could this movement possibly mean? What else could matter so much?

And on that day, that day of truce, that day when not one woman is raped, we will begin the real practice of equality, because we can't begin it before that day. Before that day it means nothing because it is nothing: it is not real; it is not true. But on that day it becomes real. And then, instead of rape we will for the first time in our lives—both men and women—begin to experience freedom.

If you have a conception of freedom that includes the existence of rape, you are wrong. You cannot change what you say you want to change. For myself, I want to experience just one day of real freedom before I die. I leave you here to do that for me and for the women whom you say you love.

Reprinted with permission of the author. Copyright © 1984 by Andrea Dworkin. First printed under the title "Talking to Men about Rape," *Out!*, vol. 2, #6, April 1984. Collected in *Letters From a War Zone*, first published in the U.S. by E. P. Dutton, currently available in paperback from Lawrence Hill Books.

ANDREA DWORKIN is the author of the nonfiction landmarks *Intercourse* (The Free Press), *Pornography: Men Possessing Women* (Dutton), and *Woman Hating* (Dutton). She has published two collections of essays and lectures, *Letters From a War Zone* and *Our Blood: Prophecies and Discourses on Sexual Politics.* Her most recent novel, *Mercy,* is about rape.

She is coauthor of legislation recognizing pornography as a violation of the civil rights of women, lectures extensively on violence against women, and is a committed political activist.

FRATERNITIES AND THE RAPE CULTURE

by Chris O'Sullivan

When I began to study group sexual assault on campus,
I found that the majority of gang rapes were perpetrated by
fraternity men. Men who don't like to live around women,
who have difficulty accepting women as equals and
relating to them, may be more likely than other men to
choose to join a fraternity; thus, men Mary Koss calls
"hidden rapists" may self-select for fraternity life.

WHEN I TOOK a teaching position at Bucknell University in 1989, there was a move afoot among the faculty to get rid of the fraternities on campus. I joined and found myself somewhat in the forefront of the movement to sever our ties with them. The faculty voted to abolish the fraternities, but the fraternity alumni threatened to withdraw financial support, and, even more upsetting to Bucknell, the fraternity alumni corporations threatened to board up their houses on campus and leave them to deteriorate. In the end, the university decided to keep the fraternities and get rid of me. I was certainly more expendable: fraternities have great wealth and influence. At many universities, most trustees are fraternity men, and the wealthiest alumni are loyal to their fraternities.

By the fall of 1991, fraternity rush had been pushed back to sophomore year, and I was collecting unemployment. None of the fraternity houses was closed. In fact, the university spent a half million dollars to renovate a fraternity house that had been trashed by its members when it was shut down because of a possible gang rape a few years before.

My opposition to fraternities derives from my professional experience as a social psychologist, from my research and the research of others, from studying the social psychology of groups, and, as a faculty member at several universities, from observing the impact of membership on my students. It does *not* come from any negative personal experience with fraternities, although fraternity loyalists insist it must.

A number of social psychological processes occur in groups that promote mistreatment of outsiders and poor decision-making processes. Combined with male socialization in our society and the connotations of masculinity in our culture, fraternal cultures at schools and colleges breed a propensity to abuse women sexually, along a continuum of behaviors. I came to this conclusion by studying gang rape on campus, which led me to study fraternities and athletic teams. The analysis applies to both, since both are "fraternal cultures."

Social cognitive processes in groups are modes of thinking to which we are susceptible because they arise from the way the human mind works. I'll note three such processes that are underpinnings of misogyny and abuse.

- The "outgroup homogeneity effect," the belief that all members of the outgroup (defined as not one's own group) are alike. Independents think that all Greeks are alike. Members of one sorority feel that their membership is diverse, but that members of another sorority all fit one stereotype.

- The natural sense of "ingroup superiority." In one experiment, participants were given false feedback that they were either "dot overestimators" or "dot underestimators." The underestimators attributed negative characteristics to overestimators and positive characteristics to themselves, and vice versa. Of course, the categories were meaningless and the trait inferences groundless, nor were the assignments of individuals to groups based on their actual performance.

- "Groupthink," a faulty decision-making process of groups, particularly elite groups. The concept was coined by Irving Janis at Yale, and the primary example was the decision to execute the Bay of Pigs invasion of Cuba. Janis delineated the reasons that groups head down the path to a really stupid decision, including an inflated belief in the group's righteousness, accompanied by an exaggerated belief in the ineptitude and unworthiness of the opposition. Dissent within the group is squelched by the isolation of critics and self-censorship of doubt.

These cognitive processes give group members a sense of invulnerability and entitlement, as well as a disdain for nonmembers that makes it easier to victimize them.

In addition, people are often more aggressive in groups than they would be individually. Strong identification with a group replaces individual ethics with group ethics. This process can lead people to behave more honorably as a group member than as an individual, but more commonly the result is the opposite. Group identification, along with alcohol, excitement, noise, anonymity, "de-individuation" (loss of a sense of self), and even darkness, has often been found to promote heedless aggression.

Socialization and social roles also contribute to group sexual aggression by men. Male friendships involve elements of competition and camaraderie. Sex as a competitive arena necessarily results in exploiting girls and women, because the motive is to "score," to impress one's male friends rather than to relate to the female. Drinking is another common arena for competition, as is risk-taking. Throughout childhood, boys' friendship groups provide support in violating adult and societal notions of propriety.

A boy's prestige with his group may be based on the degree to which he takes risks in breaking rules (although for most groups there is a boundary beyond which risky troublemaking earns disapproval of the group). Self-esteem for boys and young men typically comes from their reputation for success in these areas, as judged by their male peers. In our society, the perception of males by females counts for little, except insofar as female attention enhances their reputation among other males.

The definition of masculinity in our culture includes independence (from relationships), lack of sentimentality, sexual success (which usually means access to numbers of different women, but can also mean getting women to do things they don't want to), physical toughness, and worldly success, measured in dollars or achievements. Each of these elements of constructed masculinity has implications for a male's relationships with women. The requirement that a man be physically tough means tuning out his own pain, which also weakens his capacity for empathy. Attachment to a woman can threaten the image of independence and produce accusations that a man is "dominated" or "pussy-whipped" by his mother, girlfriend, or wife. A man's need to "score" and to push women into sexual acts that earn masculinity credits objectifies women. "Scoring" is enhanced by getting women to perform sex acts that the men consider demeaning. Thus, fellatio earns more points than intercourse, and anal intercourse more than vaginal intercourse. Of course, a woman who would do such things is not worthy of respect and must not be treated as a serious person or real girlfriend.

When I began to study group sexual assault on campus, I found that the majority of gang rapes were perpetrated by fraternity men. Athletes were also overrepresented, but interestingly only those who played team sports such as basketball, football, lacrosse, or rugby. I have isolated a number of reasons for this concentration of gang rapists among fraternity men and team athletes.

In part, this correlation has to do with *opportunity*. The perpetrators typically share housing in an all-male residence reserved for the group. They have privacy from men not in the group, from women, and from authority figures. They have bedrooms and social areas that are their exclusive territory or turf. This group residency is one reason that these men are more likely than other college men to engage in sex collectively with only one woman, but it doesn't touch on the question of why they would *want* to.

Second, these are men who have chosen to spend their college years living in a single-sex residence, or at least taking their meals and socializing in an all-male group. Men who don't like to live around women, who have difficulty accepting women as equals and relating to them, may be more likely than other men to choose to join a fraternity; thus, men Mary Koss calls "hidden rapists" may self-select for fraternity life. This explanation is less applicable to athletes. Other research has shown, however, that both athletes and fraternity men are also more likely to commit acquaintance rape *individually* than other college men. That is, the values and ways of relating to women that they learn in these all-male groups foster sexual aggression. Furthermore, women, for a variety of reasons, place greater trust in men who are members of high-prestige groups.

In addition to the common experiences of growing up male in our culture and being a member of a male friendship group, there are several practices often indulged in by these groups that may explain why fraternity men and athletes who play team sports may be more likely to be sexually aggressive, and especially to engage in group sexual assaults.

During fraternity "pledging," there are many rites that serve both to objectify women and, perhaps more importantly, to alienate men from their own sexuality. Many high school and college athletic teams have initiation rituals that are similar. The quasi-sexual, or homosexual, nature of these rituals is striking. Nudity is often involved, along with heavy drinking, to allow men to suffer the humiliations they must endure. One common example from fraternities and teams around the U.S. and Canada is a race in which pledges have to run across a room holding a grape, ice cube, or marshmallow between the cheeks of their buttocks and then drop it into a box. The last guy has to eat the first guy's grape. Wood paddles are an accoutrement of fraternity life. In one fraternity, the initiates kneel in a row for the final initiation ceremony; the president walks down the row, putting his penis in each man's mouth. There are many other examples of this kind of ritual.

In addition to the physical exposure and contact involved in the all-male contests of humiliation, some rituals involve humiliation of pledges in front of women. One example is the "elephant walk," in which men form a public procession with their pants pockets pulled inside out to form an elephant's ears and their penises hanging out for the trunk;

another rite is performing naked jumping jacks in front of a sorority house.

Still other practices involve sexual humiliation of women: in one such pledging ritual, the men surrounded sorority women at the dinner table in their sorority; one man read a lecture on Freud while another masturbated a dildo. Additionally, there is the sexual exploitation category of behavior, such as having sex with a teenager as a pledging requirement.

Many common practices of fraternity men after pledging can promote sexual aggression. These include videotaping, photographing, or merely observing through peepholes or windows a brother having sex with a woman. Most fraternity houses have collections of pornographic magazines and videos. Sexual contests are common among fraternity men. At the most benign, the contest may simply be "notch" contests over who has sex with the greatest number of women. A step up in victimizing and objectifying women, as well as alienating men from their own sexuality, are "pig contests," also called "hog contests," in which a man wins by having sex with the woman the group considers most unattractive. There is a lively verbal component to the sexual competitions, including "date reports" given in locker rooms or at fraternity meals, in which the men compete in telling the most disgusting and/or funny sexual encounter (often considered the same), encouraging the men to mock their romantic relations. Fraternity logs and newsletters, laced with scatological and obscene humor, repeat these stories and add mocking tales of brothers' sexual failures and successes.

All of these practices make sexuality dirty, exploitative, and public, rather than intimate, cooperative, and private. Men who resist this "take" on sexual relations between men and women may be ostracized by the group, or they may be left alone and excluded from full acceptance. I heard a story of a man who found a woman friend drunk, unconscious, and naked in the hall of his fraternity. He took her into his room for the night and escorted her home in the morning. His modestly gallant behavior caused a major rift in the fraternity. Some of his brothers were furious because he didn't "share" her with them.

It is a contradictory goal to establish organizations that discriminate on the basis of sex and then expect the members to consider those who are excluded as equal, full human beings. A basic, although counterintuitive, tenet of social psychology, well documented through extensive research, is that not only do attitudes guide our behavior, but also, quite powerfully, our behavior influences our attitudes. Specifically, discrimination produces prejudice.

While I know that people cling to membership associations that allow them to be "one of the guys," I hope that the social evolution of our society will make belonging to a fraternity a source of shame rather than of pride. Fraternities encourage behavior in young men that falls along a continuum of sexual violence. I believe that abolishing college fraternities will be an important step in healing a rape culture.

CHRIS O'SULLIVAN is a social psychologist who speaks and writes about group sexual assault and consults on gender-based discrimination and sexual harassment. Her studies of campus gang rapes led to an analysis of male-exclusive organizations and brotherhoods and the consequences for the men who belong to them and for the women who encounter them.

She graduated from Sarah Lawrence College, received a master's degree in linguistics at Southern Illinois University, and earned a Ph.D. in experimental psychology from the University of Oklahoma. She has taught at the University of Kentucky and at Bucknell University, where she joined a faculty movement to abolish fraternities. Her contract at Bucknell was not renewed, and she has left academia. Her book, *Nice Boys, Dirty Deeds: Gang Rape on Campus* is forthcoming from Guilford.

EROTICA VS. PORNOGRAPHY

by Gloria Steinem

In short, pornography is not about sex. It's about an
imbalance of power that allows and even requires
sex to be used as a form of aggression.

LOOK AT OR imagine images of people making love; really making love. Those images may be very diverse, but there is likely to be a mutual pleasure and touch and warmth, an empathy for each other's bodies and nerve endings, a shared sensuality and a spontaneous sense of two people who are there because they *want* to be.

Now look at or imagine images of sex in which there is force, violence, or symbols of unequal power. They may be very blatant: whips and chains of bondage, even torture and murder presented as sexually titillating, the clear evidence of wounds and bruises, or an adult's power being used sexually over a child. They may be more subtle: the use of class, race, authority, or just body poses to convey conqueror and victim; unequal nudity, with one person's body exposed and vulnerable while the other is armored with clothes; or even a woman by herself, exposed for an unseen but powerful viewer whom she clearly is trying to please. (It's interesting that, even when only the woman is seen, we often know whether she is there for her own pleasure or being displayed for someone else's.) But blatant or subtle, there is no equal power or mutuality. In fact, much of the tension and drama comes from the clear idea that one person is dominating another.

These two sorts of images are as different as love is from rape, as dignity is from humiliation, as partnership is from slavery, as pleasure is from pain. Yet they are confused and lumped together as "pornography" or "obscenity," "erotica" or "explicit sex," because sex and violence are so dangerously intertwined and confused. After all, it takes violence or the threat of it to maintain the dominance of any group of human beings over another. Moreover, the threat must be the most persuasive wherever men and women come together intimately and are most in danger of recognizing each other's humanity.

This confusion of sex with violence is most obvious in any form of sadomasochism. The inability to empathize with the "opposite sex" has become so great that a torturer or even murderer may actually believe pain or loss of life to be the natural fate of the victim; and the victim may have been so deprived of self-respect or positive human contact that she expects pain or loss of freedom as the price of any intimacy or attention at all. It's unlikely that even a masochist expects death. Nonetheless, "snuff" movies and much current pornographic literature insist that a slow death from sexual torture is the final orgasm and ultimate pleasure. It's a form of "suicide" reserved for women. Though men in fact are far more likely to kill themselves, male suicide is almost never presented as sexually pleasurable.

Sex is also confused with violence and aggression in all forms of popular culture, as well as in respectable theories of psychology and sexual behavior. The idea that aggression is a "normal" part of male sexuality, and that passivity or even the need for male aggression is a "normal" part of female sexuality, are part of the male-dominant culture we live in, the books we learn from, and the air we breathe.

Even the words we are given to express our feelings are suffused with the same assumptions. Sexual phrases are the most common synonyms for conquering and humiliation (*being had, being screwed, getting fucked*); the sexually aggressive or even expressive woman is a *slut* or a *nymphomaniac*, but the sexually aggressive man is just *normal*; and real or scientific descriptions of sex may perpetuate the same roles, for instance, a woman is always *penetrated* by a man though she might also be said to have *enveloped* him.

Obviously, untangling sex from aggression—from violence or the threat of it—is going to take a very long time. And the process is going to be greatly resisted as a challenge to the very heart of male dominance and male centrality.

But we do have a wisdom to guide us: the common sense of our bodies. Pain is a warning of damage and danger. If that sensation is not mixed with the intimacy we are given as children, we are unlikely to confuse pain with pleasure and love. As we discover our free will and strength, we are also more likely to discover our own initiative and pleasure in sex. As men no longer dominate and have to find an identity that doesn't depend on superiority, they also discover that cooperation is more interesting than submission, that empathy with their sex partner increases their own pleasure, and that anxieties about their ability to "perform" tend to disappear along with stereotyped ideas about masculinity.

But women will be the main fighters of this new sexual revolution. It is our freedom, our safety, our lives, and our pleasure that are mostly at stake.

In this wave of feminism, we began by trying to separate sex and violence in those areas where the physical danger was and is the most immediate; challenging rape as the one crime that was considered biologically irresistible for the criminal and perhaps invited by the victim; refusing to allow male-female beatings to be classified as "domestic violence" and ignored by the law; and exposing forced prostitution and sexual slavery as national and international crimes. With the exception of wife beating, those challenges were made somewhat easier by men who wanted to punish other men for taking their female property. Women still rarely have the power to protect each other.

Such instances of real anti-woman warfare led us directly to the propaganda that teaches and legitimizes them: pornography. For the same reasons that we had begun to differentiate rape from sex, we realized that we must find some way of separating pornographic depictions of sex as an anti-woman weapon from those images of freely chosen, mutual sexuality.

Fortunately, there is also wisdom in the origin of words. *Pornography* comes from the Greek root *porné* (harlot, prostitute, or female captive) and *graphos* (writing about or description of). Thus, it means a description of either the purchase of sex, which implies an imbalance of power in itself, or sexual slavery.

This definition includes, and should include, all such degradation, regardless of whether it is females who are the slaves and males who are the captors or the rare examples that are vice versa. There is certainly homosexual pornography, with a man playing the "feminine" role of victim. There is also role-reversal pornography, with a woman whipping or punishing a man, though it's significant that this genre is created by men for their own pleasure, not by or for women, and allows men to *pretend* to be victims—but without real danger. There is lesbian pornography, with a woman assuming the "masculine" role of victimizing another woman. That women rarely choose this role of victimizer is due not to biological superiority, but to a culture that is far less likely to addict women to violence. But whatever the gender of the participants, all pornography is an imitation of the male-female, conqueror-victim paradigm, and almost all of it actually portrays or implies enslaved woman and masterful male.

Even the 1970 Presidential Commission on Obscenity and Pornography, whose report is often accused of suppressing or ignoring evidence of the causal link between pornography and violence against women, defined the subject of their study as pictorial or verbal descriptions of sexual behavior that was characterized by "the degrading and demeaning portrayal of the role and status of the human female."

In short, pornography is not about sex. It's about an imbalance of power that allows and even requires sex to be used as a form of aggression.

Erotica is a word that can help us to differentiate sex from violence, and to rescue sexual pleasure. It comes from the Greek root *eros* (sexual desire or passionate love, named for Eros, the son of Aphrodite), and so contains the idea of love, positive choice, and the yearning for a particular person. Unlike pornography's reference to a harlot or prostitute, *erotica* leaves entirely open the question of gender. (In fact, we may owe its connotation of shared power to the Greek belief that a man's love for another man was more worthy than love for a woman.) Though both erotica and pornography usually refer to verbal or pictorial representations of sexual behavior, they are as different as a room with doors open from one with doors locked. The first might be a home, but the second could only be a prison.

The problem is that there is so little erotica. Women have rarely been free enough to pursue erotic pleasure in our own lives, much less to create it in the worlds of film, magazines, art, books, television, and popular culture—areas of communication we rarely control. Very few male authors and filmmakers have been able to escape society's message of what a man should do, much less to imagine their way into the identity of a woman, and even depictions of sex between men or between women often fall into the dominant-passive paradigm. Some women are now trying to portray equal and erotic sex—whether with men or with other women—but it is still not a part of popular culture.

And the problem is that there is so *much* pornography. This underground stream of anti-woman propaganda has existed in all male-dominant societies, but mass communication, profiteering corporations, and a backlash against female equality have now turned it into an inescapable flood in our streets and theaters and even our homes. Perhaps that's useful in the long run. Women can no longer pretend pornography does not exist. We must either face our own humiliation and torture every day on magazine covers and television screens, or fight back. There is hardly a newsstand without women's bodies in chains and bondage, in full labial display for the conquering male viewer, bruised or on our knees, screaming in real or pretended pain, pretending to enjoy what is hurting and killing us. The same images are in mainstream movie theaters and respectable hotel rooms via closed-circuit TV for the traveling businessman. They are brought into our own homes not only in magazines, but in videocassettes and on cable TV channels. Even video games offer such features as a smiling, rope-bound woman and a male figure with an erection, the game's object being to rape the woman as many times as possible. (Like much of pornography, that game is fascist on racial grounds as well as sexual ones. The smiling woman is an Indian maiden, the rapist is General Custer, and the game is called "Custer's Revenge.") Though "snuff" movies, in which real women are eviscerated and finally killed, have been driven underground (in part because the graves of many murdered women were discovered around the shack of just one filmmaker in California), movies that simulate the torture-murders of women are still going strong. (*Snuff* is the porn term for killing a woman for sexual pleasure. We are not even allowed the seriousness of a word like *murder*.) So are the "kiddie porn" or "chicken porn" movies and magazines that show adult men undressing, fondling, and sexually abusing children; often with the titillating theme that "fathers" are raping "daughters." Some "chicken porn" magazines offer explicit tips on how to use a child sexually without leaving physical evidence of rape. The premise is that children's testimony is even less likely to be believed than that of adult women, and as we see in the few cases of the sexual abuse of children that reach the courts, this is true.

Add this pornography industry up, from magazines like *Playboy* and *Hustler*, to movie classics like *Love Gestapo Style*, *Deep Throat*, or *Angels in Pain*, and the total sales come to a staggering ten billion dollars a year—*more than all the sales of the conventional film and record industry combined.* And that doesn't count the fact that many "conventional" film and music images are also pornographic, from gynocidal record jackets like the famous *I'm "Black and Blue" from the Rolling Stones—and I Love It!* (which showed a seminude black woman bound to a chair) to the hundreds of teenage sex-and-horror movies in which young women die sadistic deaths and rape is presented not as a crime but as sexual excitement, plus the many mainstream films and TV shows that tailor pornography to pass minimal standards. Nor do those industries include the sales of the supposedly "literary" forms of pornography, from *The Story of O* to the works of the Marquis de Sade.

If Nazi propaganda that justified the torture and killing of Jews were the theme of half of our most popular movies and magazines, would we not be outraged? If Ku Klux Klan propaganda that preached and glamorized the enslavement of blacks were the subject of much-praised "classic" novels, would we not protest? We know that such racist propaganda precedes and justifies the racist acts of pogroms and lynchings. We know that watching a violent film makes test subjects more likely both to condone violence and to be willing to perpetrate it themselves. Why is the propaganda of sexual aggression against women of all races the one form of group hatred in which the "conventional wisdom" sees no danger? Why is pornography the only media violence that is supposed to be a "safety valve" to satisfy men's "natural" aggressiveness somewhere short of acting it out?

The first reason is the confusion of *all* nonprocreative sex with pornography. Any description of sexual behavior, or even nudity, may be called pornographic or obscene (a word whose Latin derivative means *dirty* or *containing filth*) by those who insist that the only moral purpose of sex is procreative, or even that any portrayal of sexuality or nudity is against the will of God.

In fact, human beings seem to be the only animals that experience the sex drive and pleasure both when we can and cannot conceive. Other animals experience periods of heat or estrus in which sexual activity is concentrated. Humans do not. Just as we developed uniquely human capacities for language, planning, memory, and invention along our evolutionary path, we also developed sexuality as a form of expression, a way of communicating that is separable from our reproductive need. For human beings, sexuality can be and often is a way of bonding, giving and receiving pleasure, bridging differentness, discovering sameness, and communicating emotion.

We developed this and other human gifts through our ability to change our environment, adapt to it physically, and so in the very long run to affect our own evolution. But as an emotional result of this spiraling path away from other animals, we seem to alternate between periods of exploring our unique ability and feelings of loneliness in the unknown that we ourselves have created, a fear that sometimes sends us back to the comfort of the animal world by encouraging us to look for a sameness with it.

For instance, the separation of "play" from "work" is a feature of the human world. So is the difference between art and nature, or an intellectual accomplishment and a physical one. As a result, we celebrate play, art, and invention as pleasurable and important leaps into the unknown; yet any temporary trouble can send us back to a nostalgia for our primate past and a conviction that the basics of survival, nature, and physical labor are somehow more worthwhile or even more moral.

In the same way, we have explored our sexuality as separable from conception: a pleasurable, empathetic, important bridge to others of our species. We have even invented contraception, a skill that has probably existed in some form since our ancestors figured out the process of conception and birth, in order to extend and protect this uniquely human gift for sexuality that is a means of expression. Yet we also have times of atavistic suspicion that sex is not complete, or even legal or intended by God, if it does not or could not end in conception.

No wonder the very different concepts of "erotica" and "pornography" can be so confused. Both assume that sex can be separated from conception; that human sexuality has additional uses and goals. This is the major reason why, even in our current culture, both may still be condemned as equally obscene and immoral. Such gross condemnation of all sexuality that isn't harnessed to childbirth (and to patriarchal marriage so that children are properly "owned" by men) has been increased by the current backlash against women's independence. Out of fear that the whole patriarchal structure will be upset if we as women really have the autonomous power to decide our sexual and reproductive futures (that is, if we can control our own bodies, and thus the means of reproduction), anti-equality groups are not only denouncing sex education and family planning as "pornographic," but are trying to use obscenity laws to stop the sending of all contraceptive information through the mails. Any sex or nudity outside the context of patriarchal marriage and forced childbirth is their target. In fact, Phyllis Schlafly has denounced the entire women's movement as "obscene."

Not surprisingly, this religious backlash has a secular, intellectual counterpart that relies heavily on applying the "natural" behavior of some selected part of the animal world to humans. This is questionable in itself, but such Lionel Tiger-ish studies make their political purpose even more clear by the animals they choose and the habits they emphasize. For example, some male primates carry and generally "mother" their infants, male lions care for their young, female elephants often lead the clan, and male penguins literally do everything except give birth, from hatching the eggs to sacrificing their own membranes to feed the new arrivals. Perhaps that's why many male supremacists prefer to discuss chimps and baboons (many of whom are studied in atypical conditions of captivity) whose behavior is suitably male-dominant. The message is that human females should accept their animal "destiny" of being sexually dependent and devote themselves to bearing and rearing their young.

Defending against such reaction leads to the temptation of merely reversing the terms and declaring that *all* nonprocreative sex is good. In fact, however, this human activity can be as constructive or destructive, moral or immoral, as any other. Sex as communication can send messages as different as mutual pleasure and dominance, life and death, "erotica" and "pornography."

The second kind of problem comes not from those who oppose women's equality in nonsexual areas, whether on grounds of God or nature, but from men (and some women, too) who present themselves as friends of civil liberties and progress. Their objections may take the form of a concern about privacy, on the grounds that a challenge to pornography invades private sexual behavior and the philosophy of "whatever turns you on." It may be a concern about class bias, on the premise that pornography is just "workingmen's erotica." Sometimes, it's the simple argument that the objectors themselves like pornography and therefore it must be okay. Most often, however, this resistance attaches itself to or hides behind an expressed concern about censorship, freedom of the press, and the First Amendment.

In each case, such liberal objections are more easily countered than the anti-equality ones because they are less based on political reality. It's true, for instance, that women's independence and autonomy would upset the whole patriarchal apple cart: the right wing should be worried. It's not true, however, that pornography is a private concern. If it were just a matter of men making male-supremacist literature in their own basements to assuage their own sexual hang-ups, there would be sorrow and avoidance among women, but not the anger, outrage, and fear produced by being confronted with the preaching of sexual fascism on our newsstands, movie screens, television sets, and public streets. It is a multi-billion-dollar industry, which involves the making of public policy, if only to decide whether, as is now the case, crimes committed in the manufacture and sale of pornography will continue to go largely unprosecuted. Zoning regulations on the public display of pornography are not enforced, the sexual slavery and exploitation of children used in pornography go unpunished, the forcible use of teenage runaways is ignored by police, and even the torture and murder of prostitutes for men's sexual titillation is obscured by some mitigating notion that the women asked for it.

In all other areas of privacy, the limitation is infringement on the rights and lives and safety of others. That must become true for pornography. Right now, it is exempt: almost "below the law."

As for class bias, it's simply not accurate to say that pornography is erotica with less education. From the origins of the words, as well as the accurate way that feminists working against pornography are trying to use them, it's clear there is a difference of content, not just artistic or economic form. Pornography is about dominance. Erotica is about mutuality. Any man able to empathize with women can easily tell the difference by looking at a photograph or film and putting himself in the woman's skin. Perhaps the most revealing thing is that this argument is generally made *on behalf* of the working class by pro-pornography liberals who are middle or upper-class themselves.

Of course, the notion that enjoying pornography makes it okay is an overwhelmingly male idea. From Kinsey forward, research has confirmed that the purchasers of pornography are almost all males, and that the majority of men are turned on by it, while the majority of women find it angering, humiliating, and not a turn-on at all. This was true even though women were shown sexually explicit material that may have included erotica, since Kinsey and others did not make that distinction. If such rare examples of equal sex were entirely deleted, pornography could probably serve as sex aversion-therapy for most women; yet many men and some psychologists continue to call women prudish, frigid, or generally uptight if they are not turned on by their own domination. The same men might be less likely to argue that anti-Semitic and racist literature was okay because it gave them pleasure. The problem is that the degradation of women of all races is still thought to be normal. A male-dominant system must teach men that dominance over women is normal, and that's just what pornography does.

Nonetheless, there are a few well-meaning women who are both turned on by pornography and angered that other women are not. Some of their anger is misunderstanding: objections to pornography are not condemnations of women who have been raised to believe sex and domination are synonymous, for we have all internalized some degree of sexism and are struggling to dig it out. Other women's anger results from an underestimation of themselves: being turned on by a rape fantasy is not the same thing as wanting to be raped. As Robin Morgan has pointed out, the distinguishing feature of a fantasy is that the fantasizer herself is in control. (Both men and women have "ravishment" fantasies in which we are passive while others act out our unspoken wishes—but they are still *our* wishes.) And some anger, especially when it comes from women who consider themselves feminists, is a refusal to differentiate between what may be true for them now and what may be true in the future. For example, a woman may be attracted only to men who are taller, heavier, and older than she, but still understand that such superficial restrictions on the men she loves and enjoys going to bed with won't exist in a more free and less-stereotyped future; or more seriously, she may be drawn to cruel and distant men because she is still trying to get her cruel and distant father of the past to love her, but understand that a future of mutuality is possible and preferable. Similarly, some lesbians may find themselves following the masculine-feminine patterns that were our only model for intimate relationships, heterosexual or not; yet still see these old patterns clearly and try to equalize them. It isn't that women attracted to pornography cannot also be feminists who are doing their best with their own internalized demons, but that pornography itself must be recognized as a perpetuation of those demons for other women now and into the future.

Finally, there is the First Amendment argument against feminist antipornography campaigns: the most respectable and publicized opposition, but also the one with the least basis in fact. Feminist groups are not arguing for censorship of pornography through prior restraint, just as we are not arguing that Nazi literature or racist propaganda of the Ku Klux Klan cannot be published. For one thing, any societal definition of pornography by a male-dominant society (or of racist literature by a racist society) might well be used to punish the powerless even more. Freely chosen gay or lesbian expression might be deemed more "pornographic" than snuff movies, school sex education courses more "obscene" than bondage, just as generalizations about European Americans might be more punished than those about African Americans. Furthermore, censorship in itself, even with the proper definitions, might only drive pornography into more underground activity and, were it to follow the pattern of drug traffic, into even more profitability. Most important, the First Amendment is part of a statement of individual rights against government intervention that feminism seeks to expand, not contract: for instance, a woman's right to decide whether and when to have children. When we protest against pornography and educate others about it, as I am doing now, we are strengthening the First Amendment by exercising it.

The only legal steps suggested by feminists thus far have been the prosecution of those pornography makers who are accused of such crimes as murder, assault, and kidnapping; prosecution of those many who use children under the age of consent; enforcement of existing zoning and other codes that are breached because of payoffs to law-enforcement officials and the enormous rents paid to pornography's landlords; the use of public-nuisance statutes to require that pornography not be displayed in public places where its sight cannot reasonably be avoided; and the right to sue for damages the makers of any pornography (or other hate literature) that can be shown to the satisfaction of a jury to have contributed to a crime. None of these measures keeps material from being published: "prior restraint," in the terms of censorship law. Most just require that those responsible for pornography no longer be immune from prosecution for crimes committed during its production and distribution.

Perhaps the reason for this "First Amendment" controversy is less substance than smoke screen. Just as earlier feminist campaigns against rape were condemned by some civil libertarians as efforts that could only end by putting more men of color or poor men in jail, or in perpetuating the death penalty then on the books in some states as a punishment for rape, antipornography campaigns are now run on similarly high-minded grounds. When rape victims began to come forward, however, the public learned that white psychiatrists, educators, and other professionals were just as likely to be rapists as were poor men or men of color. Furthermore, changing the patriarchal definition of rape to degrees of sexual assault made the law more realistic and thus more likely to be administered, eliminated the death penalty for rape, and protected males against sexual assault, too.

Though there are no statistics on the purchasers of pornography, those who serve this clientele—clerks, movie-house owners, videocassette dealers, mail-order houses, and the like—usually remark on their respectability, their professional standing, their suits, briefcases, white skins, and middle-class zip codes. For instance, the last screening of a snuff movie showing a real murder was traced to the monthly pornographic film showings of a senior partner in a respected law firm; an event regularly held by him for a group of friends, including other lawyers and judges. One who was present reported that many were "embarrassed" and "didn't know what to say." But not one man was willing to object, much less to offer this evidence of murder to the police. Though some concern about censorship is sincere—the result of false reports that feminist antipornography campaigns were really calling for censorship, or of confusion with right-wing groups who both misdefine pornography and want to censor it—much of it seems to be a cover for the preservation of the pornographic status quo by a left/right coalition of men who are dependent on this huge industry, whether psychologically or financially.

In fact, the arguments against taking on pornography seem suspiciously like the virgin-whore divisions of the past. The right wing says all that is not virginal or motherly is pornographic, and thus they campaign against sexuality and nudity in general. The left wing says all sex is good as long as it's male-defined, and thus must be protected. Women who feel endangered by seeing ourselves as the victims, and men who feel demeaned by seeing themselves as victimizers, have a long struggle ahead. In fact, pornography in some form will continue as long as boys are raised to believe they must control or conquer women as a proof of "masculinity," and as long as society rewards men who believe that success or even functioning—in sex as in other areas of life—depend on women's subservience.

But at least now we have words to describe our outrage, and to separate sex from aggression. We have the courage to demonstrate publicly against pornography, to throw its magazines and films out of our houses, to boycott its purveyors, to take even friends and family members who support it as seriously as we would if they were supporting and enjoying Nazi literature or the teachings of the Klan.

But until we finally end the male dominance that has equated sexuality with aggression, there will be more pornography in our lives and less erotica. There will be little murders in our beds—and very little love.

—1977, 1978,
and 1993

GLORIA STEINEM is one of the country's most widely read and critically acclaimed writers and activists. She also travels as a lecturer and feminist organizer. She is a founder and now the consulting editor of *Ms.* magazine, a founder of the Ms. Foundation for Women, and president of Voters for Choice. Her most recent book, the bestseller *Revolution From Within: A Book of Self-Esteem,* was published in 1992 by Little, Brown.

TWENTY YEARS LATER:
The Unfinished Revolution

by Peggy Miller & Nancy Biele

Only slow, patient education campaigns finally began to
convince people of the truth: Most rapes go unreported
because women are not believed.

WRITING THE RECORD

The rape crisis movement in the United States started a revolution. A generation ago, we took the first steps toward changing the realities women face by sharing our personal experiences of sexual assault and finding how many other women shared our experiences. Standing in front of school classrooms or church groups, rape crisis counselors spoke the words women had always whispered: rape, victim, rapist. We took the personal stories of everyday women and children and put them in a social context, deriving statistics that have since been corroborated by the FBI, the Uniform Crime Index, and the U.S. Senate Judiciary Committee:

One in eight women will be raped in her adult lifetime, according to the most conservative published study.[1] Another estimate put that figure at one in three.[2] One in four girls[3] and as many as one in seven boys[4] will be sexually victimized before they are old enough to vote, and many will be raped repeatedly.

The rape crisis movement illuminated the fact that rape is not a personal aberration in which a solitary male overcome by lust or perversion attacks a culpable, provocatively dressed female. Instead, rape in all its forms—sexual assaults on children, incest, date rape, the manufacture of pornography, and stranger rape—is an act of violence, a violation of the victim's spirit and body, and a perversion of power, a form of control exercised over more than half of the population.

THE (UN)NATURAL HISTORY OF RAPE

Rape, the crime and its attendant myths, is as old as dirt. Under ancient Hebrew law, if a woman was raped outside the city gates, her assailant was put to death. It was assumed that she was innocent, as her cries for help would not have been heard. If a woman was raped inside the city gates, however, both she and her assailant would be stoned to death; she obviously did not resist, or someone would have heard her. Her allegation of rape was therefore held to be frivolous, and she was regarded as a consensual adulterer.

Such punishment of victims seems too cruel to be real, yet today victims are often asked to explain what they did to resist attack and thus prove their innocence, their position outside the figurative city gates. Most states do not require evidence of physical resistance on the part of the victim, but from the disappointing outcomes of those few cases of rape that come to trial, it appears that most jurors do.

Historically, rape laws were property laws. Rape was a crime not against the victim, but against the man who owned her, her husband or father. If a man raped an unmarried woman, he would pay her father some amount, usually above the bride price, and he would then marry her. She, of course, had no choice.

Although our criminal codes have gradually changed to more closely reflect a humane world in which women have full legal personhood, our attitudes still percolate with bigotry. In cases of sexual violence involving evidence of a prior consenting sexual relationship, the victim's past will be scrutinized and judged in court, even in states with rape shield laws. If women who have been used in prostitution, pornography, and other areas of the sex industry bring action for redress of grievances, they rarely stand a chance for justice.

In the early days of the rape crisis movement, our efforts to expose the myths around sexual violence were met with disbelief and doubt. People seemed to believe that women falsely accused men of rape all the time. Even quoting statistics and identifying conservative criminal justice agencies as the source of data contrary to that belief did nothing to shake its constancy at first. Only slow, patient education campaigns finally began to convince people of the truth: Most rapes go unreported because women are not believed. It's in men's interest to disbelieve, and women disbelieve because the truth frightens and appalls them.

We saw that nothing can change until women and men both acknowledge the prevalence of sexual violence and how it functions in society to keep women afraid and men powerful. For a brief time it seemed that our efforts were succeeding in bringing about change. Many states passed laws and regulations specifically criminalizing sexual violence and shielding rape victims from investigation into their pasts.

In 1991 and 1992, highly visible cases of sexual violence and harassment made the news for weeks. It is true that without decades of education, the women bringing these complaints could not have gone as far as they did; still, the cases elicited a remarkable backlash. Many of us, within and outside the movement, were startled at the level of misogyny.

Twenty years ago the facts of incest and sexual victimization of children were met with silence and utter denial. Then we moved into a period of limited acknowledgment: okay, well, maybe it happens sometimes, but only someplace else. Then, during a fleeting moment, we seemed to achieve a level of appropriate community outrage: children are being raped and abused, and this must stop. But now we are faced with a sophisticated backlash, claiming that most children's accusations are fabricated.

THE BATTLE CONTINUES

A generation into the anti-rape movement, we have a history born out of speakouts, rallies, consciousness-raising groups, and volunteer hotlines in church basements. There are rape crisis centers in almost every state. Some have coalitions for mass education, for support, and for maintaining the growth and focus of the movement. There is even a National Coalition Against Sexual Assault.

Sexism, sexual harassment on the job and at school, and other injustices used to be called by a simple term—life. But now we have educated ourselves to acknowledge that these things cost billions of dollars in lost time and productivity. We have taught employers to write policies to protect their personnel.

We know something else as well: all our efforts in education, redefinition, and personal history have brought about only minor changes in social attitudes. Moreover, it is bad speech to yell "Fire!" in a movie theater, but it is good and protected speech to portray a woman hanging from a meat hook for sexually violent fantasies and ejaculatory enjoyment. Much of the entertainment that people pay to view while eating their popcorn concerns the stalking of young women, the sexy murder of women, or crazed, male-dependent women who perpetrate crimes against innocent men.

Men rape because they can. Sexual violence is sanctioned, at worst taught, and at best excused. Once we believed that those who rape women and children had been harmed themselves as children and were acting out. They were in need of our support and understanding. But millions of women are raped, and they do not rape anyone in return. Simple cause-and-effect victimization theories are just that—simple.

Something much larger than individual pathology is involved. Rape is a hate crime, the logical outcome of an ancient social bias against women. We must not forget that it is supported by a system of language, law, and custom. The battle to eradicate sexual violence is not going to be won through information alone. Ignorance may foster hatred, but information and education will not undo it. No one has ever claimed that men rape because they don't know the statistics.

The rape crisis movement has work ahead. We have made many forward strides, but resources are limited and demands for services will only grow. We have lost some ground, too. The individualism of the 1980s exacted its toll; there is now a whole industry, comprising diagnosis, therapy, medications, books, films, and tapes, that aims to move the reality of rape from its social context to an individual problem. The treatment of survivors today may be more humane than in the days of delusions and shock treatment, but treatment is only part of our charge.

A VISION FOR THE FUTURE

If the rape crisis movement had all the necessary resources, our crisis lines could be fully staffed, education would continue, and we would keep on expanding the definition of rape prevention to include real social change instead of just locking our doors and buying dogs.

We would have the resources to dream, discuss, and create new ways of doing things. We would hold personal and policy forums to examine concepts such as freedom of speech, freedom of choice, and responsibility. Rape and the threat of rape would be seen as violations of women's civil rights. Women would honor the female power of our leaders and not compete for status on the basis of our wounds, currently a popular way to divide us. We would have feminist research institutions for our founding mothers and others who would identify emerging issues, explore ethical concerns about the methods we use to further our causes, and develop alternative systems for seeking justice.

Each person would decide every day what resources, actions, and behavior he or she would personally commit to changing the status quo. And then we would do it.

The roots of sexual violence are deep. They are part of the very foundation of society. Addressing racism, sexism, heterosexism, and classism is essential to undoing the practice of rape.

The costs of living in a rape culture are very high. Women live in fear, limiting our own freedoms. We are less productive as citizens because we cannot work together. Women all carry the scar tissue of rape whether or not an individual act of sexual violence has been perpetrated against us. The symptoms of rape also result from living in a society that hates us.

All people suffer from living in a rape culture. There has to be room for healing, for resisting the temptation to perpetuate the patterns we know too well, and for finding the information we carry in our very bones that will allow us to teach the world a radically different way to be.

This is our future.

Women are not crazy. Women are not raped because someone did not know a definition, a fact, a reality. Rape is the reality. It is the final expression of sexism, a perfectly designed weapon for social control.

Rape will not stop until both men and women are allowed our full humanity. It is difficult, if not impossible, to harm another whom one perceives as equally human. The violence that comes from bias, hatred, and inequality can change when we figure out how to relate to one another as equals; this knowledge can be one of the gifts of truth from the rape crisis movement.

We have much more to learn from the collective wisdom of all the past and future activists and advocates in the struggle to end sexual violence. And we have much to gain from making our jobs obsolete.

We have a revolution to finish.

NOTES

1. "Rape in America: A Report to the Nation," National Victim's Center and the Crime Victims Research and Treatment Center, April 23, 1992.
2. Diana E. H. Russell, *Sexual Exploitation: Rape, Child Sexual Abuse and Workplace Harassment* (Newberry Park, CA: Sage Publications, 1984), p. 49, fig. 1.5, and p. 283.
3. Diana E. H. Russell, *Sexual Exploitation,* p. 194 and p. 285.
4. David Finkelhor, *Sexually Victimized Children* (New York: The Free Press, 1979), p. 30. Diana E. H. Russell, *Sexual Exploitation,* p. 194.

PEGGY MILLER is a counselor, educator, and garden-variety activist in the movement to end sexual violence. For the past eighteen years she has worked in rape crisis centers in Saginaw, Michigan, and St. Paul, Minnesota. She has served as executive director of the Minnesota Coalition against Sexual Assault. A writer of fiction and poetry, she also teaches journal writing, is a massage therapist, and is an activist in the lesbian and gay communities.

NANCY BIELE is currently the Violence Prevention Planner in the Office of Drug Policy and Violence Prevention with the Minnesota Department of Public Safety, and she is an advocate and trainer with the Minnesota Council of Churches in the area of clergy sexual misconduct. From 1974 to 1992 she was involved in rape crisis centers as an educator and director, including service as chair of the Minnesota Coalition Against Sexual Assault and president of the National Coalition against Sexual Assault.

STRATEGIES FOR CHANGE

According to the late Audre Lorde, "The master's tools will never dismantle the master's house." The basic institutions of the rape culture—language, kinship, religion, governance, and education—must be dismantled with new tools and replaced, if people truly wish to transform their culture. The writers in this section describe the new tools they have forged for transforming the world, from changing how we raise our sons and daughters to learning to speak a language that will not lie to rethinking our relationships with one another. They share the goal of changing consciousness, of creating new commitments to the long human journey away from violence and toward abundant life.

"I just raped my wife! What are you going to do about it, Pastor?":
The Church and Sexual Violence

by Carol J. Adams

An understanding of battering and marital
rape could transform the clergy from being
unhelpful or harmful to being catalysts for safety and
change. Ministers have an opportunity that few other
service providers have of interacting with congregates who
are being battered and raped or who are doing
the battering or raping.

Where language and naming are power,
silence is oppression, is violence.
—Adrienne Rich, 1977

PROLOGUE: THE RAPE OF SHIRLEY

Let me introduce you to Shirley, a woman who was despised and rejected by men, a woman of sorrows, a woman acquainted with grief. Shirley was battered and raped, and she tried to stop the terror. Her husband at times seemed like a "perfect gentleman"—caring, playful, kind. But . . . there were other times. Once, he rammed her head into a cabinet when she was pregnant; she sustained a concussion and had a miscarriage. Another time, he spilled milk on the floor, then knocked her onto the floor and mopped the milk up with her hair and clothes. Once, when she sought refuge in her mother's house, he showed up with a knife and said, "If I can't have her, no one can." Sometimes he raped her during or after beatings. Shirley told her fundamentalist pastor about the violence; she was counseled by him to forgive her husband. She recalled a particularly savage assault:

> . . . they had had an argument and she had gone into the shower
> to try to put some distance between them. He came into the bathroom and kept ripping back the curtain. She slapped him, something she had never done before (and never did again: "That taught me"). He started socking her in the stomach until she vomited. Then he forced her to have sex. Distraught, she thought she might finally get some assistance from her pastor and quickly dialed his number. Before she could tell him what had happened, however, her husband picked up the phone on another extension and shouted, "I just raped my wife! What are you going to do about it, Pastor?"[1]

The rapist's taunt is also our question: what should the church do about sexual violence, especially marital rape? In the responses of both Shirley and her rapist to the pastor—one faithfully seeking help, one expressing extreme contempt—we find a clue to the problem that the church faces. When it fails to help the victim, it simultaneously colludes with the rapist while demonstrating its powerlessness to him. The rapist is thus enabled to view the church and its representatives with the same scorn he holds for his victim. And the victim faces further violence, deserted by her faith community and, from her perspective, by her God as well.

Even without Shirley's story, we know that ministers are doing harm when women abused by their male partners seek their counseling. We know that battered women who escape their abusers ranked the assistance they received from clergy at the bottom of their list.[2] We also know that women who turned to their clergy for guidance stayed longer with the men who hurt them. We know that battered women's shelters often shy away from working with clergy because of their poor track record.

An understanding of battering and marital rape, however, could transform the clergy from being unhelpful or harmful to being catalysts for safety and change. Ministers have an opportunity that few other service providers have of interacting with congregates who are being battered and raped or who are doing the battering and raping. Women who distrust secular authorities, who might never consider going to a shelter for battered women or calling a rape hotline, often do talk to their ministers. Moreover, unlike social workers and other service providers, pastors enter freely into the domain where most injury to women occurs—the home.

There are some specific reasons for the inadequacy of the church in responding to the issue of sexual victimization; this essay will examine the barriers to effective response and conclude by providing some suggestions for a compassionate response to Shirley and other victims of marital rape.

THE WIDESPREAD PROBLEM OF SILENCE AND NAMING

The church, like society at large, has had difficulty naming sexual violence and believing the victims who break the silence. The failure to name accurately plagues our culture, as the following anecdote exemplifies:

An anthropologist went to South America to live with the Yanomano—a people whose culture had been identified as intensely violent. In a book he later wrote about that experience, he concluded that this label was wrong. Ugly incidents may occur in this culture, but, he argued, to focus on them distorts the Yanomano way of life. When his book was reviewed in the *New York Times Book Review*, the reviewer praised the book and its approach because it refused to allow reported incidents of violence to dominate any definitive interpretation of this culture.

This book, the review, and the reaction to them help identify some of the issues that will concern us as we discuss the church and sexual violence. It turns out that a great deal of the violence in the Yanomano culture is violence against women by men. Single women beyond the age of puberty are routinely raped. Witnessing the gang rape of a woman from another village who had run away from her husband, the anthropologist was shaken with anger. Though he pondered the question of whether he should stop this violence, he finally allowed another man to pull him away.

The anthropologist left the community for a while, leaving his young Yanomano wife as well. She was put in an extremely perilous situation. When word came back that the anthropologist had died, tribesmen repeatedly raped the woman, and one of her ears was badly ripped.

In response to the book review that recounts these incidents, as well as to the conclusion that violence is not the central theme of Yanomano life, a letter was sent to the *Times*. In part it read:

> Here is a society in which the lives of half the population
> (women) are overtly controlled by the other half (men) through
> the threat and actuality of rape as an institutionalized, culturally
> sanctioned norm; in which any woman of childbearing age not
> married and subservient to a man from her own village is "rou-
> tinely raped" by the men of her own or another village. If this is
> not violence as a central theme of societal life, what would be?[3]

It could be argued that this disparity in interpretation—in which some people minimize the significance of violence while others see sanctioned cultural violence—is true for our culture as well. This has become clear when researchers have used open-ended questions in surveys and approached women about their experiences. Although the questions may not have focused specifically on violence, by their open-ended nature, they allowed for the disclosure of information on violence. In fact, it has been the case that women disclose violent acts against them to such a degree that researchers must redesign their study to take numerous instances of reported violence into account. For example, in their project to identify ways in which women's self-concepts and ways of knowing are intertwined, the authors of *Women's Ways of Knowing* report:

> Although we did not initially intend to collect information on sexual abuse, it became clear to us, after we started interviewing, that women spontaneously mention childhood and adolescent sexual trauma as an important factor affecting their learning and relationships to male authority. Midway into the study we began to survey the women systematically on their history of sexual and physical abuse. Based on our data, sexual abuse appears to be a shockingly common experience for women. . . . We believe that sexual trauma among women is a far more serious problem than is acknowledged by the medical and psychiatric establishment and the public at large.[4]

Once named and no longer invisible, sexual violence moves from the margin to the center of a discussion of women's lives. For the church to be effective, this movement of the issue of sexual violence from margin to center must occur within its own structures.

Church leaders must acknowledge that they *know* sexual violence exists in society, and, therefore, in their congregations. Are they prepared to offer helpful responses? When clergy *do* name violence from the pulpit or in their other capacities as church leaders, they report surprise at the number of people who come forward who have been personally affected by sexual violence.

Just as clergy must begin by naming violence to announce their concern, just as victims begin to regain control in their world by naming their experiences, questions of naming and interpretation must concern us first.

FROM DENIAL TO NAMING

The question of naming and perceiving violence is an urgent one for the church. The church has had difficulty naming violence. Biblical stories about violence against women are not a part of the lectionary (the assigned readings from the Bible for weekly church services). In the absence of naming violence and understanding the dynamics of sexual victimization, it is difficult to believe victims, even though they usually understate the abuse. There is also an expectation that victims will self-disclose the information about their abuse.

While silence is the opposite of speaking, *denial is the opposite of naming*. In other words, the absence of any discussion within the theological community at whatever level—in seminary or church, in counseling or sermons–might be considered "silence," but it is actually "denial." In this response, the Christian community resembles the abuser, who actively denies the violence or his responsibility for the violence. Silence "not only immobilizes victims but encourages the behavior of perpetrators."[5] As long as violence is both invisible and unnamed, it is tacitly, although perhaps unintentionally, condoned.

Paulo Freire writes: "Dialogue cannot occur between those who want to name the world and those who do not want this naming."[6] Victims need to name their world, so that the terror and violence will stop, and so that they will no longer be victimized but will become survivors. Perpetrators do not want their acts to be acknowledged through naming. How has the church faced this problem of dialogue? Some within the church have been afraid to learn about private terrors because of antiquated notions about family or marital bliss, fears of inadequacy in terms of counseling abilities, close friendships with abusers, an unwillingness to hear of the immense suffering, or because clergy are at times abusers themselves. A problem inadequately named cannot be adequately addressed.

Paulo Freire writes further that "to speak a true word is to transform the world."[7] What are the true words that must be spoken about sexual violence? First, we must admit that next to the police and the military, the home is the most violent institution in the United States. Women and children are considerably less safe in the home than are men. Rape, child sexual victimization, and physical abuse all occur behind the closed doors of parishioners' homes. We must create a climate of safety in which acts of naming can overthrow acts of violation and denial.

WHY HASN'T NAMING OCCURRED?

Our language has a tendency to mask violence. It may highlight someone's victimization while simultaneously cloaking the agency and actions of the perpetrator of that violence. Sarah Lucia Hoagland demonstrates how this works: "John beat Shirley" becomes "Shirley was beaten by John," then "Shirley was beaten," then "women beaten," and thus "battered women." Hoagland observes that "now something *men do to women* has become instead something that is a part of *women's nature.* And we lose consideration of John entirely."[8] Pushing Hoagland's insights, we see that when Shirley says, "I was raped, abused, battered," she is not only saying something about herself, she is saying something about another—the rapist, abuser, batterer. The difficulty of doing this is that you are announcing that someone has inflicted evil, that *someone has been evil.* In her moving autobiography *My Father's House,* Sylvia Fraser depicts the process of coming to the point where she can actually say "my father raped me." She is naming something about herself and her father simultaneously. This dialectic of naming—that one is saying something about oneself and another—results in a complex process of denial and resistance to naming. The maxim "do not speak ill of another" carries terrifying weight for victims of battering, rape, and child sexual abuse.

Language that excludes women will exclude their experiences. The continual use of *man* and *mankind* as generic terms implies that the male human being is the norm. It also denies women's experiences and women themselves, presupposing that they can be included within the term *man.* When women are rendered invisible through androcentric language, it is "difficult for women to recognize their own needs for health and safety as legitimate, [and] also makes recognition difficult for the entire community."[9]

Naming may not occur for many because they have no name to give to their experience. But when, through representation and identification, an image is offered by the media, naming pours forth. For instance, after the first showing of *The Burning Bed,* a film that portrays a wife who kills her husband after enduring years of beatings, women responded by an inundation of calls to shelters for battered women and hotlines.[10] Suddenly, naming became possible because what has happened to these women has been represented by the media. Similarly, after a clergyperson mentions battering from the pulpit, women abused by their partners will be more likely to approach her or him and discuss their own beatings. When one minister announced he was attending a seminar on family violence, four families in which violence was ongoing contacted him. "He was horrified at first; he thought there was an epidemic in his congregation. Then he realized that these things had always existed, but no one had ever spoken to him of them, because he had never given them a signal that he knew about them, cared about them, and thought they were appropriate subjects to deal with in the church."[11]

Women are more likely to speak about the experiences of rape that conform to society's notion of rape, i.e., violently coerced sexual acts by strangers. This, as Susan Estrich has shown, is what people think of as "real rape."[12] The further one's own experience strays from this cultural notion of being "really raped, the less likely is one to speak about one's experience as rape," and even to think of it as rape. Many women do not call nonconsensual sex "rape," or they classify it as the lesser crime of assault or battery. It is especially difficult for a wife to admit that her husband raped her: "She doesn't want to face the fact that she is living with a rapist, that she is making herself vulnerable to rape."[13] This is denial. Yet Diana Russell's monumental study indicates that marital rape is the most common kind of rape.

In her landmark survey on marital rape, Russell discovered that women who did not see themselves as raped confirmed that they had been forced to have intercourse or that intercourse had been obtained by threat. In one study, more than twice as many women were raped by their *husbands* as by strangers. Anywhere from one-third to one-half of battered women are victims of marital sexual assault.[14] In *License to Rape*, David Finkelhor and Kersti Yllo identified three categories of marital rape. The first is battering rape, in which violent sex is another aspect of controlling behavior and physical abuse by the male partner. Of the women they interviewed who were battered by their husbands, 50 percent had been sexually assaulted twenty times or more. Women are often raped as a continuation of a beating, threatened with more violence if they fail to comply with their husband's sexual requests, or forced to have sex to oblige the abuser's need to "make up" after a beating. Women who survived battering rapes often felt that it was the sexual abuse that was the most devastating. The second category is force-only rape or "nonbattering rape," in which forced sex was related to specifically sexual contexts. And the third category is obsessive rape, in which the husbands had bizarre sexual obsessions and were heavily involved with pornography. A third of the women in Finkelhor and Yllo's study reported anal rape.

Once sexual violence has been named, additional forces may make it difficult for an individual to speak about her experience of violation. Elsewhere Finkelhor and Yllo tell us: "No doubt raped wives, like battered wives, use many self-deceptions to avoid facing the realities of an intolerable marriage because the alternatives—loneliness, loss of financial security, admission of failure—are so frightening."[15]

Lack of comfort in discussing a woman's physical body compounds the problem of naming. We must be able to name female body parts—breast, clitoris, vagina—and to hear them named without feeling squeamish, if we are to name what has happened or hear it named. In the absence of comfort about the words themselves, a woman will feel awkward describing what was done to those body parts. Moreover, in a culture in which images of these body parts are so heavily eroticized, the victim who speaks of violation may be experienced as speaking pornographically.[16] The overcoming of denial by naming is complicated by this patriarchal contamination of the space into which women must speak about their experience of sexual violation.

NAMING, DENIAL, AND THE CHURCH'S RESPONSE TO SEXUAL VIOLENCE

In addition to the forces identified above that impede naming, the commitment of the church to educating its leaders on the subject of sexual violence faces several structural impediments.[17]

First, pastoral care has no category for the crises of battering, date rape, and marital rape. The classic book on pastoral counseling, Howard Clinebell's *Basic Types of Pastoral Care and Counseling*, proposes that the vast majority of pastoral care in the church occurs around life crises, and identifies two kinds of crises: *developmental crises* "that occur around the normal stressful transitions in the life journey" and *accidental crises*.[18] What Clinebell reveals is something many survivors have experienced: pastoral care has no category for ongoing, nondevelopmental crises perpetuated by someone with whom the victim is in a caring relationship, such as childhood sexual victimization, marital rape, and wife battering. Without such a category, pastoral care has attempted to "fit" the crises of sexual and domestic violence into preexisting categories. As a result, what is actually a chronic problem (the abuser's behavior) is treated within an inadequate crisis framework.

Second, ministers have a tendency to minimize the lethality of sexual and domestic violence by focusing instead on relationship issues. This distorts the responsibility of the abuser. Because of this focus on the relationship rather than on the violence, reconciliation may be encouraged before the abuse has been stopped. Or, as in the case of Shirley, forgiveness may be encouraged, even though the abuser has not repented of his behavior.

Third, inadequate counseling techniques are taken as adequate. For instance, domestic violence protocol holds that couples counseling when battering is ongoing may contribute to increasing, rather than decreasing, the violence. Yet pastoral care courses often encourage couples counseling without noting when it is inadvisable. When untrained to identify and act on the evidence of sexual and domestic violence, ministers will put women at risk if they follow traditional counseling techniques.

Fourth, criminal behavior has been defined as a psychological problem for the victim. Questions about her behavior enter into the counseling, again minimizing the abuser's accountability by implying the victim's provocation. The psychological focus also means that the victim must go through "recovery" rather than achieve justice. Moreover, often uncomfortable with the use of secular resources, the church has difficulty seeing the role of criminal justice in Christian justice.

Fifth, there is a lack of clarity on the issue of confidentiality. While reporting requirements for child sexual abuse may or may not be seen to apply to clergy—and many clergy do not want to be held to this reporting requirement—it is sadly the case that clergy often call the perpetrators after learning from their victims about abuse. Without the permission or knowledge of the victims, this violation of confidentiality can seriously endanger them.

Finally, there is little comprehension that abuse provides rewards for the abuser, and that he is thus unlikely to stop without intervention. Several issues are apparent here:

(1) Sometimes clergy identify with the abuser, especially if he is a church member. Thus the tendency is to see the violence as an aberration rather than as a chronic problem. This protects the offender.

(2) Often the church believes in the abuser's contriteness, and thus emphasizes forgiveness, especially when there is any sign of remorse.

Abusers can manipulate religious language in their own interest. Remorse is confused with repentance. But forgiveness without any guarantee that the abuser has changed, has truly repented, will not stop the abuse. It also short-circuits the legitimate anger of the victim while endangering her.

(3) There is a misapprehension of the meaning of the marriage covenant, and when the covenant is broken:

> A woman victimized in an abusive domestic relationship feels serious ethical/spiritual dilemmas about the marriage covenant. She has made promises that are still important and meaningful to her. One of those is that the relationship will be a lasting one. To stay in the relationship means to suffer further abuse, but to leave (temporarily or permanently) makes her feel as if she is breaking her promise. Many women thus stay and suffer the abuse, precisely because they take their commitment seriously. Seldom does it occur to the victim of the abuse (at least in the beginning)—or to friends, family, or the church—that the covenant has already been broken by the behavior of her partner. . . . The victim who seeks safety, or eventually decides to seek separation or divorce, *is* acknowledging that the covenant which she had established with another no longer exists, *but she is not the one breaking the covenant.*[19]

In other words, rather than asserting that the family must stay together, the church could acknowledge that violence has already sundered the family, and it is the abuser who has broken the covenant.

NAMING, GOD-TALK AND SEXUAL VIOLENCE

Men who abuse and rape their partners are men who seek to control others. In being abusive, they are not out of control; rather, they establish control.[20] Images of control, authority, and maleness combine in traditional representations of God as Father, which upholds the petit-godhead established within each family by the abusive husband. In this, God the Father sacralizes domination by a father/husband who in turn usurps the role of this patriarchal God: assigning guilt, punishing, and controlling. Sallie McFague argues that we need language appropriate for our time, not language that supports hierarchical, dualistic, external, unchanging, atomistic, and deterministic ways of understanding the relationship between God and the world, but language that understands the God-world relationship as open, caring, inclusive, interdependent, changing, mutual, and creative.[21] Were we to replace the harmful monarchical language about God—king, ruler, lord, sovereign—with language that embedded God within the world, the abuser would lose the sacralized reinforcement of authoritarianism.

It is not surprising that an abuser might gravitate to any hints of misogyny in the Christian tradition. This tradition provides excellent raw material for his authoritarianism. What Rosemary Radford Ruether terms patriarchal anthropology has proclaimed women as sinful, women as the cause of sin, and subjugation to men as the punishment for women's sinful behavior.[22] This positioning of women provides several legitimations for rapist behavior—seeing woman as temptress and each woman's duty as submission to her husband. From Eve, who was sinful, who tempted Adam, who deserved God's punishment, through to the New Testament and the apparent absence of female disciples, the Biblical tradition appears to be on the side of the abuser. This tradition gets incorporated into justifications for the abuser's behavior. Just as an abuser twists everything—claiming as reasons for his actions such things as adding mushrooms to a pizza, vacuuming a room at the wrong time of day, taking a job, or refusing to have sex—how much more salient are selected texts from the Bible about women being obedient or sinful.

Of course, twisted Biblical interpretations seem to confirm women's subjugation to abuse as well. In a search for the meaning of her abuse, the victim may see Jesus' suffering as a model for her own and think that she must accept her cross (especially if this is what her clergyperson exhorts). She may think sinfulness lies in her assertion of self and believe that she must become more self-denying. She may conclude that forgiveness is required by her toward all who have hurt her.

It is understandable why battered and raped women might gravitate to this idea of Jesus' suffering and his forgiveness of his abusers to cope with the abusive behavior of their partners. Our culture encourages the sacrifice of wives and mothers. Women are said to be the caretakers and nurturers of the family. Women's self-development is sacrificed to the family and this sacrifice is considered redemptive for all involved, including the woman.[23] The perceived Christian emphasis on sacrifice as something good matches the way girls are taught to consider others rather than themselves, to be self-sacrificing in a social situation. *The religious meaning of sacrifice is thus layered on top of the social view of women as sacrificial.* The idea that bodily suffering is spiritually redemptive also intersects with the traditional Christian notion of denial of the body. Thus, women's bodies are separated from the idea of being redeemed in and of themselves, of having bodily worth or bodily integrity.

By failing to provide a prophetic word against interpretations that, on one hand, justify domination and, on the other, reinforce subordination, the church becomes complicit in perpetuating these images and ideas so ripe for misapplication. The church becomes a party to dominant-subordinate relationships.

In the face of this appeal to authority by the abuser, and the gravitation to Biblical messages that entrap the victim, the church must side, clearly, with the abused. It must challenge interpretations that accept abuse as appropriate, offering instead a liberating, prophetic word about setting captives *and* rape victims free. It must declare to the assaultive man and his victim that the person who has been violent is the person who has endangered this marriage. It must remind victims of marital rape and battering that when Jesus had the opportunity to stop or prevent suffering, he did. Often, the suffering individuals were women: the woman whose bleeding would not stop, the woman taken in adultery, the Samaritan woman. If Jesus were ministering today, would he say, "Yes, continue suffering as I did"? Or would he say, "Stop suffering! Whenever I could, I stopped suffering, and your suffering can be stopped."

Furthermore, the church must proclaim that God is not male, and that the male—especially in his own home—is not God. It must challenge the domination-subordination model of the God-human relationship and proclaim that for victims of rape and battering, sin is not self-assertion, love is not self-sacrifice, forgiveness does not involve condoning or excusing abusive behavior. The church has been unable to do this, in part, because marital rape and battering are seen as interpersonal problems rather than as widespread institutional violence against which the church must take a firm stance.

SEXUAL VIOLENCE IS INSTITUTIONAL VIOLENCE

Prologue: The Rape of Maria Goretti

In July 1902, Maria Goretti, a 12-year old Italian girl, was stabbed in a sexual assault and died. Although details of the story have been influenced over the years by constant retelling and adaptation, the basic facts are as follows: Maria Goretti was from a poor rural family. Home alone one day, Maria was attacked by a young man, Alessandro Serenelli. He threatened to kill her if she did not have sex with him. Maria refused, and he stabbed her repeatedly with a knife. She died 24 hours after the attack. Serenelli was caught and tried for murder. He was sentenced to 30 years in prison. When he was released, Serenelli went to live with an order of monks. Reportedly, Maria appeared to him in a vision during his imprisonment. She forgave him, and he repented of his sin. When she was canonized by the Roman Catholic Church in 1950, Serenelli was present, along with Maria's mother and her family.[24]

What for Maria was a murderous rape was described as "an attractive pleasure" in Pope Pius XII's homily at her canonization.[25] Here Pope Pius XII, like the dominant culture, resists seeing the violence in sexual assault. Rape is not "an attractive pleasure" for the victim, nor is the victim of rape sinful. As Marie M. Fortune points out, the major problem with the religious attention to the murder of Maria Goretti is that the wrong lessons are drawn: "Unfortunately, this story does not teach women to resist male sexual aggression *for the right reasons,* i.e., because it is violent and aggressive and women have a right to maintain their bodily integrity."[26]

The minister's response to Shirley was that she should pray for her assailant and forgive him; this is the message derived from the story of the suffering of Maria Goretti as well, that the sexually victimized should forgive their abusers. To be adequately understood, the rape of Shirley and the attempted rape of Maria Goretti—and these embarrassingly inadequate responses—must be set within the framework that sexual violence is institutional violence and that sexual violence will no longer be minimized, misnamed, and misunderstood.

Elsewhere I have identified what I consider to be the major components of institutional violence.[27] For something to be *institutional violence, it must be a widespread, unethical practice* in a society. As this anthology demonstrates, a large number of children and women are at risk of being battered, raped, or sexually victimized. In addition, institutional violence consists of six interrelated factors:

1) *Institutional violence is an infringement on or failure to acknowledge another's inviolability.* Sovereignty over our own bodies is a basic right. It is this sovereignty that is undermined, this inviolability made violate by sexual violence. Abuse is aggressive, destructive behavior that violates and often annihilates another human being. Sexual violence is a violation of right relationships: it is evidence of the abuser's alienation, brokenness, estrangement. It also causes alienation, brokenness, and estrangement in the victims. Abuse involves destruction of the ego. For women who are battered and raped by their partners, the assault on their self-esteem accompanies assaults on their bodies. Children who are sexually victimized live in a climate of constant danger. Dissociation "becomes not merely a defensive adaptation but the fundamental principle of personality organization."[28]

Victims of rape and sexual abuse often feel dirty, embarrassed, and guilty. In the face of the violation of their bodies, they also carry the stigma in our culture that it was their fault.

David Finkelhor and Kersti Yllo's *License to Rape: Sexual Abuse of Wives* argues that "rape by intimates in general is more, not less, traumatic than rape by strangers" because the rapist continues to live with his victim. Moreover, women victimized by battering rapes said that rapes were especially traumatizing because of "the more personal, intimate nature of the sexual abuse," as opposed to the sense that the "beatings seem[ed] more external."[29]

If we listen to the victims, we can learn precisely how they feel about losing their sense of inviolability. They felt devastated, demeaned, humiliated, degraded, despondent, depressed, shocked, defiled, betrayed, powerless, isolated, entrapped. Moreover, because they were raped by their husbands, some felt like prostitutes, and many worried whether they would be able to trust intimates again.

2) *Institutional violence is any treatment and/or physical force that injures or abuses.* By treatment, I mean *ongoing* conditions that are abusive or injurious. By physical force, I mean *specific* actions that cause

injuries. Incest, rape, and battering are violent and coercive acts that provide to the husband, father, or partner the ability to control, intimidate, and subordinate his wife, his daughter or son, or his partner.

Child sexual abuse often begins when a child is between the ages of four and eight and continues until the child reaches adolescence and is able to escape from the abuse. The average age of a child who is being sexually victimized is between eight and eleven. The average length of time of an incestuous relationship is three years. Child sexual abuse "may include fondling, masturbation, genital penetration, or exhibitionism. It is a crime in every state."[30]

Battering is "assaultive behavior occurring in an intimate, sexual, theoretically peer, usually cohabiting relationship, a *pattern* of behavior, not isolated individual events. One form of battering builds on another and sets the stage for the next battering episode."[31]

Sexual violence "includes any physical, visual, verbal or sexual act that is experienced by the woman or girl, at the time or later, as a threat, invasion or assault, that has the effect of hurting her or degrading her and/or takes away her ability to control intimate contact."[32]

These are all physical violations that produce trauma and somatic responses. The trauma of marital rape can cause nausea and vomiting, soreness, bruising, muscle tension, headaches, fatigue, and injuries to the genital area. The marital rape victim may feel strain and stress because she is constantly reminded by the presence of her rapist husband of the incident and the possibility of another attack. Women can experience flashbacks as well as haunting nightmares for years after an assault.

3) *Institutional violence involves a series of denial mechanisms that deflect attention from the violence.* Denial of the extent and nature of violence is an important protective device for maintaining institutional violence. It communicates that the violence that is an integral part of our culture is neither troublesome nor severe. The pastor who told Shirley to forgive her husband was denying the criminal actions of her husband. Pope Pius XII, in misnaming the act of rape, was denying it.

To accomplish denial, *false naming* is a major component of institutional violence. False naming means that we can avoid responsibility. False naming creates false consciousness. As the church struggles with the issue of violence, it often relies on terms such as "marital aggression" or "husband-wife violence," "the incestuous family" or "the battering system." These terms avoid assigning responsibility, thus cloaking who the incest offender is, who the batterer is, who the rapist is, and who the victim is. This false naming inadvertently sends a message to the perpetrator that he has still not been "found out," that the church is not concerned specifically with what he is doing. As with the perpetrator himself, these efforts minimize the violence and deny responsibility. Contrary to these terms, the facts are that husbands and fathers perpetrate the majority of sexually and physically abusive acts; women and children are the victims and suffer emotional, medical, and spiritual consequences.

Perpetrators deny, evade, or minimize their actions. Denial occurs through the perpetrators' excuses: victims are portrayed as having enjoyed the experience. (Even rapists who used weapons think that their victims enjoyed it.) The child sexual abuser often sees himself as providing a positive experience for the victim. Other denials by perpetrators include refrains such as "She asked for it," "She enjoyed it," "She deserved it," or "I did it for her."

Where there is denial, *there is no call to accountability* to the perpetrators of sexual violence. Rape, child sexual victimization, and battering are all against the law (though marital rape is not yet criminalized in every state). Ministers, police, doctors, and other authorities have often discouraged rather than encouraged the reporting of sexual violence. Studies, statistics, and individual testimony demonstrate clearly that the most effective way to stop violence against women and children is to hold the abuser accountable. As long as individual women and children who are sexually and physically abused seek help from the church, without any direct cultural message that names the abuse as illegal and the abuser as a sinner or names the violence as illegal and the abuser as a perpetrator, the violence will most likely not stop. Indeed, it may escalate. When Shirley finally escaped to a shelter, her furious husband sought her out there: "She was frightened to death, she remembers, so immobilized that it was all she could do to crawl upstairs to safety on her hands and knees."[33] Even after Shirley's divorce, her husband hid in her bedroom closet and then forced her to do something he knew she hated—oral sex.

In the absence of accountability, abuse continues. The problem is that crimes of sexual violence are the least likely to be reported and have the lowest conviction rate: "On a national average, one rapist in twenty is arrested, one out of thirty is prosecuted, and one in sixty is convicted."[34] Despite this, criminal prosecution should be encouraged for several reasons. First, it is the only way to establish that sexual violence is criminal activity rather than interpersonal problems gone awry. Second, continued appeal to the criminal justice system eventually brings about some reforms, as has been seen in some cities where successful prosecution of batterers resulted in a decrease in incidents of violence. And third, there is even less accountability when legal sanctions are not invoked.

What should the minister Shirley called have done? He should have said to her rapist, "You have just told me that you broke a law. You have also violated the church's most basic ethical position on covenantal relationships. Will you call the police or shall I?" This offers the opportunity to say to the assailant: "What you did was wrong. You need to get counseling to learn more appropriate ways of responding. I know that court-ordered counseling is often the only way that perpetrators actually participate fully in the counseling program. Through the prosecution for your offense, you are being offered the chance to change, to learn more effective ways of interacting, and to respect your partner. I will support you in this."

4) *Institutional violence targets "appropriate" victims.* Ideology makes the existence of "appropriate victims" appear to be natural and inevitable. If one raped or sexually assaulted one's boss, professor, clergyperson, or doctor, the assault would clearly be seen and responded to as the criminal act that it is. Women and children are "appropriate" victims in our culture, which sees the adult (white) male as the normative person. We can find cultural definitions of women and children as male property; for that reason, fathers and husbands believe they have the right to control and punish.

The misapplication of certain Biblical passages is evident in the making of appropriate victims. Fathers and husbands come to believe that their authority is divinely mandated, that God ordains men's authority in marriage and women's and children's subordination. Problematic passages such as Genesis 2, 1 Timothy 2:12–14, 1 Corinthians 11:8, and Ephesians 5:22–24 are taken as affirming theological justification for women's subordination. In fact, it has been found that egalitarian, democratic families are less likely to have an abusive husband or incest offender than families in which fundamental religious beliefs are held and sex role stereotypes are rigidly adhered to.

A logic of domination accompanies the making of appropriate victims. Differences of age and differences between the sexes have been deemed to carry meanings of superiority and inferiority. According to a logic of domination, that which is morally superior—maleness and/or adulthood—is morally justified in subordinating that which is not—femaleness and/or childhood.[35] We find the equation of masculinity with dominance and power in sexual relationships, the view that male aggression is a natural and normal part of sexual intercourse, and the eroticization of male domination. Many see rape as related to our culture's contempt for female qualities. They also argue that rape is an act of social control that keeps women in their place.[36] The fact that marital rape was not outlawed for many years indicated precisely who are the appropriate victims.

The church in its emphasis on certain virtues reinforces marital rape and married women as the appropriate victims. Social conventions about women's duty in marriage are often parroted within religious communities. Thus women who believe it is their duty to have sex with their husbands whenever it is desired, that it is part of their roles as wives, may tragically find this belief confirmed by church authorities to whom they turn for assistance. When this occurs, the church provides a mirror for the abuser's reality. Moreover, married women may come to believe that God has made them the appropriate victim, that is, that God is punishing them.

The difference between the ways women resist stranger rape versus marital rape illustrates the making of appropriate victims. While gouging the rapist's eyes, kicking him in the groin, running out of the house, calling the police, and brandishing or using a weapon are all possible responses to stranger rape, they are seldom enacted against husbands. Finkelhor and Yllo report that they "heard remarkably few stories of successful resistance to marital rape."[37] Instead, tactics of appeasement were more frequently found: keeping the peace, giving in, preventing anal rape or oral sex by substituting vaginal rape. Women found that trying to talk their husband out of it was ineffective and that running away and hiding brought about broken doors. Some did threaten to leave, some did leave temporarily, some did leave and divorce, and some did use violence. But, overall, the decisions to choose appeasement over outright resistance revolved on several perceptions: the perception of the husband's strength, the presumption that if the wife resisted she would be hurt even worse (especially if there was a history of battering), that resistance prolonged the assault, that appeasement protected the children, that unless she was ready to leave she would have to face the man again, that it was good to "keep the peace," and that she believed herself to be wrong, at fault. Catharine MacKinnon has pointed out that the strategies needed for day-to-day survival of violence are the exact opposite of those needed for ending violence. Appropriate victims are those for whom surviving day-to-day violence overwhelms the ability to end the violence; thus they must find ways to accommodate the rapist rather than resist him, they find themselves feeling guilty rather than angry, and they keep the peace rather than holding the husband accountable. "An inability to respond with anger is one way in which multiple experiences of sexual abuse destroy women."[38]

A rapist's sinful acts should be understood as a consequence of his own brokenness and alienation, not as in any way caused by the woman. There are no appropriate victims.

Misunderstanding of theological issues such as suffering, forgiveness, and redemption contributes to maintaining women and children as appropriate victims. They may begin to interpret their suffering as ordained by God, as acceptable because it recalls Jesus' suffering, as having a purpose in redeeming another. In place of the legitimate anger and rage they should feel for the violation of their bodies, they are encouraged to forgive their abusers. Instead of repentance *by* the abuser, their victims are encouraged to be forgiving *of* their abusers, like Christ from the cross. The victim should not be asked to forgive her abuser, as Maria Goretti was in her enormous pain. In the absence of the abuser's repentance— which would include both accepting responsibility for having been abusive and *stopping the abuse*—women and children will continue to be abused. Forgiveness in the absence of repentance by the abuser is a salve for the conscience of society, but it is not a healing experience for the victim.

In the absence of a liberation theology that clearly sides with the violated, traditional theological formulations encourage the victims to find meaning in their abuse, rather than resisting that abuse. Sermons that speak generally on topics such as the necessity for forgiveness or the inappropriateness of anger, without recognizing how they are heard specifically by survivors, can perpetuate victimization.

5) *Institutional violence has identifiable detrimental effects on society as a whole.* Besides the obvious unethical behavior manifested in sexual violence, there are other costs to the human community. More than

one-third to one-half of all homeless women are fleeing domestic violence. Runaway children are often running away from sexual abuse. "It is estimated that over seventy-five percent of all adolescents involved in prostitution—female and male—were victims of prior sexual violence: rape, incestuous abuse, or molestation."[39] We have no adequate way to measure the effect on society as a whole of the fact that for numerous women and children basic trust relationships have been violated, and the result of this is that they rightly have difficulty trusting others.

6) *Institutional violence manipulates others into passivity regarding its practices.* Like the anthropologist mentioned at the beginning of this article, we are pulled away from considering just how we might stop the violence. The result is that the violence continues. We are not empowered to *believe* that we can stop it. We have difficulty recognizing that violence is a choice, one of several options. Rather than asking judgmental questions such as "Why doesn't she leave?" about a battered woman, "What was she wearing or doing?" about a rape victim, and "Can we believe her?" about a child abuse victim, we need to ask, "Why does he choose to batter, rape, and abuse?"

In fact, the seminary community has most likely not equipped ministers to respond to the issue of violence in their own congregations. Though often shocked by information about violence and feeling the urgency for action, ministers do not know what to do. Or they may be afraid to act. Or, if they do respond, they may rely on general counseling techniques that they may later learn were totally inadequate.

MARITAL RAPE: A PASTORAL RESPONSE

Calling upon Paulo Freire's insights again, we must acknowledge that "no one can say a true word alone—nor can s/he say it *for* another, in a prescriptive act which robs others of their words."[40] I envision a community that invites the saying of a true word, not alone, but in a supportive presence. Such a community does not describe and delimit by asking the question, "Have you been abused?" Instead it invites someone to expand her relationship with the outer world, to transform herself by stating what is happening now, to begin to change the now into the reconstructed and liberating future. Sexual violence requires that we respond appropriately and directly. It requires that we name the violence, that we offer protection and advocacy for the victims, that we hold the perpetrator accountable, and that we work as a society to prevent further abuse.

Freire observes that "to exist, humanly, is to *name* the world, to change it."[41] The power of naming is the power of self-authorization. This is what the church must offer survivors of sexual violence.

Women and children see their abuse as a spiritual issue and seek out religiously affiliated people, such as pastors, to help them interpret their experience. Some religious women may not trust secular resources that do not acknowledge the religious crisis they may be undergoing. A secular program that offers safety without addressing deeply important issues such as spirituality and a religious institution that addresses spiritual issues divested from safety issues are fragmented responses.

Three qualities of the pastoral counselor are essential when survivors disclose their experiences: the ability to process information about the dehumanizing violence enacted by one person against another; the ability to provide practical assistance; and the ability to reflect theologically. Most importantly, these three abilities must be constantly balanced, and the boundaries between them must be understood and maintained. So many of the "don'ts" of pastoral care in this area involve respecting the difference between process, practical advice, and theology, and not substituting a response from one area when a response from another area is called for. If clergypersons act shocked or horrified, they have failed to process the information adequately. If they offer a general prayer for someone's suffering or discuss forgiveness, they have relied on the theological dimension in an unrealistic way that ignores the victim's safety. The primary goal that must be pursued is the victim's safety; this requires practical advice. Diana Russell observes:

> It seems to me that if wives were in a position to threaten to leave
> the marriages in which husbands were violent toward them, and
> if they really meant to and were able to convey this to their hus-
> bands, we would be at least halfway toward a solution to the prob-
> lem of violence against wives.[42]

In order for a woman to speak the truth about her situation, to be able to say "John has been battering me" or "John anally raped me last night," she must feel safe and be assured that the information she provides will be kept confidential. *Insuring sufficient time and safe space for a discussion is essential.* Questions that allow for disclosure should be asked, rather than questions that sound like accusations, including questions that focus on her own background ("What was your family life like?") or that focus on her action ("What did you do?"). Instead, beginning with the obvious can be helpful:

> "You seem so unhappy. Do you want to talk about it? I'd like to listen, and I'll keep it between us." Even if she rejects the offer, your observation about her unhappiness supports her by affirming some of her feelings. And you've left the door open for a confidential conversation in the future.[43]

Once naming has occurred, the church must insure that the pastoral response does not do damage, does not revictimize but instead empowers the victims and holds the abusers accountable. The counselor must offer to be with a woman in her suffering and her healing. The solidarity model of counseling that I envision has at the minimum these components:[44]

1) *Caring.* First, the counselor can say, "I am sorry this happened to you." She has been courageous in breaking the silence; this should be acknowledged. She should be assisted in grieving the loss of safety and security. She can mourn what she has lost. She should be told no one ever deserves to be hit or hurt. We can affirm that her reactions are normal; she is not going crazy even though she has never experienced such a range of emotions before. Validate her feelings: "It's all right to feel betrayed, hurt, angry, etc." Questions might include "How are you doing?" and "How are you sleeping?" Solidarity begins with caring.

2) *Concern for safety.* Immediately, however, counseling must acknowledge the trauma of marital rape and the life-threatening nature of battering. The violence must be unequivocally challenged. Women must be encouraged to take their husband's violence seriously and to find support for challenging this violence. It is not their duty to submit to their husband's violence. The marital rape victim's first moral responsibility is to herself. Questions to be asked focus on safety, such as "Are you safe?" and "What would it take for you to be safe?"[45] Referral is essential. Information should be repeated; she should know the name of a hotline and be aware of resources for battered women. Referral ensures that neither the clergyperson nor the victim interprets the violence as an interpersonal problem and that the response is placed where it appropriately lies—with the community. The clergyperson could offer to

accompany her to meet with a hotline representative if she shows some hesitancy about relying on secular services.

3) *Empowerment.* She should be reassured that it is possible to reestablish control over her life. She has choices. There are resources available. Prosecution of her assailant is an important resource. She could benefit from the creation of new support groups, help in increasing her problem-solving skills, and help in increasing her sense of responsibility toward herself. By asking questions such as "What can I do?" the pastoral counselor empowers her to make decisions. We can help her understand her alternatives while increasing her sense of control. We can ask her, "What decisions have you made so far? What are your concerns?"

Affirmations are extremely valuable. Her courageous act of speaking about the violence should be affirmed. She should be told:

> I believe you.
> I care about you.
> I'm glad you told me.
> You are not alone.
> Violent behavior toward you is never appropriate or deserved.
> It's okay to be afraid.
> I'm glad you survived.
> It's okay to be angry with your husband.
> It's okay to be angry with God.
> You deserve a nonviolent life.
> You can change your life.
> You are not responsible for your husband's behavior.
> You have the right to make choices.
> You are not to blame.
> You have a right to privacy.
> I do not believe that God is punishing you for a sin.
> I believe that God does not want you to suffer.
> Whatever you did, you did not deserve to be raped.

Once safety issues have been addressed, many religious issues may come up. Most importantly, if she feels abandoned by God we need to ask, "What kind of God do you feel has abandoned you?" Before her images of God are refuted, she must have the space to describe just how she has experienced her God during her victimization. Feelings such as betrayal and anger at this God are legitimate and should not be short-circuited by attempting to substitute a benign and loving God for the punishing or absent God she has experienced. As Annie Imbens and Ineke Jonker observe about incest survivors:

> We found that it is vital for these women to have the room to express their rage and sorrow about God. Even more crucial is the response. One reaction given to her oppressive image of God and the problems she still has with it is: "Well, God isn't like that, you're looking at it all wrong. That's a false image of God you're describing." This response does not take her seriously and it gives her no room to liberate herself from her oppressive image of God. "This God" should not be the subject of these discussions. It is more pleasant for the priest or minister, because it takes a great deal of resilience and restraint to talk about God in the way that incest survivors need to talk about their oppressive image of God. When the minister or priest starts talking about "this God" during such a conversation, he or she creates a safe distance from his or her own experience of God, and then he or she cannot feel how threatening it is for a woman like Nell to express her rage and sorrow about God in her experience. For *her*, God is not "this God," which people are not supposed to struggle with. For her, it is her only image of God. And that's why she still has so many problems with it.[46]

Women must be provided with the space to discuss their experience of the images of God that have been imposed on them by others. *Then* they can begin to seek their own image of God. "This makes them more resistant in their lives. The space that is created when they liberate themselves from their oppressive images of God should be left open."[47] Only then can a God who abandoned them be abandoned *by* them. Only then can a God who would ordain a woman's suffering as punishment for some sinful act on her part, a God who would require submission to rape as marital duty, a God who would not want the abuser called to accountability, a God who would be content with injustice, be told: "You are not my God."

We all must say, to anyone we know, "If you've been given advice to stay or submit because that is your duty, or because God ordains it, if you are told to forgive the rapist, *you have talked to the wrong person*. If you are given this advice, no matter who the counselor is, no matter how inspiring or spiritually attuned he or she is, you have the wrong advisor. It is not you who are mistaken for resisting this advice, it is the counselor who is mistaken for suggesting it. You have the right to be safe."

What, finally, should the minister have told Shirley when informed of her sexual and physical victimization at the hands of her husband? These are the words I believe Shirley should have heard when she bravely overcame the silence about her victimization:

> Shirley, being long-suffering should not be confused with being *actively* engaged in change. Whatever you have suffered, you know somehow, by talking to me, and by exploring this issue, that that suffering is enough. No more suffering is necessary. The question now is how do we create the reality by which those beatings and rapes can be stopped? To continue to suffer is, in part, to deny the validity of your past suffering. You can say, "It is enough. The suffering is finished. I deserve a life free of violence. My moral responsibility must be, at this moment, to myself. It is time to move on to new life."

NOTES

I would like to thank Pat Davis, Marjorie Procter-Smith, Nancy Tuana, Mary E. Hunt, and Meredith Pond for their suggestions, and Marie M. Fortune for her encouragement. This article incorporates material from "Naming, Denial, and Sexual Violence," *Miriam's Song V* (Priests for Equality).

1. Shirley's story is told on pp. 19–21 of David Finkelhor and Kersti Yllo, *License to Rape: Sexual Abuse of Wives* (New York: Holt, Rinehart and Winston, 1985).
2. See Lee H. Bowker, *Beating Wife-Beating* (Lexington, MA & Toronto: Lexington Books, 1983).
3. Lynn Hecht Shafron, letter to the *New York Times,* responding to Tim Cahill's review of Kenneth Good's (with David Chanoff) *Into the Heart: One Man's Pursuit of Love and Knowledge Among the Yanomano. New York Times Book Review,* January 1991.
4. Mary Field Belenky, Blythe McVicker Clinchy, Nancy Rule Goldberger, Jill Mattuck Tarule, *Women's Way of Knowing: The Development of Self, Voice, and Mind* (New York: Basic Books, 1986), pp. 58, 89.
5. Anne L. Horton and Judith A. Williamson, *Abuse and Religion: When Praying Isn't Enough* (Lexington, MA and Toronto: Lexington Books, 1989), p. 9.
6. Paulo Freire, *Pedagogy of the Oppressed* (New York: Penguin, 1972, 1978), p. 61.

7. Ibid., p. 60.
8. Sarah Lucia Hoagland, *Lesbian Ethics: Toward New Values* (Palo Alto: Institute for Lesbian Studies, 1988), pp. 17–18.
9. Marjorie Procter-Smith, "Reorganizing Victimization: The Intersection between Liturgy and Domestic Violence," *Perkins Journal* (October 1987), pp. 20–21.
10. *Albany Times Union*, 11 October 1984.
11. Peggy Halsey, "Will the Silence Be Unbroken," *South of the Garden* 9, no. 3, p. 3.
12. See Susan Estrich, *Real Rape: How the Legal System Victimizes Women Who Say No* (Cambridge: Harvard University Press, 1987).
13. Finkelhor and Yllo, *License to Rape*, p. 115.
14. Ibid., p. 22.
15. David Finkelhor and Kersti Yllo, "Rape in Marriage: A Sociological View," in *The Darker Side of Families: Current Family Violence Research*, eds. David Finkelhor, Richard J. Gelles, Gerald T. Hotaling, Murray A. Straus (Beverly Hills: Sage Publications, 1983), p. 121.
16. "Perhaps men respond sexually when women give an account of sexual violation because sexual words are a sexual reality, in the same way that men respond to pornography, which is (among other things) an account of the sexual violation of a woman. Seen in this way, much therapy as well as court testimony in sexual abuse cases is live oral pornography." Catharine MacKinnon, *Toward a Feminist Theory of the State* (Cambridge: Harvard University Press, 1989), p. 152.
17. The following section is from a work-in-progress on *Theology, Woman-Battering, and Pastoral Care*, examining the reasons why pastoral care has been so inadequate in responding to battering and marital rape.
18. Howard Clinebell, *Basic Types of Pastoral Care and Counseling: Resources for the Ministry of Healing and Growth* (Nashville: Abingdon Press, 1966 and 1984), p. 35.
19. Mitzi N. Eilts, "Saving the Family: When Is Covenant Broken?" In Horton and Williamson, p. 212–13. Emphasis is in the original.
20. See Ann Jones and Susan Schecter, *When Love Goes Wrong: What to Do When You Can't Do Anything Right* (New York: HarperCollins, 1992).
21. Sallie McFague, *Models of God: Theology for an Ecological, Nuclear Age* (Philadelphia: Fortress Press, 1987), p. 13.
22. See Rosemary Radford Ruether, *Sexism and God-Talk: Toward a Feminist Theology* (Boston: Beacon Press, 1983), pp. 94–99.
23. See Carol S. Pearson, *The Hero Within: Six Archetypes We Live By* (San Francisco: HarperSanFrancisco, 1986, 1989), p. 99.
24. Kathleen Z. Young, "The Imperishable Virginity of Saint Maria Goretti," *Gender & Society* 3, no. 4 (December 1989), p. 475. Young notes the numerous discrepancies in the story depending on the source.
25. Ibid., p. 477.
26. Marie M. Fortune, *Sexual Violence, the Unmentionable Sin: an Ethical and Pastoral Perspective* (New York: The Pilgrim Press, 1983), pp. 65–66.
27. See "Feeding on Grace: Institutional Violence, Christianity, and Vegetarianism,"

in *Good News for Animals? Contemporary Christian Approaches to Animal Well-Being*, ed. Jay McDaniel and Charles Pinches (Maryknoll, NY: Orbis Press, 1993).

28. Judith Herman, *Trauma and Recovery* (New York: Basic Books, 1992), p. 102.
29. Finkelhor and Yllo, *License to Rape*, pp. 127, 135.
30. Lee W. Carlson, *Child Sexual Abuse: A Handbook for Clergy and Church Members* (Valley Forge, PA: Judson Press, 1988), p. 11.
31. Anne L. Ganley, "Integrating Feminist and Social Learning Analyses of Aggression: Creating Multiple Models for Intervention with Men Who Batter," in *Treating Men Who Batter: Theory, Practice, and Programs*, ed. P. Lynn Caesar and L. Kevin Hamberger (New York: Springer Publishing, 1989), p. 202.
32. Liz Kelly, *Surviving Sexual Violence* (Minneapolis: University of Minnesota, 1989), p. 41.
33. Finkelhor and Yllo, *License to Rape*, p. 21.
34. Carole J. Sheffield, "Sexual Terrorism," in *Women: A Feminist Perspective*, third edition, ed. Jo Freeman (Palo Alto, CA: Mayfield Publishing Company, 1984), p. 11.
35. For an analysis of the logic of domination, see Karen Warren, "The Power and the Promise of Ecological Feminism," *Environmental Ethics* 12, no. 3 (Summer, 1990), pp. 128–33.
36. See Susan Brownmiller, *Against Our Will: Men, Women, and Rape* (New York: Simon & Schuster, 1975).
37. Finkelhor and Yllo, *License to Rape*, p. 100.
38. Diana E. H. Russell, *Rape in Marriage: Expanded and Revised Edition* (Bloomington & London: Indiana University Press, 1982, 1990), p. 318.
39. Marie M. Fortune, *Sexual Abuse Prevention: A Study for Teenagers* (New York: United Church Press, 1986), p. 9, quoting Jennifer James, Principal Investigator, "Entrance into Juvenile Prostitution," August, 1980, and "Entrance into Juvenile Male Prostitution," August, 1982.
40. Freire, *Pedagogy of the Oppressed*, p. 61.
41. Ibid.
42. Russell, *Rape in Marriage*, p. 321.
43. Jones and Schecter, *When Love Goes Wrong*, p. 307.
44. I am not delineating here long-term counseling such as described in Herman's *Trauma and Recovery*. I am sketching the counseling needs of women still trapped within victimizing relationships, those issues that Herman addresses in part in her chapter on "Safety."
45. Space does not allow me to discuss in detail the safety issues that a pastoral counselor can raise with a victim of marital rape or battering. For a more in-depth description, see my forthcoming book, *Woman Battering*, a part of the Creative Pastoral Care and Counseling Series of Fortress Press.
46. Annie Imbens and Ineke Jonker, *Christianity and Incest* (Minneapolis: Fortress Press, 1992), pp. 209–210.
47. Ibid., p. 210.

CAROL J. ADAMS is the author of the forthcoming book *Woman Battering*, which will be part of the Creative Pastoral Care and Counseling Series of Fortress Press. She teaches a course on sexual and domestic violence at Perkins School of Theology and has been involved in the violence against women movement since the mid-1970s. She is also the author of *The Sexual Politics of Meat: A Feminist-Vegetarian Critical Theory* (Continuum, 1990) and the editor of *Ecofeminism and the Sacred* (Continuum, 1993).

CONVERSATIONS OF CONSENT:
Sexual Intimacy without Sexual Assault

by Joseph Weinberg & Michael Biernbaum

We can't control someone else's feelings, though the rapist
may have the illusion that he does. One astounded male
college athlete demanded, "Do you mean that if I grab a
woman's crotch, that could be rape? That's unfair!"

ALL ACROSS THIS country antisexist men are talking to other men about rape, providing honest and factual information about sexual assault. (We use the terms "rape" and "sexual assault" interchangeably throughout this article.) Clarifying what constitutes sexual assault is necessary, for there is an astounding lack of information about it out there among men. Examples abound. We still hear, for example, that the rape of women is an "excess of sex," and how could that be bad? And when we talk about the males who are raped, many—particularly high school-aged men—assume the perpetrator to be a "beautiful, older woman"! Most men still don't know or *haven't had to know* what constitutes rape. This doesn't excuse or exonerate our behavior, but does point to education as the most important way to break the cycle of sexual violence.

Until now, rape has been an invisible issue for most men. Say the word *rape* to most women and there is a shudder, an involuntary muscular reaction, or some other visceral response. Certainly not all women understand the dynamics of rape culture, but most have a strong body sense of what rape means. Mention rape to most men and there is not a comparable physical response. (The twenty percent of men who have experienced incest or other sexual assault by age eighteen, and older male survivors, often carry a palpable imprint. To them rape is not invisible. Nor is it invisible to partners and friends of those who have been raped, who increasingly are identifying themselves and seeking to know more about the monster that has entered their lives and the lives of the survivors.)

Since most of us men do not carry the body-centered terror and pain of rape, the idea of "not raping" also carries little psychophysical feeling or relief. It's an idea or vision that stays intellectual for most of us. One young man wanted to know, "What's the payoff?" "That you don't rape," we replied. "Yeah, but what's the payoff?" Exasperated, we countered, "That you don't rape!" "But what's the payoff?" he persisted. "That you don't rape," we shouted. What more did he need? *What more do we need?*

INTENSIFYING THE CONFUSION

We were recently called by a magazine editor. "Are men reeling?" she asked. "In light of the William Kennedy Smith, Clarence Thomas, and

Mike Tyson cases, are men reeling?" "No," we had to tell her, "we don't exactly see men reeling, but there are rumblings of doubt." Pressure cracks are appearing in the "real man" facades many of us live behind, and unsightly feelings of uncertainty, fear, and vulnerability are beginning to show through, particularly among younger men. For all our past bravado, we now have questions and doubts.

We were in a high school the day the William Kennedy Smith verdict came down—when he was found rich and white. From the twenty-four young men there that day, questions came pouring out: "What is consent?" "What if a girl says yes, then changes her mind?" And "How do we know what they want?" (Echoes of Sigmund Freud.) It's great to hear these questions. While the threat of legal sanction may get men's attention for a moment, that distant threat does not start the changes in behaviors and attitudes that stop the raping. We encourage uncertainty and confusion, allowing a man to see that what he has accepted as normal can be rape—that he may be raping by doing exactly what he thinks he is "supposed" to be doing. This can shake him from his insouciant "hey-no-problem-with-me-man" mask. This can make it more difficult for him to continue his high-risk activities just because he has "gotten away" with rape in the past (i.e., has not been accused or charged with assault).

These responses can be part of a psychological disruption in which the stereotypes about rapists that keep *them* distant from *me* (a rapist is the stranger out there, the isolated "sick" guy, someone—anyone—else) begin to fall apart. At a gut level men may begin to feel this is me we're talking about; I think I've done this.

This discomfort is something we are happy to see, for if the normal expression of male sexuality is seen as a moving, even runaway, train—linear, rushing forward, with "too much momentum to stop"—then braking to a halt and even rolling backward a little is a desirable response. In our experience, nothing gets men to put on the brakes like the combination of clear, factual information and emotional confusion.

EMOTIONAL RESPONSES

When men begin to experience this confusion, they may identify one or more of the following feelings: resentment, panic, anger, or shock.

Some express resentment at male figures in their lives—fathers, brothers, uncles, and male friends—for feeding them lies about sexual "conquest," "the hunt" for women, and all the other strategies for obtaining sex that were laid on them as they were growing up. Their anger draws on feelings of belittlement by older men for the younger one's possibly inadequate masculinity. (Remember being asked, "You younger guys must be getting it all the time, *aren't you?*") Here some of the lies that form the foundation of our participation in the patriarchy can begin to be named, identified, and rejected.

Hopelessness and panic can be seen in the response of one fraternity man: "If this is rape then every one of us has raped! We can't do anything." This moment of incipient recognition is familiar to us; a large number of us have done something that could qualify as rape. His fearful pronouncement resonates for many men. One man's fear and panic was so strong—and so illustrative of the multiple and confused expectations about being a man that he'd internalized—that his response reached a truly absurd height, and he exclaimed, "With this new definition of rape, we could end up in prison for not satisfying a woman sexually!" (Now while that could be a wickedly funny discussion for some women or men, we felt we had to reassure him that no man is in prison anywhere in the universe for premature ejaculation.)

A fear of false charges also arises. "We have no protection. All she has to do is say we raped her." But statistically, the false report is a minute occurrence. We find it important here to talk of the hellish experience reported by women (and men) who report an assault to disbelieving, insensitive, and unprofessional authorities, and the further indignities they experience in carrying the case through our judicial system. The fact is that the odds are extremely small that any middle- or upper-class white man in this country will ever be imprisoned for rape. Racism and a racist judicial system make the story entirely different for African-American men: in the U.S., where ninety-six percent of the reported perpetrators of rape are white, eighty percent of the men in prison for rape are black!

We also hear anger expressed by some men at all or some women for "causing" a problem (rape) where, in their opinion, none exists. In the discussion of sexual assault it is important to separate this bogus and reactionary blaming of women from the issue of the responsibility of female perpetrators (twenty percent of sexual violence is perpetrated by females upon male victims, usually boys or infants). The same power/ experience differential necessary for abuse is present. While there is no excuse for denying women's pain and these men's anger is misdirected, some angry men (and others who are defensive or seemingly resistant to hearing the truth about rape) are themselves survivors or "significant others" of survivors. Some angry men may be reactionary jerks, but not all are. It is dangerous, fatuous and perhaps even willful to pretend otherwise. If victims can only be female, then females can only be victims.

Perhaps men's most remarkable reaction is amazement that having assaulted her, they cannot "unassault" her. It comes as a rude shock that they can't "un-say" her feelings, interpret her experience for her, and have the last word on what happened. We are entitled to our perceptions, but it is not under our control to decide for our partners whether they have been sexually assaulted.

We are slowly moving to a new paradigm: if our partners feel assaulted, then they *have been* assaulted. Men are aghast that their intent doesn't really matter, whether they rape with a *complete* sense of what they are doing or *no* sense. We can't control someone else's feelings, though the rapist may have the illusion that he does. One astounded male college athlete demanded, "Do you mean that if I grab a woman's crotch, that could be rape? That's unfair!"

CONSENT: EXPLICIT AND VERBAL

Often, when the accused in a date rape case is interviewed in the media, he says (no doubt under advice of counsel), "Well, I had consent and then she changed her mind." Whenever we hear this, we shout back, "What was the *conversation* like that established consent?" His assumption is that since she (1) ate dinner with him; (2) went back to his room; (3) didn't say "no" (even though she had passed out or had fallen asleep); and (4) etc., she must have wanted sex and was agreeing to whatever he had in mind.

The old saw "She got herself raped" reveals the operating paradigm: it's all *her* responsibility to say "no" and to attempt to set *my* limits. Rape occurs when *she* doesn't succeed. This is an analysis that is familiar to many men and women whose victim-blaming usually revolves around this point. The process of consent seeks to redress this disastrous imbalance, charging men with the responsibility for our behavior and for respecting the integrity of our partner.

To us, consent is the continual process of explicit, verbal discussion, a dialogue, brief or extended, taken one step at a time, to an expressed "yes" by both parties and a shared acknowledgment that at this moment what we are doing together is safe and comfortable for each of us. Consent is what establishes that the interaction (including sex) is between equals in power. We feel safe enough to say anything we need to—without incapacitation of either party, coercion or threat, implied or actual—to protect ourselves from violation. Both parties are autonomous at each moment and can change their minds at any time. We share control of the situation with each other. Our responsibility is to be as sure as possible that what we are doing is not felt as violation.

This process may be new historically. When (or if) Dad sat us down for *that* talk, he never told us about having this kind of discussion nor did he admit his own questions. We have learned instead to "read" body language, a too often self-fulfilling prophesy that invites us to hear and see only what *we* want to. How many of us think we can read our partners' body language as confirmation of their desire for sexual contact and their (implied?) agreement with what we have in mind? Using body language this way is a sham; we're merely justifying self-deception or pretending that we've established more than mere acquiescence or submission.

Consent is not a panacea. Teaching men the process of explicit verbal consent for sexual contact will stop much rape, but will not stop all rape. There are men who know exactly what rape is and will persist. "You need this, you deserve this, you asked for this, and you will be a better wife after this." These are the words of men who know exactly what they are doing. But even for these men, convicted or not, this persistent discussion of consent can bring home the meaning of rape in a new way. Due to the myths about who the "real" rapist is and what rape is, the definition of rape is often misunderstood even by the convicted rapist!

Most of the men in prison are there for the rape of strangers, though stranger rape represents less than twenty percent of reported rapes. We have found in our workshop experiences in prisons that some rapists, admittedly guardedly and tentatively, are perplexed by the idea that most rape is forced intercourse or sexual contact without consent with an *acquaintance, partner, friend,* or *spouse.* Some of them begin to understand they have *also* raped people they know and can begin to see this as similar (in the effect on the victim) to the stranger rape that they're in for. They show the same shock that other men do when they begin to feel the truth about rape. (After all, the main difference between them and most of the rest of us men is that they were caught.)

Can any man become empathetic to women and their experience of rape? The process of consent offers a challenge to men who hate women, who say that women "don't know what they want," are "vindictive," "out to get us," etc., to look at themselves. We ask, what is sex like when we feel this way? Sex will remain terrifying and fraught with danger, with high risk for those of us committing sexual assault, as long as we don't care about ourselves. Consent opens up possibilities for a man to understand and love himself as a person, to recognize the riskiness of the choices he has been making and become empathetic to his own state—frightened, lacking communication skills, unsure of what he wants from women. Consent raises the issue of personhood—ours *and* hers. The linkage is unavoidable. If we men have not been taught to be empathetic to ourselves, how can we extend that empathy to women, who are seen as alien or "other"? Facing or accepting our own fears of vulnerability and intimacy, our own histories of victimization *and* abusing, can open men to hearing women's experiences with us and other men, to hearing their fears and desires. We have seen many men move out of a hardened, defensive posture through this process and start making the connections.

WHAT ARE WE ASKING?

What is going on when we "ask"? Many men explain that they don't ask because they might hear "no." We respond, "Would you rather rape than risk hearing 'no'?" Nobody wants to be turned down—especially for something as potentially pleasurable as sexual contact—but asking a question means being prepared to hear what we may not want to hear. Asking for an answer and then refusing to accept it is *not* asking. The exact question is not as important as: am I prepared to accept the answer, whether or not it's one I want to hear?

"No" is only the least of what we might hear. We may hear that she (or he) is a survivor of incest or other sexual assault. Our own intimate history together may be brought up for review and discussion. There may be some revelations, some surprises. It's important to take all the time we need to vocalize our feelings and questions when we are feeling unsure about how clear or truthful we or our partner are being. After all, most of us don't have lots of experience in this sort of frank and honest exchange of feelings.

The question and answer is the first step in a trust-building exchange. The discussion has to be allowed all the time necessary to be as sure as we can be that we are both clear and OK with what is happening. Sometimes the exchange will take far longer than we might imagine or desire, particularly if we are used to very little, if any, verbal exchange around consent, or if there is a history of unsafe experiences (e.g., unwanted touches, groping, forcing, etc.) between us.

We hear many men complain or worry about getting "mixed messages." Aside from a statement that patently and absurdly contradicts itself, such as "Touch me, don't touch me," the claim of a mixed message is an excuse, an after-the-fact justification. Regardless of how we interpret or want to read our partner's physical movement or expression, direct explicit language is the only sure way to ascertain our partner's intent and meaning. If we are uncertain for any reason about the answer we've received, there's plenty of time to check it out with another exchange. We might ask, "Are you sure?" or "Did you mean that. . . ." The less sure we are of what's been agreed to, or the more we are disbelieving of the answer, the *higher* the risk of assaulting and the *more* responsibility we have to ourselves to establish verbal consent to sexual contact. There's a legal implication, too. In the William Kennedy Smith case, for example, the more the defense team tried to establish Patricia Bowman's instability/insanity, the more they proved his guilt. Smith called her "a real nut." According to the *New York Times*, "At other times, [Smith] said, the woman was erratic, hysterical and irrational." If she were those things, then legally she *couldn't* consent to his supposedly "innocent" advances.

Of course, absolute safety cannot be guaranteed. As in all interactions between people, there is no 100 percent guarantee of mutual understanding. The process of establishing consent is not a fixed legal contract that can obligate the parties to "consent" to their own assault (see "Warning on 'Dating Contracts'" in *Changing Men* #20), and the idea of taking lawyers to bed with us (as witnesses?) is really a perversion.

There's going to be some resistance to asking, even for those who want to try. It's new and can feel awkward at first, so practicing and becoming comfortable with asking is critical. The process seemed so mysterious to us when we began that we found it useful to start with general questions, such as "How do you feel about this?", "How are we doing?", and "Is everything OK?" These kinds of gentle "check-in" questions allow us to open the process of consent with our partner without feeling so foolish or weird that the purpose is lost. We can also adopt a slower pace, so a mistake or confusion has less chance of becoming a severe violation or assault.

Since the principle underlying this process is the sharing of power, we seek out the "little" moments when we can check in and negotiate a consentual moment together. We ask about holding hands or exchanging hugs: "I'd like to hold hands. How would you feel if we did that?" We are not only holding hands; we are agreeing to, wanting to, even looking forward to holding each other's hand—and we're telling each other so. Depending on the answer, the experience is being entered into consentually, and more than that, with desire. If she says "no," we've gotten some information that has helped us to avoid unwanted touch, and suggests, in case we had it in mind, that she's probably not interested in intercourse (!) at that moment. Think that you know that she/he absolutely wants to hold hands? Then what's the harm in asking?

One way to begin is to ask a question about the question "one step removed" from the actual move. We are asking about asking, finding out how receptive our partner is to hearing something we want to ask. "Would you be interested in hearing something about the way I feel about you?" "How would you feel about kissing?" instead of saying, "I want to kiss you" or kissing without checking it out first. If the answer is "no," it is the opening that has been rejected—not me or my opinion. I have not made myself prematurely vulnerable again. The rejection was about "asking about," not a rejection of my feeling or idea. I am protecting myself when I ask first about whether my partner wants to even hear what I've got to say or how I feel, rather than shoving right in with it without asking.

CULTURAL BLOCKS TO CONSENT

There's lots of discussion nowadays among the mythopoetic folk about initiation. It's the foundation upon which Robert Bly and other male essentialists and apologists build their edifice of anger-driven reaction. We are poorly initiated, they insist. To us it's not that we have been poorly initiated, but that we've been initiated *too* well—though certainly not the way we might be by some wise, caring, gentle, humorous father. We have grown to be the men that patriarchy needs and forces us to be, "real men," angry at and frightened of women, other men, and ourselves. We inflict rape and other violence; we are cannon fodder in war and compulsive consumers of worthless products, unquestioningly remaining within oppressive gender, racial, and economic systems. Oh, we are brilliantly, coldly, efficiently initiated! We are initiated by our fathers and brothers with the same scarring, humiliating rites that they experienced. We are calling for men to examine how the process by which each of us becomes a man can hurt all of us; we are calling for men to refuse to rape.

Maybe millions of rapes have soured the possibility for an idealized, nonverbal, intuitive interaction with a generous, sensitive partner. Maybe that model of romance has always been a pornographic myth. Using pornography is one of our stickier rites (rights) of passage. It helps keep us on the Masculine, Straight-acting Path. A potential partner is reduced to *something* to ejaculate into. The sex language men use—I *porked* her, *stuck* it to her, *ripped off* a piece of ass—mirrors pornography's purposeful blurring of sex and violence. Men are also *bilingual* when it comes to sex talk: we use one set of words to talk to men, and a second, cleaned-up, insincere version to talk to women. Is honest communication possible with this kind of split? Pornography and locker room double-talk may teach us that rape is sex, but the process of consent we're talking about here makes possible a sex that is not rape.

Consider also the insidiousness of the "double standard" for women that we've been taught and that's encoded in our language. What are the positive words for a sexually active woman? There aren't any in popular usage, though we hear some fascinating attempts: liberated (!), mother (?), generous (!). Contrast this with the dozens of supposedly positive words for a sexually active man: stud, stallion, player, womanizer, pile driver, lady's man, Don Juan, Romeo, Casanova, etc. There are more than a thousand negative words for a sexually active woman. We say we crave a partner who initiates sex, yet we have no positive words or images to express the reality of a fully embodied, complex, active partner! What sort of joyous, spontaneous, self-defined sexual expression does this forced invisibility allow women? We have chosen to settle for far less in our language and our conceptions, and to this degree we are constantly recreating a rape culture inside our heads.

EROTICIZING CONSENT

Can we be turned on by sex that is not violent? Is sex inevitably violent? Can power-*with* (instead of pornographic power-*over*) be erotic? We will not be able to break the addiction to aggressive, violating sexual behavior unless the new feelings of power-*with* are felt to carry the same sort of sexual rush and pleasure.

Talking to each other can be hot, especially for those for whom emotional trust intensifies our expression of passion. And for many of us, feeling safe and more in control of our choices in our intimate sexual play can be a real turn-on. The situation is full of possibility. It can be an extraordinary emotional/sexual rush to open to each other in ways that we did not dream of doing before. The conversations of consent open the door to this kind of information and feeling exchange.

The erotic charge of our interactions also may intensify. Nothing is forbidden because nothing is forced. Within the "safer space" we create as part of the consent-exchange between us, we have abundant time to check things out. Being together in close, intimate, verbal—even humorous—presexual ways can intensify the erotic charge between us. Checking in often with each other becomes one of the intimate things we like to do together, and it may be one of the things we do really well together. By opening this space we also open a new place in which to play together with lowered risk of violation.

"No" *is* hard to hear. But what about a heartfelt "yes!" What about "more" or "now!" or "harder" or "faster" or any other expressions that we may have longed to hear in our fantasies and dreams of desire. What would it be like to create a space where partners can speak their wishes, express what feels good, and tell us how to help pleasure them? Here is communication in a safer space that can be trusted and played with. "Kiss me this way." "Touch me here." This is information that can bring us closer in sexual intimacy, without assault.

And what about romance? Can consent be romantic and safe? Can safety be romantic? Some men and women have said, "The uncertainty, the ambivalence, the hunt, is exciting, even romantic." Ironically this is how many men defend what they've been doing, as if their planned scenarios, which too often result in assault, were genuinely "spontaneous and romantic." We need to jettison "romantic" as it has been practiced, replete with abuse and confusion, no one getting what they want.

Let's *reinvent a romance* that is safer to play with than false images and silence. When we experience what consent feels like—some deep and abiding body sensation of openness and safety—we may feel a body warning when it is not present. Its absence can be felt, and we can do what we have to do to restore that sense of comfort and minimize our risk of raping. We may start to feel adventure and excitement in this feeling of comfort. We may find it "sexy" *and* "romantic."

When young men plaintively ask, "Isn't there some way, other than asking, to find out if she wants sex?" they're saying that communication sounds like a crazy idea and a losing proposition.

Well, consent sounds crazy because it hasn't been tried. And the real losing proposition is the way that men have done it for the last five thousand years.

And what might we gain?

Deeper, more trustworthy relationships based on intimacy without assault, a new way of being together.

Originally published in *Changing Men* #25, Winter/Spring 1993, pages 28–32.

JOSEPH WEINBERG lives in Madison, Wisconsin, where he works as a rape-prevention educator, presenting speeches, trainings, and workshops at colleges, universities, high schools, conferences, businesses, and prisons nationwide. He is past president of Men Stopping Rape–Madison, a mask maker and collector, and a carpenter of fifteen years.

MICHAEL BIERNBAUM is a cofounder of Men Stopping Rape–Madison and teaches "Confronting Assaults, Protecting Ourselves," a program of nonviolent intervention skills and body-centered strategies to increase personal safety, prevent sexual assault and other hate-motivated crimes on individuals and communities, and confront violence in our schools through "communities for safety."

Biernbaum lives in Madison. He is board chair of Protective Behaviors, Inc., a U.S./Australia abuse prevention and antivictimization program for safety with adventure. He is managing editor and art editor of *Changing Men* magazine, an international profeminist journal on "issues in gender, sex and politics." He is a father of two and primary caregiver for a partner with AIDS.

THE LANGUAGE OF RAPE

by Helen Benedict

Some might argue that changes in our language can only
follow changes in legislation and the social balance
of genders, but I believe changes in language
can also lead the way.

FEMINIST LINGUISTS HAVE pointed out for some years now the sexist bias in the English language. Dale Spender, for example, told us in 1980 that there are 220 words for a sexually promiscuous woman and only 20 for an equally promiscuous man. This antiwoman bias in our language not only reflects the culture of rape, but encourages it, because it portrays women as sexual objects, fair prey for the hunter-man. In short, English is a language of rape.

By "a language of rape," I mean vocabulary that portrays women as sexual, subhuman, or childlike temptresses, and that perpetuates the idea of women as legitimate sexual prey. I also mean the vocabulary used to describe rape itself as an act of pleasure, or of comedy, rather than of violence.

Take, as illustration, the tradition of treating rape as a joke. Last night, it just so happened, I watched the 1967 British comedy *Bedazzled* starring Peter Cook as the devil and Dudley Moore as a pathetic, short-order cook version of Faust. I had loved that movie as a teenager, but as an adult feminist I had quite a different reaction. The film was still amusing, but its misogyny was relentless, culminating in two full scenes making fun of rape. In the first, Eleanor Bron, the object of Moore's desires (and I use the word "object" decidedly), cries rape when Moore leaps on her, and keeps on crying it after the devil has caused him to vanish into thin air. The scene leaves her lying on her back, screaming "Rape!" and kicking, with no one else in the room—enacting the traditional view of rape as a figment of a frigid woman's imagination, or, more accurately, as something that doesn't exist.

In the second scene, a police inspector is showing bodies to Bron in the morgue. He mentions that he has dealt with a lot of rape cases recently and immediately follows with the sentence, "And that's a nice dress you're wearing, as well," or some such sequitur. He then goes on to say, "Mind you, the girls always bring it on themselves, you know."

I may not have the exact words, but I certainly have the gist: rape is sex, rape is attraction, rape is the woman's fault, i.e. rape doesn't exist.

That film was made twenty-six years ago, but its attitude, and the language in which the attitude is expressed, has barely changed. I spent the last five years looking at newspaper coverage of rape over the past decade, and I found that same language of rape everywhere, in ordinary people's comments ("He had plenty of girls, he didn't need to rape her"), in lawyers' arguments ("It was Jennifer [Levin] who was pursuing Robert

[Chambers] for sex . . . that's why we wound up with this terrible tragedy"), in the jokes of friends I told about my work ("A book about rape? Are you for it or against it?"), and, most of all, in the language of the reporters and headline writers themselves.

Here are some examples of the words I found used by newspapers for female victims of sex crimes: pretty, hysterical, attractive, flirtatious, bright, bubbly, petite, pert, vivacious, girl (for a grown woman). These words, never used for men, either infantilize women (the woman is bright, the man intelligent; the woman is bubbly, the man energetic; the woman is hysterical, the man terrified; the woman is a girl, the man is a man), or, in the context of a sex crime, make them sound like sexual temptresses (a male crime victim is *never* described as attractive, pretty, or the suggestive equivalent). To see the bias, simply change the subject's gender: "Petite, bubbly John Harris took the witness stand today," or, "Friends described Robert Smith as a pert vivacious boy who liked to flirt in the bars," or, "Alan Peterson ran from the scene half-naked, crying hysterically."

Examples of the vocabulary I found used to describe rape and sexual assault are "fondled," "caressed" and "had sex with," all words written by so-called objective journalists who were unconsciously reflecting the rapist's point of view. These words were not being used to describe an ambiguous case of date rape, but the brutal and bloody attack by at least seven youths in 1989 on the woman who came to be known as the Central Park jogger.

True, the language of rape is insidious, used unconsciously, quickly, carelessly; yet I maintain that we need not sit passively in the face of its bias. Language can be and has been reformed in the media and, symbiotically, in everyday life. The media, for instance, long ago learned not to use the word "Negro" and is switching from "black" to "African-American" as I write; it has also dropped the routine use of "Miss" and "buxom blonde" in its reference to women. The media, therefore, can learn to reform its language about rape. Reporters and editors can be taught to apply a simple test to the words they use about women and crime victims: "Would I use this word for a man? What does this word imply in context?"

Some might argue that changes in our language can only *follow* changes in legislation and the social balance of genders, but I believe changes in language can also lead the way. Again, take the media. If we grew used to seeing women treated as equal to men in the news, if we read and heard descriptions of sex crimes as only horrible and not titillating, of female victims as ordinary people, not as whores or martyrs, it would be harder to accept the status quo of women as objects of prey. The media reflects public opinion, to be sure, but it also shapes it, for it is through the media that the public receives all its news and most of its information. The media, therefore, can lead the reform of the language of rape.

Journalists can begin this reform by fighting for a fairer and less sexist use of vocabulary, and consumers can do their part by writing in to object to biased language. Everyone concerned—reporters, columnists, consumers, feminists, writers, and upcoming editors—must argue until the established media is ready to accept a feminist view of rape: that rape is an act of torture in which sex is used as the weapon; that desire and lust have nothing to do with rape except in the sickest of ways (the assailant is aroused by his own acts of sadism, anger, and violence); and that women are not objects of prey but human beings who must be treated with the same respect and consideration a civilized society would like to accord its male citizens.

Once the media accepts the feminist view of rape as neither extreme nor radical, but merely realistic, then perhaps women will no longer have to cry "Rape!" to an empty room.

HELEN BENEDICT is the author of *Virgin or Vamp: How the Press Covers Sex Crimes* (Oxford University Press, 1992), upon which this article is based. She has also written extensively about rape for magazines and newspapers over the past fifteen years and is the author of four other books, two of which concern rape and sexual assault: *Recovery: How to Survive Sexual Assault* (Doubleday, 1985) and *Safe, Strong, and Streetwise* (Little, Brown, 1987). Her other books are a novel, *A World Like This* (E.P. Dutton, 1990), and *Portraits in Print* (Columbia University Press, 1991). Benedict is a professor at The Graduate School of Journalism at Columbia University and lives in New York with her husband and two children.

I THOUGHT YOU DIDN'T MIND

by Elizabeth Powell

We must hold rapists responsible, but we must also
develop skills that will empower us to change the culture.
Practically speaking, it has not worked to just "ask" the
male power structure to please change things.

SHOPPING FOR LAMPS one day last summer, I stood in front of a counter and idly glanced down into a showcase. I saw some brass plaques. On the first was printed, Women Are Like Boats—You Pay More for the Rigging Than You Do for the Hull. I was offended. But I had not yet felt the impulse to take action. My eyes wandered to another, smaller plaque, obviously made to tack onto a door. It read, Screw Room. My adrenalin was beginning to rise. I glanced at the next plaque. It said, Women Trespassers Will Be Violated. My anger shot over the edge.

Within one minute I had asked for the manager (who was not in), told the person waiting on me to take the message that this plaque was very offensive because it makes fun of rape, told him that I would never shop there again if this kind of merchandise was being sold there, and asked for their business card in case I wanted to take further action.

All of this was relatively easy, because I was familiar with basic assertive skills. I was confident and, although enraged, could take control of the situation and make my point. Yet such actions might not even have occurred to many women. Where could they have picked up these skills? All the media scenes of their lifetimes would not show them even one small act of sexual assertion. From whom would they obtain emotional support if their assertion elicited a negative response? In many circles such behavior would be shocking and in most groups, unfeminine. Yet, if every woman had these skills and the confidence to be assertive, our definition of what is socially acceptable would be transformed. Just as large numbers of nonsmokers spoke out and changed the acceptability of public smoking, disapproval of sexist actions could eventually change society. If sexism were seen to be as offensive and hurtful as cigarette smoke, people would become desensitized to assertive remarks, and such comments would no longer be perceived as inappropriate.

We live in a culture whose belief system is based on massive distortions about women's sexual availability. Like any oppressed people, women must lose no chance to correct these misimpressions. They must speak up, and they must know what to say. Assertiveness at its best does not accept the responsibility for the intruder's actions; rather, it demands change in the *other*. And, yes, we need to hold men responsible with our assertive words, whenever possible.

To insist that women need to be assertive is not to blame victims. Rapists are entirely responsible for their decision to rape. And at the actual point of rape, assertiveness may not be helpful. It is long before rape is attempted—out in the rape-prone culture—that assertive skills can make the biggest difference. We must hold rapists responsible, but we must also develop skills that will empower us to change the culture. Practically speaking, it has not worked to just "ask" the male power structure to please change things.

Many women are angry over the suggestion that we might have to take action when it is others who perpetrate crimes against us. Let men change. But if you tell me you are going to travel through the territory of a hostile tribe, and I know some techniques with which you might protect yourself, I'd prefer to teach them to you—now—in addition to spending a few more decades working on pacifying that tribe. Perpetrators are not the only people affected by your speaking up. Assertiveness may sometimes cause an acquaintance rapist to back off, but it offers another, more salient advantage. Assertive retorts can chip away at the underpinnings of false assumptions on which the rape culture rests. The more frequent the objections to sexism, the sooner the rape culture will be transformed.

Our assertive remarks can raise the consciousness of well-meaning citizens who simply don't get it. For example, I have noted that among my students who saw the film *Pretty Woman*, seventy percent do not remember that it contained a prolonged rape attempt. I have wondered why this is so, and have concluded that throwing a woman down on a couch and tearing her clothes off is just not that unusual in American films. And, after all, she *knew* him. Rape is thought to be a crime committed by strangers. I hope that, if you see a film like this, you all comment so that others do not assume you are neutral in the face of this affront.

There are two vital areas where we need to use assertiveness skills: in personal sexual encounters, and out in society. There is a third, nonassertive level of response that may thwart some rape attempts, and that is aggression. But far more significant is the power of our words.

What kinds of assertive skills are needed in the first level of assertiveness training? First, we need to know how to respond on a personal level to events that impinge on our sexuality. For example, how can you explain how far you want to go sexually on a date? How can you resist verbal pressure from someone who is pushing you sexually? How can you respond on the job when being sexually harassed? When pressured to have unprotected intercourse with someone whose HIV status is unknown?

In responding to verbal pressure, there are simple skills that can be helpful. Let's say your date keeps asking you to come up to his room in the fraternity house. If it is merely a repeated request, you could respond at a low level of assertiveness: "No, I wouldn't be comfortable up there." Another, slightly stronger, method is to turn the pressure on the other person: "Why do you keep pressuring me like this?"

Sometimes assertion is threatening to a young woman who wants her date to like her. At this level she would like to be assertive yet pleasant. But in her mind assertiveness is angry and essentially unfeminine. Perhaps her date is not using force—just words–to persuade her to go further sexually. He thinks he's only fulfilling the male script. She wants to go out with him again. But she doesn't know how to be pleasantly firm. Given the option between an angry assertive confrontation and passivity, she may opt for avoiding his disapproval. She should have several assertive options in her repertoire. In this situation there's room for assertive remarks that deflect or decline rather than confront. These remarks fall into the category of "polite" or "nonconfrontive" assertion.

For example, you have a date with someone who keeps wanting you to go away for the weekend and stay in his brother's place. You like him, but you're not ready for sexual intimacy. You may not need to confront him ("I get mad when you keep bugging me"). At this early level, he's only asking. You might say, "No thanks, I need to stay in town." Or "I might like to sometime, but I want to get to know you better first."

These skills are relatively simple to learn. As the woman learns to move toward more confrontive assertion, she can often start with a simple formula. Filling in the blanks in a straightforward sentence will suffice for many situations: "I feel _____ when you _____." I feel nervous when you keep touching me, I feel angry when you won't listen to my refusal, I feel upset when you keep reading those pornographic magazines right beside my desk, I feel furious when you stare at my breasts while I'm talking to you.

But becoming assertive on an individual level is just the first step. Let's say your boss is harassing you and you speak up. You tell him, "I feel very uncomfortable when you keep talking about my body. I want you to stop." He stops. You feel you've done your bit for stopping sexual harassment. Suppose that night you go to a party and someone is telling blonde jokes:

Do you know how to get a blonde's eyes to light up?
Shine a flashlight in her ear.

If you say nothing about that joke, you're perpetuating sexual exploitation. You're giving someone permission to laugh at a woman's "stupidity." Others will think you do not mind.

But we need to admit it—witty jokes are cleverly written, and we might laugh before we realize the implications. Some jokes are hilarious in *style*, yet when they combine laughter with sexism they desensitize us to the put-down. But what other group would laugh when it is the brunt of such jokes? Could we say, "Do you know how to get a Catholic's eyes to light up?" No, women are the only group in which a large number will laugh at prejudiced remarks against its own.

Some other opportunities to assert at a societal level might be:

Your friend has an explicit magazine that treats women like playthings. It's not the nudity of which you disapprove, it's the insipid portrayal of women. You say something like, "I really find that kind of magazine offensive. Women aren't playthings, they're people."

If your consciousness isn't raised enough to recognize sexist films, ponder the fact that Dracula sinks his long teeth into the bleeding neck of a woman as she writhes and moans in pleasure. This is the quintessential rape theme, the most dangerous portrayal of sexual force —when the woman loves it. You may see a movie with a date or with friends who don't notice the sexism. One in eight American films contains a rape, so you won't have any trouble finding something on which to comment. You could say something along these lines: "You know, I really don't like to see movies where women are afraid of men. It makes me very uncomfortable." Otherwise, if you are silent, who will know that you mind?

We need to talk about our observations to the people with whom we view these sexist media presentations. Let the fear of being judgmental die with the eighties. Let's *make* judgments and let's talk about them. And afterwards—at the coffee break, at the party, maybe even at the family table over the holidays. One does not have to be constantly unpleasant in order to drop in a well-placed comment: "Gee, Dad, I felt really sad seeing that woman being hurt." Or: "Must we watch a program about another woman being pursued by a crazy man? Surely there's another program. Come on, folks." If every woman knows the first levels of nonconfrontive, "polite" assertion, we can enlist more people to raise consciousness.

The young heterosexual woman who wants to get along with the nicer guys in Fraternity X is not going to be comfortable screaming in rage at the first sexist remark she hears. She is not going to align herself with what the culture perceives as the "man-hating feminists." Why should we not provide her with training in how to respond with "polite assertion"? For example, "I really get uncomfortable when people joke about people's bodies like that." Maybe her intuitive feeling has some accuracy—attitude change can occur by the efforts of those who remain on the inside. Another place for "polite assertion" might be teaching women how to cope with co-workers joking on the job, when a bit of testing goes on in the form of "mildly" sexist remarks.

We need to teach young people that they can often be assertive without seeming to be a stuffed shirt or a bitch. We could even reframe non-confrontive assertiveness as a kind of manners. It's a mannerly way to express anger and personal rights without becoming aggressive. We can reserve angry or confrontive assertion for other situations.

We need to make assertiveness feminine. We need to make assertiveness nice. One can be a nice woman and still assert. We need to have assertive responses available for women of all cultural and educational levels. Yes, there will always be those who are offended by the strong woman. But assertion does not always have to be offensive in order to work. There is room for all of our styles in this battle. Laura may, whenever possible, avoid behavior for which she can be labeled as a crazy woman and dismissed. Chris may feel so strongly that she uses confrontive assertion at every opportunity.

This second level of assertion—angry or confrontive methods—involves more powerful, intense statements. These remarks are for situations in which the offended individual is not interested in politeness or in maintaining the good will of the other, but in making a strong, and often militant, statement. The remarks can still qualify as assertive and not aggressive. For example, I know a college professor to whom a female student complained about being stalked. The professor suggested she report the stalking to the campus police. The police officer came to take the report and said to the student, "No wonder he's stalking you—look at how you're dressed." The student was speechless. Upon learning about this incident, the professor was outraged and told the officer, "I am furious that you would blame this student for someone else's crime!" Within a half hour, the professor had delivered a letter of complaint to the officer's superior.

The battle against sexism compares in many ways to the campaign against racism. How did African-Americans make it socially unacceptable to utter racist remarks on television? How did the Jews raise consciousness about anti-Semitic remarks? The answer is simple: they protested.

But there is a critical difference between ethnic groups and women. The former, while they may have many justifiable fears of retaliation when they speak up, do not fear losing love in an intimate relationship. In order to speak up about sexism, the heterosexual woman has to do something that is considered unfeminine and, therefore, unlovable. The average woman has to do something that she fears may cut her off from the major relationship she has sought, perhaps all her life. Often she will not realize that such a man is not worth having; she may not even be acquainted with any other type of man. Or, perhaps she is afraid that assertive remarks will alienate her not only from him, but from everyone in her environment. A woman may have no one with whom to commiserate when she is the object of prejudice or discrimination. Everyone where she works, for example, may have thought that Anita Hill was lying or cheered for William Kennedy Smith. The woman does not realize that by speaking up she has some power to shape the very men with whom she's attempting to have a relationship. Already sexist, these men are unaware of the limits of her tolerance. Thus it is a circular problem: I may reject you if you have the nerve to risk my rejection by speaking up. Be quiet so I can assume you don't mind.

An assertive woman is a terrible threat to an insecure male. If his masculinity depends upon power over a woman, the more power she gets, the less masculine he is. Ever since Eve, blaming the "evil woman" has been an easy out, and probably even extends back to the time when the cause of birth represented an awesome mystery. This frightening power of women then suggested the witch, the sorceress, the temptress, the bitch. One can observe throughout our society the belief that the sexually attractive woman must be deliberately tempting the man. Because their sexuality threatens men, women are suspect for their sexual power. This is due to the defense mechanism of projection: If I am attracted to you, *you* must be attracted to *me*. If I want to seduce you, you must be trying to seduce me. And so you wear those clothes just to seduce me, and when you say *no*, you're a tease. We are unable to insult a man without insulting a woman's sexuality: bastard, son-of-a-bitch. There is even a graphic insult accusing people of incest with their mothers. We will not challenge this view unless we speak up precisely and frequently and with a variety of voices that feel comfortable and appropriate in the various subcultural and socioeconomic groups in which we find ourselves. Assertiveness training must allow for the needs of all women. And also for the men who report sexual exploitation.

We Americans cannot really be blamed for having no assertive responses on the tips of our tongues. We have little familiarity with response options between passivity and aggression. Ask anyone who's angry why expressing it to the other person is so difficult, and the usual reply is, "I was afraid I would lose my temper and do something I would regret." Not knowing there is an option that is firm and powerful, the angry American believes "losing it" is the only way to defend the self.

It is no wonder we fail to absorb simple assertiveness skills the way we absorb, for example, simple good manners like "please" and "thank you." To respond with violence is our national script for the way to deal with anger. Hollywood makes millions by showing us how to be violent.

Research is beginning to support the fact that assertiveness helps change attitudes in other people. Edward Donnerstein at the University of California studied the reactions of young men and women who watched films together, showing women being victimized in various ways. When the woman viewer commented to the man that she did not like the sexual aggression, the studies showed that the man tended to change his attitude in a positive direction. If the woman was silent, he assumed she did not mind. This response suggests that women's silence does contribute to men's sexual beliefs. In addition, the researchers followed up by asking the men about women's great fear—that if they are assertive, they will be rejected. The fear did not prove to be realistic. The men's attitudes toward the assertive woman remained the same.

This research contains a powerful message. Speaking up can change attitudes. And assertiveness does not have to cause a woman to be rejected. Despite the fact that at times we need to protest regardless of others' opinions, the possibility of assertion without rejection is vitally important. If the penalty for speaking up is rejection, only the most secure and confident women will assert themselves.

There are some other studies that show how an immediate assertive response can stop a negative behavior. A study of junior-high gossip by Donna Eder at Indiana University found that if one student initiates gossip, and if the immediate reply to the first gossiping statement is critical, the gossip stops cold. Repeatedly, we see that assertion can completely derail negative remarks. When children do something undesirable and adults do not intervene, it has the same effect as if the child was rewarded for the action. Again, passivity is interpreted as approval: I thought you didn't mind.

Some of our assumptions about men's strong beliefs in rape myths may not be correct. There seem to be three groups of men with respect to this issue. There are hard-core, completely macho, insensitive, and callous males. Nothing will change them; their personalities are probably so insecure that they *need* to control women. At the other extreme are sensitive males who decry the rape culture and don't need their consciousness raised. But in between there are millions of males who are not emotionally invested in misogyny—they just go along with it.

Those men in the middle need to be set straight. There is much hope for them. They need to be reminded that the cultural messages are inaccurate. They need to hear someone say, "I don't like jokes that put women down." They need to have peers, friends, teachers, and sisters who speak up when they are hurt, scared, or offended. Otherwise this culture will brainwash men with such overwhelming frequency that they will have no reason to think anyone disapproves.

Again, this kind of societal assertiveness is not women's *responsibility*. It is a choice: to empower ourselves, to take every opportunity to set things right. Its message is, "I am powerful enough to insist on respect."

We must provide a variety of options with which women and men can respond when sexist assumptions are present. We must realize that there are assertive responses that most women can find acceptable if phrased in their language and responsive to their needs.

We must be strong, feminine, and courageous, and we must empower our less experienced sisters by supporting them in finding new ways to communicate. We must offer hope that when they speak up they will not be cut off from others. There is no downside to owning our own strength. The only people who don't like it are abusers.

Yes, we do mind.

ELIZABETH POWELL is a licensed psychologist and author of *Talking Back to Sexual Pressure* (CompCare, 1991), which won the 1992 Midwest Book Association Award for the best self-help book of the year. Powell is also the scriptwriter/presenter of "Avoiding Date Rape: Talking Back to Sexual Pressure" (CompCare, 1992), a videotape that trains women and men in rape avoidance. She holds an M.S. degree in clinical psychology from Purdue University and an M.A. degree in family counseling from Webster University. She is professor of psychology at St. Louis Community College, where she teaches Human Sexuality and founded the AIDS task force. She appears frequently on radio and television to speak about how to use assertiveness to cope with harassment, sexually transmitted disease, and acquaintance rape.

CLARENCE, WILLIAM, IRON MIKE, TAILHOOK, SENATOR PACKWOOD, SPUR POSSE, MAGIC . . . AND US

by Michael S. Kimmel

What is it about groups that seems to bring out the worst
in men? I think it is because the animating condition
for most American men is a deeply rooted fear
of other men—a fear that other men view us
as less than manly.

THE 1990s may be remembered as the decade in which America took a crash course on male sexuality. From the national teach-in on sexual harassment that emerged from Clarence Thomas's confirmation hearings, to accusations about sexual harassment against Senator Robert Packwood, to the U.S. Navy Tailhook scandal, to Magic Johnson's revelation that he is infected with the HIV virus, to William Kennedy Smith and Mike Tyson's date rape trials, to the trials of lacrosse players at St. John's University and high school athletes at Glen Ridge, New Jersey, we've had a steady discussion about male sexuality, about a sexuality that is more about predatory conquest than pleasure and connection.

And there's no end in sight—which explains the title of this essay. In the immediate aftermath of the Clarence Thomas confirmation hearings, the media claimed, as if with one voice, that the hearings would have a "chilling effect" on American women—that women would be far less likely to come forward and report incidents of sexual harassment for fear that they would be treated in the same shameful way as Anita Hill was by the Senate Judiciary Committee. Have the media ever been more wrong?

Since then, we've had less of a "chilling effect," and more of a national thaw, as women have come forward in record numbers to report cases of sexual harassment, date rape, and acquaintance rape. "Every woman has her Clarence Thomas," commented one woman, sadly surveying the workplace over the past two decades. In an op-ed essay in the *New York Times*, novelist Mary Lee Settle commented that Anita Hill had, "by her heroic stance, given not only me but thousands of women who have been silenced by shame the courage and the need to speak out about what we have tried for so long to bury and forget."

Currently, corporations, state and local governments, universities, and law firms are scrambling to implement procedures to handle sexual harassment. Most seem motivated more out of fear of lawsuits than out of general concern for women's experiences; thus, they are more interested in adjudicating harassment *after the fact* than in developing mechanisms to prevent it. In the same way, colleges and universities are developing strategies to handle the remarkable rise in date and acquaintance rape, although only a few are developing programs on prevention.

With more women coming forward now than ever before, many men have reacted defensively; "Men on Trial" has been the common headline linking Smith and Thomas in the media. But it's not *men* on trial here, it's *masculinity*, or, rather, a definition of masculinity that leads to certain behaviors that we now see as problematic and often physically threatening. Under prevailing definitions, men have been and are the "politically incorrect" sex.

But why have these issues emerged now? And why are issues such as sexual harassment and date rape the particular issues we're facing? Since it is certain that we will continue to face these issues for the rest of the decade, how can we understand these changes? And, most important, what can we do about it? How can we change the meanings of masculinity so that sexual harassment and date rape will disappear from our workplaces and our relationships?

THE SOCIAL CONSTRUCTION OF MALE SEXUALITY

To speak of transforming masculinity is to begin with the way men are sexual in our culture. As social scientists now understand, sexuality is less a product of biological urges and more about the meanings that we attach to those urges, meanings that vary dramatically across cultures, over time, and among a variety of social groups within any particular culture. Sexual beings are made, not born. John Gagnon, a well-known theoretician of this approach, argues in his book *Human Sexualities* that

> People learn when they are quite young a few of the things that they are expected to be, and continue slowly to accumulate a belief in who they are and ought to be through the rest of childhood, adolescence, and adulthood. Sexual conduct is learned in the same ways and through the same processes; it is acquired and assembled in human interaction, judged and performed in specific cultural and historical worlds.

And the major item in that assemblage, the chief building block in the social construction of sexuality, is gender. We experience our sexual selves through a gendered prism. The meanings of sex to women and to men are very, very different. There really are a "his" and "hers" when it comes to sex. Just one example: think about the difference in the way we view a man or a woman who has a lot of different partners—the difference, say, between a stud and a slut.

The rules of masculinity and femininity are strictly enforced. And difference equals power. The difference between male and female sexuality reproduces men's power over women, and, simultaneously, the power of some men over other men, especially of the dominant, hegemonic form of manhood—white, straight, middle-class—over marginalized masculinities. Those who dare to cross over—women who are sexually adventurous and men who are sexually passive—risk being seen as *gender*, not sexual, nonconformists. And we all know how homophobia links gender nonconformity to homosexuality. The stakes are high if you don't play along.

Sexual behavior confirms manhood. It makes men feel manly. Robert Brannon has identified the four traditional rules of American manhood: (1) No Sissy Stuff: Men can never do anything that even remotely suggests femininity. Manhood is a relentless repudiation and devaluation of the feminine. (2) Be a Big Wheel: Manhood is measured by power, wealth, and success. Whoever has the most toys when he dies, wins. (3) Be a Sturdy Oak: Manhood depends on emotional reserve. Dependability in a crisis requires that men not reveal their feelings. (4) Give 'em Hell: Exude an aura of manly daring and aggression. Go for it. Take risks.

These four rules lead to a sexuality built around accumulating partners (scoring), emotional distance, and risk taking. In locker rooms and on playgrounds across the country, men are taught that the goal of every encounter with women is to score. Men are supposed to be ever ready for sex, constantly seeking sex, and constantly seeking to escalate every encounter so that intercourse will result, since, as one of my students once noted, "It doesn't count unless you put it in."

The emotional distancing of the sturdy oak is considered necessary for adequate male sexual functioning, but it leads to some strange behaviors. For example, to keep from ejaculating "too soon," men may devise a fascinating array of distractions, such as counting, doing multiplication tables in their heads, or thinking about sports.

Risk taking is a centerpiece of male sexuality. Sex is about adventure, excitement, danger. Taking chances. Responsibility is a word that seldom turns up in male sexual discourse. And this of course has serious medical side effects; the possibilities include STDs, impregnation, and AIDS—currently the most gendered disease in American history.

To rein in this constructed male "appetite," women have been assigned the role of asexual gatekeeper; women decide, metaphorically and literally, who enters the desired garden of earthly delights, and who doesn't. Women's sexual agency, women's sense of entitlement to desire, is drowned out by the incessant humming of male desire, propelling him ever forward. A man's job is to wear down her resistance. One fraternity at a college I was lecturing at last year offered seminars to pledges on dating etiquette that appropriated the book of business advice called *Getting to Yes.*

Sometimes that hum can be so loud that it drowns out the actual voice of the real live woman that he's with. Men suffer from socialized deafness, a hearing impairment that strikes only when women say "no."

WHO ARE THE REAL SEXUAL REVOLUTIONARIES?

Of course, a lot has changed along the frontiers of the sexual landscape in the past two decades. We've had a sexual revolution, after all. But as the dust is settling from the sexual revolution, what emerges in unmistakably fine detail is that it's been women, not men, who are our era's real sexual pioneers. Of course, we men like to think that the sexual revolution, with its promises of more access to more partners with less emotional commitment, was tailor-made for male sexuality's fullest flowering. But in fact it's been women's sexuality that's changed in the past two decades, not men's. Women now feel capable, even *entitled,* to sexual pleasure. They have learned to say "yes" to their own desires, claiming their own sexual agency.

And men? We're still dancing the same tired dance of the sexual conquistadors. Look, for a minute, at that new late-night game show "Studs." Here are the results of the sexual revolution in media miniature. The men and women all date one another, and from implicit innuendo to explicit guffaws, one assumes that every couple has gone to bed. What's not news is that the men are joking about it; what *is* news is that the women are equally capable of it.

Now some might argue that this simply confirms that women can have "male sex," that male sexuality was victorious because we've convinced women to be more like us. But then why are so many men wilting in the face of desiring women? Why are the offices of sex therapists crammed with men who complain not of premature ejaculation (the most common sexual problem twenty years ago—a sexual problem that involves being a bit overeager) but of what therapists euphemistically call "inhibited desire." That is, these men don't want to have sex now that all these women are able to claim their sexual rights.

DATE RAPE AND SEXUAL PREDATION, AGGRESSION, AND ENTITLEMENT

As women have claimed the right to say "yes," they've also begun to assert their rights to say "no." Women are now demanding that men be more sexually responsible and are holding men accountable for their sexual behaviors. It is women who have changed the rules of sexual conduct. What used to be (and in many places still is) called male sexual etiquette—forcing a woman to have sex when she says no, conniving, coercing, pushing, ignoring efforts to get you to stop, getting her so drunk that she loses the ability (or consciousness) that one needs to give consent—is now defined as date rape.

In one recent study, by psychologist Mary Koss at the University of Arizona, forty-five percent of all college women said that they had had some form of sexual contact against their will. A full twenty-five percent had been pressed or forced to have sexual intercourse against their will. And Patricia Bowman, who went home with William Kennedy Smith from Au Bar in Palm Beach, Florida, knows all about those statistics. She testified that when she told Smith that she'd called her friends, and she was going to call the police, he responded, "You shouldn't have done that. Nobody's going to believe you." And, indeed, the jury didn't. I did.

I also believed that the testimony of three other women who claimed they were sexually assaulted by Smith should have been allowed in the trial. Such testimony would have established a pattern not of criminal assault, but of Smith's obvious belief in sexual *entitlement*, that he was entitled to press his sexual needs on women despite their resistance, because he didn't particularly care what they felt about it.

And Desiree Washington knows all about men who don't listen when a woman says no. Mike Tyson's aggressive masculinity in the boxing ring was sadly translated into a vicious misogyny with his ex-wife Robin Givens and a predatory sexuality, as evidenced by his behavior with Desiree Washington. Tyson's "grandiose sense of entitlement, fueled by the insecurities and emotions of adolescence," as writer Joyce Carol

Oates put it, led to a behavior with women that was as out of control as his homosocial behavior inside the ring.

Tyson's case underscores our particular fascination with athletes, and the causal equation we make between athletes and sexual aggression. From the St. John's University lacrosse team, to Glen Ridge, New Jersey, high school athletes, to dozens of athletic teams and individual players at campuses across the nation, we're getting the message that our young male athletes, trained for fearless aggression on the field, are translating that into a predatory sexual aggression in relationships with women. Columnist Robert Lipsyte calls it the "varsity syndrome—winner take all, winning at any cost, violence as a tool, aggression as a mark of masculinity." The very qualities we seek in our athletes are exactly the qualities we do not want in young men today. Rather, we want to encourage respect for others, compassion, the ability to listen, and attention to process rather than the end goal. Our task is to make it clear that what we want from our athletes when they are on the playing field is *not* the same as what we want from them when they are playing the field.

I think, though, that athletes only illustrate a deeper problem: the problem of men in groups. Most athletes play on teams, so much of their social life and much of a player's public persona is constructed through association with his teammates. Another homosocial preserve, fraternities, are the site of most gang rapes that occur on college campuses, according to psychologist Chris O'Sullivan, who has been studying gang rape for several years. [See "Fraternities and the Rape Culture," pp. 23–30.] At scores of campus and corporate workshops over the past five years, women have shared the complaint that, while individual men may appear sympathetic when they are alone with women, they suddenly turn out to be macho louts capable of the vilest misogynistic statements when they are in groups of men. The members of the U.S. Navy Tailhook Association are quite possibly decent, law-abiding family men when they are alone or with their families. But put them together at a convention, and they become a marauding gang of hypermasculine thugs who should be prosecuted for felonious assault, not merely slapped on their collective wrists.

I suppose it's true that the members of Spur Posse, a group of relatively affluent Southern California adolescent boys, are also "regular guys." Which makes their sexual predation and homosocial competition as chilling as it is revealing of something at the heart of American masculinity. Before a large group of young women and girls—one as young as ten!—came forward to claim that members of Spur Posse had sexually assaulted and raped them, these guys would have been seen as typical high school fellas. Members of the group competed with one another to have sex with the most girls and kept elaborately coded scores of their exploits by referring to various athletes' names as a way of signifying the number of conquests. Thus a reference to "Reggie Jackson" would refer to 44, the number on his jersey, while "David Robinson" would signify 50 different conquests. In this way, the boys could publicly compete with one another without the young women understanding that they were simply the grounds for homosocial competition.

When some of these young women accused the boys of assault and rape, many residents of their affluent suburb were shocked. The boys' mothers, particularly, winced when they heard that their fifteen-year-old sons had had sex with 44 or 50 girls. A few expressed outrage. But the boys' fathers glowed with pride. "That's my boy," they declared in chorus. They accused the girls of being sluts. And we wonder where the kids get it from?

Spur Posse is only the most recent example of the way masculine sexual entitlement is offered to boys as part of their birthright. Transforming a rape culture is going to mean transforming a view of women as the vessels through which men can compete with one another, trying to better their positions on the homosocial ladders of success and status.

What is it about groups that seems to bring out the worst in men? I think it is because the animating condition for most American men is a deeply rooted fear of other men—a fear that other men will view us as less than manly. The fear of humiliation, of losing in a competitive ranking among men, of being dominated by other men—these are the fears that keep men in tow and that reinforce traditional definitions of masculinity as a false definition of safety. Homophobia (which I understand as more than the fear of homosexual men; it's also the fear of other men) keeps men acting like men, keeps men exaggerating their adherence to traditional norms, so that no other men will get the idea that we might really be that most dreaded person: the sissy.

Men's fear of being judged a failure as a man in the eyes of other men leads to a certain homosocial element within the heterosexual encounter: men often will use their sexual conquest as a form of currency to gain status among other men. Such homosocial competition contributes to the strange hearing impairment that men experience in any sexual encounter, a socialized deafness that leads us to hear "no" as "yes," to escalate the encounter, to always go for it, to score. And this is occurring just at the moment when women are, themselves, learning to say "yes" to their own sexuality, to say "yes" to their own desire for sexual pleasure. Instead of our socialized deafness, we need to become what Langston Hughes called "articulate listeners": we need to trust women when they tell us what they want, and when they want it, and what they don't want as well. If we listen when women say "no," then they will feel more trusting and open to saying "yes" when they feel that. And we need to listen to our own inner voices, our own desires and needs. Not the voices that are about compulsively proving something that cannot be proved, but the voices that are about connection with another and the desires and passions that may happen between two equals.

Escalating a sexual encounter beyond what a woman may want is date rape, not sex; it is one of the most important issues we will face in the 1990s. It is transforming the sexual landscape as earlier sexual behaviors are being reevaluated in light of new ideas about sexual politics. We have to explore the meaning of the word *consent*, explore our own understandings, and make sure that these definitions are in accord with women's definitions.

FROM THE BEDROOM TO THE BOARDROOM

Just as women have been claiming the right to say "yes" and demanding the right to say "no" and have it listened to and respected in the sexual arena, they've also transformed the public arena, the workplace. As with sexuality, the real revolution in the past thirty years has been women's dramatic entry into the labor force in unprecedented numbers. Almost half of the labor force is female. I often demonstrate this point to my classes by asking the women who intend to have careers to raise their hands. All do. Then I ask them to keep their hands raised if their mothers have had a career outside the home for more than ten years. Half put their hands down. Then I ask them to keep their hands raised if their grandmothers had a career for ten years. Virtually no hands remain raised. In three generations, they can visibly see the difference in women's working lives. Women are in the work force to stay, and men had better get used to having them around.

That means that the cozy boy's club—another homosocial arena—has been penetrated by women. And this, just when that arena is more suffused with doubt and anxieties than ever before. We are, after all, a downwardly mobile culture. Most Americans are less successful now than their parents were at the same age. It now takes two incomes to provide the same standard of living that one income provided about a generation ago. And most of us in the middle class cannot afford to buy the houses in which we were brought up. Since men derive their identity in the public sphere, and the primary public arena where masculinity is demonstrated is the workplace, this is an important issue. There are fewer and fewer big wheels and more and more men who will feel as though they haven't made the grade, who will feel damaged, injured, powerless—men who will need to demonstrate their masculinity all over again. Suddenly, men's fears of humiliation and domination are out in the open, and there's a convenient target at which to vent those anxieties.

And now, here come women into the workplace in unprecedented numbers. It now seems virtually impossible that a man will go through his entire working life without having a woman colleague, co-worker, or boss. Just when men's economic breadwinner status is threatened, women appear on the scene as easy targets for men's anger. Thus sexual harassment in the workplace is a distorted effort to put women back in their place, to remind women that they are not equal to men in the workplace, that they are still just women, even if they are in the workplace.

It seems to me that this is the context in which to explore the meaning of sexual harassment in our society. The Clarence Thomas confirmation hearings afford men a rare opportunity to do some serious soul searching. What is sexual harassment about? And why should men help put an end to it?

One thing that sexual harassment is usually *not* about, although you couldn't convince the Senate Judiciary Committee of this, is a matter of one person telling the truth and the other person lying. Sexual harassment cases are difficult and confusing precisely because there are often a multiplicity of truths. "His" truth might be what appears to him as an innocent indication of sexual interest by harmless joking with the "boys in the office" (even if those "boys" happen to include women workers).

"Her" truth is that those seemingly innocent remarks cause stress and anxiety about promotion, firing, and sexual pressure.

Judge Thomas asserted during the course of his testimony that "at no time did I become aware, either directly or indirectly, that she felt I had said or done anything to change the cordial nature of our relationship." And there is no reason to assume that he would have been aware of it. But that doesn't mean his words or actions did not have the effect that Professor Hill states, only that she was successful in concealing the resulting trauma from him—a concealment that women have carefully developed over the years in the workplace.

Why should this surprise us? Women and men often experience the same event differently. Men experience their behavior from the perspective of those who have power, women from the perspective of those upon whom that power is exercised.

If an employer asks an employee for a date, and she declines, perhaps he has forgotten about it by the time he gets to the parking lot. No big deal, he says to himself. You ask someone out, and she says "no." You forget about it. In fact, repairing a wounded male ego often *requires* that you forget about it. But the female employee? She's now frozen, partly with fear. What if I said yes? Would I have gotten promoted? Would he have expected more than a date? Will I now get fired? Will someone else get promoted over me? What should I do? And so, she will do what millions of women do in that situation: she calls her friends, who counsel her to let the matter rest and get on with her work. And she remembers for a long, long time. Who, therefore, is likely to have a better memory: those in power or those against whom that power is deployed?

This is precisely the divergence in experience that characterizes the controversies spinning around Senator Bob Packwood. Long a public supporter of women's causes, Senator Packwood also apparently chased numerous women around office desks, clumsily trying to have affairs with them. He claims, now, that alcoholism caused this behavior and that he doesn't remember. It's a good thing that the women remember. They often do.

Sexual harassment is particularly volatile because it often fuses two levels of power: the power of employers over employees and the power of men over women. Thus what may be said or intended as a man to a woman is also experienced in the context of superior and subordinate, or vice versa. Sexual harassment in the workplace results from men using their public position to demand or exact social relationships. It is the confusion of public and private, bringing together two arenas of men's power over women. Not only are men in positions of power in the workplace, but we are socialized to be the sexual initiators and to see sexual prowess as a confirmation of masculinity.

Sexual harassment is also a way to remind women that they are not yet equals in the workplace, that they really don't belong there. Harassment is most frequent in those occupations and workplaces where women are new and in the minority, like surgeons, firefighters, and investment bankers. "Men see women as invading a masculine environment," says Louise Fitzgerald, a University of Illinois psychologist. "These are guys whose sexual harassment has nothing whatever to do with sex. They're trying to scare women off a male preserve."

When the power of men is augmented by the power of employer over employee, it is easy to understand how humiliating and debilitating sexual harassment can be, and how individual women would be frightened about seeking redress. The workplace is not a level playing field. Subordinates rarely have the resources to complain against managers, whatever the problem.

Some men were confused by Professor Hill's charges, others furious about sexual harassment because it feels as though women are changing the rules. What used to be routine behavior for men in the workplace is now being called sexual harassment. "Clarence Thomas didn't do anything wrong that any American male hasn't done," commented Dale Whitcomb, a thirty-two-year-old machinist. How right he was. The fact that two-thirds of men surveyed said they would be complimented if they were propositioned by a woman at work gives some idea of the vast gulf between women's and men's perceptions of workplace sexual conduct.

Although men surely do benefit from sexual harassment, I believe that we also have a stake in ending it. First, our ability to form positive and productive relationships with women colleagues in the workplace is undermined by it. So long as sexual harassment is a daily occurrence and women are afraid of their superiors in the workplace, innocent men's behaviors may be misinterpreted. Second, men's ability to develop social and sexual relationships that are both ethical and exciting is also compromised. If a male boss dates a subordinate, can he really trust that the reason she is with him is because she *wants* to be? Or will there always be a lingering doubt that she is there because she is afraid not to be or because she seeks to please him because of his position?

Currently, law firms and corporations all over the country are scrambling to implement sexual harassment policies, to make sure that sexual harassment will be recognized and punished. But our challenge is greater than admonition and post hoc counseling. Our challenge will be to prevent sexual harassment *before* it happens. And that means working with men. Men must come to see that these are not women who happen to be in the workplace (where, by this logic, they actually don't belong), but workers who happen to be women. And we'll need to change the meaning of success so that men don't look back at their careers when they retire and wonder what it was all for, whether any of it was worth it. Again, we'll need to change the definition of masculinity, dislodging it from these misshapen public enactments, including the capacity to embrace others as equals within it, because of an inner security and confidence that can last a lifetime. It is more important than ever to begin to listen to women, to listen with a compassion that understands that women's and men's experiences are different, and an understanding that men, too, can benefit from the elimination of sexual harassment.

AIDS AS A MEN'S DISEASE

Surely, men will benefit from the eradication of AIDS. Although we are used to discussing AIDS as a disease of gay men and IV drug users, I think we need to see AIDS as a men's disease. Over ninety percent of all AIDS patients are men; AIDS is now the leading cause of death for men aged thirty-three to forty-five nationwide. AIDS is American men's number one health problem, and yet we rarely treat it as a men's issue. But AIDS is also the most gender-linked disease in American history. No other disease has attacked one gender so disproportionately, except those to which only one sex is susceptible, such as hemophilia or uterine or prostate cancer. AIDS *could* affect both men and women equally (and in Africa that seems to be closer to the case). But in the United States, AIDS patients are overwhelmingly men.

(Let me be clear that in no way am I saying that one should not be compassionate for women AIDS patients. Of course one must recognize that women are as likely to get AIDS from engaging in the same high-risk behaviors as men. But that's precisely my point. Women don't engage in those behaviors at rates anything like men.)

One is put at risk for AIDS by engaging in specific high-risk behaviors, activities that ignore potential health risks for more immediate pleasures. For example, sharing needles is both a defiant flaunting of health risks and an expression of community among IV drug users. And the capacity for high-risk sexual behaviors—unprotected anal intercourse with a large number of partners, the ability to take it, despite any potential pain—are also confirmations of masculinity.

And so is accumulation—of money, property, or sexual conquests. It's curious that one of America's most lionized heroes, Magic Johnson, doesn't seem to have been particularly compassionate about the possibility of infection of the twenty-five hundred women he reported that he slept with. Johnson told *Sports Illustrated* that as a single man, he tried to "accommodate as many women as I could, most of them through unprotected sex." Accommodate? When he protested that his words were misunderstood, he told the *New York Times*, "I was a bachelor, and I lived a bachelor's life. And I'm paying the price for it. But you know I respect women to the utmost." (I suppose that Wilt Chamberlain, who boasted in his autobiography that he slept with over twenty thousand women, respected them almost ten times as much.)

As sociologists have long understood, stigmatized gender identity often leads to exaggerated forms of gender-specific behavior. Thus, those whose masculinity is least secure are precisely those most likely to enact behavioral codes and hold fast to traditional definitions of masculinity. In social science research, hypermasculinity as compensation for insecure gender identity has been used to explain the propensity for homophobia, authoritarianism, racism, anti-Semitism, juvenile delinquency, and urban gangs.

Gay men and IV drug users—the two largest risk groups—can be seen in this light, although for different reasons. The traditional view of gay men is that they are not "real men." Most of the stereotypes revolve around effeminacy, weakness, passivity. But following the Stonewall riots of 1969, in which gay men fought back against a police raid on a gay bar in Greenwich Village, New York, and the subsequent birth of the Gay Liberation Movement, a new gay masculinity emerged in major cities (see Kleinberg, 1990; Levine, 1991). The "clone," as the new gay man was called, dressed in hypermasculine garb (flannel shirts, blue jeans, leather); had short hair (not at all androgynous) and a mustache; and was athletic, highly muscular. In short, the clone looked more like a "real man" than most straight men.

And the clones—who comprised roughly one-third of all gay men living in the major urban enclaves of the 1970s (see Bell and Weinberg, 1980)—enacted a hypermasculine sexuality in steamy back rooms, bars, and bathhouses, where sex was plentiful, anonymous, and very hot. No unnecessary foreplay, romance, or post-coital awkwardness. Sex without attachment. One might even say that, given the norms of masculinity (that men are always seeking sex, ready for sex, wanting sex), gay men were the only men in America who were getting as much sex as they wanted. Predictably, high levels of sexual activity led to high levels of sexually transmitted diseases, such as gonorrhea, among the clones. But no one could have predicted AIDS.

Among IV drug users, we see a different pattern, but with some similar outcomes when seen from a gender perspective. The majority of IV drug users are African-American and Latino, two groups for whom the traditional avenues of successful manhood are blocked by poverty and racism. More than half of the black men between eighteen and twenty-five in our cities are unemployed, and one in four are in some way involved with the penal system (in jail, on probation, under arrest). We thus have an entire generation structurally prevented from demonstrating its manhood in that most traditional of ways—as breadwinners.

The drug culture offers an alternative. Dealing drugs can provide an income to support a family as well as the opportunity for manly risks and adventure. The community of drug users can confirm gender identity; the sharing of needles is a demonstration of that solidarity. And the ever-present risk of death by overdose takes hypermasculine bravado to its limits.

WHO ASKED FOR IT?

The victims of men's adherence to these crazy norms of masculinity—AIDS patients, rape victims, victims of sexual harassment—did not become victims intentionally. They did not "ask for it," and they certainly do not deserve blame. That some women today are also sexual predators, going to swank bars or waiting outside athletes' locker rooms or trying to score with male subordinates at work, doesn't make William Kennedy Smith, Mike Tyson, Magic Johnson, or Clarence Thomas any less predatory. When predatory animals threaten civil populations, we warn the population to stay indoors, until the wild animals can be caught and recaged. When it's men on the prowl, women engage in a voluntary curfew, unless they want to risk being attacked.

And the men—the date rapists, the sexual harassers, the AIDS patients—are not "perverts" or "deviants" who have strayed from the norms of masculinity. They are, if anything, overconformists to destructive norms of male sexual behavior. Until we change the meaning of manhood, sexual risk-taking and conquest will remain part of the rhetoric of masculinity. And we will scatter the victims, both women and men, along the wayside as we rush headlong towards a testosterone-infected oblivion.

THE SEXUAL POLITICS OF SAFETY

What links the struggle against sexual harassment, date and acquaintance rape, and AIDS is that preventing all of them require that *safety* become the central term, an organizing principle of men's relationships with women, as well as with other men. The politics of safety may be the missing link in the transformation of men's lives, in their capacity for change. Safety is more than the absence of danger, although that wouldn't be such a bad thing itself. Safety is pro-active, the creation of a space in which all people, women and men, gay and straight, and of all colors, can experience and express the fullness of their beings.

Think for a moment about how the politics of safety affects the three areas I have discussed in this essay. What is the best way to prevent AIDS? To use sterile needles for intravenous drug injections and to practice "safer sex." Sterile needles and safer sex share one basic characteristic: they both require that men act responsibly. This is not one of the cardinal rules of manhood. Safer sex programs encourage men to have fewer partners, to avoid certain particularly dangerous practices, and to use condoms when having any sex that involves the exchange of bodily fluids. In short, safer sex programs encourage men to stop having sex like men. To men, you see, "safer sex" is an oxymoron, one of those juxtapositions of terms that produce a nonsensical outcome. That which is sexy is not safe, that which is safe is not sexy. Sex is about danger, risk, excitement; safety is about comfort, softness, and security.

Seen this way, it is not surprising to find, as some researchers have found, that one-fourth of urban gay men report that they have not changed their unsafe sexual behaviors. What is, in fact, astonishing is that slightly more than three-fourths *have* changed and are now practicing safer sex.

What heterosexual men could learn from the gay community's response to AIDS is how to eroticize that responsibility—something that women have been trying to teach men for decades. Making safer sex into sexy sex has been one of the great transformations of male sexuality accomplished by the gay community. And straight men could also learn a thing or two about caring for one another through illness, supporting one another in grief, and maintaining a resilience in the face of a devastating disease and the callous indifference of the larger society.

Safety is also the animating condition for women's expression of sexuality. While safety may be a turnoff for men (comfort, softness, and security are the terms of postorgasmic detumescence, not sexual arousal), safety is a precondition for sexual agency for women. Only when women feel safe can they give their sexuality full expression. For men, hot sex leaves a warm afterglow; for women, warmth builds to heat, but warmth is not created by heat.

This perspective helps explain that curious finding in the sex research literature about the divergence of women's and men's sexualities as they age. We believe that men reach their sexual peak at around eighteen, and then go into steady, and later more precipitous, decline for the rest of their lives; while women hit their sexual stride closer to thirty, with the years between twenty-seven and thirty-eight as their peak years. Typically, we understand these changes as having to do with differences in biology—that hormonal changes find men feeling soft and cuddly just as women are getting all steamed up. But aging does not produce such changes in every culture; that is, biology doesn't seem to work the same way everywhere.

What biological explanations leave out is the way that men's and women's sexualities are related to each other, and the way that both are shaped by the institution of marriage. Marriage makes one's sexuality more predictable—the partner, the timing, the experience—and it places sex *always* in the context of the marital relationship. Marriage

makes sex safer. No wonder women find their sexuality heightening—
they finally feel safe enough to allow their sexual desires to be expressed.
And no wonder men's sexuality deflates—there's no danger, risk or
excitement left.

Safety is a precondition for women's sexual expression. Only when a
woman is certain, beyond the shadow of a doubt, that her "no" means
"no," can she ever say "yes" to her own sexual desires. So if we men are
going to have the sexual relationships with exciting, desiring women that
we say we want, then we have to make the environment safe enough for
women to express their desires. We have to make it absolutely certain to
a woman that her "no" means "no"—no matter how urgently we feel the
burning of our own desires.

To do this we will need to transform the definition of what it means
to be a real man. But we have to work fast. AIDS is spreading rapidly,
and date rape and sexual harassment are epidemic in the nation's colleges
and workplaces. As AIDS spreads, and as women speak up about these
issues, there are more and more people who need our compassion and
support. Yet compassion is in relatively short supply among American
men, since it involves the capacity of taking the role of the other, of seeing ourselves in someone else's shoes, a quality that contradicts the
manly independence we have so carefully cultivated.

Sexual democracy, just like political democracy, relies on a balance
between rights and responsibilities, between the claims of the individual
and the claims of the community. When one discusses one's sexual
rights—that each person, every woman and man, has an equal right to
pleasure—men understand immediately what you mean. Women often
look delighted and a little bit surprised. Add to the Bill of Sexual Rights
a notion of responsibility, in which each of us treats sexual partners as if
they had an integrity equal to our own, and it's the men who look puz-
zled. "Responsibility? What's that got to do with sex? I thought sex was
about having fun."

Sure it is, but it's also political in the most intimate sense. Sexual
democracy doesn't have to mean no sex. It means treating your partner
as someone whose lust is equal to yours and also as someone whose life is
equally valuable. It's about enacting in daily life one's principles, claiming our rights to pleasure, and making sure that our partners also feel safe
enough to be able to fully claim theirs. This is what we demand for those
who have come to America seeking refuge—safety—from political

tyranny. Could we ask any less for those who are now asking for protection and refuge from millennia of sexual tyranny?

NOTE: My thinking on these issues has benefitted enormously from collaborative work with Michael Kaufman and the late Martin Levine. The material in the sections on sexual harassment and AIDS draws from that collaborative work, and I am grateful to them for their insights and support. Thanks also to the editors of this book for the invitation to bring together these seemingly disparate themes.

MICHAEL S. KIMMEL is one of the nation's foremost educators on men and masculinity. He is Associate Professor of Sociology at SUNY at Stony Brook, where he teaches courses on the Sociology of Men, Social Theory, and Sex and Society. His books include *Changing Men* (Sage, 1987), *Men Confront Pornography* (Crown, 1990; paperback Penguin, 1991), and *Against the Tide: Pro-Feminist Men in the United States, 1776–1990*, a documentary history of men who have supported women's equality (Beacon Press, 1992; paperback, 1993). His anthology, *Men's Lives* (co-edited with Mike Messner), has been adopted in virtually every college-level course on men in the nation. Kimmel also writes for general audiences and is a regular contributor to *The Nation* and *Psychology Today*, where he has been a Contributing Editor. He is the National Spokesperson for the National Organization for Men Against Sexism, the nation's pro-feminist men's organization. His new book, *Manhood: The American Quest*, a history of the idea of manhood in America, will be published in 1994 by HarperCollins.

CREATING REDEMPTIVE IMAGERY:
A Challenge of Resistance and Creativity
by Sandra Campbell

The goal of our speaking must be to develop a new
understanding that violence is the resort of the
resourceless; that poverty, sexism, and racism provide
the seedbed for its development; and that all prevention
must be grounded in this perspective.

THIS ESSAY IS a meditation on the pervasiveness of violence in our popular imagery, sounds, and stories, and an exploration of the basic beliefs that promote violence. The challenge to artists and to individuals is to counter this pervasiveness so that a new lexicon of redemptive imagery can be created. As we engage in this challenge, we will facilitate the development of a new paradigm for a violence-free reality that will help us heal centuries of violence. This paper emerges from three years of work—since the massacre of fourteen women engineering students at the Université de Montreal—on developing alternatives to violence.

THE CHALLENGE: RESISTANCE AND CREATIVITY TOGETHER, CONCURRENTLY

There is a growing intolerance to the prevalence of violence and a mounting resistance to its seeming inevitability. Thus, we now have a very real possibility of shifting public consciousness towards an abhorrence for violence. This shift will happen as we respond as individuals and artists to two interconnected challenges. The first challenge is to refuse to comply with the worldview that is now being conveyed. The second challenge—to be undertaken simultaneously with the first—is to create images, sounds, and stories that articulate difference, that illuminate paths towards alternatives, indeed that describe the unfamiliar. Further, we need to engage in these interconnected challenges in ways that both inspire and nurture hope. Hope is the elixir for change, and as we honor its magic, our resistance will be emboldened and our creativity enlivened.

One of the essential qualities of being human is our need for stories. Stories provide a context in which life has meaning. They shape our emotional attitudes, provide us with life purpose and energize our actions. At present, mainstream popular culture force-feeds us a steady diet of stories of domination and violation, which leaves us starved for stories that foster hope for ourselves and our future.

Because stories that engender despair are familiar, our task must be to illuminate the unfamiliar. How do we do this? First, we must imagine a world in which destruction of the "other" is not valued in any way. To do this, we must begin by removing the limitations on our imaginations imposed by our outmoded assumptions about what is possible and what is human. Then, as we engage in the process of removing these barriers to our imaginations, alternative images, sounds, and stories will emerge that recognize conflict and the range of human feelings that give rise to it, but that abhor the expression of these feelings through violence. A new lexicon of redemptive imagery that both reflects and supports a world without violence will be the reward for our engagement in this process of resistance and creativity.

To produce this new lexicon, we need to engage in three ongoing, interrelated undertakings. We must first embrace these as individual, personal acts of reflection. Then we must carry our own personal take on violence into discussion and diverse action in the public domain, using each of our voices as the primary instrument of change. By doing this we will lead the way to the establishment of structures and supports for artists and others in our cultural industries to develop, to market, and to disseminate a wide range of alternatives.

As we engage in these undertakings we will give birth to new stories of what it is to be human, what it is to be alive on this planet—stories that celebrate everyday human experiences of connection, of community, of diversity and difference, of reciprocity, of deep feeling and its human expression, and most importantly, of human conflict *without* destruction of the other. This rich tapestry of redemptive images, sounds, and stories will facilitate our healing from the destruction and devastation caused by centuries of violence.

STEP ONE: ASSESSING WHERE WE ARE

The current popular culture serves to validate all forms of violence, including men's violence against men, men's violence against women, and acts of sexism, racism, and other prejudices. As individuals, we must honestly define how this current reality affects us. How does it shape our worldviews, including our beliefs about our life possibilities? What happens to our relationships when the popular depiction of gender roles posits the male as the invulnerable, unfeeling aggressor, and the female as the silent, submissive victim? What happens to our sense of personal potential as women when the genre of films like *Fatal Attraction* and *Basic Instinct* depicts women initiators as dangerous and psychopathic threats to male privilege, thus reinforcing the working hypothesis that women must be dominated? What happens to our sense of female sexuality when violence against women is consistently eroticized, with sex often used as a weapon? What happens to our attitudes about conflict when violence between men is presented as a valiant and noble power struggle in which might is right—the sine qua non of masculinity?

We must ask, too, how our media environment affects our children. The process of image internalization works outside rational thought, and for this reason the absorption of images and sounds requires no special gift, no level of education, no minimum age. Words carried by music remain in the rhythm of our heartbeat, whether we desire recollection or not. Therefore our children are as affected by our cultural artifacts as we are. Whether we like it or not, the coming generation absorbs the values represented in contemporary icons, perpetuating their underlying beliefs. How does the toy and video-game culture of super-hero as white, male, omnipotent dominator influence their beliefs and attitudes about gender and race, about difference, and about resolving conflict? How does this shape their behavior as boys and girls, and how will this affect the kinds of adults they become? What happens to children's developing sense of appropriate sexual behavior when their primary instruction comes from music videos such as those of Guns N' Roses that depict bondage and rape as erotic, and from mainstream "slasher" films such as *The Silence of the Lambs* and *Cape Fear* that children watch on home videos? An image once perceived is absorbed indelibly in memory. What is the impact of the Nintendo video-game culture that rewards absorption of violence through the imitation of the behavior of brutally violent media bullies such as in *Robocop* and *Terminator*?

There are four basic, related beliefs that are the foundation of the violence reflected in our popular culture. Our personal process of assessment needs to include determining how these assumptions have shaped our own beliefs, values, and behaviors.

As we understand the impact of these assumptions on each of us, so we will be better equipped to resist and change them.

1 / Belief: Violence Is Innate to the Human, Inevitable, Erotic

Popular adages from "might is right" to "go ahead, make my day" to "consider this a divorce" indicate how commonly held is the belief that violence is the necessary and inevitable response to any human conflict. When the bonds of connection, affection, or reason are too difficult to sustain, violence is considered an appropriate form of self-expression. Violence and violent sexuality are thus linked to power. In addition, since violence is one of the few ways in which people are seen to relate, popular culture further links violence with sexuality. One writer commented on *Basic Instinct*'s earning $100 million in box-office business within weeks of its release: "Mix up some sex and violence, throw in a psycho killer, and you've got yourself a hit."

2 / Belief: Hierarchy Is the "Natural" Order

A belief in hierarchy disrupts the bonds of empathy between people, allowing for the dehumanization of those designated "other" and the seeking of power over them. Implicit in the hierarchical view is the assumption that male is better than female and that whiter skin is better than darker skin. And so our popular images and stories present women as subordinate, objectified as sexual bodies, which are considered the domain for male aggressive sexuality and, ultimately, violence.

3 / Belief: Individualism Is Paramount

This belief assumes a denial of the facts of nature—that humans are innately social beings, biologically programmed to live in connection and community with others. Instead, the only relationship that is possible between people is a competitive one, as they jockey for position in hierarchy. The representation of human relations in television sitcoms often has a competitive base, portraying them as encumbering, inadequate, disappointing—merely setups for jokes and put-downs at others' expense. This representation is also exemplified in the media presentation of the relationship of Hillary Clinton and Tipper Gore as adversarial, portraying any indications to the contrary as suspect.

4 / Belief: The Consequences of Violence Are of No Significance

According to this belief, there is no interdependence among humans, no relationship, no action, and no reaction. The consequences of violence are never anticipated, nor considered reasons for not acting. As the human is an isolate, without bonds or connection to the other, one person's impact on another—except of course for domination through violence or violent sexuality—is of no consequence. Fittingly, this belief allows the creation of sensational, extreme images in which the visual impact of physical violence can be emphasized, dissociated from the pain it causes. Psychological violence of the kind present in many thrillers is used as primer and prelude for the physical violence that follows—a way of revving up the motor. A profoundly disturbing enactment of this idea is the coverage of the Gulf War of 1991 as a video game. Where in the media was there an expression of grief for the hundreds of thousands of human casualties of that war?

As we analyze the problem of violence and see how our own categories of thought contribute to it, we will understand that we are each both victim and potential agent for solution. As we distinguish between what is absolutely unacceptable to us as individuals and what is tolerable, we will move to a new understanding of the difference between the two. This understanding will enable us to move to the next step: actions that facilitate solutions.

STEP TWO: DARING TO DREAM

In order to build a society that abhors violence we have to be able to imagine it. We have to dare to dream what our stories will be in a world that honors all human feeling, including anger, rage, hatred, and aggression, but that dishonors their expression in ways that violate the other.

Our imaginings can be informed by an understanding that violence is the violation of the psychic and physical integrity of the other. This violation occurs as a kind of invasion, a rupture of relation, a disconnection. Nonviolence then is the absence of invasions and disconnection and the presence of bonds and secure boundaries. It is not, however, the absence of conflict, for conflict is a fundamental fact of all existence. Humans have always had to negotiate the tensions that arise from clashes of needs and wants, beliefs and values. Thus our imaginings and our creativity need to focus on representations of the means to manage and express these conflicts nonviolently.

As we envision this, new stories and images will come to life. Violent behavior will be portrayed as learned rather than intrinsic. It will be perceived that its societal roots are embedded in injustice and inequity; its individual roots in the experiences of childhood, including socialization into particular gender roles and attitudes. Ways of resolving conflicts without subjugation, control, or destruction will be explored, and the full range of all human feelings and their diverse expressions will be celebrated.

And what other possibilities could emerge? These could include representations that celebrate, without hierarchy, difference between male and female experience, feelings, beliefs, and behavior, as well as diversity of ethnicity and age. Human relationships—including sexual ones—of equality, mutuality, and reciprocity will be presented. In addition, our similar and differing creative approaches to shared human challenges will be presented.

The new lexicon will reflect a reverence for interdependence, for the relatedness and connectedness that characterize all human activity and all life on this planet. Protagonists of both genders and every ethnicity will live out stories that reflect the deep human need for community. Stories will explore how personal histories are inextricably connected to the social, political, and cultural history of family, community, country, and planet. Valuing interconnection, these stories will demonstrate that individuals who are unable to act interdependently with the people with whom they live, love, and work are aberrant, and unlike the dominator super-heroes of today, their behavior will be seen as pathetically inadequate.

Finally, our imaginings will lead to representations of the ways in which all human actions have consequences. Positive consequences are those that facilitate the ability of both genders and all people to live, love, and work in ways that do not include the violation of the other either psychically or physically. Negative consequences are those that manufacture compliance to inequity, domination, or subjugation of one group/gender by another. The consequences of violence—an illegal activity—will be fully depicted as ruptures in community, breaches of trust, undermining the safety and well-being of all members.

STEP THREE: HOW TO GET THERE

At step three, we must translate our personal assessments and imaginings into actions. At present there are many indicators that demonstrate a growing intolerance for the glamorization of violence in popular culture. Twelve-step recovery programs, incest and child-abuse survivor groups, men working to redefine the masculine without patriarchy, and environmental action groups all reflect the growing desire to build an ethical and just society informed by spiritual values of self-esteem, self-actualization without oppression, and an honoring of interdependence, diversity, and difference.

In the last twenty years, we've seen radical change in attitudes toward pollution, smoking, and drinking and driving. These attitude changes have preceded new initiatives in public policies, regulation, legislation, and education. The creative spark for these changes was ignited by individuals who repeatedly voiced their refusal to submit to the prevailing cultural norm, while presenting a deeply felt alternative vision. For example, local garbage recycling initiatives began with people individually and collectively expressing their concerns, defining solutions, and implementing them. Similarly, Mothers Against Drunk Driving (MADD) has had a powerful impact on our attitudes about drinking and driving.

We need to remember that the most significant and the most powerful instrument we each have is our own voice, articulating both resistance and alternatives in our unique ways. Simply saying "no" is the place to begin. Additionally, we must consider very carefully what we say, whom we speak to, and the ways we speak. And what/whom we say "yes" to.

What do we say? Our speaking needs to name the many dimensions of the problem and its solutions. On the problem side these can include: an exploration of the roots of violence; its dynamics and consequences, including myths about violence and gender behavior; the particular vulnerability of children to socialization into violence because of their experiences with media; an analysis of who owns and who benefits from our current popular culture and how this influences what we experience; the power of stories and images to inform and direct us for good or ill; the challenges and responsibilities of free speech. On the solution side, we can start by defining the possible, describing examples of music, stories, and images from plays and films that present alternatives (e.g., *Daughters of the Dust* and *Strangers in Good Company*). Then, we need to focus on what needs to happen in the short term to protect children now and to nurture their learning positive social skills. Solutions need to include an exploration, perhaps informed by the experience of other countries, of employment and funding strategies that provide the kind of support to artists and others in the cultural community that will ensure that alternatives are created, marketed, and widely disseminated.

The goal of our speaking must be to develop a new understanding that violence is the resort of the resourceless; that poverty, sexism, and racism provide the seedbed for its development; and that all prevention must be grounded in this perspective. We must facilitate a new understanding that individual violent behavior is learned and not a concomitant of being male or human. To do this, we need to challenge prevailing myths about violence and gender behavior, myths that valorize, glamorize, and eroticize its expression by men and vilify it in women. The enormous personal and societal costs of perpetuating the racial and gender stereotyping in mainstream media must be re-articulated. Finally, our speaking needs to make explicit that in most societies, acts of physical violence, apart from formal declarations of war, are illegal and are defined as assault. And many acts of psychological violence, as expressed by racist and sexist discriminatory practices, are also illegal.

Our focus on children must serve to build a deep respect for the fact that all early childhood experiences have profound significance for the development of the character and behavior of the adult. We must define how behaviors of domination are learned. The child's unique susceptibility to media messages about human nature, gender behavior, and conflict resolution must be made explicit so that children's current experience of media is no longer trivialized and is instead understood as having the potential to be a major impediment to their healthy development. This can be achieved by informing our listeners about how children learn and how their current experience of media, whether broadcast, videos, video games, or toys, interferes with their learning of such basic life skills as speaking and listening with respect for the other, collaborating and cooperating, empathizing, and behaving with responsibility for one's actions. Our speaking must shed new light on the perspective that a whole community, not just parents and teachers, educates a child. We can make explicit how everyone involved in the lives of children, including sports and recreation people, health providers, retailers, and entertainers can *support* parents and teachers to empower children in positive social relations and develop their creativity and resourcefulness to solve the problems and conflicts that are always part of every life.

Our speaking needs to build a new understanding that stories and images as disseminated through media have enormous potential to shape our beliefs and inform our behavior. We need to develop a widespread consciousness that cultural artifacts are never neutral, that they always reflect the attitudes, values, and unique perspective of their creators. For this reason, it matters most profoundly *who* makes, *who* funds, and *who* distributes those artifacts. Such a discussion will enable people to understand that what we have at present is not in any way a reflection of the universal.

Finally, the current popular understanding of the nature of free speech needs to be explored. We should ask what *free* speech is when the only voices that have access to widespread distribution are those that support the monetary interests of very few. The implications of the fact that seventy-five percent of commercial network television time and fifty percent of public television is paid for by the hundred largest corporations (of a total of 450,000 corporations) can be explored. We can reconsider the rights to broadcast via telecommunications technologies as a privilege that also entails social responsibilities. Then we can describe the kinds of regulations that might reflect this consciousness. We can communicate that a free and democratic society places reasonable restrictions on its citizens. For this reason, there must be a balance between individuals' rights to freely express their sadistic fantasies and the right of women, for example, to live without threat of violence. We can explore the potential of a harms-based definition of free speech such as that articulated in Canada in February 1992 (in a Canadian Supreme Court ruling in the case of Donald J. Butler). This decision states: "Depictions of degrading and dehumanizing sex and sex with violence harm society by poisoning attitudes towards women." To curtail this poisoning of attitudes towards women, the Supreme Court ruled unanimously that "the undue exploitation of sex or depictions of sex involving violence, degradation, dehumanization [of women] and [sex involving] children is illegal and a justifiable infringement of freedom of expression guaranteed in the Charter of Rights and Freedoms."

To whom do we speak? At the beginning, it is important to focus on the sympathetic, those in our immediate circle of family, friends, colleagues, and neighbors who do not necessarily need convincing but need a language to name the problem and explore solutions. If we begin with this focus, our energy will not be diverted by those who would trivialize our perceptions. It also facilitates the gathering of like-minded people who together can become a chorus that will drown out the naysayers.

If the dream of a new paradigm about violence is to be realized, we need to overturn the unidimensional worldview that is currently being conveyed. Artistic production always reflects the beliefs and values of its creators; diversity of creators will lead to a variety of alternatives. For this reason, artists reflecting all races, ethnicities, and ages and both genders need to be supported to create productions that truly reflect their differing realities.

To remove barriers to the production of alternatives we need to examine critically how cultural institutions, agencies, and foundations that support new endeavors allocate their resources. Does the distribution of funding and awards reflect principles of gender parity? Does it reflect the racial and ethnic diversity of the applicants?

In Canada, one of our major cultural institutions, the National Film Board, which produces over one hundred films annually and has been nominated for fifty-eight Academy Awards, made an organizational commitment to equality and diversity in its production. To achieve this, its employment and training practices as well as its production funding priorities have been redefined over the last twenty years. The result of this commitment has been the creation of real alternatives in films of world-class quality, including such woman-directed classics as the Academy Award-winning *If You Love This Planet*, about the arms race; *The Goddess Remembered*, about women's spirituality; and *Not a Love Story*, about pornography. By identifying and supporting alternatives, we can counter the familiar response that nothing can be done.

Leaders of film and television production institutions must hear our voices. We can speak most directly through the ways we choose to spend our dollars, in our absolute refusal to consume that which glorifies or eroticizes violence, and in our clear articulation of the rationale for refusal. Additionally, as the environmentalists have done, we can lobby to engage writers, producers, directors, and actors in an education process, enabling them to become change agents in shifting public attitudes.

We can speak to our elected representatives at municipal, state, and national levels to forge cooperative relationships that will ensure that regulations and legislation are instituted that reflect an abhorrence of glamorized or eroticized public expressions of violence. These regulations should include home-video and video-game classification systems, based on current psychological research, to protect children from further desensitization and socialization into violence. We can also address, using the same research, their particular susceptibility to exploitation through media advertising.

Finally, the manner in which we voice our resistance needs careful consideration. To declare a war on violence is to replicate the culture that has to change. Therefore, while we need to honor personally and privately our very legitimate anger about this problem, we need to temper our public expression of it so that we do not become violators ourselves. We need to speak with clarity and simplicity, without naiveté but with critical consciousness. Our language needs to demystify what at first might seem complex, grounding it in the reality of our listeners' individual lives. In these ways we will seed new thoughts, knowledge, and concerns, which give our listeners the means to articulate the problem and act on it. And to the degree that we address the problem by providing examples of alternatives, case studies of difference, we will engender hope as well.

It is in all these ways that each of us, informed by our heads and our hearts, can use our voices as primary instruments and can become the agents for transforming our culture by creating images that foster hope for ourselves and our future. Each of these activities has the potential to be significant in and of itself; when combined, they will enable us to realize what may seem at this time almost unimaginable, a new lexicon of imagery that will lead the way to transforming our rape culture and healing centuries of violence.

SANDRA CAMPBELL has worked in the field of education, including educational TV, for seventeen years. She heads her own consulting firm, VIVA Associates, which provides research and education services that address issues arising from violence in children's lives, particularly the combination of violence in media and in society. Her clients include: The National Film Board of Canada, the Ontario Institute for the Prevention of Child Abuse, Canadian broadcasters, as well as teachers' federations and mental health services. She is currently completing a resource book of strategies to counter media/toy violence for parents and teachers, which is based on her research with children.

The mother of a daughter and a son, Campbell lives in Toronto, where she is active in feminist and anti-violence community groups.

HOW RAPE IS ENCOURAGED IN AMERICAN BOYS
and What We Can Do to Stop It

by Myriam Miedzian

In order to significantly decrease violence, including rape,
we must begin to protect boys from violent entertainment
and to teach them, from the youngest age, to view
themselves as future nurturing, nonviolent,
responsible fathers.

WHEN A UNIVERSITY of Florida administrator was asked to comment on high rates of gang rape on college campuses, he responded, "The men almost cannot say no, because if they do their masculinity will be in question."[1]

In her book *Fraternity Gang Rape*, Peggy Sanday, a University of Pennsylvania professor of anthropology, comments that "those men who object to this kind of behavior run the risk of being labeled 'wimps' or, even worse in their eyes, 'gays' or 'faggots'."[2]

If we are serious about *significantly* decreasing our rape rates, we must move men, and especially young boys, away from a definition of masculinity that centers on toughness, power, dominance, eagerness to fight, lack of empathy, and a callous attitude towards women. For as long as these values (which I refer to as "the masculine mystique") prevail among many men, rape will continue to be viewed by them as proof that they are "one of the boys," that they are "real men."

When dominance and power define masculinity, men rape as a way of putting "uppity" women in their place. Many men feel deeply threatened by the achievements of the women's movement. Some react to the greater freedom, independence, and power of women with rage and violence, including rape, battering, and killing.

Masculinity must be redefined to include caring, nurturance, and empathy along with positive "masculine" traits such as courage, strength, initiative, and adventurousness. But, in fact, we have been defining masculinity in the opposite direction. We have witnessed in recent years an extreme escalation of the values of the masculine mystique. Part of the problem is that in our unprecedented age of advanced technology, boys and men are presented with endless violent, sadistic, rapist male role models in the media. Another part of the problem lies in the increasing number of boys growing up without fathers in the home. While most single mothers succeed in raising perfectly decent sons, social science research reveals that the presence of a caring, *nonviolent,* involved father puts a boy at lower risk of violent behavior. On the other hand, if a father is physically abusive, this increases the odds that his son will be violent, and the son is better off without him.

In order to significantly decrease violence, including rape, we must begin to protect boys from violent entertainment and to teach them, from the youngest age, to view themselves as future nurturing, nonviolent, responsible fathers. As we shall see, in doing so we would be encouraging all men, including those who never become fathers, to move away from the values of the masculine mystique.

ENTERTAINMENT

Surrounded by TV, films, videos, disks, tapes, Walkmans, and video games, children today spend more time being entertained than they spend with their parents or in school. By the age of eighteen, the average teenager has watched an estimated twenty-six thousand murders on TV alone, most of them committed by men. A major part of our children's socialization now lies in the hands of the entertainment business, whose primary goal is not helping to cut down on rates of rape or other forms of violence, but maximizing profit.

Over two hundred thirty-five studies have been done in the last forty years on the effects of viewing violence on the screen. A vast majority indicate that the catharsis hypothesis, according to which viewing violence helps viewers get violent impulses out of their system, is mistaken. Viewing violence encourages violent behavior.

Seeing women being raped or threatened with rape desensitizes male viewers and facilitates rape. For example, in their book *The Question of Pornography*, psychologists Edward Donnerstein, Daniel Linz, and Steven Penrod describe a research study in which they sought to test the desensitizing qualities of slasher films. These films graphically depict people being dismembered, chopped up, burned alive, raped, or endlessly threatened with rape. While men are victimized, the main thrust is usually the pursuit of one or more young women.

For the study, fifty-two men were chosen out of a larger group because they seemed *"least likely to become desensitized"* (my emphasis). They were then shown one slasher film a day for five days. Changes occurred in the men's evaluation of how violent, degrading, and offensive scenes were. Material that the men had earlier found anxiety-provoking and depressing became less so. After being exposed to large doses of filmed violence against women, they judged that female victims of assault and rape were less injured than did men in a control group. They were less able to empathize with *real-life* rape victims. The authors point out that the frequent juxtaposition in slasher films of extremely violent scenes with relaxing music or mildly erotic scenes is very similar to the techniques used in desensitization therapy to get people to engage in behavior that was previously too anxiety-provoking—stimuli that provoke anxiety are combined with stimuli that promote relaxation.

This desensitization to violence and rape starts at a very early age. Horror/slasher films are a favorite genre of young boys. While they are rated R, this voluntary rating is seldom enforced. When I went to see *Nightmare On Elm Street Part IV*, which features a young woman being dismembered and other teenagers being burned alive and drowned, there were children in every row of the theater, some as young as three or four years.

If these films desensitize even men who were carefully chosen because they seemed "least likely to become desensitized," one can easily imagine the effect they might have on some of the millions of boys and men in the U.S. who are at above average risk for violence due to physical conditions such as mild mental retardation, a severe learning disability, or Attention-deficit Hyperactivity Disorder (ADHD). What about men suffering from serious emotional disorders? Not only do these films desensitize, they also serve as detailed, gruesome blueprints for violence. Even if only a small percentage of these men are affected, the results are disastrous.

Besides the results of studies on viewing violence, we know from child-development research that children learn by imitating those they admire. So-called adventure films (they are in fact nonstop violence films), starring, among others, Sylvester Stallone, Arnold Schwarzenegger, and Jean-Claude Van Damme as heroes, encourage boys to associate masculinity with dominance and power and to accept violence as a normal response to conflict, anger, or frustration.

When it comes to sports, there has been an increase in recent years in fistfights, dirt-throwing, and verbal insults among professional and even college athletes. Much of this appears on TV and is viewed by young boys. A substantial number of these sports "heroes" have been charged with rape. For many athletes, and for millions of men who played competitive sports as children, training in violence and the denigration of women (and gay men) starts early. Far too often in youth and high school sports, boys insult each other by yelling "girl," "wuss" (a cross between woman and pussy), or "faggot." Already at this level, some coaches encourage winning at any cost and an obsessive concern with dominance. Too often the result is "scoring at any cost" with girls and women.

Some heavy metal and rap lyrics encourage young boys to connect sex with dominance and rape. A song by the heavy metal group Poison, which reached number three on the Billboard pop charts and sold over two million copies, includes lines like "I want action tonight . . . I need it hot and I need it fast. If I can't have her, I'll take her and make her." The very popular rap group Two Live Crew has a song called "Dick Almighty," which describes a young woman's enormous desire and effort to have oral sex with "this big black cock." It goes on to say, "He'll tear the pussy open, 'cause it's satisfaction . . . Dick so proudful, she'll kneel and pray . . . Suck my dick, bitch, it'll make you puke."

A recent addition to entertainment for boys are "killer cards" glorifying murderers, cannibals, and rapists such as Ted Bundy, David "Son of Sam" Berkowitz, and Richard Speck. Modeled on baseball cards, each card has a picture on one side and a record of "achievement" on the other. Descriptions often have cutesy touches. In one set, Richard Speck's bio informs us that just as he was beginning to tie up, rape, and murder a group of student nurses, "One, then two more nurses came home. They joined the party." And this set may not even be the most sophisticated. Some come with coding symbols—for example, the sketch of a behind informs us that this fellow was a sodomist.

In light of all this, is it surprising that crime rates among minors have soared, and that perpetrators are getting younger and younger? In 1992, in Indianapolis, two seven-year-old boys were accused of raping a six-year-old girl. In Washington state a ten-year-old boy was charged with raping five children between the ages of two and six.

Because of their abhorrence of censorship, many well-intentioned Americans, including some feminists, continue to ignore the very strong evidence that this kind of entertainment plays an important role in encouraging violence. Even Donnerstein, Linz, and Penrod, whose research was discussed earlier, are so concerned about censorship that in discussing this issue they downplay the implications of their own and others' research lest it lead to the conclusion that some regulation is desirable. All of these First Amendment buffs fail to distinguish between censorship aimed at adults and regulations to protect minors.

In researching my book *Boys Will Be Boys*, it became clear to me that to significantly decrease our rates of male violence, we must begin to treat American children as a precious national resource rather than a commercial market. In the course of developing recommendations for the protection of children from an exploitative culture of violence, I consulted with four First Amendment law professors. They pointed out that we have a long legal tradition of regulations to protect children, including liquor, child labor, and pornography laws, and that laws to protect children from violent entertainment would be in that tradition. Unlike laws aimed at adults, they would have an excellent chance of passing Supreme Court muster.

I strongly recommend that with respect to films, videos, disks, killer cards, toys, etc., we begin to adopt regulations of the kind that already exist in many European countries, including Sweden, Belgium, and Germany. In these countries, governmental regulations and serious penalties for infractions keep movie theater owners from allowing children to see gratuitously violent films.

When it comes to television, legal experts advised me that attempts to regulate content to protect children would be very unlikely to pass Supreme Court muster because such regulations would interfere with the First Amendment rights of adults. With respect to television, I therefore recommend a major educational campaign (similar to public health campaigns to discourage cigarette smoking) to render parents aware of the effects of viewing violence on their children, particularly their sons. Parents should also be urged to acquire TV lock boxes, which permit them to program their sets so that they can control what their children watch. Just like safety belts and safety seats for children in cars, lock boxes should eventually become mandatory with the sale of every TV set.

To complement lock boxes, we need to create a Children's Public Broadcasting System with two channels, one for younger and one for older children, dedicated to top quality TV programming that is entertaining, prosocial, nonsexist, devoid of any gratuitous violence, and appealing to children of all social classes.

RAISING BOYS TO BE NURTURING FATHERS

A growing number of psychoanalytically-oriented psychologists and sociologists, Dorothy Dinnerstein and Nancy Chodorow among them, analyze the difficult psychological process through which boys, who are almost all raised primarily by women, develop a masculine identity.

These boys' primary identification is with their mother or female care-taker. When they begin to realize that they are not like her, that they will not be able to have a baby, nurse it, develop breasts, etc., their efforts to develop a male identity often include depreciating and rejecting every-thing feminine, and embracing the qualities of the masculine mystique.

These observations are supported by sociological studies that reveal that a disproportionate percentage of violent boys come from fatherless homes with no consistently present male figure they can identify with and model themselves on. Sociologists use the term "hypermasculinity" to describe the extreme concern of these boys with proving their masculinity.

Cross-cultural anthropological studies indicate that violent behavior is often characteristic of males in cultures where fathers are absent or play a small role in their son's early rearing. In these cultures, boys are usually taken away from the women after a certain age and put through often excruciatingly painful and desensitizing initiation rites intended to turn them into "real men." Analogously to sociologists, anthropologists con-clude that boys raised by women alone, or mainly by women, often lack a primary sense of masculine identity. In order to develop such an iden-tity many of them reject everything feminine and embrace "protest masculinity."

In our society, the greater tendency towards violence on the part of fatherless boys is exacerbated by the culture of violence described above, which surrounds them with violent and often sadistic male role models and desensitizes them to violent, rapist behavior.

Boys raised with nurturing, involved fathers develop a *primary* male identity. They identify with and model themselves on their fathers from the youngest age. They do not need to prove that they are "real men" by rejecting everything "feminine," by being tough and violent. Their model of masculinity includes nurturance, caring, and empathy, which they experienced from their fathers. If there is no father, the presence of an involved, caring uncle, grandfather, male friend, or "Big Brother" can be a great benefit.

A twenty-six-year longitudinal study of empathy lends further sup-port to the importance of an involved father in deterring violence.[3] Researchers found that the single factor most highly linked to the devel-opment of empathy in boys (and girls) was the level of paternal involve-ment in child care. Empathy is inversely related to violence.

Nurturant fathering has another beneficial side effect. A mother who raises her children together with their father is far less likely to be overwhelmed both financially and emotionally by the enormous demands of child-rearing, and is less likely to physically abuse her children. Boys who are battered by either their father or mother are more likely to become violent. If they have been abused by their mothers, wife battering, murder, and rape can be an expression of early rage and a form of revenge. In the words of one rapist: "My sisters asked me why I raped and I told 'em I wanted to hurt you females in my family, just like I'd been hurt. They knew my real mom abandoned me and that my stepmom beat the hell out of me all the time."[4]

At the deepest psychic level, the completely helpless, dependent baby experiences the person who fulfills its needs as all-powerful. It follows that as long as solely women fulfill the needs of young children, men's emotional reactions to women will be overdetermined. The rapist quoted above is aware of the displacement of his early anger, but many men are unaware that their rage at and violence towards women grows out of often repressed early feelings of rage at mother. The desensitization and violent role models furnished by the media often facilitate the transition from anger to action.

The fact that we are the least child-oriented of any advanced industrialized country only aggravates the problem of mother-directed rage. Lack of parental leave and flexible work hours, lack of quality day-care and after-school programs, and lack of adequate medical care leave us with millions of angry, neglected young children and older latchkey children. All of this is aggravated in the case of working mothers who are single.

To significantly decrease our violence rates, including those for rape, we must do everything possible to encourage nurturing, nonviolent, responsible fathering (and mothering) and create a society that *genuinely* values children and helps parents in the all-important task of child rearing.

Probably the single most effective intervention in terms of these goals would be the introduction of mandatory child-rearing classes in our schools, starting at the very latest in fifth grade. In the course of searching for programs that would discourage violence for boys, I visited parenting classes at a private school and at several inner-city elementary, junior high, and high schools, where many, if not most, children are fatherless. Before observing these programs, I was skeptical about their impact on boys. My research had made me aware that by first grade many boys consider anything having to do with babies as "girls' stuff" and won't go near it. My hunch was that most of the boys wouldn't be very interested. I was therefore all the more amazed by the level of interest and enthusiasm demonstrated by virtually every boy, regardless of race, ethnicity, or social class. I came away convinced that most boys are as capable of being interested and involved with children and child rearing as girls. Unfortunately, our culture discourages this interest and involvement from the youngest age.

When classes in child rearing are mandatory, boys are given permission to express that interest. The elementary and junior high school child-rearing program I visited centers on a mature parent bringing a baby or toddler to class once a month. Students observe the child's behavior, interact with the child, and ask questions about what it is like to be a parent. They keep a chart of the child's progress and keep a workbook to encourage observation, psychological insight and sensitivity. In the high school classes, teachers impart basic knowledge about child development to juniors and seniors at an appropriately sophisticated level.

These programs in child rearing deter violence in three ways: They encourage nurturing, caring, informed fathering; they make boys feel that empathy, sensitivity, and caring are acceptable, even desirable male qualities; and they strongly discourage child battering. Sons of single teenage mothers are at particularly high risk for violence. Teachers and administrators involved in the programs report a decrease in teenage pregnancy. When girls and boys fully understand the awesome demands of responsible parenting, they decide to put off having children until they are financially and emotionally better able to deal with the responsibility.

In terms of public policy, if all women *and men*, including those in positions of political power, had taken child-rearing classes when they were in elementary and high school, we would be a society imbued with a much deeper sense of the importance of good parenting and far more willing to provide support for it.

It will not be easy to bring about programs that encourage caring, nurturance, and empathy in boys. Only if large numbers of Americans pressure their state legislators and school boards to appropriate funds and develop child-rearing classes is there any hope. It will be even more difficult to effect the changes necessary to protect children from a culture of violence that encourages rape, battering, and murder. Only the most intense and persistent pressure on legislators could turn protective regulations, mandatory lock boxes, and a Children's Public Broadcasting System into a reality.

The school programs, recommendations for protecting children from violence in entertainment, and research studies referred to in this essay are described in detail, and discussed at length in Myriam Miedzian, *Boys Will Be Boys: Breaking the Link Between Masculinity and Violence* (New York: Anchor, 1992).

NOTES

1. The *New York Times*, 17 February 1986.
2. Peggy Reeves Sanday, *Fraternity Gang Rape* (New York: New York University Press, 1990), p. 11.
3. Richard Koestner, Carol Franz, and Joel Weinberger, "The Family Origins of Empathic Concern: A 26 Year Longitudinal Study," *Personality & Social Psychology*, 58 (1990), pp. 709–17.
4. Timothy Beneke, *Men on Rape* (New York: St. Martin's Press, 1982).

This article is based on **MYRIAM MIEDZIAN**'s book *Boys Will Be Boys: Breaking the Link Between Masculinity and Violence* (Anchor, 1992). Miedzian holds both a Ph.D. in philosophy and a master's degree in clinical social work. She has served on the faculties of several universities, including Rutgers and the City University of New York. She has written and lectured extensively on male socialization, the psychology of criminal behavior, the breakdown of ethical values in contemporary American society, and a variety of women's issues.

ON BECOMING ANTI-RAPIST

by Haki R. Madhubuti

If we men, of all races, cultures, and continents would just
examine the inequalities of power in our own families,
businesses, and political and spiritual institutions, and
decide today to reassess and reconfigure them in
consultation with the women in our lives, we
would all be doing the most fundamental
corrective act of a counter-rapist.

There are mobs & strangers
in us
who scream of the women
we wanted and
will get
as if the women are ours for the
taking.

I N 1991 THE CRIME of rape in the United States entered our consciousness with the power of the dissolution of the U.S.S.R. The trials of William Kennedy Smith (of the Camelot family) and Iron Mike Tyson, former heavyweight boxing champion of the entire world, shared front pages and provided talk-show hosts with subject matter on a topic that is usually confined to women's groups and the butt jokes of many men. Since women are over fifty percent of the world's population and a clear majority in this country, one would think that the question of rape would not still be hidden in the minor concerns files of men.

However, what is not hidden is that Mr. Kennedy Smith and Mr. Tyson both tried defenses that blamed the women in question. For Smith that tactic was successful; for Tyson, it failed. Pages of analysis have been written in both cases, and I do not wish to add to them. But one can safely state that no woman wants to be raped, and that if men were raped at the frequency of women, rape would be a federal crime rivaling those of murder and bank robbery. If car-jacking can command federal attention, why are we still treating rape as if it's a "boys will be boys" sport or a woman's problem as in "blame the victim"? In the great majority of sex crimes against women in the United States, the women are put on trial as if they planned and executed their own rapes.

Male acculturation (or a better description would be males' "seasoning") is antifemale, antiwomanist/feminist, and antireason when it comes to women's equal measure and place in society. This flawed socialization of men is not confined to the West but permeates most, if not all, cultures in the modern world. Most men have been taught to treat, respond, listen, and react to women from a male's point of view. Black men are not an exception here; we, too, are imprisoned with an intellectual/spiritual/sexual understanding of women based upon antiquated male culture and sexist orientation—or should I say miseducation. For example, sex or sexuality is hardly ever discussed, debated, or taught to black men in a nonthreatening or nonembarrassing family or community setting.

Men's view of women, specifically black women outside of the immediate family, is often one of "bitch," "my woman," "ho," or any number of designations that demean and characterize black women as less than whole and productive persons. Our missteps toward an understanding of women are compounded by the cultural environments where much of the talk of women takes place: street corners, locker rooms, male clubs, sporting events, bars, military service, business trips, playgrounds, workplaces, basketball courts, etc. Generally, women are not discussed on street corners or in bars as intellectual or culturally compatible partners. Rather the discussion focuses on what is the best way to "screw" or control them.

These are, indeed, learning environments that traditionally are not kind to women. The point of view that is affirmed all too often is the ownership of women. We are taught to see women as commodities and/or objects for men's sexual releases and sexual fantasies; also, most women are considered "inferiors" to men and thus are not to be respected or trusted. Such thinking is encouraged and legitimized by our culture and transmitted via institutional structures (churches, workplaces), mass media (*Playboy* and *Penthouse*), misogynist music (rap and mainstream), and R-rated and horror films that use exploitative images of women. And of course there are the ever-present, tall, trim, "Barbie-doll" women featured in advertising for everything from condoms to the latest diet "cures." Few men have been taught, really taught, from birth—to the heart, to the gut—to respect, value, or even, on occasion, to honor women. Only until very recently has it been confirmed in Western culture that rape (unwelcomed/uninvited sex) is criminal, evil and antihuman.

> our mothers, sisters, wives and
> daughters ceased to be the
> women men want we think of them as
> loving family music & soul bright wonderments.
> they are not locker room talk
> not the hunted lust or dirty
> cunt burnin hos.
> bright wonderments are excluded by association as

> blood & heart bone & memory
> & we will destroy a rapist's knee caps,
> & write early grave on his thoughts
> to protect them.

Human proximity defines relationships. Exceptions should be noted, but in most cultures and most certainly within the black/African world-view, family and extended family ties are honored and respected. One's sexual personhood in a healthy culture is nurtured, respected, and protected. In trying to get a personal fix here, that is, an understanding of the natural prohibitions against rape, think of one's own personhood being violated. Think of one's own family subjected to this act. Think of the enslavement of African people; it was common to have breeding houses on most plantations where one's great-great-grandmothers were forced to open their insides for the sick satisfaction of white slave owners, overseers, and enslaved black men. This forced sexual penetration of African women led to the creation of mixed-race people here and around the world. There is a saying in South Africa that the colored race did not exist until nine months after white men arrived. This demeaning of black women and other women is amplified in today's culture, where it is not uncommon for young men to proclaim that "pussy is a penny a pound." However, we are told that such a statement is not meant for one's own mother, grandmother, sister, daughter, aunt, niece, close relative, or extended family. Yet the point must be made rather emphatically that incest (family rape) is on the rise in this country. Incest between adults and children is often not revealed until the children are adults. At that point their lives are so confused and damaged that many continue incestuous acts.

> it will do us large to recall
> when the animal in us rises
> that all women are someone's
> mother, sister, wife, or daughter
> and are not fruit to be stolen when hungry.

Part of the answer is found in the question: Is it possible or realistic to view all women as precious persons? Selective memory plays an important role here. Most men who rape are seriously ill and improperly educated. They do not view women outside of their "protected zone" as precious blood, do not see them as extended family, and do not see them as individuals or independent persons to be respected as most men respect other men. Mental illness or brain mismanagement blocks out reality, shattering and negating respect for self and others, especially the others of which one wishes to take advantage. Power always lurks behind rape. Rape is an act of aggression that asserts power by defaming and defiling. Most men have been taught—either directly or indirectly—to solve problems with force. Such force may be verbal or physical. Violence is the answer that is promoted in media everywhere, from Saturday morning cartoons to everyday television to R-rated films. Popular culture has a way of trivializing reality and confusing human expectations, especially with regards to relationships between men and women. For too many black people, the popular has been internalized. In many instances, the media define us, including our relationships to each other.

Women have been in the forefront of the anti-rape struggle. Much of this work has taken place in nontraditional employment, such as serving in police and fire departments, as top professors and administrators in higher education, as elected and appointed public servants in politics, and in the fields of medicine and law. However, the most pronounced presence and "advancement" of women has been seen in the military. We are told that the military, in terms of social development, remains at the cutting edge of changes, especially in the progress of blacks and female soldiers. However, according to Gary A. Warner in the *San Francisco Examiner* (December 30, 1992), the occurrence of rape against women in the military is far greater than in civilian life:

> A woman serving in the Army is 50 percent more likely to be raped than a civilian, newly released military records obtained by the Orange County Register show.
>
> From 1981 to 1987, 484 female soldiers were raped while on active duty, according to Department of the Army records released after a Freedom of Information Act request.
>
> The Army rate of 129 rape cases per 100,000 population in 1990 exceeds nationwide statistics for the same year compiled by the FBI of 80 confirmed rape cases per 100,000 women. The 1990 statistics are the latest comparable ones available.

The brutality of everyday life continues to confirm the necessity for caring men and women to confront inhuman acts that cloud and prevent wholesome development. Much of what is defined as sexual "pleasure" today comes at the terrible expense of girls and often boys. To walk Times Square or any number of big city playgrounds after dark is to view how loudly the popular, throwaway culture has trapped, corrupted, and sexually abused too many of our children. In the United States the sexual abuse of runaway children, and children sentenced to foster care and poorly supervised orphanages, is nothing less than scandalous. The proliferation of battered women's shelters and the most recent revelation of the sexual abuse of women incarcerated in the nation's prisons only underscores the prevailing view of women by a substantial number of men, as sex objects for whatever sick acts that enter their minds.

Such abuse of children is not confined to the United States. Ron O'Grady, coordinator of the International Campaign to End Child Prostitution in Asiatic Tourism, fights an uphill battle to highlight the physical and economic maltreatment of children. Murray Kempton reminds us in his essay "A New Colonialism" (The *New York Review of Books*, November 19, 1992) of Thailand's "supermarkets for the purchases of small and disposable bodies." He goes on to state that:

> Tourism is central to Thailand's developmental efforts; and the attractions of its ancient culture compare but meagerly to the compelling pull its brothels exercise upon foreign visitors. The government does its duty to the economy by encouraging houses of prostitution and pays its debt to propriety with its insistence that no more than 10,000 children work there. Private observers concerned with larger matters than the good name of public officials estimate the real total of child prostitutes in Thailand at 200,000.
>
> The hunters and others of children find no border closed. They have ranged into South China carrying television sets to swap one per child. The peasants who cursed the day a useless girl was born know better now: they can sell her for consumers overseas and be consumers themselves. Traffickers less adventurous stay at home and contrive travel agencies that offer cheap trips to Kuala Lumpur that end up with sexual enslavement in Japan or Malaysia.

That this state of affairs is not better known speaks loudly and clearly to the devaluation of female children. The war in Sarajevo, Bosnia, and Herzegovina again highlights the status of women internationally. In the rush toward ethnic cleansing and narrow and exclusive nationalism, Serbian soldiers have been indicted for murder and other war crimes. The story of one such soldier, Borislav Herak, is instructive. According to an article by John F. Burnes in the *New York Times* (November 27, 1992) entitled "A Serbian Fighter's Trial of Brutality," Mr. Herak and other soldiers were given the go-ahead to rape and kill Muslim women:

> The indictment lists 29 individual murders between June and October, including eight rape-murders of Muslim women held prisoner in an abandoned motel and cafe outside Vogosca, seven miles north of Sarajevo, where, Mr. Herak said, he and other Serbian fighters were encouraged to rape women and then take them away to kill them in hilltops and other deserted places.
>
> The indictment also covers the killings of at least 220 other Muslim civilians in which Mr. Herak has confessed to being a witness or taking part, many of them women and children. (Also see the January 4, 1993 issue of *Newsweek*.)

Much in the lives of women is not music or melody but is their dancing to the beat of the unhealthy and often killing drums of men and male teenagers. Rape is not the fault of women; however, in a male-dominated world, the victims are often put on the defensive and forced to rationalize their gender and their personhood.

> Rape is not a reward for warriors
> it is war itself
> a deep, deep tearing, a dislocating of
> the core of the womanself.
> rape rips heartlessly
> soul from spirit,
> obliterating colors from beauty and body
> replacing melody and music with
> rat venom noise and uninterrupted intrusion and beatings.

The brutality of rape is universal. Most modern cultures—European, American, African, Asian, religious, and secular—grapple with this crime. Rarely is there discussion, and, more often than not, women are discouraged from being a part of the debates and edicts. Rape is cross-cultural. I have not visited, heard of, or read about any rape-free societies. The war against women is international. Daily, around the world, women fight for a little dignity and their earned place in the world. And men in power respond accordingly. For example, Barbara Crossette reported in the *New York Times* (April 7, 1991) about an incident in Batamaloo, Kashmir:

> In this conservative Muslim Society, women have moved to the forefront of demonstrations and also into guerrilla conclaves. No single event has contributed more to this rapidly rising militancy among women than reports of a gang rape a month ago by Indian troops in Kunan, a remote village in northwestern Kashmir.
>
> According to a report filed by S. M. Yasin, district magistrate in Kupwara, the regional center, the armed forces "behaved like violent beasts." He identified them as members of the Fourth Rajputana Rifles and said that they rampaged through the village from 11 P.M. on Feb. 23 until 9 the next morning.
>
> "A large number of armed personnel entered into the houses of villagers and at gunpoint they gang-raped 23 ladies, without any consideration of their age, married, unmarried, pregnancy etc.," he wrote. "There was a hue and cry in the whole village." Local people say that as many as 100 women were molested in some way.

As a man of Afrikan descent, I would like to think that Afrikans have some special insight, enlightened hearts, or love in us that calms us in such times of madness. But my romanticism is shattered every day as I observe black communities across this land. The number of rapes reported and unreported in our communities is only the latest and most painful example of how far we have drifted from beauty. However, it is seldom that I have hurt more than when I learned about the "night of terror" that occurred in Meru, Kenya, on July 13, 1991, at the St. Kizito boarding school. A high school protest initiated by the boys, in which the girls refused to join, resulted in a night of death, rapes, and beatings unparalleled in modern Kenya, in Africa or in the world. As Timothy Dwyer reported in the *Chicago Tribune* (April 18, 1991):

> The night of terror a month ago at the boarding school near Mount Kenya has torn the soul of the Kenyan people. What had the girls done to invoke the wrath of their male schoolmates?

They dared say no to the boys, who wanted them to join a protest against the school's headmaster, according to police and to those girls who lived through the night.

In Kenya, one-party rule has resulted in a tyranny of the majority. Dissent, even in politics, is not welcome. "Here, the minority must always go along with the majority's wishes," said a businessman who has done a lot of work with the government in the last 15 years and asked not to be named. "And it is said that a woman cannot say no to a man."

Woman's groups have said the rapes and deaths were an extreme metaphor for what goes on in the Kenyan society. The girls of St. Kizito dared to say no to the boys, and 19 paid with their lives while 71 others were beaten and raped. . . .

There have been many school protests in Kenya this year. This summer alone, some 20 protests have turned into riots resulting in the destruction of school property. There have been rapes at other schools when girls have refused to join boys in their protests.

A growing part of the answer is that we men, as difficult as it may seem, must view all women (no matter who they are—race, culture, religion, or nationality aside) as extended family. The question is, and I know that I am stretching: Would we rape our mothers, grandmothers, sisters, or other female relatives, or even give such acts a thought? Can we extend this attitude to all women? Therefore we must:

1. Teach our sons that it is their responsibility to be anti-rapist; that is, they must be counter-rapist in thought, conversations, raps, organizations, and actions.

2. Teach our daughters how to defend themselves and maintain an uncompromising stance toward men and boys.

3. Understand that being a counter-rapist is honorable, manly, and necessary for a just society.

4. Understand that anti-rapist actions are part of the black tradition; being an anti-rapist is in keeping with the best Afrikan culture and with Afrikan family and extended family configurations. Even in times of war we were known to honor and respect the personhood of children and women.

5. Be glowing examples of men who are fighting to treat women as equals and to be fair and just in associations with women. This means at

the core that families as now defined and constructed must continually be reassessed. In today's economy most women, married and unmarried, must work. We men must encourage them in their work and must be intimately involved in rearing children and doing housework.

6. Understand that just as men are different from one another, women also differ; therefore we must try not to stereotype women into the limiting and often debilitating expectations of men. We must encourage and support them in their searching and development.

7. Be unafraid of independent, intelligent, and self-reliant women. And by extension, understand that intelligent women think for themselves and may not want to have sex with a particular man. This is a woman's prerogative and is not a comment on anything else other than the fact that she does not want to have sex.

8. Be bold and strong enough to stop other men (friends or strangers) from raping and to intervene in a rape in process with the fury and destruction of a hurricane against the rapist.

9. Listen to women. Listen to women, especially to womanist/feminist/Pan-Africanist philosophies of life. Also, study the writings of women, especially black women.

10. Act responsibly in response to the listening and studying. Be a part of and support anti-rape groups for boys and men. Introduce anti-rape discussion into men's groups and organizations.

11. Never stop growing, and understand that growth is limited and limiting without the input of intelligent women.

12. Learn to love. Study love. Even if one is at war, love and respect, respect and love must conquer, if there is to be a sane and livable world. Rape is anti-love, anti-respect. Love is not easy. One does not fall in love but *grows* into love.

We can put to rest the rape problem in one generation if its eradication is as important to us as our cars, jobs, careers, sport-games, beer, and quest for power. However, the women who put rape on the front burners must continue to challenge us and their own cultural training, and position themselves so that they and their messages are not compromised or ignored.

A significant few of their
fathers, brothers, husbands, sons

and growing strangers
are willing to unleash harm onto the earth
and spill blood in the eyes
of
maggots in running shoes
who do not know the sounds of birth
or respect the privacy of the human form

If we are to be just in our internal rebuilding we must challenge tradition and cultural ways of life that relegate women to inferior status in the home, church/mosque/temple, workplace, political life, and education. Men are not born rapists; we are taught very subtly, often in unspoken ways, that women are ours for the taking. Generally, such teachings begin with the family. Enlightenment demands fairness, impartiality, and vision; it demands confrontation of outdated definitions and acceptance of fair and just resolutions. One's sex, race, social class, or wealth should not determine entitlements or justice. If we are honest, men must be in the forefront of eradicating sex stereotypes in all facets of private and public life. I think that being honest, as difficult and as self-incriminating as it may be, is the only way that we can truly liberate ourselves. If men can liberate themselves (with the help of women) from the negative aspects of the culture that produced them, maybe a just, fair, good, and liberated society is possible in our lifetime.

The liberation of the male psyche from preoccupation with domination, power hunger, control, and absolute rightness requires an honest and fair assessment of patriarchal culture. This requires commitment to deep study, combined with a willingness for painful, uncomfortable, and often shocking change. We are not where we should be. That is why rape exists; why families are so easily formed and just as easily dissolved; why children are confused and abused; why our elderly are discarded, abused, and exploited; and why teenage boys create substitute families (gangs) that terrorize their own communities.

I remain an optimistic realist, primarily because I love life and most of what it has to offer. I often look at my children and tears come to my eyes because I realize how blessed I am to be their father. My wife and the other women in my life are special because they know that they are special and have taken it upon themselves, at great cost, to actualize their dreams, making what was considered for many of them unthinkable a few years ago a reality today. If we men, of all races, cultures, and continents would just examine the inequalities of power in our own families, businesses, and political and spiritual institutions, and decide today to reassess and reconfigure them in consultation with the women in our lives, we would all be doing the most fundamental corrective act of a counter-rapist.

It is indeed significant, and not an arbitrary aside, that males and females are created biologically different. These profound differences are partially why we are attracted to each other and are also what is beautiful about life. But too often due to hierarchical and patriarchal definitions one's sex also relegates one to a position in life that is not necessarily respected. Sex should not determine moral or economic worth, as it now does in too many cultures. In a just society, one's knowledge and capabilities, that is, what one is actually able to contribute to the world, is more valuable than if the person is male or female.

Respect for the woman closest to us can give us the strength and knowledge to confront the animal in us with regards to the women we consider "others." Also, keep in mind that the "others" often are the women closest to us. If we honestly confront the traditions and histories that have shaped us, we may come to the realize that women should be encouraged to go as far as their intellect and talents will take them—burdened only by the obstacles that affect all of us. Most certainly the sexual energies of men must be checked before our misguided maleness manifests itself in the most horrible of crimes—rape.

No!
Means No!
even when men think
that they are "god's gift to women"
even after dropping a week's check & more
on dinner by the ocean,
the four tops, temptations and intruders memory tour,
imported wine & rose that captured her smile,
suggested to you private music & low lights
drowning out her inarticulated doubts.

Question the thousand years teachings
crawling through your lower depths and

don't let your little head
out think your big head.
No! means No!
even when her signals suggest yes.

As a writer, publisher, and educator, **HAKI R. MADHUBUTI** serves as a pivotal figure in the development of a strong black literary tradition, emerging from the era of the sixties and continuing to the present day. Over the years he has published eighteen books and is one of the world's best-selling authors of poetry and nonfiction, with books in print in excess of three million. He has convened workshops or served as guest/keynote speaker at more than a thousand colleges, universities, and community centers in the United States and abroad. A proponent of independent black institutions, Madhubuti is the founder of Third World Press and the Institute of Positive Education in Chicago. He is the president of the African American Book Center, also located in Chicago, and editor of Black Books Bulletin. Madhubuti is a founding member of the National Black Wholistic Retreat Society and the Organization of Black American Culture Writers' Workshop (OBAC). He is a founding member of the African American Booksellers, Publishers, and Writers Association and is currently its president. Madhubuti is professor of English and director of the Gwendolyn Brooks Center at Chicago State University. He received the 1991 American Book Award for *Black Men: Obsolete, Single, Dangerous* (Third World Press, 1991) and was named Author of the Year by the Illinois Association of Teachers of English in 1991. Madhubuti earned his MFA from the University of Iowa. He lives in Chicago with his wife and children.

RAISING GIRLS FOR THE 21ST CENTURY

by Emilie Buchwald

Our daughters were able to tell us about their experiences
of harassment, knowing that we would do everything we
could to help. At the time, though, neither they nor we
knew enough to connect personal traumas to societal
patterns. That connection was made when we
recognized the truth of the phrase
"the personal is political."

"The great question that has never been answered and which I have not yet been able to answer, despite my thirty years of research into the feminine soul, is *What does a woman want?*"

—Sigmund Freud, to Marie Bonaparte (ca. 1935)

A GENERAL RECOGNITION is dawning that our culture will need both women and men who are strong, wise, and generous if the future is to be better than the present. The nurture and education of girls must emphasize the importance of their role in that future. What a girl wants, what a woman wants, is what Freud knew is held precious by every man: self-determination, autonomy within reason, life without undue fear, liberty without causing harm to others, and the ability to pursue one's happiness. None of those desires can be fulfilled for women so long as we live in a rape culture.

LEARNING GENDER

In my robe and hospital slippers I spent long, delightful minutes staring through the glass panel into the hospital nursery at the babies in their wheeled bassinets, some crying and kicking, some asleep, a few being changed. I was flooded with an emotion I couldn't identify. What I felt was so powerful that I wasn't sure whether I wanted to laugh or weep. I was struck by the sight of an entire room filled with lives just begun, one of them our daughter's. An ID bracelet at the ankle identified the infants by name. Each wore a white knit cap whose blue or pink pom-pom signaled male or female. The nurses on duty sometimes had as many as twenty babies to care for. They were quick as well as deft. I am sure they thought they were tending the babies identically, but I noticed that they hefted and handled baby boys with a heartiness that said, "He's a male, he can take it." I know that they spent minutes of their precious time combing our baby girl's hair into a miniature topknot, tied with a pink ribbon. Her gender life was already under way.

A child is born with the potential ability to learn Chinese or Swahili, play a kazoo, climb a tree, make a strudel or a birdhouse, take pleasure in finding the coordinates of a star. Genetic inheritance determines a child's abilities and weaknesses. But those who raise a child call forth from that matrix the traits and talents they consider important.

A child is born with a sex determination but without innate knowledge of what it means to be a woman or a man. Even before its birth, the preconceptions of the parents seal a child's gender fate, and moments after birth the infant is swaddled in gender definition. Our self-image as a female or a male is a major force in creating the person we become. We exaggerate gender differences rather than celebrate what we share as human beings. Male and female are distanced from one another, made into polar opposites, as if a division into yin and yang were mandated. We sunder brother from sister and create a lifelong distrust.

Our gender lives are further burdened by thousands of years of propaganda written by men that define the nature and role of male and female. This propaganda both demonizes and trivializes women as inferior in every particular of character and ability. I was reminded of the ancient nature of misogyny when I read the quotes in *The "Natural Inferiority" of Women,* a compilation by Tama Starr of men's slanders of women over the past five thousand years. Women are reviled by some of the sages she quotes for being licentious and promiscuous and by others for being frigid and asexual. Women are described matter-of-factly as the physical, intellectual, and moral inferiors of men. In the words of St. John Chrysostom, around 380 A.D., "What else is woman but a foe to friendship, a cosmic punishment, a necessary evil, a natural temptation, a desirable calamity, a domestic peril, a delectable detriment, a deadly fascination, a painted ill!"[1]

Men of every age, including our own, have added poisonous brush strokes to the unflattering portrait of womankind. Their words of scorn, contempt, exclusion, and hatred continue to feed the male notion that women are—less. Henry Miller's comment in a 1975 interview conveys the idea: "Women have been a definite influence on my life. I adore women as a whole. I enjoy them as a breed, like a dog. They're another species that you become endeared to. I don't mean that derogatorily, but in an admiring sense, like someone would appreciate a fine breed of horse. It's like treading on eggs not to offend these people, the women's libbers. They're touchy, always on the defensive. What are they so worried about?"[2]

Freud would never have thought to ask, *What does a man want?* His vexed question speaks to his belief that women are a different, inferior kind of being, hence impossible to understand. Women are subordinate to men *by nature*. As inferiors women must always be kept in protective custody, under the control of men. When Freud's fiancée offered to go to work to enable them to marry sooner, Freud replied, "It is really a stillborn thought to send women into the struggle for existence exactly as men. If, for instance, I imagined my sweet gentle girl as a competitor it would only end in my telling her . . . that I am fond of her and that I implore her to withdraw from the strife into the calm incompetitive activity of *my* home." [italics mine][3]

Boys take in misogyny with their Wheaties. They are shown by mentors and peers that it won't do to spend much time with girls and women. No boy wants to "throw like a girl," or to be told to go home to mama. When your teachers and your buddies tell you that girls are not only physically weaker but lack all the important virtues, including courage, strength, and rationality, why would you respect girls? It's easy to move from the idea that women are inferior to treating them as inferiors.

The effect of this poison on women is equally potent. Like successful advertising, the message is designed into our lives and repeated until it becomes part of stored memory, until it is thought of as a received truth, an article of faith. Sexist messages, such as "no girls in this game," have been internalized by women as well as by men.

Ideas are powerful shapers of behavior. No idea has had graver consequences than this: one group is superior to another *by nature*. Most societies have been built on the bedrock of that idea. It has been the basis for racism, sexism, nationalism, imperialism, and speciesism.

For example, many societies have considered slavery an acceptable condition for those conquered in battle or seized by force (hence, inferior) or for children born into a state of servitude. As long as people *believed* that it was proper for human beings to be bought and sold, slavery persisted in this country. Emancipation in the United States came after public sentiment was galvanized by abolitionists—the radicals of their day—who regarded slavery as neither natural nor legitimate. We will not see the end of a rape culture until a critical mass of people believe that violence against women is neither natural nor legitimate. And that will require rethinking and reshaping attitudes internalized from childhood. When the destructive messages that sexism broadcasts are recognized as dangerous to a worthwhile future civilization, we will have relationships based on mutual trust, true peer relationships built from the ground up. Built on mutual respect.

THE PERSONAL IS POLITICAL

For years I thought that acts of sexual violence were the irrational, unrelated acts of deranged strangers. Experience and study lead me to conclude that a malevolent tradition and woman-hating gender training have everything to do with the universality of violence against women. The outcome of that training is evident in the imbalance of power between genders in our private and public lives but is most painfully visible when it erupts as sexual violence.

Preparing for this book has shown me how well and for how long I suppressed my own experiences of living in a rape culture when I was growing up. At that time I didn't understand the meaning of a number of unpleasant experiences. I remember the day I first saw a man unzip his fly and expose his penis in the secluded front entry area of a subway car. I was on my way to junior high school in Manhattan. I had been staring out the front panel of the train into the void of tunnel, hypnotized by the dazzling passage of colored lights. A blurred motion of his hand caught my attention. He was looking at my face, waiting for a reaction. I knew instinctively that his behavior was inappropriate, bizarre, and I turned and found a seat in the center of the subway car.

My best friend and I often took the long way home from school, walking across Central Park, to have more time to talk. Occasionally men followed us as we strolled across the park, but we learned that if we kept a certain distance ahead of them and didn't respond to their chitchat, they would eventually leave us alone. We weren't sure why grown men would waste their time stalking high-school girls.

During rush hour on the subway, a man would sometimes get close enough to rub his pelvis against my body, something I decided I would not put up with. I became expert in getting away through the crowd or, if the crush was too great, in thrusting my lumpy schoolbag between us. I pretended to ignore those men.

The summer I was fourteen, I hitched a ride back to our rented summer cottage from the little upstate town where I had been shopping. A man who had been watching me from across the street turned his car around and volunteered to drive me home. On the seven-mile drive back, he made a sexual offer that felt extremely menacing. I talked glibly about the fact that I was already late and that my parents were probably out looking for me. To my intense relief he dropped me off at my road without another word. I've read the newspaper stories about women hitchhikers found raped and murdered by the roadside. My life might have ended that way.

I wouldn't have known how to describe these incidents to my parents without using words about parts of the body they never named or spoke of and that I sensed they didn't wish to speak of. I never mentioned these incidents to anyone because they had to do with sex, and sex in the '50s was a taboo subject, an ugly, secretive activity that people were ashamed of. There was no public discussion of rape. No one said the word out loud. Each woman was alone with what had been done to her. And there were no statistics.

The faces of our daughters look out at me from old grade-school photographs. Their expressions are hopeful. Days at school were an adventure that might or might not go well, yet each well-loved face wears the smile the photographer requested. I had learned, as most parents do, that I could not pack happiness into their lunches with the sandwich and the apple. My love and my desire to protect did not give me the power to keep them from pain and trouble. Yet I sent them off, hopeful myself that no one would deliberately make them unhappy.

Our four daughters grew up in a pleasant suburb of a midwestern city. They were not subject to the pressures of living and going to school in a core city.[4] They attended reputable coed schools and colleges. Their father and I told them to fight back against classroom and neighborhood bullies, but the sexual bullying and harassment they encountered as they grew up could not be dealt with so simply or directly:

In a biology lab between classes one day, a male high-school classmate grabbed one of our daughters from behind. He held her and fondled her, despite her vigorous protests, until she was able to break his hold.

As an eight-year-old, one of our daughters was walking home from a friend's house a few blocks away when a man stopped his car beside her on the street, opened the passenger-side door, exposed himself to her, and told her to get into his car. Instead, she turned and ran for home. For months she was frightened that the stranger might come back and "get her."

One of our daughters, at fifteen, was hassled and propositioned every school-day afternoon by the loungers she had to pass on her way from the bus stop to her dance class a block away.

When one of our daughters was a college freshman, a casual friend who lived down the hall in her dorm attempted to rape her in her room. A passing student heard her call out and intervened. The would-be rapist told her that no one would believe she hadn't "asked for it" by allowing him into her room.

At seventeen, one of our daughters found a summer job as a waitress in a busy restaurant where tips were good. The mandatory uniform, a short skirt and form-fitting top, drew frequent sexual comments and propositions. She held her tongue and kept the job for the summer, although she was angry that she was considered "fair game" because she was a woman working in a service-oriented job.

As a college sophomore, one of our daughters was assigned a room in a frat house that had recently been converted into a dorm. She was terrorized for an entire semester by the ex-fraternity men next door. They threatened to beat her up and rape her because she wouldn't move out of her room, a room they thought should go to a fraternity buddy of theirs. When she complained to the dean of students, he told her that he had no power to prevent these men from threatening her. He suggested that she be cautious about walking across the campus after dark.

One of our daughters was stalked for several months by an acquaintance. Even after she assured him that she never wanted to see him again, he wouldn't leave her alone. He didn't take her "no" seriously. Only after he received a call from another man, her father, did he cease and desist.

During their teen years, three of our four daughters received obscene phone calls, some random, others from people who obviously knew them from school. Several times we had to change the number of our children's line to stop the frightening calls.

These experiences are the ones that come readily to mind, although there were others, including sexual name-calling on the school bus and in high-school corridors. At the time, I minimized them as much as I could in order not to frighten my daughters further. As I write down these stories, I am surprised by how many there were, and by how unwilling I was then to understand what they represented. They were expressions of forces I didn't dare think about too much.

I cite these incidents not because I believe that our daughters were singled out for harassment but because, on the contrary, what they experienced is all too customary. As our daughters grew up, they heard similar stories from their friends. We began to realize that girls leading ordinary lives in supposedly safe surroundings were in fact living in an environment latent with hostility and sexual threat.

Our daughters were able to tell us about their experiences of harassment, knowing that we would do everything we could to help. At the time, though, neither they nor we knew enough to connect personal traumas to societal patterns. That connection was made when we recognized the truth of the phrase "the personal is political." Women sharing their experiences of sexual violence and harassment with other women in the '70s and '80s broke the silence of centuries. Their stories allowed air and light into the darkness of women's sexual ignorance and sexual abuse. This was a time when women opened rape crisis centers and educated the police and the courts to become more aware that rape was an issue that called for sensitivity and proper training. Because of feminism, because of the women's movement, because of the daring and the dedication of thousands of women who applied social and political pressure to bring violence against women into the open and to quantify the issue, we finally have a statistical idea of the enormity of the problem.

The National Crime Victims Survey lists 2.3 million rapes and attempted rapes during the ten-year period from 1973 to 1982. The National Women's Survey estimates that 12.1 million American women have been the victims of forcible rape in their lifetime, about one out of every eight adult women, a staggering number. Twenty-nine percent of those rape victims are under the age of eleven and another thirty-two percent are between the ages of eleven and seventeen. In addition, the Department of Justice estimates that 18.7 million females were the victims of violent attack (aggravated and simple assault) between 1979 and 1987.[5] Add to that the girls and women who have been intimidated by sexual name-calling, taunting, threatening behavior, unwelcome touching, and working in a sexually hostile environment: those affected in some way include every woman I know.

The fear of sexual assault that is part of the daily life of women in this country takes up a continent of psychic space. A rape culture is a culture of intimidation. It keeps women afraid of being attacked and so it keeps women confined in the range of their behavior. That fear makes a woman censor her behavior—her speech, her way of dressing, her actions. It undermines her confidence in her ability to be independent. The necessity to be mindful of one's behavior at all times is far more than annoying. Women's lives are unnecessarily constricted. As a society, this one issue hampers the best efforts of half our population. It costs us heavily in lost initiative and in emotional energy stolen from other, more creative thoughts.

THE DAMAGE TO GIRLS GROWING UP NOW

Girls and boys are themselves quite aware of the differing cultural situations that confront them. In a 1992 newspaper survey, thousands of schoolchildren were asked whether they would prefer to be a man or a woman. Both boys and girls commented frequently that a woman is vulnerable to assault, rape, and murder.[6] Here are three of the responses:

The worst thing about being a woman is we get raped and killed. Women can get killed by their prettiness.
                                —fifth-grade girl, age 10, Mounds View, Minnesota

The up side to being a woman is you can manipulate men with your body. There isn't anything a man wouldn't do for a gorgeous woman. . . . Even though it might be fun to be a woman for a while, I wouldn't want to be one full time. Why? Because no matter how you slice it, men are in control in today's society just as they have been ever since man and woman existed. That's where I like to be.
                                —tenth-grade boy, Elk River, Minnesota

The best thing about being a man is that I can do what I want, be as rude and disgusting as I want, and no one says anything.
                                —eleventh-grade boy, age 16, Grey Eagle, Minnesota

Here, in the words of those who know, is the truth about the way things are today. American girls grow up in an atmosphere of gender-based pressure. Although they are the objects of aggression from the time they enroll in grade school, the situation grows steadily worse in junior high and high school. The air in such an atmosphere is unfit for girls to breathe, unhealthy and depressing. It's not surprising that a number of studies have shown that the self-esteem of girls plummets when they reach adolescence.

RAISING GIRLS TO KNOW THEIR STRENGTHS

What can we do to remedy the damage? What can we teach girls that will help them to grow up strong enough to resist and to change a rape culture?

• **Tell your daughters what helped you to survive growing up.** I begin by taking Thoreau's advice and looking into my own life to judge what may be learned from it. Since I was as unscathed by adolescent feelings of anxiety and low self-esteem as anyone in hormonal overload can be, I have tried to understand why that was so. Raised in a blue-collar neighborhood by immigrant parents, my life was bare bones in terms of what we could afford. My father worked long hours to make a go of a fledgling business, and my mother was often sick and depressed. But both my parents gave me the feeling that I was important and worth their time and interest. The feeling of being valued for one's self is probably at the base of most people's self-estimate.

I learned to express myself physically, to trust and enjoy using my body. As a city kid I had no parks, but I roller-skated and played long games of jump rope, stoopball, stickball, and, most glorious of all, rode my two-wheeler on long bike hikes.

I had one teacher who cared about my future. My sixth-grade teacher, Mrs. Pauline Hill, suggested that I try to test into Hunter College junior high school, a New York City public school that offered an excellent education for girls who wanted a college preparatory course of study. My parents were doubtful about whether to allow a thirteen-year-old to travel by subway into the city each day, but they finally agreed that I could enroll. I consider that decision pivotal in shaping my life. Because of it, I bypassed the usual coed competition and social anxiety.

I was part of a society of girls and women from seventh grade until I graduated from high school. The atmosphere was informal. I didn't worry about what I was going to wear; a few skirts and blouses saw me through. Today Hunter would be called multicultural, because the girls came from every imaginable ethnic group and from all the boroughs of the city. My friends were remarkably different, one from another, in temperament and background. We got to know each other through the extracurricular clubs and groups where I spent every school afternoon from three to six o'clock.

My role models in school were women. Without thinking too much about it, I absorbed the knowledge that women were intellectual, proactive, good leaders, firm friends, and simply fun to be with.

I was encouraged academically. My teachers were women who, for the most part, cared about their students and urged them to speak in class and to go beyond what was called for in an assignment.

I was empowered by my peers. I ran for student government office, I had a small part in a school play, I joined the staff of the magazine, I was a mentor to younger girls through a Big Sister organization. My friends, too, had their activities and roles in some facet of school life—the athletic association, the French club, the school newspaper, the honor society. No one needed to talk to us abstractly about the importance of women participating in the social or political life of our school.

Coming out of that experience, I had great enthusiasm for going on to college and into the working world. I had learned that I could work toward a goal I cared about and have a reasonable chance of achieving it. And I never thought that my gender might be a hindrance.

Some women who have studied at a single-sex school have a different and much less enthusiastic opinion. Women have said to me, "We live in a coeducational world. Girls should learn to get along with boys in school." I agree wholeheartedly, in principle. If girls were treated as equals in the classroom, coeducation might be ideal.

I doubt that I could have convinced any of my daughters to attend a girls' school, even if one had been available. But I firmly believe that girls should have some place—a club or a team or an organization with a social goal—where they can come together to meet each other as friends and as allies.

Girls need that comradeship as relief from the social-sexual competition that makes the junior-high and high-school years so dreadful that girls can easily slip into a victim mentality. Even the matter of what to wear becomes a problem in that social pressure cooker, because appearance in these years is much more important than achievement. No one who hasn't witnessed it can imagine the self-loathing and despair that can accompany the simple act of getting dressed for school.

• **Give girls your attention and your approval. Teach them to be independent.** A girl should be raised to feel that she is a valuable person who will be taken seriously. Children's stories are sometimes serious allegories: Margery William's velveteen rabbit wishes to be a "real" rabbit, not a toy to be played with and abandoned at the whim of its owner. Pinocchio longs to be flesh and blood, not a marionette controlled by even a kind master. It is essential that a girl think of herself as valuable in her own right, as a "real person," not a toy or a marionette dancing on strings held by the men in her life.

Girls must hear repeatedly, from as many sources as possible, that their lives are as important as those of their brothers. Girls must be told that they have the right to aspire to work they care about.

Parents complain that teenage girls won't talk to them about their problems and don't seem to value their parents' input. The time to establish a talking relationship that will last a lifetime is early in a girl's life. She will recognize the fact that her parents think she is worth talking and listening to.

For centuries girls were taught that they had to commit a kind of psychic suicide. They were required to efface any quality of self that was rebellious or enterprising or merely curious and imaginative. Girls were directed to be meek and gentle, docile and submissive, because such qualities were appropriate to woman. A woman was obedient. A woman did not question, much less look directly at, a man. The idealized woman, painted as a madonna, is always portrayed with her head down, gaze lowered and averted. Girls were trained for subservience, not for personal satisfaction. Girls trained in this way do not often grow up to become independent women.

The most important gift anyone can give a girl is a belief in her own power as an individual, her value without reference to gender, her respect as a person with potential. I have heard the gratitude and satisfaction in an adult woman's voice when she speaks of a father or a mother or a teacher who showed her early in her life that she mattered. Yes, a woman can overcome being shut up and toned down as a child, but getting to the other side of that wall takes an enormous amount of time and energy. The girl with a rambunctious feeling of knowing her own strengths will become a person who empowers others out of the abundance of her self-respect.

• **Encourage fathers to become active allies in remaking the culture.** Society now acknowledges what was long denied and long concealed—the fact that there are sexually abusive fathers as well as fathers who regularly batter their children. There are also fathers who permanently scar their daughters by openly preferring their sons. The misogyny of our culture is at least in part at the root of these men's actions and attitudes.

We ought to recognize, though, that there are millions of supportive, nurturing fathers in this country whose efforts to promote gender equity make a large, positive difference in the lives of their daughters.

In my own life and in the lives of our daughters, it would be hard to overestimate the effect of having had a father who showed us his love and his confidence. Busy and tired as he was, my father found time to have long conversations with me, to walk with me in the evening and tell me stories, to explain his taste in music and literature. He listened without laughing to my half-baked plans for the future. In short, he treated me with respect as a person who had interesting thoughts and opinions.

Our daughters each spent considerable time with their father right from the beginning: he took on the 2 A.M. feedings, and he was the one they chose to throw up on in the middle of the night when they had stomach flu. When our daughters were young and fascinated by the process, they wanted to shave like their dad; he gave them a play razor and lathered them up. No matter how cold or wet the weather, he took them trick-or-treating. He went fishing with the ones who didn't mind baiting their own hooks. He was the one who had to be restrained at least once a year from calling on a teacher who was "unfair." He danced around the living room as they did to music they loved, but he didn't miss a chance to lobby on behalf of the music he cared about. He rearranged his schedule to attend their school plays, gymnastic meets, dance recitals, debates, soccer matches, and birthday parties. His pride in them is evidenced in the yard of photo albums on our bookshelf that chronicle their days in colorful detail.

The ongoing father-daughter kitchen-table debates and skirmishes about political issues and any other topic worth discussing, continue to this day whenever they are together. They disagree, creatively and at length, on a variety of issues. They agree that they can disagree and still love one another. That's vital knowledge for a girl to have when she is learning to partner in her adult life.

Daughters can bring awareness to fathers of the prevalence of harassment in their everyday lives. For most men, sexual violence is an invisible issue, and the huge and incontrovertible fact that America is the most sexually violent country in the world literally has no impact on their consciousness. The fear of being sexually assaulted is simply not on a man's mind as it always is on a woman's. I would go further and say that sexual violence is a *non-issue* for most men, with none of the clout, say, of the state of the economy or the standing of a favorite baseball/football/basketball team.

How do we make this enormous shadow on the lives of women visible to the millions of men who are not rapists or molesters or seducers? How do we reach the men most of us know, the men who flinch at the thought of being put into the category of perpetrator but who are socialized to agree tacitly with the beliefs of a rape culture?

I believe that a father's love for his daughter, and his knowledge of what his own male socialization was like, might inspire him to look at the familiar clubby world of male privilege through a different lens: to recognize the effect that gender inequity has on his daughter's life, to be outraged by the harassment and violence that touches her in some way every day. The former navy officers who were fathers of the women officers hassled at Tailhook were furious and indignant about the male notion of sexual privilege expressed in sexual harassment at that convention.

I believe that fathers of daughters should actively promote the idea that sexually violent men are not "real" men at all but cowards and bullies. I would like to see men's groups undertake a campaign to make sexual violence not only repulsive to men but—and this could be crucial —unfashionable, uncool, unmasculine.

Fathers of daughters, step forward and turn your love and energy into practical efforts to remake this culture into one that actively promotes the growth and happiness of girls and women. Your efforts are needed and welcomed. They could make a profound difference to this society.

• **Tell girls the truth: Replace sexual ignorance with sexual knowledge.** We've simply got to recognize that protecting girls means giving them the knowledge that will allow them to make intelligent, principled decisions about sexuality. We as a society—preferably through a parent or parents—should teach girls at an early age about the sexual functioning of their bodies. It is a mistake to wait until a girl is "old enough."

My father and mother were themselves unsure what to say to a girl about the life of her body, so they said nothing. My mother had been trained to deny that she knew anything remotely connected with the sex act or its consequences. Once I asked her the meaning of the word *abortion*. She looked as if I had struck her and told me never again to use such a word in her presence.

Of course I read whatever I could get my hands on about sex in an attempt to understand why there was so much mystery and secrecy. My high school didn't get around to sex education until junior year, when Miss Mildred Duffy gave her popular course, called Health Education 6, a euphemism for sex education.

Even though we should have been given such a course much earlier in our lives, Miss Duffy's students in the late '50s and early '60s were an immensely privileged group. We were among the tiny percentage of women in all of recorded history given accurate information—and actually taught—about human reproduction.

Miss Duffy was careful not to talk about the implications to us personally of what we were learning; she didn't teach about sexuality as a source of pleasure, nor did she speak about sexual violence against women. Nonetheless, her class was a door to what used to be called carnal knowledge, knowledge forbidden to us because we were girls and because such knowledge might tarnish our innocence.

An innocent is literally one free of guilt or sin, lacking in knowledge. The girls in my class qualified as innocents. We had little or no concept of the physiology of sexuality or reproduction. We didn't know there was an estrus cycle that regulates conception. Several years after we began wearing sanitary napkins each month, we were taught the reason women menstruate.

I wish that Miss Duffy could also have told us that boys were being socialized to become sexual marauders and to see women as sexual prey.

Our mothers and certainly their mothers went to their marriage beds "innocent." A woman learned about sex not from books or wall charts but from what she could glean from the hints of other women or from the experience of being sexually assailed on her marriage bed. No woman considered virtuous by her community knew anything significant about sex before she married.

Moreover, lack of information was made a *virtue* in a woman. To be pure was to be unaware of basic physical facts, to be ignorant, uninformed, hence vulnerable, pliable, obedient to the wishes of the husband who knew, more or less, what to do. A proper girl was raised to be a sexual lamb, docile and tractable. Ignorance was dressed up and paraded to women as innocence. Innocence was touted as fostering a high level of morality.

The male authority that kept girls and women ignorant of their physiology is intact in many places in the world today, and that deliberate ignorance of anything to do with her sexuality is part of the market value of a prospective bride. Even in the United States, sexual ignorance continues to make girls easy pickings for the molester and the seducer. Recently, I read a newspaper story that quoted the mother of a ten-year-old who had become pregnant. The mother lamented that she couldn't understand how such a thing could have happened when she had purposely withheld any information about sex.

Ignorance is not and never should have been a virtue. To deliberately keep a girl ignorant of the way her body functions sexually is disrespectful and detrimental. Early and thorough education for girls and boys about their sexuality is a basic need that even in the '90s is being met rather poorly. Sex education coupled with sexual harassment curricula could form the basis for school programs that talk about ethical sexual behavior.

• **Arm them with the knowledge that they can be a part of cultural change.** Teach girls the importance of cultural history, including the history of the women's movement, and let them know it's a live movement that they can become part of. They will be heartened to know that society has changed in the past and will continue to change in response to pressure. The definition of what is innate and "natural" shifts remarkably from country to country and from one era to the next. Customs that seemed intrinsic to human nature have been abandoned or redirected. Human sacrifice was once practiced extensively. Consigning feeble newborns, the very sick, and the old to death by exposure and starvation was once routine. Societies change their sentiments, their habits of mind, and their practices.

Women have only begun to recognize and to use their political clout. Girls who grow up with a desire to work for social justice will become politically aware and active.

Girls will recognize that eradicating sexual violence is a formidable goal but no more so than cleaning up pollution on the planet, a recognized cultural objective we have embraced as worthy of time and support. The knowledge that we can—by a dedicated effort—bring about the end of so much suffering must motivate us.

• **Enlist women mentors and role models.** We don't live in close-knit villages or have readily accessible extended families where our daughters can find other listeners and guides. However, grandmothers, aunts, honorary aunts, neighbors, and family friends, no matter how far away, can become a tremendous source of stimulation and companionship. A girl might be able to turn to one of these adult women as an additional source of encouragement and advice. Older women are a girl's link to history, her personal knowledge of the past. Such mentors can enlarge her horizons and help her reflect upon her own future.

• **Find ways for girls to play and work together.** Athletic programs are an excellent way for girls to gain strength and competence, especially now that schools have recognized that it's not only the few girls who make a varsity team who should be trained and strengthened. All girls should be included in some athletic program and instructed in physical activities. Being able to swim or run or play volleyball can help a girl survive a socially cutthroat school.

Many studies have demonstrated the boost to self-esteem when girls become active in sports and recreational activities. The Women's Sports Foundation reports that girls who participate in sports are ninety-two percent less likely to get involved with drugs, eighty percent less likely to have an unplanned pregnancy, and three times more likely to graduate from high school.[7] A recent study of pre-teen girls supports the idea that girls derive a strong, positive self-image from the challenge, achievement, skill development, and risk-taking of sports involvement. The study makes a number of recommendations, including creating single-sex teams where girls can play and try new activities in a safe, uncritical environment.[8]

I recommend that parents of girls investigate what's available through their daughters' schools and in their communities, and that they help to develop new programs that allow girls the experience of working cooperatively. Organizations like the Girl Scouts and the Y should become much more important to girls, not only as a source for camaraderie and good times, but as places where their skills and leadership abilities will be encouraged.

• **Teach girls to be media critical.** Often women don't tell the truth about the damage that fear of sexualized violence does to us. There is strong evidence that men exposed to repeated doses of violence and rape in films become increasingly desensitized to violent acts and to the effect of that violence on the victims. What is the effect of repeated doses of sexual violence on women and girls? How much anger do women have to repress every time they watch a TV program or a film in the company of a man and see women being stalked, raped, tortured, murdered? A few women say they get up and leave. Others think they need to show their tough-mindedness by watching with outward composure, although they may be quite uncomfortable. Many women don't say anything to the man they're with, because, after all, sexual violence in the media is such a common and popular prop for a plot that women would have to walk out on most of what's commercially available. And perhaps that's what women should be doing.

How can anyone quantify the damage done to a girl who daily sees a stream of images of women being pursued, threatened, sexually assaulted, and killed? What happens to a girl's sense of adventure, her zest for living an interesting life, in the face of a world obviously hostile to women? The cumulative effect of media violence on girls is difficult to estimate, but I believe that over the years the results are visible in the lessening of their self-esteem, and in their belief that they cannot effectively fight a predation that appears to be universal.

We demonstrate to girls repeatedly that being beautiful and seductive are the qualities society prizes in adult women. At the same time, girls cannot help but observe that in the media beautiful and seductive women are the most likely candidates to be sexually assaulted. A successful woman, in this unspoken double bind, is set up to be a victim of violence. As the Minnesota fifth-grader wrote, "Women can get killed by their prettiness." The media portrayal of women prepares girls to become victims, just as surely as it teaches men to be comfortable perpetrators of violence.

Because of the heavy penetration of media and popular culture into the lives of children, watching television or a film with one's child can be a springboard for questions about what is happening on the screen: how are female and male characters presented? do they seem real? how do they relate to one another? what are their goals? A parent can ask, for example, "How would you have handled that situation?" If girls learn from adults at an early age that the messages being broadcast at them are not necessarily in their best interests, they have the chance to reject those messages. Children can quickly become critical and reflective about what they see, hear, and read.

We ought to have alternative media, some of them created by children themselves, that give girls other visions and other outlets. Parents' groups should band together to discuss strategies to influence media presentation of women. Women characters who are three-dimensional humans rather than clothes pegs, sex objects, or villainous sexual manipulators are badly needed in the media's global village.

• **Choose toys and stories that don't reinforce gender stereotypes.** Barbie must go. The male erotic ideal is so deeply seated within us that we buy it for our daughters. Thirty years after "Free To Be You and Me" took on some of our worst cultural stereotypes and replaced them with role models for a more egalitarian world, Barbie dolls and their wardrobes reign supreme in the marketplace. Let's be realistic about who Barbie is and what she means. Barbie is the chesty, trim, blond, fashion-obsessed woman that men who buy *Playboy* and *Hustler* prefer. Her feet are curved to wear heels; she looks as if she might be a chorus girl but not an athlete.

While we are working to change the adult culture, we can't ignore those who are growing up in it. Girls will want a Barbie look-alike doll as long as they see women who look like Barbie rewarded by money, fame, and male attention. It's not easy to deny a child what "everybody else has." But Barbie and her empty-headed friends perpetuate the sex-kitten stereotype for girls. Demand worthy substitutes for Barbie, toys that we don't have to apologize to ourselves for buying.

Fairy tales may be all right, as Bruno Bettelheim suggests, to introduce children to the terrors of life, but frankly they are dreadful gender role models for girls. Most of the heroines are ladies-in-waiting: Cinderella waits humbly in the ashes for a transformation or a prince; Snow White waits primly in her bed-coffin to be kissed and awakened by a man into a real-life existence. All those multiple princesses wait in their towers to be rescued, the "pretty women" of their day. Being beautiful is a storybook heroine's stock-in-trade, but waiting is her primary activity. Passivity encourages victimization. Video games haven't improved the situation. The Nintendo women, scantily clad, also wait to be rescued.

Girls want to be heroes. Find stories and books that give them women heroes worth identifying with.

• **Be a part of the solution yourself.** Whatever you can find the time and energy to do that makes this society more hospitable and more just for women helps to make positive change. Your actions register more deeply than you suspect with your daughters. Your behavior and your relationships with others are critical shapers of a girl's image of who she can and should become. For good or ill, parents are primary role models for their daughters.

• **Encourage girls to be ecstatic.** At twelve, I rode my bike in the warm last light of summer evenings, swooping down the long hill just past my block, past St. Teresa's parochial school where my friends learned every day that their bodies were provocations to evil, down another block, and then another and another, until I knew that I was late for dinner and would be in trouble when I finally pedaled home. I have never been more completely alive than in those moments, in sync with the whir of the spokes and the air I displaced. I had no word then for the ecstatic, but that was the emotion. I knew what it was to feel joyful and alive, on my own but not lonely, mind and body working together.

Joy and playfulness are regarded as childish emotions, instead of being recognized as lifelong resources that strengthen and invigorate. We rarely speak about those emotions, the causeless happiness that floods us and makes us grateful to be alive. The ability to feel deeply is a power and a resource that Audre Lorde speaks of magically in her essay "Uses of the Erotic: The Erotic as Power." Whether we call it the ecstatic or the erotic, we are talking about an emotion that is a source of creativity and love, that nourishes a healthy sense of self and allows a human being to feel keenly with others. This source of happiness can be kept and counted on, available and infinitely renewable.

In this culture that so often and so early makes girls feel meek and powerless, whatever nourishes playfulness, joy, and the ecstatic must be cherished and cultivated every day.

NOTES

1. *The "Natural Inferiority" of Women,* compiled and edited by Tama Starr (New York: Poseidon Press, 1991), p. 19.
2. Ibid., pp. 87–88.
3. Ibid., p. 181.
4. Caroline Wolf Harlow, *Female Victims of Violent Crime,* U.S. Department of Justice, January 1991, NCJ-126828. A girl growing up in a low-income city neighborhood faces the likelihood of being in physical danger and experiencing psychic abuse on a daily basis. The victims in sixty-nine percent of rapes and attempted rapes committed from 1973–1982 had annual family incomes of less than $15,000.
5. Ibid., p. 1. Also: Bureau of Justice Statistics Bulletin, *Female Victims of Violent Crime,* U.S. Department of Justice, 1985, NCJ-126826 p. 1; 6.; "Rape in America: A Report to the Nation," National Victim Center, April 23, 1992.
6. From the *Star Tribune,* Mind Works section, p. 1, October 6, 1992.
7. Reported in the Minnesota Women's Fund News, vol. 6, no. 1, pp. 2, 4.
8. Lynn Jaffee and Rebecca Manzer, "Girls' Perspectives: Physical Activity and Self-Esteem," *Melpomene Journal,* vol. 11, no. 3, Fall 1992.

EMILIE BUCHWALD is the publisher, cofounder, and editor of Milkweed Editions. She was educated at Barnard College (B.A.), Columbia University (M.A.), and the University of Minnesota (Ph.D.). Buchwald is the author of two award-winning children's books, *Gildaen* and *Floramel and Esteban* (Harcourt Brace Jovanovich). A poet and fiction writer, her work has been frequently anthologized. Buchwald was a recipient of the governor's "Marvelous Minnesota Woman" award in 1991. She is married to Henry Buchwald and is the mother of Jane, Amy, Claire, and Dana, who provided ideas, insights, and valued suggestions for this book.

RELIGION AND VIOLENCE:
The Persistence of Ambivalence
by Joan H. Timmerman

The traditional acts of mercy need to be updated to fit our
times. More often than not, the wounded individual
found at the side of the road by the good
Samaritan is a woman.

RELIGION, WITH ITS evocative symbols, is one of the few institutions capable of speaking to the unconscious levels that arouse and fuel violence in people. With its global reach and historical memory, religion is perfectly placed to challenge those patriarchal structures that legitimate violence. But is it so complicit with those structures that it cannot change them? How persistent is its ambivalence of word and action with regard to violence, especially violence against women?

Newspapers record acts of violence, and as they accumulate in our consciousness we recognize that we live in a culture of violence. Yet violent acts are seldom condemned with the moral outrage that customarily greets deviations from sexual norms. Surely rape is a more antisocial phenomenon than is a peaceable same-sex partnership.

A number of questions need to be asked. What have the churches done (or failed to do) to prevent the glorification and perpetration of violent force? Why has the transforming power of institutional religion been ineffective against a rising tide of violence? Is there, in fact, a sacralization of violence that can only be termed religious, that is masked, tolerated, and enabled, if not perpetuated, by the churches? What evidence exists of particular church communities or religious leaders taking a prophetic, counter-cultural stance, condemning violence as blasphemy against people and as a perversion of human energies? What will motivate the churches, and by that I mean the people of the churches, to work as conscientiously for the transformation of attitudes and structures that produce violence as they have worked to identify and root out excessive or variant sexual behavior? When will they put the same energy into preventing violence as they have traditionally spent on compassion for its victims?

Religion plays two roles in society that are particularly relevant to the topic at hand: the first is to give meaning to familiar aspects of life by a process of sacralization, establishing *everyday realities* (the way things are) as holy and meaningful, and providing a psychological basis for religious fulfillment. A second function of religion is to be *prophetic*, that is, proclaiming what ought to be, and providing a vision of holiness and meaning far beyond the realities we know around us.

Death and the need for food, both critical and problematic universals, acquire religious meaning by this process of sacralization. Male dominance and the rituals that consecrate it—the honor and courage of making war, and the sacred authority of the head of the family—have also been sacralized in traditional religion. Many passages in the Hebrew scriptures, especially those written before the sixth century B.C., detail the experience of the Hebrew people as led by Yahweh in the conquest of land and people. In this context war becomes holy, and victory a manifestation of God's favor and support. The theme carries through Christian epistles and writings of the Fathers of the Church that assume God's agents should impose God's authority on those unwilling (or too weak or corrupt) to accept it freely. From the justification of violent force for "just" purposes it is a small step to the justification of violence for "necessary" purposes. And who is going to distinguish them?

Religion's prophetic power has been exercised in quite another natural realm. Perhaps because the people who lived in the lands near the Hebrews constructed a religious universe in which sexuality and fertility, especially the female principle, were sacralized, the early and late prophets of the Scriptures railed against sacred sexuality. It was not so much sexual pleasure in itself they condemned as the promise of religious fulfillment through it. Their sovereign lord, Yahweh, claimed absolute worship and therefore Hebrew priests condemned the pagan sexual practices as idolatrous.

The prophetic impulse in religion recognizes in certain signs of the times and places that things are not as they should be. A prophetic voice is then raised to confront those actions and to name as evil those who do them. Both in the past and at present, the prophetic power of religion in America has been summoned against pleasure and against value for the feminine principle, while the unleashed force of violence is deplored but allowed as necessary, or named as simply a good impulse gone astray. Recent examples include the widespread religious opposition to the use of condoms; the refusal of the sacrament of communion to pro-choice activists; and the condemnations of feminism from the pulpit of the 1992 Republican National Convention.

In some ways the conditioning that has connected sexual arousal with violence is new and unique to the American experience. An anomalous, even sociopathic, response that finds acts of rape and assault exciting becomes common, even normal, in nightly media coverage of the news and in entertainment programming. While religion has not been actively responsible for this marriage of sexual arousal and violence, it has, by default, enabled it. In the name of opposing evil and stopping perpetrators, cop and detective shows feature exploitative scenes of terror in which vulnerable females are brutalized. When I have personally suggested to priest and minister friends that they preach against rape and battering of women, I have been told repeatedly that "our people" do not do these things. Not in the least embarrassed to assume their congregations need advice about adultery, birth control, and abortion, they cavil at the thought that there might be patterns of violence present in the lives of members. What sort of selective vision assumes that the good people who attend church need to be addressed on the temptations of illicit pleasure, whether from material possessions or bodily stimulation, but are not at risk for temptation to abuse power? It is clear, though almost incredible, that a deep preference for violence over pleasure characterizes the patriarchal roots of the original religious traditions.

There are, however, glimmers of change. In a prophetic gathering in August 1991, religious and community leaders in Minnesota condemned the growth of ethnic, racial, and sexual violence in society and called for intensified and coordinated responses to it. These included the leadership of Jewish, Catholic, and Lutheran congregations. The Minnesota Council of Churches at that time supported the local religious community in addressing violence through social programs, sexual and domestic abuse workshops, and informational training. In practice, however, the motivation for these programs was not religious. It was based on the fears of individuals for their own and others' safety, as well as the dollar costs to our society of the levels of violence now commonplace. A theological analysis that offers religious reasons for creating a society free of violence against women still awaits formulation. The key question of the New Testament, Who is my neighbor?, has not yet been answered in such a way as to include women. In many areas and mentalities it is still not a crime for a man to beat his wife or to use fear, force, or trickery to have intercourse with a woman. Religious valorization for sexual pleasure without violence is still awaiting acceptance.

I do know of one promising development, an unprecedented prophetic critique of present practice regarding "conjugal" violence. *A Heritage of Violence?* was published recently by the Social Affairs Committee of the Assembly of Quebec Bishops.[1] It appears to be the first document of its kind, the result of a mandate given by the bishops of Quebec to a commission of "women and men of different socioeconomic milieus" to study the problem of violence against women and to prepare a study paper dealing with "appropriate attitudes toward the situation of women who are victims of violence" (7). As a consciousness-raising document and a pedagogical tool for priests, pastoral workers, and educators, this represents something that is being done in Canada that could be replicated effectively by the leadership of other churches.

A Heritage of Violence? is a welcome sign that at least some religious groups are aware of the issue of violence and ready to speak to it. The motivation for change that it represents is clearly religious motivation: the authors see it as part of their task of evangelization and humanization, an expression of their commitment to the call of Jesus to love, not possessively but with respect for another's "physical and psychological integrity, of the other's freedom and dignity" (8). The context is that of liberation theology, a mode recognized for more than a decade by feminist theologians as applicable to the situation of North American women, but one not generally invoked by Catholic bishops in this country as the foundation for their reflection on the relationship between the sexes. The Quebec paper concludes with explicit reference to its theological grounding:

> If we use the word "liberation," it is because women have, in fact, been bound and oppressed. This liberation has neither occurred everywhere, nor been completed where begun. It is, therefore, a Christian issue consistent with the fundamental option of Jesus Christ (56).

The theoretical part of the document gathers the most significant research available on the phenomenon of conjugal violence and offers it, along with ecclesial and gospel principles, to educate its readers. Its intent is explicit: to become involved in the social struggle against conjugal violence (10). The various types of violence are described, as well as the known patterns of escalation, cycles, and consequences for the family. In a second chapter the causes of violence against women are discussed, both as an individual and a social problem with theological roots. Born of the patriarchal system and reinforced by economic structures, violence against women has survived many revolutions, reforms, and movements toward equality and liberty in male-defined societies. One thing is abundantly clear—that men's negative vision of women is deeper than the behavioral problems of individuals.

The document's third chapter proposes a path toward solutions and is intended to challenge members of the Christian community, indeed any persons actively involved in church or society, to break their silence and join forces with the work of groups already involved in preventing and opposing violence.

The prophetic vision of a transformed society, "a new heaven and a new earth," is integral to Christian revelation (Rev. 21:1). Feminist movements have begun to provide the pressure for that transformation. It will, however, be neither profound nor complete until some important insights take root:

—Transformation begins with conversation of hearts and consciences of people.

—It comes out of a greater sensitivity to oneself, to others, to events, and to the presence of the Spirit.

—It results from acknowledgment that familiarity can prejudice one against truth.

—It brings about a transformation of patriarchal, social, and economic structures (44).

Deployment of the forces of such transformation have been described, helpfully I think, in terms of various paths—of *reflection*, of *compassionate response*, of *conscientization*, of *education*, and of *social transformation*. Sometimes persons are deterred from expressing their commitment against violence because the path of activism is not congenial to them; active involvement does not draw upon their strengths or is incompatible with other commitments. Identifying alternative, but equally valued strategies, can summon these people's energies to the cause in more effective ways.

The path of *reflection* provides a necessary, deep foundation for action, and mobilizes the thinkers in theology, sociology, psychology, and the researchers, teachers, and students in all areas of human endeavor to the fray. It also engages the contemplatives and those to whom life has assigned the path of solitude and interiority. There is nothing more destructive than uncentered activism. One of the greatest insights of religious history is the power of the combination of contemplation and action. Practically, deploying this power would mean:

—making recent developments in theology, biblical exegesis, and Christian anthropology available to people to update the prevailing perception of women and their role, as well as ethical discourse on the subjects of marriage and the family;

—recognizing by word and liturgical action that men and women are equal partners with equal dignities;

—listening receptively to the theological reflection offered when women name God, speak of Mary, and read the Bible;

—supporting the feminist movement, so that the Christian community may be more accepting of the humanistic and evangelical values that it defends. To a great extent, the United States Council of Catholic Bishops has advanced a caricature of feminism as incompatible with Christian values, an intellectual and political error that one would think would have been prevented by reflection on the embarrassment of past positions regarding democracy and Marxism. Not only intellectual integrity but justice requires acknowledgment and acceptance of the positive fit between gospel values and feminist insight.

The path of *compassion* calls for active involvement to assist victims and make aggressors aware of their responsibility. To do this, priests and pastoral ministers must:

—receive warmly those coming to confide their problem;

—direct those who have been assaulted to the proper resources, giving special support to those for whom access to services is made more difficult by their ethnic origin, their culture, or the place where they live;

—direct aggressors to appropriate programs, for there is great hope if someone can take part in a process of rehabilitation;

—support the community in its commitment against violence so that active charity toward victims may be triggered among those who are in a position to help.

The traditional acts of mercy need to be updated to fit our times. More often than not, the wounded individual found at the side of the road by the good Samaritan is a woman.

The path of *conscientization* is one well known and powerfully used by church leadership. The pulpit has an awesome power to increase public awareness of any issue; it has been used for years to urge victims to patience and forgiveness, as well as to reinforce bias against gays and lesbians and others in unconventional lifestyles. Without intending that effect, it may have helped to incite self-righteous action against others. Now the churches need to exert their influence to increase public awareness of the problem of violence against the vulnerable, seen as a global reality. In order to accomplish this, we will need to denounce violence against women by stating clearly that it is unacceptable in all its physical, emotional, and psychological forms; and call for collaboration by all levels of organizations that should be concerned about this problem.

The path of *education* is crucial to the solution, even as it has added to the problem. Progress on this path requires:

—informing people, especially young people preparing for intimate relationships in their lives, about the causes and consequences of violence and teaching them that autonomy and respect are essential in a couple;

—pursuing, together with professionals in the fields of human relations, a process of reflection on conflict resolution and stress management;

—encouraging those who reflect on the status of men and who promote a new concept of manhood, and promoting understanding that the abuse of power and control is not an essential component of manhood, nor an affirmation of masculinity;

—redefining and reemphasizing paternity as a man's equal responsibility for life and for the child;

—rediscovering what it means to reconcile love of the other with love of oneself and what it means to be a man or woman free of stereotyped and predetermined gender roles; and

—including in the formation of future priests sensitization to the causes and consequences of violence against women, and training for appropriate pastoral intervention.

The ending of relationships, including rituals for uncoupling and divorce, must be shown to have evangelical value; they are a part of living that should at times be experienced as blessed rather than blame-filled. Violence may erupt when individuals are unable to accept the loss of someone they believe they "own" in some transcendent way. The churches' traditional (patriarchal) rituals of marriage bear some responsibility for giving men this false impression. Many of these rituals have been reformed in light of the dignity and autonomy that is recognized today as belonging to women, but education, especially the Christian education of men regarding the meaning of sexuality and marriage, has been neglected.

Finally, the path of *social transformation* calls members of the Christian community to encourage political and economic authorities to take action aimed at correcting abusive aspects of the economic system. A form of capitalism, or its administration, that uses power and money against the most vulnerable members of society and is insensitive to the rights and needs of women and children rewards exploitation. This prophetic role of the community and its members includes:

—denouncing to public authorities oppressive situations that could cause rebellion, such as unemployment, homelessness, and all kinds of exploitation;

—mobilizing and coordinating efforts to demand fair and equitable social policies for disadvantaged members of society; and

—raising social consciousness by using symbolic actions, on appropriate occasions, in support of the poorest of the poor.

Without doubt, some religious communities, parishes, and agencies are already playing this prophetic role. All too often, however, it is an ad hoc, localized, and specialized response that can too easily be identified with one or another individual or "wing" of the community.

Will the problem of violence be resolved if left to chance or to individual networks of vested interests—support groups for victims, legal action against selected perpetrators, and media campaigns? Lewis Thomas puts some of the immediate concern about problems like violence in evolutionary perspective, thus giving long-term, biological reasons for hope. "What we call contemporary culture may turn out, years hence, to have been a very early stage of primitive thought on the way to human maturity. . . . If we can stay alive, my guess is that we will amaze ourselves by what we can become as a species."[2] In his serene long view, our present troubles could be the equivalent of the juvenile delinquency of the race, a temporary phase in the experience of the human species. Are we in the midst of the "boys-will-be-boys" period of human technological development? Is the suffering of women and children, even of whole peoples, to be seen as the sacrificial "wild oats" that will be sown before humanity reaches maturity?

While no source of meaning or hope should be regarded with disdain, this one reminds me of a cartoon by Frank and Ernest. It takes place in the Robotics department where two robots are discussing people and their constant tinkering to change the "hardware." "Selective breeding, recombinant DNA, genetic surgery . . . I don't get it," says the first robot. "Yeah, why go to all that trouble," says the other. "Why don't they just rewrite their software?!" The gift and task of religion in the lives of people is to "rewrite the software": to give vision, information, motivation, and strategies for transformation.

NOTES

1. Antoinette Kinlough, trans., *A Heritage of Violence? A Pastoral Reflection of Conjugal Violence* (Quebec: Social Affairs Committee, Assembly of Quebec Bishops, 1988). This paper, available from the Peacepower Foundation (Angela Mislans, Trustee) is quoted throughout unless otherwise indicated.
2. Lewis Thomas, *The Fragile Species* (New York: Charles Scribner's Sons, 1992), p. 81.

Born in Dickeyville, Wisconsin, **JOAN H. TIMMERMAN** has a Ph.D. in religious studies from Marquette University in Milwaukee (1974). She has been a professor of theology at the College of St. Catherine in St. Paul since 1968. Her interest in systematic and philosophical theology continues to be reflected in her teaching of contemporary theologians and methodologies. She also teaches in the areas of sacramentality, sexuality, social justice, and spirituality. During her twenty years on the faculty of the College of St. Catherine, she has been chair of the theology department, director of the Master of Arts program in theology, and initiator of the Theological Insights program, now in its sixth year.

A lecturer and writer in addition to her academic position, she has previously published *The Mardi Gras Syndrome: Rethinking Christian Sexuality* (Crossroad, 1984) and *Sexuality and Spiritual Growth* (1992). She is coeditor of *Walking in Two Worlds: Women's Spiritual Paths* (North Star Press, 1992) and writer of a chapter in *The Spiral Path*, edited by Theresa King (Yes International, 1992).

MAKING RAPE AN ELECTION ISSUE

by John Stoltenberg

Imagine a candidate declaring on national television,
"As president, I will commit the resources of my
administration to making the United States
a rape-free zone." Sounds utterly
farfetched, but *why?*

THE THIRD SATURDAY of October is BrotherPeace Day: An International Day of Actions to End Men's Violence. Every year on that day, in scores of cities, ad hoc bunches of profeminist men demonstrate their commitment to ending rape, battery, pornography, and various other human-rights violations committed in men's name. These ragtag actions are diverse and imaginative, and the chant "Break the silence, end men's violence!" is frequently heard shouted antiphonally by voices that are pitched toward tenor, baritone, and bass—turning heads of astonished passersby who can scarcely conceive of such a possibility.[1]

In the fall of 1992—with the presidential election looming—a New York profeminist men's group I belonged to wheat-pasted posters all around town calling for a speakout, march, and vigil on BrotherPeace Day with the banner headline "MAKE RAPE AN ELECTION ISSUE." Our posters also bore this shocking statistic: "400,000 women in NYC have been RAPED." In small print, we spelled out more bad news: "Thirteen percent of all women living in the U.S. have been raped at least once. . . . The position papers of Bill Clinton and George Bush don't even mention the word 'rape' once."

That whole fall I heard exactly one campaign radio spot that mentioned "rape and violence," but the ad merely touted the candidate's commitment to hiring more and more police officers. Otherwise, so far as I know, our ragtag demo was about the only time the subject of rape was broached publicly during the presidential contest of 1992.

Four years earlier, in 1988, Massachusetts Governor Michael Dukakis, then the Democratic candidate for president, blundered in his third televised debate against Republican George Bush when asked this question about his wife: "If Kitty Dukakis were raped and murdered, would you favor an irrevocable death penalty for the killer?" Dukakis gave a rambling and irrelevant reply—about the crime rate in Massachusetts and "the avalanche of drugs that's pouring into the country."[2] Many believe this dumbfounding display of insensitivity demolished forever his dwindling chances for the presidency. At around the same time, the Bush campaign was airing a TV spot featuring one Willie Horton, a black man convicted for rape who had been furloughed from a Massachusetts prison only to commit rape again. It was an inflammatory commercial that many believe helped boost Bush to victory.

Election after election, political candidates of all stripes slug it out across the country, seeing who can wave the flag the hardest, who can beat on their chest the mightiest, who can speak most worthily to people's troubles and fears, people's longing for security and a better life. Yet likely as not, all their zealous electioneering sheds no light upon our national epidemic of rape.

Rape is difficult to quantify because the crime is notoriously under-reported. According to a government-financed survey released by the National Victim Center in April 1992, a criminal rape happened to seventy-eight women in the U.S. every hour of 1990.[3] Perhaps more to the point, almost every woman lives with the terror that a rape could sometime happen to her.[4] There are significant odds that it already has. Research by sociologist Diana E. H. Russell based on face-to-face interviews with 930 women residents of San Francisco—selected at random from a scientific probability sample of households—found that forty-four percent had suffered a criminal rape or an attempted rape at least once in their lifetime.[5] The National Victim Center study—which did not tabulate rape attempts—found that thirteen percent of U.S. women have been criminally raped at least once in their lifetime (this is the percentage cited on our BrotherPeace posters in combination with U.S. Bureau of the Census figures for the local adult female population).[6] Extrapolating from both studies, there is a rape-survivor population in the U.S. of somewhere between twelve million and forty-one million living Americans.[7]

Rape is a crisis of national security if anything is. For any political candidate who is concerned with the safety of *all* the folks who live here, rape would seem to be a problem that desperately needs solving. Living in fear of forced and violent sex is much like living in a state of siege in occupied territory. Yet one candidate after another will declaim about defending this country's interests against *foreign* aggressors. Why doesn't local, homegrown, day-in-and-day-out *sexual violence against women* make it even to the bottom of their list of major social-policy questions?

Imagine candidates stumping for public office debating how best to stop rape. Imagine them inspiring us with new ideas and new programs to eliminate crimes of sexual violence completely. Imagine them promising bold and innovative leadership to set a national priority to "denormalize" rape, to refute myths about rape through all the mass media, to educate young people about personal rights and bodily integrity throughout the public school system, to create a national climate of opinion in which ending rape matters—because it gets talked about and cared about and people take it seriously. Even among groups of men there would emerge a new kind of peer pressure, discouraging rape rather than encouraging it, labeling coercive sex as one of the most not-cool things a guy can do. Imagine a candidate declaring on national television, "As president, I will commit the resources of my administration to making the United States a rape-free zone."

Sounds utterly farfetched, but *why*? Why isn't stopping rape an election issue?

There used to be a National Center for Prevention and Control of Rape. There isn't anymore. In 1986, because of the Reagan administration's budget cuts, this federal agency was absorbed into another, the antisocial-and-violent-behavior branch of the National Institute for Mental Health.

There used to be a National Clearinghouse on Rape. There isn't anymore. In 1986, because of the Reagan administration's budget cuts, it was quietly defunded.

These offices were not closed because the U.S. rape rate—which is the highest of any Western nation[8]—had suddenly plummeted. Far from it. The FBI acknowledges that the rate of criminal rapes in 1990 was twelve percent higher than in 1986 and twenty-four percent higher than 1981.[9] In one year alone, between 1990 and 1991, that rate rose fifty-nine percent.[10] So why *isn't* rape an election issue? I believe there are real answers to that question—a series of interlocking explanations that, taken as a whole, signal a deep and disturbing truth about this country right now.

Answer #1: **A lot of women don't like to think about rape.** As a strategy for survival, most women get through each day by blocking out consciousness about sexual violence against other women. If they can't protect themselves from the violence, they can at least protect themselves from the information. Ignorance gives the illusion of strength, and their denial is like a drug. For any candidate, this is an applecart of delusion not to upset.

Even some self-professed feminist women give rape short shrift when it comes to matters of public policy. For a while Dukakis's campaign manager was Susan Estrich, an *expert* on rape. A tenured Harvard Law School professor, Estrich had argued in her 1987 book, *Real Rape*,[11] that the law must respond not only to aggravated rape (by a stranger for instance), but also to "simple rape" (as when a woman is victimized by a friend or acquaintance). Whatever Estrich did or did not argue once she joined the Dukakis campaign, on the subject of rape the Duke himself kept mum.

There is evidence, however, that women in the electorate are becoming more inclined to voice their concerns about rape. For its cover story "Women Face the '90s," *Time* magazine polled one thousand women about which issues concerned them most. Rape ranked third (eighty-eight percent of the women said the issue was important to them), just below equal pay (ninety-four percent) and day-care (ninety percent). It was somewhat *more* important than abortion (seventy-four percent) and considerably more important than sexual freedom (forty-nine percent).[12] Notwithstanding *Time's* own data, the accompanying story (cheeringly titled "Onward, Women") did not mention the word *rape.*[13] Clearly women's deep concerns about rape are not being spoken to.

Although the abortion controversy has often been pitched into electoral politicking, rape remains a campaigner's no-no. The pro-choice side has generally tried to keep these two highly charged issues—reproductive freedom and sexual violence—pristinely separate. But that sleight of hand may prove to be a serious strategic mistake. A woman's right to control her own body once she's pregnant is a rather moot abstraction for all the women whose bodies are already colonized through forced sex. If pro-choice advocates were more candid about the social reality of forced sex, they might persuade women on the anti-abortion side to reexamine their forced-pregnancy position. Moreover, if pro-choice advocates were more honest about the relationship between forced sex and forced pregnancy, they might successfully put pressure on *both* major parties' platforms to acknowledge women's body rights without equivocation. So long as candidates think women voters can be counted on to keep silent about their human right not to be raped, the candidates can pretend to speak to women as full citizens—and really only address men.

Answer #2: **A lot of men don't want to hear about rape.** As things stand now, a candidate for elected office probably could not talk forthrightly about rape without alienating enormous numbers of men—and that's not just because rapists, too, vote. Violence against women is perceived by campaign managers and a huge share of the electorate as a "special interest" issue, a pejorative by definition because it affects mainly women. So the trick for the campaigner is to give the appearance of concern for women's interests—child care, for instance—while reassuring men that all their gender-class interests will still be served. A candidate may be tough on crime, a staunch defender of law and order, but he dare not breathe a word about crimes like rape and battery—which hit too close to home.

Answer #3: **To be soft on rape is to be soft on war.** Rape is a significant motivating force in military strategy.[14] Uncle Sam needs to keep men's taste for rape alive—in order to forge unified combat platoons across racial and class animosities and in order to get out there and blow the heads off "the enemy."

Military-supported brothels have long been a fixture of U.S. bases around the world, with virtually every PX proffering an ample line of pornography as well. The bodies of uncounted indigenous women, garrisoned and variously impaled in the service of our far-flung armed forces, have borne silent witness to Nietzsche's dictum that "man shall be trained for war, and woman for the recreation of the warrior."[15]

The fair-haired son of a U.S. diplomat in Southeast Asia once told me how his father used his position to secure sexual favors from Asian women in the war zone. Taken as a youth one night on a prove-your-manhood prowl of brothel life in a small town in Thailand, he watched in inner horror as his father ogled and patronized the young Thai women—some of them silicone-breasted, their eyes surgically sliced to look Caucasian and therefore more desirable to GIs. "It was simple," he told me, "the Cong were gooks to be snuffed; women were cunts to be fucked."

During the mud-and-trenches Vietnam War, a training refrain from boot camp was widely reported: "This is my weapon, this is my gun [the man points to his crotch]; this one's for killing, this one's for fun." During the high-tech Persian Gulf War, this chant reverberated as news slipped past military censors that pilots on the aircraft carrier USS *John F. Kennedy* had watched pornographic movies before flying bombing missions.[16] The pedagogy was all too familiar: inciting men's aggression and training men to view "the other" as the enemy through sexualized hate and fear.

Electoral politics do not disrupt the status quo of militarism, and they therefore do not disrupt the status quo of rape.

Answer #4: **Rape sells, so rape pays.** You won't find the pro-rape lobby in any Washington, D.C., office. But you will find them marketing pro-rape scenarios in film and video pornography and defending their pro-rape propaganda in "civil liberties" circles and high-toned journals of liberal opinion. To these folks, some of whom donate generously to campaign war chests, the rapist appetite creates a lucrative market segment—for heavy-metal sadism, for hate rap, for slasher films, for masochistic fashion. It's the classic American combination of free speech and free enterprise, and no candidate for office wants to catch flak from this powerful contingent. Consider, for instance, the woes of nomination contender Albert Gore in the 1988 presidential primary when his wife, Tipper, suggested a link between sexual violence and pornographic media: the music press especially treated her like a prudish cartoon. Candidate Dukakis found in his campaign manager Susan Estrich someone who could perhaps keep him out of this fray. After all, in a 1985 case before the United States Court of Appeals for the Seventh Circuit, Estrich had signed her name to an amicus brief that, among other things, categorically denied a link between rape and pornography and in fact lauded pornography as an empowering opportunity for women to explore their rape fantasies.[17]

To really stand up forcefully to the pro-rape lobby, a politician would need to be unusually high-minded—and have unusually deep pockets.

Answer #5: **There's a widespread belief that you can't really do anything to end rape.** "Some men will inevitably rape. It's probably men's nature—who knows? Rape—like death and taxes—will always be with us. The best that can be hoped is a few legal reforms, more humane treatment for victims, and—if you're a woman—dumb luck." This is a profoundly nihilistic view, one that is tacitly shared across most of the political spectrum, from left to right. It seems that only radical feminists still believe rape is stoppable. They are the vocal optimists—and also the "man-hating extremists," according to everyone else.

A candidate for political office won't articulate a vision of basic change if people don't believe in the possibility of basic change. And vice versa: People don't believe in the possibility of basic change in part because their leaders do not want them to.

If this deafening silence continues to surround sexual violence against women, are we as a nation left to conclude that we have both the leaders *and* the rape rate we deserve?

I fervently hope not.

President George Bush, on his way to a 1989 speech before the American Association of University Women, happened to spend some time talking with women in a runaway shelter in New York City. Hearing of the brutality of their experiences reportedly so moved him that later in his speech he made this special (and, for a male politician, quite atypical) point:

> I am angered and disgusted by the crimes against American women and the archaic and unacceptable attitudes that all too frequently contribute to those crimes. . . . Fundamentally, violence against women won't subside unless public attitudes change. We must continue to educate police and prosecutors, judges and juries, and we must engender a climate where the message our children get from television and films, from schools and parents, is that violence against women is wrong.[18]

Fine words well spoken—but without any perceptible follow-through.

Could a president or campaigning presidential candidate make specific policy proposals about ending rape—and then actually achieve them in office? I believe so. And I have several concrete ideas about where to begin.

• **Rally the private sector.** Provide presidential leadership to enlist corporations, the Advertising Council, and print and broadcast media to mount a public-information campaign to refute myths about rape and to encourage rape reporting. Launch a media blitz even more massive than current ones against drug use (such as Partnership for a Drug-Free America) and HIV transmission (America Responds to AIDS). If you need to cost-justify it, tally the medical expenses and productivity losses due to sexual violence. Many good anti-rape media materials already exist. Find them, improve them if necessary, and—with clear-cut White House support—roll them out nationally.

• **Get behind sex education in public schools—seriously.** Call for the development and funding of comprehensive curricula that teach not just the facts of life, not just information about safer sex, but also the meaning of informed consent and bodily integrity, together with personal self-esteem values and sexual communication skills. For a model of what can be done to promote self-respect in the young, note the training program for the prevention of child sexual abuse that was in place throughout the California public school system, the legacy of California state legislator Maxine Waters (until Governor Deukmejian abruptly defunded it in 1990).

• **Make rape a real crime—a crime someone gets *convicted* for.** Promise to get tough with institutions receiving federal funding: hold them accountable, vow to withhold federal monies from colleges, for instance, if they do not turn campus rape complaints over to law-enforcement agencies, and if they do not implement meaningful rape-prevention education. Use your influence to urge Congress to make rape and other forms of sexual violence prosecutable as gender-bias crimes. Beef up sex-crimes prosecutorial staffs. Make sure they know what they're doing so they do it right.

• **Speak out against the pornography industry as a purveyor of pro-rape propaganda.** Does pornography "cause" rape? From a purely scientific point of view, causality is no more or less than *increased probability.* And there is no doubt whatever that some rapes are committed that would not have been committed without the influence of pornography. Just because we can't be certain *which* rapes and *which* pornography does not mean there is no link. Sociologist Russell, reviewing the extensive clinical and psychological evidence, points out that pornography "intensifies the predisposition" of some men to rape (and various researchers have found that twenty-five to sixty percent of college-age males are already so predisposed, by their own admission). Russell also points out that pornography "undermines some men's *internal* inhibitions against acting out their rape desires" (and as various researchers have found, measuring penile tumescence, twenty to thirty percent of young male subjects are sexually aroused by depictions of sex forced on a woman, and another ten percent are aroused by extreme sadism as well). Citing data correlating rape with pornography distribution and consumption, Russell further points out that pornography "undermines some men's *social* inhibitions against acting out their desires." As Russell observes, in response to those who say there is no causality in all the available evidence, "If researchers had insisted on being able to ascertain why Mr. X died from lung cancer after 20 years of smoking but Mr. Y did not before being willing to warn the public that smoking causes lung cancer, there would have been a lot more deaths from lung cancer."[19] Much pornography is actually a *documentary* of coercion and sexual abuse, and some rape-crisis centers report more and more rapes involving videotaping by perpetrators. So forget pro-family moralizing. Forget posturing about social purity. Speak to the real issue of human harm: Pornography that promotes rape is wrong. Pornography that is made from rape is wrong.

Then, once you're in office, commission a Justice Department task force to eventually replace our useless hodgepodge of obscenity laws with legislation that would allow victims of pornography to sue for violations of their civil rights. Under current laws, a movie of a rape is considered "protected speech," and it can be sold anywhere. Commit your administration to confront pornography as a civil-rights issue—and take the profit motive out of rape.[20]

NOTES

1. BrotherPeace is a project of the Ending Men's Violence Network, a national organization for profeminist projects and individuals whose work emphasizes community-based action projects to stop battery, rape, and pornography. For information, write EMV Network, 54 Mint Street, Suite 300, San Francisco, CA 94103.
2. A transcript of the debate, broadcast live October 13, 1988, appeared October 14 in the *New York Times*.
3. National Crime Victim Center, "Rape in America: A Report to the Nation," April 23, 1992.
4. See Margaret T. Gordon and Stephanie Riger, *The Female Fear* (New York: The Free Press, 1989).
5. Survey conducted in 1978 by Diana E. H. Russell (using California statutory definition of rape) and reported in her book *Sexual Exploitation: Rape, Child Sexual Abuse, and Workplace Harassment* (Beverly Hills: Sage Publications, 1984), p. 35.
6. National Crime Victim Center, p. 2.
7. National Crime Victim Center, p. 2. Russell extrapolation calculated at forty-four percent of half the total urban population, which in the 1990 census was 187,053,487 (U.S. Census Bureau).
8. Arthur F. Schiff, "Rape in Other Countries," *Medicine, Science and the Law 11*, no. 3 (1971), pp. 139–143, cited in Russell, p. 30.
9. Federal Bureau of Investigation, *Uniform Crime Reports: 1990* (Washington, D.C.: U.S. Department of Justice), pp. 15–17.
10. "Survey of Victims Shows Increase in Violent Crime," *New York Times*, 20 April 1992, p. B12.

11. Susan Estrich, *Real Rape* (Cambridge: Harvard University Press, 1987).

12. "Onward, Women," *Time*, 4 December 1989, p. 82.

13. Ibid., pp. 80–89.

14. See, of course, the classic *Against Our Will: Men, Women and Rape*, by Susan Brownmiller (New York: Simon and Schuster, 1975).

15. Friedrich Nietzsche, *Thus Spake Zarathustra* in *The Philosophy of Nietzsche* (New York: The Modern Library, 1954), p. 69.

16. "U.S. Censors Story on X-Rated Films," *Boston Sunday Globe*, 27 January 1992, p. 16.

17. "Brief Amici Curiae of Feminist Anti-Censorship Taskforce, et al." in *American Booksellers Association, Inc., et al.* v. *William H. Hudnut III, et al.*, April 8, 1985.

18. As reported in the *Boston Globe*, 27 June 1989.

19. Diana E. H. Russell, "Pornography and Rape: A Causal Model," *Political Psychology 9*, no. 1, March 1988, pp. 41–73.

20. For more background and a bibliography, see "Confronting Pornography as a Civil-Rights Issue" in John Stoltenberg, *Refusing to Be a Man* (New York: Penguin USA/Meridian, 1990). See also Andrea Dworkin and Catharine A. MacKinnon, *Pornography and Civil Rights: A New Day for Women's Equality* (published by Organizing Against Pornography, 1988, distributed by Southern Sisters, Inc., 411 Morris Street, Durham, North Carolina 27701).

JOHN STOLTENBERG (M.Div., M.F.A.) is the author of *Refusing to Be a Man: Essays on Sex and Justice,* a revolutionary examination of male sexual identity (Penguin USA/Meridian, 1990), and *The End of Manhood: A Book for Men of Conscience* (Dutton, 1993). He is a frequent lecturer at colleges, conferences, and antisexist men's gatherings. A longtime profeminist activist, he is cofounder of Men Against Pornography in New York; he conceived and cofounded BrotherPeace: An International Day of Actions to End Men's Violence; he is featured in *Sex & Selfhood: New Issues for Men of Conscience,* a video series for sexual-assault prevention education (Minneapolis: Kundshier/Manthey Video Design, 1992); and he has spoken and lobbied for passage of the Dworkin-MacKinnon civil-rights antipornography ordinance, which would empower victims of pornography to fight back through civil lawsuits.

ACTIVISM

A college teacher uses the collaborative writing of plays to help her students come to consciousness; men and women learn and teach one another to care for victims of the rape culture; legislative activists lobby for change; reformers work to transform school curricula and the military from within. Their reports describe a broad spectrum of possible changes. Their activism rides the crest of change. Some of the work is deeply controversial and potentially in conflict with other social values like freedom of speech and market freedom. These writers point out that behind the screen of "freedom," however, are dangers to women's safety and welfare.

THE DATE RAPE PLAY:
A Collaborative Process

by Carolyn Levy

We thought we were prepared for the response,
but we were amazed at the outpouring of emotion from
spectators. They greeted the play with joy and pain. For
some, it reaffirmed that they were not alone in their
experiences. For others it opened a topic for discussion that had previously been closed tight.
For still others, it raised questions about
behaviors and attitudes.

(House lights down. Eight actors enter and face the audience. A man steps forward.)

Man: Every six minutes someone in America is raped. The vast majority of them are raped by someone they know.

(He checks his watch. A bell rings. Blackout. Throughout the play the bell will ring every six minutes.)

IN 1992 I created a play with a group of my students at Macalester College about the troubling issue of date rape. We titled our play *Until Someone Wakes Up*. The project grew out of our department's interest in community-based theater; we wanted to create an experience for our students that was outside the Broadway model of a five-week rehearsal period of a set script.

My own background had been in another form. For eight years I was the artistic director of the Women's Theater Project in the Twin Cities where we had created new plays by and about women. As a collaborative enterprise, we had worked with a wide variety of writers, designers, performers, and directors as well as community groups and women's organizations. It was this experience I wanted to bring to my students, to teach them another mode of working, one that is central to some of the best theater being made in this country. We chose to do a community-based project and then cast about for appropriate subject matter.

The subject of date and acquaintance rape seemed to be everywhere around us. When I read Robin Warshaw's book, *I Never Called It Rape*, and learned that one in four college women has been or will be the victim of rape or attempted rape, I found I could not walk into any gathering of students without mentally counting off the women ("One, two, three, *four*"), knowing that a fourth of them had likely experienced this violence in their lives. But I read on and learned that women are not alone in being victims: men are raped, too. I found that if I looked hard at the society and culture in which we are living, if I really examined forces at work on our students as they grow up, then the rape statistics were not a surprise. The climate is ripe for such things to happen. We are not taught well what it is to be a man or a woman. We don't have a lot of good models for healthy relationships. We receive confusing messages about whom to be and how to be—both men and women. The issue had lots of gray areas—perfect for theatrical exploration.

Mom: Georgie Porgie, pudding pie,

Boy: Kissed the girls and made them cry!

Voice: One in twelve of the male students surveyed had committed acts that met the legal definition of rape or attempted rape.

Girl: Mommy, Gary threw snowballs at me today and it hurt.

Mom: Oh honey, that means he likes you.

Voice: Only twenty-seven percent of the women whose sexual assault met the legal definition of rape thought of themselves as rape victims.

Many groups collaborated on this project. Foremost was the support of the Dramatic Arts and Dance Department; the process owed its existence to the department's philosophy. In addition, many other groups helped in the research and development of the piece: the Sexual Assault Work Group, and their sponsors in Residential Life and Health Services, provided invaluable assistance, as did Campus Programs, the dean's office, and members of other academic departments who provided their expertise, notably anthropology, sociology, and the Women's Studies Program. Finally, we enlisted the support of organizations in our community—rape crisis centers, treatment facilities, counselors, and the media.

The collaboration of all these groups made this a truly community-based project. In addition, however, we found that the work was intensely personal. All of the participants examined their own lives and behaviors, and our collaborating groups not only helped us in our research but also made it possible for us to get support and counseling for the participants in the process and ultimately for the members of the audience who found they needed it.

Man: . . . It's not as if I am some rapist or something. It isn't like I beat her up or anything. And I was comforting her the whole time. I told her I didn't want her to miss out on a perfect opportunity. . . . It bothers me. I thought the first time having sex was supposed to be something great. Something special.

I spent fall semester 1991 deep in my own research on the subject. Assisted by several students, I began to work out the details of an interim class (our intensive January term) to research and develop the play. We assembled books, videotapes, and speakers, and we put classified ads in the student newspapers of the seven colleges in the Twin Cities for rape survivors and their loved ones who were willing to be interviewed. A counselor in a treatment center for sex offenders brought perpetrators who agreed to speak to us. As the project proceeded and word of what we were doing spread, more and more people sought us out to share their stories.

In interim term 1992 I taught a course with the cumbersome title "Community-Based Theater: Script Development Workshop." Twenty-one students (ten men and eleven women) participated in what turned out to be a crash course on date rape and sex in our culture. We began with the research in books and tapes. We heard speakers and learned about interviewing. Every member of the class conducted at least one interview with a rape survivor or perpetrator. They transcribed these and used them as the basis for monologues. We created improvisation based on this material. We examined different aspects of our culture—TV, music, commercials, magazines, toys, novels, and children's literature, etc. We discussed the lack of adequate sex-education programs. We noted the way our language expresses society's biases about sex and relationships. And we talked about ourselves and our own lives.

Writing began to pour out, some of it intensely personal. Some grew from the interviews we conducted. Some came in response to our "culture watch." Some was filled with agony, and some spoke to our desperate need for humor. By the end of January we had enough material for ten plays, maybe more.

Barbie: (Giggles.) Hi.

GI Joe: Well, hello.

Barbie: Where are you going?

GI Joe: On a dangerous secret mission to slay my evil enemies. And you?

Barbie: Malibu.

GI Joe: Perhaps we should go together.

Barbie: (Giggles.) You'll have to put my shoes on first.

GI Joe: No! I'll carry you! (Slings her over his shoulder.)

Barbie: Ooo! You're much more interesting than Ken!

What followed was a period of writing, rewriting, editing, and organizing. Ultimately I worked with a small group of students to synthesize
the material that had been generated in the class. From that work, we
created a spine of scenes that examined how we grow up in this culture,
from earliest nursery rhymes to college dating. We arranged them
chronologically, as if one set of children were growing up through a
series of scenes, and then we took the stories of rapes told by survivors
and perpetrators in monologues, scenes, triplets, and duets and placed
them between the scenes in the spine. What emerged, with humor where
we found it appropriate, chronicled the years of maturation and simultaneously told female and male tales of painful experiences.

The rewriting overlapped with the casting and rehearsals. When I cast
the show in February, I knew I needed four men and four women to play
a variety of roles. I looked for a diverse group of actors to tell the many
stories in the play. The cast included some members of the interim class
and some new people. With a production team, many of them class
members, we began the next phase of the project—workshop rehearsals
for public presentation. We always billed our play as a work-in-progress
and allowed ourselves the freedom to change material right up until the
closing performance. The whole company experienced the workshop
process, where their own input in a given rehearsal might be reflected in
the next night's rewrites. New scenes were born from rehearsal improvi-
sations, and old scenes were reconceived.

Waiter: Would you like some coffee?

Woman: Yes, please.

Waiter: Just say when. (*Starts to pour.*)

Woman: There. (*He keeps pouring.*) That's fine. (*He pours.*)
         Stop! (*She grabs the pot; there is coffee everywhere.*)
         What are you doing? I said *stop.*

Waiter: Yes, ma'am.

Woman: Well, why didn't you stop pouring?

Waiter: Oh, I wasn't sure you meant it.

Woman: Look, of course I meant it! I have coffee all over my lap! You nearly burned me!

Waiter: Forgive me, ma'am, but you certainly looked thirsty. I thought you wanted more.

Woman: But—

Waiter: And you must admit, you did let me *start* to pour.

Woman: Well, of course I did. I wanted some coffee.

Waiter: See, there you go. A perfectly honest mistake.

We thought we were prepared for the response, but we were amazed at the outpouring of emotion from spectators. They greeted the play with joy and pain. For some, it reaffirmed that they were not alone in their experiences. For others it opened a topic for discussion that had previously been closed tight. For still others, it raised questions about behaviors and attitudes. The groups that had helped so much with the research were also there to help at performance time. The Sexual Assault Work Group and the Rape Crisis Center provided volunteers to hand out literature and to provide immediate help to any audience member who needed to talk. We created a program with steps to take if rape has happened to oneself or to a friend. For everyone, the play seemed to provoke discussion. We handed out response forms. Most poignant were those from several college students who said they wished they had seen the play in high school. Another woman wrote, "I wish I had seen this when I was a lot younger (I'm fifty-six). I was raped when I was twenty-one and had to deal with it alone." One woman wrote, "As a victim, it forced me to go back, get in touch, deal, and move forward to become a survivor."

In addition to informal responses from the members of the audience, we also asked two outside reviewers to critique the piece. A director and a playwright, both of whom have a great deal of experience workshopping new scripts, wrote critiques and met with us to discuss the play. From their ideas and from our own perspectives of how the play worked in front of an audience, we took a new look at the structure and the content. As we studied what we had done, several scenes seemed unnecessary; others seemed to need more focus in the writing; and still others needed additional material. Overall, our evaluation was positive: we felt that the piece accomplished what we set out to do and, with a minimum amount of rewriting, could be staged again.

The responses from the Macalester campus and from the other young people and educators who saw the show prompted our decision to take it on tour. We tackled the demands of rewriting and streamlined the staging to make the production more portable, and then we hit the road in September. Again, the purpose was twofold. We were anxious to bring the play to audiences who would benefit (we had already performed the play for one high school group that discussed it for months). In addition, the theater students who enjoyed the experience of creating and workshopping a new play were able to take that play on the road and learn about touring, about doing long-term work on a role, and about meeting the variety of audiences outside the walls of our college. The whole notion of "community-based theater" comes full circle when you create a play out of the words and experiences of a community and then take the play back to that community for performance.

> Woman: When we're babies, we're born knowing that if we
> scream at night, someone will take care of us. And I just want
> to know where that ability goes. Because sometimes I feel like
> screaming now, just yelling, until someone wakes up.

All quotes are from the play *Until Someone Wakes Up,* conceived and directed by Carolyn Levy and written by Carolyn Levy, Laura Bradley, C. Todd Griffin, Marcy Laughinghouse, David Page, Josh Schultz, Deborah Sengupta, Elizabeth J. Wood, Cara McChesney, Christopher Berg, C. Brianna Merrick, P. Jeffrey Nelsen, Philip Park, Tina Pavlou, K. Siobhan Ring, Alejandro Aguilera, Matt Lewis, Andrew Lyke, Laura E. Meerson, Jessica Mickens, Danielle O'Hare, and Jonathan Saltus.

CAROLYN LEVY is a theater director, teacher, and writer. She is the founder and artistic director of the Women's Theatre Project, which from 1980 to 1988 produced new plays by women about issues of importance to women and brought those plays out into the community in the Twin Cities and beyond. Most notable of these works were: *The Women Here Are No Different,* about battered women; *Red Light/Green Light,* both a play and videotape about adolescent girls; and three touring shows, coauthored by Levy: *Life in the Pink Collar Ghetto,* about women and work; *Make It Better,* about nurses; and *Daughters Arise,* about women in religion. These plays were performed all over the country, often in workplaces, and at schools and conferences.

As a teacher, Levy has developed theater programs for students in kindergarten through graduate school. She has taught at Macalester College and Hamline University. She has also consulted on curriculum development and has created programs for training in the arts. Levy lives in St. Paul with her two daughters, Rose and Georgia.

OUTSIDE IN: A MAN IN THE MOVEMENT

by Richard S. Orton

Ultimately, it is the job of men to wake other men up. But
if social change is a goal of rape crisis centers and shelters,
is it not in the best interest of these groups to challenge,
support, and educate men to do this work—
men who, in turn, challenge, support, and
educate other men to do the work?

IN 1978 I BECAME public education director of the Austin Rape Crisis Center. I was unaware of just how unusual it was to hire a man at a rape crisis center at that time, but the woman who hired me, Sylvia Callaway, knew that it would be controversial. She had also carefully considered her rationale for this action. She believed that the elimination of sexual violence involved women taking the initiative to reorient and reeducate receptive men on the sources of this violence and, in the process, creating a new partnership for social change.

In the years I have done this work, the term "odd man out" has acquired a special meaning for me, not just because I have often been the only male in a room full of women, but also because most of the men I have met who do anti-sexual violence work do so *outside* of rape crisis centers and shelters. In the earlier days I sometimes felt that being hired to work in a center was somehow less appropriate than creating my own organization, such as R.A.V.E.N. in St. Louis or E.M.E.R.G.E. in Boston.

Another source of confusion over the years has been the contrast between my relationships with female colleagues in Austin and the rhetoric on "men in the movement" expressed at conferences of the National Coalition Against Sexual Assault (NCASA). For the most part, I have worked with self-confident women who could separate their personal anger at men from their valuing of us as allies. Contrary to the rhetoric, they were willing to invest time and energy in individual men whom they considered educable. I understand that many women do not believe it is their role or responsibility to do this, and I respect that attitude. I am not saying that I feel *entitled* to this attention from women, only that I am grateful it has been offered.

I have always understood women's willingness to invest time in men as coming from a particular vision of social change, which I came to share. That vision defines rape crisis centers and shelters as, *in part,* places where women and men relearn how to interact with each other, replacing relationships based on power with relationships based on balance and respect. Such an objective is clearly secondary to the need to provide safe space for healing, but it complements the community education component most centers and shelters have. In addition to being healing places, centers and shelters can be places where women and men do some of the practical work of redefining male-female relationships— not the *only* places, but good places if both parties are willing. Most men have no experience with woman-centered and woman-led organizations. Such environments can require men to confront their power and entitlement issues and give them the opportunity to view reality from a radically different perspective.

I want to approach the "men in the movement" question from within the much larger and more important issue of social change. For me, social change is a process of *un*learning gender- and power-based behavior that has proved dysfunctional, then *re*learning respectful, empowering behavior with no reference to gender (or race, or sexual orientation, etc.). This process, as usual, takes time and practice to fully realize. It is as if we—women and men—are waking up from a long, dulling sleep. (For some, it is a nightmare.) Some of us are already awake, others in various stages of waking. The landscape we see as we begin to open our eyes looks unfamiliar and, perhaps, a bit threatening at first. But, after looking around for a while, we find something strangely attractive about it.

Since 1978 I have been in a "waking up process" induced by working in a rape crisis center, and I have observed other men engaged in the same process, at least partially as a result of their training and work at the center. This is not an end in itself. Ultimately, it is the job of men to wake other men up. But if social change is a goal of rape crisis centers and shelters, is it not in the best interest of these groups to challenge, support, and educate men to do this work—men who, in turn, challenge, support, and educate other men to do the work?

I want to propose that recruiting men into rape crisis centers and shelters as staff and volunteers can facilitate the goals for social change of the anti-sexual violence movement. One way to evaluate this proposal is to examine the life changes men working within rape crisis centers or shelters undergo in those environments over a period of time, then ask to what degree, if any, that transformation motivates them to work for social change. In other words, can the practice of bringing men into woman-centered programs create new agents for social change who happen to be men? This is an important question if you believe, as I do, that ending men's violence requires the proactive involvement of profeminist men with other men, in concert with the work feminist women have done and continue to do.

I know of no way to approach this question objectively. Outside of

Austin I have no idea how many men work in these programs or what their experiences might be like. I can only speak for myself.

If there is a constant to what I have experienced over the years it is that the full meaning of key experiences was not readily apparent to me. In the early years, especially, I had experiences that, in a most profound way, were unprecedented in my insulated male existence. It was only after much time had passed that I was able to understand what these experiences meant.

Two events stand out for me: my first lesson in male humility occurred less than a year after being hired at the Austin Rape Crisis Center (ARCC). Sylvia Callaway, then the executive director at ARCC, and I went to the first conference of the National Coalition Against Sexual Assault (NCASA) held in Lake Geneva, Wisconsin, in August of 1979. The conference took place at a rustic camp on the lake, complete with bunk beds and dining hall. Out of more than two hundred conferees I was one of six men. Although accustomed to being in a minority, I was more self-conscious than usual. I was pleased with my involvement as a man on the "right side" of the issue, but I was not at all sure how I would be regarded here. After all, this was hardly Austin, where I was supported by Sylvia, who had hired me, and the other women with whom I worked. There I represented a philosophical issue made concrete—a man working to stop rape from *inside* the movement. On this issue, the Austin Rape Crisis Center was a pioneer. So my attendance at the founding conference of NCASA was a venture into unknown territory.

Everyone seemed to take my presence right in stride. No overt hostility, no angry glares, no rude remarks. Just business as usual. But, for the most part, the conferees weren't particularly warm either. The "I'm so glad a man is here" remarks were less common than my feeling of "I'm not being noticed at all," a feeling to which I was unaccustomed.

The first workshop I attended stands out most for me. I was the only man in a group of twenty-five or thirty women. I remember nothing about the substance of the workshop, only the feeling I had after being there for an hour and a half, a new feeling. I was vaguely confused, as if I were there, yet *not* there. I felt *invisible*. The women went about their business *without reference to me*.

It took me years to figure out what had happened that afternoon. As a male—as a *white* male—I was accustomed to having women defer to me. Not in a pronounced way, but more out of politeness than anything else. Though I was never conscious of expecting such deference, I missed it when it wasn't there. My sense of self, my identity, was conditioned by having women regard me as something special.

Many years after that first NCASA conference I was at a conference for profeminist men. One of the keynote speakers, Harry Brod, was talking about his experiences with men who viewed feminism and feminists as "antimale." In commenting on where he thought this attitude comes from, he made a statement that took me back to Lake Geneva and sat me down again in that workshop. He said that what many men most misunderstand about feminism (a misunderstanding that leads them to view feminism as antimale) is that *it is not about men at all.* And this, he said, is what is so frightening about feminism to so many men.

What those women were doing in that workshop at Lake Geneva *was not about me.* While I did not experience it as being *against* me, I did experience their way of being together without including me as something completely new. And I did not know what to make of it.

That experience, though I did not comprehend it at the time, was a great gift to me. It was the first time I was forced to confront my own belief in masculine entitlement, something that had been invisible to me before. Masculine privilege is often so subtle and unremarkable in practice that it is easily missed. The process of discovering cultural truths rendered invisible by centuries of denial and political suppression may threaten men's comfortable view of themselves and their place in the world. For many men, *not about me* translates into *against me* because it challenges the idea that women exist to take care of men.

I regard my experience at Lake Geneva as a necessary balance to the support I was receiving at ARCC. Indeed, it made me aware for the first time just how much I took the traditional male-female roles for granted, and just how subtle and invisible they can be. Since then I have often felt as if I were doing a balancing act between two parts of myself—the old patriarchal, traditional male part (relatively benign, but still very much alive) and the newer, less defined part that I always seemed to be in search of. Men who take this work seriously and find themselves getting deeper and deeper into it may feel as if they are aiming themselves into a void. Role models are hard to find. For all the discussion and general verbiage generated by the so-called men's movement, only the profeminist wing challenges us to confront the part of ourselves that has caused pain in the world, while also affirming our innate worth as human beings.

Perhaps this is the tightrope that we must learn to walk. But tightrope walking is difficult. Sometimes we fall. Success involves learning how to balance opposing forces. It involves, in this case, transforming old, dysfunctional gender habits into new, workable, mutually affirming ways for women and men to be together in the world.

The second experience occurred within a year of the first.

Almost all of my work at ARCC had involved coordinating the educational outreach of ARCC to the community, including doing educational presentations and training and supervising a volunteer speakers' bureau. One or two years before, as a newly hired staff person, I had gone through our training program for volunteers. I had some experience on the hotline, but had never done crisis intervention face-to-face. That was not part of my job and not something I particularly wanted to do, though, as a staff person, I knew that I had to be prepared for it.

One Saturday night around midnight the hotline volunteer called, and I had to go to the hospital emergency room. I was the only person available. As I drove down there, like anyone in that situation for the first time, I was nervous and trying to remember all the points made in training about crisis intervention. Plus, there was the fact that I was a male. I had no idea how the woman I was to meet would respond to that. Our policy was to provide a female volunteer if a male was unacceptable, but no one else was available that night.

As I entered the emergency room I saw a young woman wearing a green hospital gown sitting on a bed. A nurse was standing beside her doing something to her hair. I introduced myself, asked her how she felt, and hoped she couldn't hear the pounding in my chest. She replied, calmly, that she was doing better now. The nurse, I saw, was washing blood out of the woman's long brown hair. A doctor had just put twenty-four stitches in her scalp. She told me her name was Sandy. Sandy, it appeared, was calmer than I was.

I knew, of course, that a "normal" response for a person in Sandy's situation could be almost anything. I was greatly relieved that she seemed glad I was there and that we were able to communicate comfortably. Sandy had recently graduated from a midwestern university and was newly hired in Austin. She told me that as she was leaving a shopping mall that afternoon a young man had approached her, saying that his car wouldn't start. He asked her to give him a ride to a friend's house nearby. He was about her age, polite—and she was accustomed to helping people out, having grown up on a farm.

She ended up in a ditch outside of town where he raped her, then beat her with a pistol. She found help at a farmhouse.

Sandy had to have X-rays and a rape exam before we could leave. In the several hours it took for her release, she said many of the things a woman in that situation says, and I responded as best I could. Other than the relief I felt at Sandy's acceptance of me, I don't remember much about how I felt while I was there. I was trying hard to do everything "right" and must have put my own feelings on hold.

Around four or four-thirty in the morning she was ready to be released. The only friends she had in Austin were her boss and his wife, since she had been in town such a short time. Sandy asked me to call her boss's wife, tell her what had happened, and ask if she could stay with her. That done, we got in my car and headed for a new subdivision on the outskirts of town. Upon our arrival we went in, sat, and talked for a while with her friend. Then Sandy went to bed.

The sun was coming up as I left. I felt strange. Fatigue, I thought. I was numb from the previous six or seven hours. But about halfway home the numbness ended, and I broke down. One moment I was fine, the next I was sobbing uncontrollably. I didn't see this coming, and I was unable to control it when it did. I was shocked and frightened at what was happening to me. I had never experienced anything like this before and now here I was, driving down the highway at daybreak falling apart.

As before, it took me several years to put this experience in perspective. Nothing that I had to do that night surprised me. I had an idea of what to expect in the emergency room from the training I had received, and I had heard rape survivors tell their stories. But that information was all *in my head.* I had read Brownmiller's *Against Our Will* and other writers of the time. I *knew* the dynamics of rape and the cultural context of such acts. I *talked* about it in educational presentations. But I did not *feel* it in my gut until that night.

Much more than my experience in Lake Geneva, that night with Sandy in the emergency room confronted me with blank spaces in my life that I associate with growing up male. Thirty-odd years of life had not prepared me to assimilate emotionally what happened to her. Women have an understanding of sexual assault born of their "at risk" status, which comes from *being* a woman. For me, and for most men, there is no such understanding, only a blank space.

It is easy to avoid the emotions associated with rape as long as we do not feel vulnerable to it.

Until that night, my work at the rape crisis center had been a job—an interesting job, a job that I enjoyed and found stimulating and challenging—but a job nonetheless. As I look back on it now, I think my time with Sandy began the process of turning a job into a lifetime commitment. Something in me changed forever that night.

Working in a rape crisis center has given me access to the world as women experience it; it has given me a chance to feel their vulnerability, their fear, and their sense of injustice. These feelings have created in me a personal imperative: the need to work for change.

But this opportunity is not available to many men. Trust and power issues keep many women in centers and shelters from being comfortable with men in their programs. Their concerns are easy to understand. Men created the problem of sexual violence, and most still do not grasp the connections between everyday sexism and violence. This creates mistrust.

But if women and men are to overcome their history and be able to redefine power in relationships, they, at some point, must *come together*, face-to-face, and learn to do this in real life—over the dinner table, in the workplace, and, in my view, in settings where women's experience is validated and women's leadership is guaranteed. Rape crisis centers and shelters are such places.

NOTES

1. It would be difficult to overstate the boldness of Sylvia Callaway's decision to hire me. Her willingness to take this chance, and her faith that I could learn what I had to learn, demonstrated her commitment to making allies of men instead of holding us at arm's length or assuming that we could be of no use in the struggle. She took a lot of heat in NCASA for that decision.

RICHARD S. ORTON moved to Austin, Texas, in 1971, after living in West Africa for two years as a U.S. Peace Corps volunteer. After completing a master's degree in musicology at the University of Texas in 1975, he worked with several nonprofit art organizations until being hired by the Austin Rape Crisis Center in 1978 as its public education director.

In 1984 he helped found the Child Assault Prevention Project in Austin, serving as its first executive director until mid-1986. He returned to the Austin Rape Crisis Center in 1989 as a member of its education staff and recently accepted a position with the Texas Department of Health as a sexual assault program specialist.

TRAINING FOR SAFEHOUSE

by Claire Buchwald

I understand that I have escaped violence at home not
because I am particularly strong or exceptional, but
because I have been lucky. . . . When I am half-asleep,
my partner lifts his hand and gently caresses my hair. I
cannot help but think about those women on whom a
hand is descending, a hand that is not gentle.

I SIT SHOULDER TO shoulder with two other women while we watch the videotape on the raised TV set. There are seventy-two of us in all, men and women, students and workers, survivors and the more fortunate.

Women on the screen tell us the truths of their existence, not philosophy but fact—the fact of events and of deep emotions. They bravely face the camera, revealing scars, wounds, and bruises on their bodies. They tell about how they tried to stop the violence, how they tried to shield the children, how they tried to be understanding of and loving to the men who abused them, how they often pleaded for their own lives, lives that no one had the right to bruise or threaten.

These are not weak or cowardly women; they are not meek. They are intelligent, creative, and beautiful. They are white, black, Hispanic, Native American, heterosexual and homosexual, married and not, rich, poor, and middle class. They are truly among the bravest people I have ever learned about.

In addition to the threats, the insults, the blows, and the rapes these women suffered from their lovers or husbands, they were beaten down by attitudes. Their families, former friends, therapists, and the "justice" systems of their communities asked them over and over, "What did you do to make him act that way?" or, "Why didn't you just leave?" with the implication, "This could never happen to me." Each of these women saw that the pain would be made out to be her fault. Somehow, she deserved to have her head beaten bloody against the kitchen floor. Somehow, she deserved to be tied down and raped.

People did not ask: "How could he make the choice to hurt you, systematically and powerfully, in every way he knew? How could he take advantage of your love?" Nor did they ask the equally important question: "Why do we—police, neighbors, family members, coworkers, law writers, and voters of our communities—allow this violence?"

I, who never go to horror movies, have just seen one. I realize that the actresses who simulate being clawed, burned, beaten, tied up, raped, and murdered on Hollywood sets are enacting, and perhaps setting an example for, those things that happen in real life, every day, to real women. Battering is the single major cause of injury to women. Half of all women will experience physical abuse from a spouse or partner in her lifetime. According to recent U.S. Department of Justice figures, every fifteen seconds a woman is seriously injured by her husband or partner.

That's 360 real women injured or killed during the hour-and-a-half viewing time of a violent movie that was made for the public's pleasure.

We have spent three hours discussing violence against women, children, and, occasionally, men. I feel too numb to participate in a brief discussion about what we have viewed. I know that letting this information into my life has changed me. I have been given the gift and the anguish of seeing more of the world and seeing it more clearly than ever before.

Outside, my partner, my most cherished friend, waits for me. In our years together, he has never hurt me, never tried to isolate me or lower my self-esteem. While I cry, he holds me gently. This warm fall evening I understand that I have escaped violence at home not because I am particularly strong or exceptional, but because I have been lucky. I wish that no woman ever had to experience the fear and isolation that the women in the videotape eloquently expressed.

On the long walk home, I tell him about the training session. The statistics and the stories I heard pour out of me. He is silent, but I can feel his shock. We are both newly aware as we walk and talk that, around us in the night, in the houses and apartment buildings we pass, violence is taking place in secret. At home we eat a snack, straighten the house together, and then cuddle in bed. When I am half-asleep, feeling safe and loving, my partner lifts his hand and gently caresses my hair. I cannot help but think about those women on whom a hand is descending, a hand that is not gentle.

Everyone in the group is tired the next morning. We are all yawning in the bright room of tiered, purple seats and smooth, white, curved desks. This is the second day of training to work in Safehouse, the shelter for battered women and children run by the local organization called the Domestic Violence Project, which is staffed primarily by volunteers. Founded in 1978, this is the oldest shelter in the state of Michigan.

At first I think that there are only a few survivors of domestic abuse at this meeting. Gradually, as the day progresses and people talk about experiences from their lives, I realize that maybe a third of us or more have been physically and emotionally battered and/or sexually abused, as adults or in childhood. I'm thinking about the fact that many people I know have probably been hurt in one of these ways and have felt that there was no recourse for them.

On this second day, we are learning to talk knowledgeably to battered women over the telephone, to give them information, and to help them come to terms with their feelings and their options. We are not allowed to tell anyone what to do, to give unasked-for advice, or to present our views. We are there to answer questions with honesty and candor. We can name the precious few resources available. We can help women sort through their own feelings. In answer to their questions, we may have to tell women some difficult truths:

—Yes, what they are living through is battering.

—No, there is no guarantee that their partner will change. There is no guarantee that peaceful times between violent episodes means the violence will not occur again.

—Yes, in most cases, the violence will become more severe and more frequent.

—No, leaving their partner—and usually, their money, possessions, family members, friends, and sometimes children—will not necessarily make them safe. In fact, they will be seventy-five percent more likely to be killed at the time they leave, separate from, or divorce their partner.

—Yes, in spite of the fact that they did nothing to bring on the abuse, it may well haunt them all their lives.

—And yes, if he asks for it, the husband is more likely than the wife to be given custody of the children, even when there is documentation that a husband has abused his wife and children.

Some of us will compose an on-call team of people who go out to provide support and information to women whose husbands or partners have been taken into custody. They may arrive to find a woman bleeding and in pain, a woman with weals on her body, or grooves on wrists and ankles where she has been tied. There will be children in these homes who have watched their father brutalize their mother. There will be children with marks of their own. The team will, at some places, meet with denial that *anything* happened at all. They will definitely encounter fear and isolation so great that it would be a cruel lie to call the woman free to leave. They will experience these situations in palatial homes and in low-income housing, in dormitories, apartments, and condominiums. And they will have to be out of the residence in an hour before the abuser, released on his recognizance, comes back.

We might be assigned to lobby for legislation in a system oftentimes shortsighted and lacking in sympathy, a system that finds it easier to blame victims than to hold criminals responsible for their actions.

Some of us will work as child-care providers and teachers to the children of battered women. We will try to show children that there are men and women who do not abuse. We will try to help them feel trust, confidence, and happiness. We will do our best to free them from guilt, shame, the constraint of secrets, and feelings of responsibility for the abusive behavior. We will build block castles with children who flinch when we lift our arms to put a high block in place. We will read sunny books to children who have been raped by their fathers or other relatives. We will listen to children talk about their waking or sleeping nightmares. We will try with all our ability to divert them into a solacing make-believe, to help them create with their own hands, to help them play together without looking fearfully behind them.

Others will speak to groups of people, many of whom don't believe that there really is such a thing as domestic violence. Some people will disregard what we have to say because they have defined us with a label—feminist, activist, do-gooder—that negates what we say. We will be introduced at community meetings by businessmen looking for an easy laugh, with comments such as "Does this mean I have to stop beating my wife?"

After this second day of training, I have conflicting emotions. I feel proud of what we are being trained to do. Yet knowing that we are relatively few and that the obstacles are great makes me deeply, bitterly sad. Programs like this one will have to be mighty and fortunate seeds to make a difference.

When I get home, I ride my old stationary bike. The wheels of the rusty orange cycle turn with a sound too close to the sound of screams. I count off the time elapsed. I need to manage forty or fifty minutes before I can stop and stretch out. As the minutes go by, I think about the women who are being hurt. Will they meet with additional distaste or distrust if their abusive lover is a woman? If they are poor, if they are not white, will they feel the unspoken words, "Naturally you get beaten. What's the big deal?" I cannot understand why this abuse continues to happen to so many women in this country. Why should anyone be hurt in her own home? I stop cycling after half an hour, feeling slightly sick to my stomach. I curl up and try to block out the anger. I make speeches in my head to inform people about the reach of violence into the lives of women and children everywhere, but that seems like such a slow way to help those who need help now, this day.

The third day of training; I'm no longer numb. I want to learn everything I can. Today the subject is child abuse, child sexual abuse, and neglect. After the sessions I wonder which of the scrubbed, well-dressed children in my suburban elementary school were tied up, hit, or used for sex at home and had to keep the secret to themselves for years, perhaps for always.

I meet some women I would like to talk with again. We'll see each other in two weeks for more training, but we exchange phone numbers so that we can talk in the meantime. We've all had friends ask, "Why are you spending time learning this stuff when they're not even paying you?" or sometimes with near disdain, "What does this have to do with *you?*" We need to talk to people who understand our fury.

That evening, I clumsily smash my bare foot into the bedroom door frame. I drop to the floor, rocking back and forth, holding my foot, feeling stupid for walking into a stationary object. And at the same time, I am filled with horror. What if this pain had been caused not by my carelessness but by someone whose object was deliberately to hurt me? What if that someone were the person who says he loves me? In ten minutes or so, my foot will no longer hurt. But what if I knew that pain and the anticipation of pain were going to be a daily part of my life and the lives of my children? How could I stand that knowledge?

For weeks afterwards, I am in a fervor of feeling. I read through the manual I bought at Safehouse. I study and memorize the facts. I consider the attitudes that have allowed and still permit and even foster violence by men against women and children. I want to be free of the burden of these sad truths, free of the need to fill every phone call, every conversation, with the statistics and examples I have to give.

Sitting at the kitchen table one evening preparing to speak to high school students about domestic violence, my thoughts wander to questions the training has raised for me: How can we make domestic violence more of a public issue? How can we change the climate of opinion so that men and women know that brutalizing someone you love is never justifiable? Are education and social pressure sufficient to change the behavior of abusers?

I make up my mind that I will not let daunting questions such as these keep me from acting on what I know. I will think instead about what I can do to reach others and involve them. If I refuse to be dissuaded from working to create change, I will move from being overwhelmed by the questions to being part of the answers.

CLAIRE BUCHWALD has been a public speaker for the Domestic Violence Project in Washtenaw County, Michigan, and in 1991 led a workshop on domestic violence at the University of California Women's Conference. Buchwald has a B.A. from Amherst College and an M.A. in Communication from the University of California, San Diego, where she is in a doctoral program. In 1990 and 1991, she cowrote and cohosted a University of California, San Diego, campus radio program about women's issues called "A Show of Our Own with a View." Buchwald writes about education and about gender issues in American culture, and she is the author of *The Puppet Book* (Plays, Inc., 1990).

MODEL FOR A VIOLENCE-FREE STATE

by Susan J. Berkson

Transforming a culture is not the work of an individual, a
summer, or a single week. The violence-free idea,
powerful as it is, carefully crafted as it is, has an effect
only if we continue to work on it.

Three conditions are necessary for true fellowship: The possession of a common ideal
involving a complete release from selfishness and
division. The discharge of a common task big
enough to capture the imagination and give
expression to loyalty. And the comradeship, the
'togetherness,' thus involved as we find out the
joy and power of belonging to an organic society. . . . We can find it at its fullest extent where
the ideal is highest and most exacting, where the
task extends and integrates every ounce of our
strength and every element of our being. . . .

—C. E. Raven[*]

Want to transform a culture?
Don't dictate.
Don't theorize.
Inspire.
Include.
Challenge.
Eliminate loopholes.
Prepare to be disappointed.
Carry on.

THE SUMMER OF 1991 was the worst summer in recent memory
for Minnesotans. Murder after murder, rape after rape, left women
enraged and ready to take all the usual actions: rallies, vigils, phone
calls, lobbying for stiffer sentencing.

I had lobbied, rallied, and vigiled before, to little effect.

One day, I passed a sign calling the surrounding neighborhood a
drug-free zone. Immediately I thought, why not a violence-free zone?
Why not make Minnesota the first violence-free state in the world? It
may be impossible, but so is the way we live now.

The idea seemed powerful, and equally appealing to men, who don't
see stopping the war on women as being in their self-interest. But a violence-free state was an idea behind which every citizen—female or male,

---

*Canon C. E. Raven, British theologian, quoted in *Alcoholics Anonymous Comes of Age*, Alcoholics
Anonymous Publishing, Inc., 1957, p. 276.

politician, business owner, civic leader, parent, child—could stand.

To involve four million people, the idea had to be intriguing yet broad, inclusive, and as nonthreatening as possible. Revolution was necessary, but so was revolutionary thinking and language.

But what did a "violence-free state" mean? How were we to get there? How do you make an entire state—4,375,099 people, 87 counties, 84,402 square miles—violence-free?

The most effective way to bring about this revolution was *not* to define the parameters. This would serve two purposes: (1) involving the citizenry in the creation, giving them ownership; and (2) avoiding the pitfalls of didacticism and conflicting theories. If four million people are involved in the creation of something, they are more likely to feel invested in it. In choosing this course, I was following the partnership model laid out by Riane Eisler in *The Chalice and the Blade.*

Every word counted in the statement of values. Instead of being a committee or a consortium, we called ourselves a *campaign*, something active. Our campaign was working toward an *ideal*, something to which we could aspire. We thought making Minnesota the *first* such state would inspire other states. And we let people know that every one of them—those already working toward the idea, those who wanted to help, and those who didn't have a clue—was critical to the success of our mission. As we said in our promotional material:

> Campaign for a Violence-Free Minnesota is working toward the ideal of making Minnesota the first violence-free state. The campaign depends upon the voluntary commitment of all parts of the Minnesota community, from individuals to major institutions, to accomplish its mission.

> Campaign for a Violence-Free Minnesota strives:

> 1. to serve as a clearinghouse for those already working to end violence,
> 2. to serve as a resource for individuals and groups who seek to end violence,
> 3. to challenge those not committed to ending violence,
> 4. to be a rallying point, an ideal, to which Minnesotans can aspire.

Our very existence posed a challenge, and we restated it in our mission statement. We crafted this mission statement to be as inclusive as possible, to challenge people everywhere we could, and to provide them with every available tool, increasing the chance of their participation:

> The Campaign for a Violence-Free Minnesota challenges Minnesotans to create a violence-free state, including, but not limited to homes, schools, workplaces, neighborhoods, and towns; to increase public awareness of the causes and costs of violence; and to provide resources for learning nonviolent alternatives to individuals and families, schools, businesses, organizations, and municipalities.

We hoped that this vision, crystal clear to us, would inspire every citizen. To provide a road map for reading a violence-free state, we next formulated these campaign goals and objectives:

• Create informed and supportive workplaces:

The Campaign for a Violence-Free Minnesota works with businesses to create safe workplaces where employees find an environment that is informed about the causes and costs of violence; that discourages language and images that encourage violence; that neither endorses nor sells products that encourage violence; and that educates management and employees on nonviolent conflict resolution.

In 1991 and 1992, Campaign for a Violence-Free Minnesota will:

1. create a violence-free workplace resolution,
2. encourage adoption of the workplace resolution,
3. establish and publicize a Violence-Free Minnesota information center.

• Increase public awareness about violence and nonviolent alternatives:

Campaign for a Violence-Free Minnesota can be a powerful vehicle for communicating to Minnesotans the causes and costs of violence. The campaign helps artists, arts institutions, and the entertainment industry reach audiences with work that responds to violence and promotes nonviolent alternatives. It engages the media in ways that promote broader public awareness and discussion. The campaign will:

1. Design a violence-free logo for stickers.
2. Initiate dialogue about images and language that encourage violence.
3. Organize a media watch to empower audiences to register their concerns.

• **Encourage Minnesotans to make their homes violence-free:**

Campaign for a Violence-Free Minnesota seeks to reinforce the right of every child, woman, and man to live free from the fear of violence within the home. In 1991 and 1992, the campaign will design guidelines for a violence-free home.

• **Encourage schools to take the violence-free pledge:**

Providing children with violence-free schools, educating them about the causes of violence, and guiding them to nonviolent alternatives are key to a violence-free Minnesota.

• **Challenge organized religion to respond:**

Campaign for a Violence-Free Minnesota challenges clergy to take a leadership role in the campaign by making their houses of worship violence-free zones and inspiring their congregations to work to end violence.

MAKING THE WORDS FLESH

We envisioned ourselves in a small central office where information about all available resources could be entered and accessed in a computer. We wanted an 800 number so that we could serve as a violence-free resource center for individuals, families, businesses, schools, organizations, and municipalities throughout the state. By providing this collective, coordinated approach, we could make current programs and efforts more widely known, better utilized, and ultimately more effective.

Achieving a consensus on this vision was challenging. Striving to adhere to an egalitarian partnership model, we backtracked to explain and justify our work to newcomers who attended later meetings. We strove to work in concert with established antiviolence groups, utilizing their expertise, sometimes assuaging their suspicions. We worked on building broad community support, calling politicians, schools, and community, religious, and business leaders. Difficult and time-consuming as it was, this helped us to clarify and refine our vision, making us better advocates for the violence-free idea.

One of those attending every meeting, from the first general meeting to each of the small violence-free Minnesota meetings, was a staffer from the governor's office. One day she called and asked to meet in the capitol cafeteria, where she pulled out a press release announcing the governor's declaration of the first violence-free Minnesota week. She showed me a poster, press kit, and other collateral with a violence-free logo.

The governor had been having a hard time selling a "Men Against Violence Week" when the "Violence-Free Minnesota" idea was mentioned. This he liked, and a full-court press was on, including letters to businesses, schools, churches, and synagogues, asking them what they were doing to make Minnesota violence-free. Also included in the program were fund-raising, posters, personal appearances, and a great deal of publicity.

With a flourish of pomp, press, and my language and ideas, the governor inaugurated Violence-Free Minnesota Week. Newspapers editorialized on the idea. Schools included it in their curriculum.

Minnesota has since marked its second annual violence-free Minnesota week. Not that we are violence-free for a week, or even a day. St.

Paul has had a record number of homicides. Minneapolis ranks second per capita in rapes in the U.S.

We have the week, the logo, and the poster. Funding for a State Office of Violence Prevention was provided for a year. A Committee to End Violence and Sexism in the Media was formed. People are more aware, more concerned—and more violent.

Transforming a culture is not the work of an individual, a summer, or a single week. The violence-free idea, powerful as it is, carefully crafted as it is, has an effect only if we continue to work on it. In the hands of state government, it is but a week. The long-range work of increasing public awareness of the causes and costs of violence; of serving as a resource for those who seek to end violence; of creating informed and supportive workplaces, homes, and schools—this is nothing short of a revolution, and governments don't make revolutions.

Neither could we. We're going to have to settle for evolution.

The task is big. The ideal is high and exacting. While the rate of violent crime has continued to grow, so have disgust, outrage, and a general sense that something must change. The status quo is no longer acceptable to the majority of people.

By itself, the campaign for a violence-free Minnesota does limited good. In concert with other efforts, it can help transform the rape culture. The transformation is best undertaken in many ways, at many levels. No one has a monopoly on method.

In remarks made to a 1992 audience at the University of Minnesota, Anita Hill said, "We cannot stand back and expect that leadership will take the initiative on gender issues and race issues, and so what I want to do is challenge you to do what I have committed myself to do: to talk about these issues, to urge leadership on these issues, to urge us to continue to move forward. We have a window of opportunity here. We've got the world's attention."

One week a year, the attention of the state of Minnesota is focused on the idea of freedom from violence. We, who came to think of ourselves as *trusted servants of the idea,* are committed to taking this one-week window of opportunity and talking about it, pushing leadership on it, and continuing our forward movement.

This is the part we can play in this evolution.

SUSAN J. BERKSON is a writer and broadcast commentator whose column appears in the Minneapolis *Star Tribune*. Berkson, who attended Princeton University and holds degrees from Macalester College and the University of Minnesota, writes often on politics and gender.

Her work has appeared in the *Chicago Tribune*, the *St. Paul Pioneer Press*, the *Minnesota Women's Press*, and the *San Diego Union-Tribune*. *Minnesota Monthly* and *Mpls.St.Paul* are among magazines where her writing has appeared.

In the summer of 1991, Susan J. Berkson founded the Campaign for a Violence-Free Minnesota, for which she received a commendation from the governor. In addition to her *Star Tribune* column, Berkson is currently working on a book and on her second film.

COMMODIFICATION OF WOMEN: Morning, Noon, and Night

by Sarah Ciriello

Companies that conduct business meetings, luncheons, or dinners at topless and strip clubs need to realize that expense-accounting their employees' participation at these clubs sends a confusing message to all their employees. At a time when companies are adopting policies that address the serious issue of sexual harassment in the workplace, they are communicating that it's all right to treat women as sex objects during the course of business entertainment.

THROUGHOUT HISTORY, ANY imagined or real forward movement by women has been seen by many men as a threat, and unfortunately such antifeminist feelings are shared by some women. Given this tendency, it is no wonder that we are now seeing an increasing amount of sexism and misogyny in the general entertainment, leisure, and service industries. This saturation has increased the exploitation of women while at the same time creating an illusion that women who are used as the means to an end (read: profit) are really sexually liberated women who, unlike feminists, appreciate men and either enjoy the status of sex object or deny such status altogether. I want to show the ways in which the pornography industry has filtered into the general entertainment, leisure, and service industries. By looking at some of the current trends in these industries, we can see how such industries, along with the help of the mass media, (1) sexualize women's labor, (2) condone and contribute to sexual harassment, and (3) put real women in danger. After examining the impact of these forms of *entertainment, leisure,* or *service,* I will address some solutions that individuals and groups are adopting in order to fight back, as well as other forms of direct action that we can take to change our culture and thus improve the status of women in our society.

CURRENT TRENDS IN THE LEISURE, ENTERTAINMENT, AND SERVICE INDUSTRIES

Consider the current themes and visual displays of popular pinball games. Over the years these games have become sexist and sometimes misogynist. Although many people dismiss them as annoyances, we ought to consider the images and messages being sold to children, adolescents, teens, and adults through this type of general entertainment.

The "Playboy" pinball game is one of many that use sexist images. Next to the game stands a cardboard display of a *Playboy* bunny. The game's display board includes women in bikinis and men in business suits. Every time the ball hits the target, the player, and anyone nearby, hears the moaning and groaning of a woman supposedly having an orgasm.

This particular game and the forms of entertainment, leisure, and service to be discussed below share a common theme: they are all examples of the demarcation of leisure by gender in a heterosexist and homophobic society. Women are the entertainment, men the entertained. By mainstreaming this demarcation, we sanction and perpetuate the objectification of women and the attitudes and behaviors associated with this view of women.

A review of the recent trend in "breastaurants" demonstrates how some entrepreneurs have managed to sexualize the job of serving food and drink. Hooters of America, Inc., has made its way around the country. Hooters, which just happens to be one of many slang terms for women's breasts, began in 1983 in Clearwater, Florida. By February 1993 there were 96 restaurants in 23 states[1]; the company expects to reach 200 by the end of 1994. The initial investment for a Hooters franchise is around $400,000 in addition to the lease, but if the owners play by the rules they're guaranteed a sizeable return.[2]

Hooters, which does not hire male servers, refers to its female servers as "Hooters Girls." Their uniform consists of running shorts, midriff-bared T-shirts, and running shoes. The Hooters logo of an owl with eyes in the form of a woman's breasts and nipples appears on the front of their T-shirts with the slogan "More than a mouthful" on the back. These T-shirts, Hooters hats, calendars of Hooters Girls, and videotapes of Hooters Girls frolicking at a swimming pool are sold in retail outlets at every Hooters restaurant. Annual income from this merchandise is $6 million[3]; combined merchandise and restaurant sales totaled $100 million in 1991.[4]

The high profits of Hooters are dependent upon the simultaneous acceptance and denial of the sexual exploitation of women, where women's labor is devalued and trivialized by skimpy outfits and the low wage of $2.06 an hour. In addition, management asks the women to volunteer in charity drives "to soften the bimbo image."[5] *Forbes* notes that "the restaurants pay the *girls* [my emphasis] $10 an hour to serve as animated billboards" at local golf tournaments, football games, and charity events.[6] In September 1992, a Minneapolis Dodge dealership used Hooters Girls to draw potential customers to a reception; it must have slipped management's mind that fifty-five to sixty percent of their customers are women.

In our society, a woman still has an excellent chance of becoming famous if she sheds her clothes for a commercial film or for a pornographic magazine. Not surprisingly, Lynn Austin, who appeared as a

1986 centerfold in *Playboy*, later became Hooters' prize billboard *girl*. *Forbes* describes this as "the kind of big break other Hooters girls—mostly local college students—are waiting for. Which is one reason why they'll work for only $2.06 an hour, compared with an average starting wage of $5 at McDonalds."[7] Such remarks show that *Forbes* is part of the men's club that believes women want to take their clothes off. A framed *Playboy* cover appears on the wall at Hooters, along with a sign reading: Men: No shirt no shoes no service; Women: No clothes free food.

Mike McNeil, marketing vice president of Hooters of America, Inc., believes that Hooters "doesn't cross the line of what the majority of people think is acceptable."[8] He obviously didn't discuss this statement with a representative sample of women in the United States. A restaurant listing in one of Minneapolis's weekly newspapers describes Hooters as a restaurant with an "adult" setting. Isn't it time to start replacing the term "adult" with "sexist" where appropriate?

Ed Droste, one of the six founders of Hooters, claims that "the only market we don't appeal to is teen-agers."[9] This is an interesting statement when we know that radio stations and newspapers carry Hooters ads, with one breast-eyed owl ad reading: "Touchdown at Hooters after the game! Fun Fun Fun 'til your daddy takes the T-Bird away!" In the Minneapolis area, feminists learned that a coupon book being distributed by the local Boy Scouts of America contains a Hooters coupon that reads: "Only a Rooster Gets a Better Piece of Chicken!!!"

What do the women get besides $2.06 an hour? According to *Forbes*, tips can run as high as $150 a night. In exchange, these women have the *opportunity* to work for a company whose slogans depend on sexual innuendos: "More than a mouthful," "You'll love our Hooters," and "Only a Rooster Gets a Better Piece of Chicken!!!" (Not coincidentally, *Forbes* titled its article "How do you like our Hooters?") The servers can also do the twist with hula hoops for lunchtime crowds. Most importantly, these women get to work in an environment where, according to *Forbes*, "appropriate activities . . . include winking, leering, nudging and smirking. But not slobbering."[10] The owners of Hooters, however, have enjoyed annual growth rates of twenty percent, including a sixteen percent profit in 1991. The appeal of such profits has stimulated the opening of other restaurants, mostly in Florida—Mugs & Jugs, Melons, and Knockers—that also use women's breasts in their marketing.[11]

In fact, Florida has been hit heavily by establishments that feature bare-breasted women, usually dressed in G-strings and high heels, performing menial tasks. In addition to the restaurants mentioned above, a topless car wash in Fort Lauderdale enjoys business described as "very active" no matter what the weather brings. Another sexist establishment in Florida is a topless donut shop. Word about the car wash became national news for men through *Playboy* in January 1992. Also in January, Boston's television station WFXT-25 brought word about the donut shop to New Englanders. Then a national television show informed Americans about a topless hot-dog stand and housecleaning service. When asked about the dangers of entering a man's house in the required attire, one woman replied that the housecleaners sometimes travel as a team of two or bring along a man. If winking, leering, nudging, and smirking are considered appropriate behavior at places like Hooters, what do you suppose is appropriate behavior for a man who is watching a topless woman clean his house?

Recent years have seen an increase in the number of topless bars and strip clubs, with the media describing this as a trend in "sophisticated" clubs. Most women don't see anything sophisticated about women publicly performing sexual acts for men. In addition to appealing to college males, these clubs often target businessmen, sometimes through direct mail. The so-called quality strip clubs, which charge a ten- or fifteen-dollar cover charge, assure men that their establishments are for men who deserve the "best" of strippers and topless performers, seven days a week, morning, noon, and night.

In April 1992, the *New York Times* reported that according to *Gentleman's Club* magazine, a trade magazine for the $3 billion-a-year topless industry, there are about eleven hundred "quality" topless clubs in forty-seven states, compared to about eight hundred in forty-five states in 1987.[12]

These "quality" strip clubs offer a range of activities that encourage men to bond with each other at the expense of objectifying, degrading, and sometimes violating women, who are treated as things that perform sex acts and take commands from men. In these clubs, men are not threatened by women; the women are there to please the men, who control the situation. Some clubs, such as Scores in Manhattan, offer widescreen televisions and basketball courts for men who now and then might want to take a break from staring at women's bare breasts. Not surprisingly, many clubs often show pornographic films in the main rooms or private booths. Such places as the Gold Club in Atlanta, the Men's Club in Houston, or Cabaret Royale in Dallas have high-priced menus, executive dining rooms, conference rooms equipped with fax machines, and bare-breasted women to shine shoes or perform secretarial tasks.[13] Again, we see the sexualizing of labor—the kinds of labor that women tend to do in a sexist society. The Foxy Lady in Providence, Rhode Island, offers a variety of events, including "legs and eggs" for breakfast, "lingerie day," "fantasy costume night," "double showers" with audience participation, "couch dancing," "table dancing," "bachelor parties," and last, but not least, "bachelorette parties," to avoid being accused of sex discrimination. Other "quality" clubs offer "lap dancing" and "wet-body shows" where men shoot water at nude female dancers.

In March 1989, Solid Gold opened its doors in Minneapolis. It offers a "free businessman's luncheon" with "beautiful ladies, eye contact, conversation, impeccable hospitality, and sensuous, sophisticated entertainment."[14] At Solid Gold men can order women off the menu as appetizers. These clubs are marketed as "sophisticated enough for businessmen and professionals who enjoy the finer things in life." Among the finer things are female boxing and wrestling with audience participation as well as watching female dancers who are locked in large gold cages. These clubs serve to further normalize sexism and exploitation; that is, in the clubs the drink or lunch happens to be accompanied by topless women or strippers.

In the summer of 1990, Deja Vu opened in Minneapolis to compete with Solid Gold. Deja Vu was able to obtain a city ordinance for a hundred percent nudity and admittance of eighteen-year-olds because it serves free juice and soft drinks rather than alcohol. City-granted liquor licenses permit localities to supervise operating hours and the conduct of dancers; without such a license, Deja Vu enjoys a lot of freedom. In addition, after the bars that serve alcohol close at 1:00 A.M. on weekends, Deja Vu enjoys an additional wave of customers.[15] Deja Vu uses print ads, billboards, and cable television commercials to attract customers; its ads, along with those for telephone sexual services, have appeared during Big Ten sporting events as well as between cartoons, as early as 7:30 A.M.

THE IMPACT OF CURRENT TRENDS IN THE LEISURE, ENTERTAINMENT, AND SERVICE INDUSTRIES

The "Playboy" pinball game described earlier may seem like nothing compared to all the breast-oriented establishments and strip clubs. But each one does its part to perpetuate the subordinated status of women in our society.

The ways in which Hooters and other breast-oriented restaurants treat, present, and use their female servers does influence our perceptions of women. Hooters' name, their uniform, logo, and slogans tell the public that these women are sex objects who serve food. It is outrageous that Hooters would have the audacity to request that these women volunteer in charity drives in order to "soften the bimbo image" that Hooters *itself* has created. Using the women as billboards at local events to attract a male crowd and potential restaurant customers is sexist and insulting to women. It teaches all of us that women, unlike men, are things. Positioning women in a work situation that encourages men to wink, leer, nudge, smirk at, or slobber over the women condones sexual harassment. It tells women that their job is not only to serve food but to accept sexual harassment as a way to make a living. (As of this writing, a group of former servers have filed a sexual harassment suit against Hooters.[16])

When we address the topless and strip club industry, whether it includes dancing, stripping, housecleaning, or shoe-shining, we need to look at this industry from another perspective. Rather than ask the same old question, "Why do women do it?", we ought to ask, "Why do men do it?" Why do men feel it is their right to have access to women's bodies for whatever leisure activity or service they desire—being waited on at a donut shop, restaurant, or bar; having their cars washed; or having their toilet bowls cleaned? All of these businesses are examples of the extension of the pornography industry into general leisure, entertainment, and service industries.

Some people believe that the increase in "quality" topless and strip clubs is due, in part, to the fear of singles bars at a time when so many people are contracting HIV. Are they saying that going to a place where women take off their clothes so that men can be sexually aroused is safe sex? Is it sex? For whom is it safe? For the men who are caught up in voyeurism? Certainly such a place is not safe for the women who work there. Wendy Reid Crisp, director of the National Association of Female

Executives, believes that the "apparent popularity of the bars may be part of the male backlash against social, economic and political gains made by women." Threatened by these advances, males frequent such establishments as their way of "trying to reestablish a masculinity that is familiar to them."[17]

The consequences of these forms of entertainment reach into every aspect of our lives. Companies that conduct business meetings, luncheons, or dinners at topless and strip clubs need to realize that expense-accounting their employees' participation at these clubs sends a confusing message to all their employees. At a time when companies are adopting policies that address the serious issue of sexual harassment in the workplace, they are communicating that it's all right to treat women as sex objects during the course of business entertainment. Women who work in offices where men consider such clubs an appropriate place to hold business meetings are affected in at least two ways. First, if they are excluded from such events, it is an extension of the "old boys' network." Second, if women are taken to such places, the experience is a form of sexual harassment. As Reid Crisp points out, "It can be dangerous for the male executive to entertain female clients or colleagues there. It could lead to a sexual harassment complaint."[18] Either way the attitudes toward women spill over into the ways men view and treat women. What do men think of their female coworkers and managers when they return to the office after ordering a woman off the menu?

What about the women who work in the clubs? The mass media would have us believe that the women who work in such clubs *freely* choose to be there; and if they don't like it, they should get out. Peggy Miller, executive director of the Minnesota Coalition Against Sexual Assault [and co-author of "Twenty Years Later: The Unfinished Revolution" see pp. 47–54] notes that people who are uncomfortable facing the harsh realities of women's status in the areas of poverty, harassment, battering, and rape tend to dismiss these places simply as bars where women work *willingly*. "Only in the sex industry," she notes, "do we justify its existence by the participation of those it uses. We don't condone illicit drug trafficking by citing the people who buy drugs."[19]

Many people—especially women—are unaware of the emotional, physical, and sexual abuse women are subjected to in strip clubs. In these clubs it is common for women to have to endure being called "bitch," "slut," or "whore."[20] Many women who work or have worked in such clubs report being grabbed, fondled, bitten, vaginally or anally penetrated, or masturbated on. Some have reported being raped by customers upon leaving the club. Others have been pressured or forced into prostitution. In a few cases, women have also reported that club owners filmed them without their knowledge and that owners continued to film them after the women refused their consent.

The activities women are expected to perform serve to degrade and humiliate them. For example, in "table dancing," a woman stands on a portable platform so that her crotch is eye-level with the customers and so that she can move from table to table. In addition to featuring women locked in large gold cages, another Solid Gold activity is an auction in which men climb on stage and wrestle an oiled woman to the ground or place bids to *manage* one or two women in a boxing ring. Prior to the *match*, the women lie on their backs with their legs spread and pointed upward while the *managers* saturate the women's crotches with shaving cream.[21]

Stress associated with sexual harassment in the workplace results in physical and psychological symptoms, including insomnia, headaches, muscle pain, stomach ailments, decreased concentration, diminished ambition, listlessness, depression, and feelings of helplessness, vulnerability, alienation, and humiliation. When a victim reports sexual harassment and receives no redress "she becomes less trusting and her expectations about fairness, loyalty, and justice are compromised."[22] In the case of topless and strip clubs, enduring sexual harassment is part of a woman's job description. Many of the physical and psychological effects noted above are intensified.[23]

Contrary to popular belief, women who work in strip clubs don't get rich. Most clubs do not pay women a salary; instead, women must compete to perform the kinds of sex acts that the business has taught them will get men to part with their money, and that may cost the women fines. In places such as Solid Gold, most of the women are independent contractors. There are no salary benefits because there is no salary.[24] The clothed owners are the ones who reap the profits. Seasoned club owner Michael J. Peter from Fort Lauderdale, who owns or operates twenty-four "quality" topless clubs, estimates that he spent around $2 million in lawyer's fees alone during an eighteen-month period just to keep his clubs open. Alcohol sales from each of his own clubs can easily amount to $30,000 to $100,000 a week.[25]

ACTIONS WE CAN TAKE

There are many things we can do to reverse the tide. The important thing is that we do something that will influence change. Complaining among ourselves may help to relieve anger, but it doesn't change the situation. We need to take action.

After being introduced to the "Playboy" pinball game at a theater owned by General Cinema Corporation, one woman wrote a letter to the manager. She explained that she could not take her daughters to a children's film without being bombarded with the sights and sounds of a so-called game that defined women as objects for the sexual pleasure of males of all ages. Within a week she received a call from a General Cinema executive who apologized, explained that he was unaware that the theater had installed the game, and told her it had been removed.

Not every community accepts Hooters without a fight. In Baltimore, the media covered protests from feminists, the mayor, the city council, and the Chamber of Commerce. In order to secure its lease, Hooters agreed to drop some of the sexual double entendres from its menu and its "More than a Mouthful" slogan from the backs of female servers. In Fairfax, Virginia, feminists, the mayor, and city council members organized a protest group.

In greater Minneapolis, feminists are leading a fight against a Hooters located in a new $625 million shopping center, which features ten nightclubs, thirty restaurants, almost four hundred stores, a seven-acre amusement park, and over thirteen thousand parking spaces. The mall, appropriately named the Mall of America, opened in August 1992 and is expected to attract more international tourists than Disney World.

Hooters secured this lease before complications arose. However, through its newsletter, networking, letters to newspapers, and television and radio interviews, the Action Committee to End Sexism and Violence Against Women in the Media is educating residents and visitors about Hooters and other sexist businesses at the Mall of America. Action Committee members are asking the public to join them in a boycott against Hooters and the Mall of America, which refuses to reconsider its lease with Hooters. A recent telephone poll taken on a radio show indicated that thirty-three percent of hundreds of callers would boycott the Mall of America because Hooters is there.[26] By developing a rapport with sympathetic reporters, Action Committee members are able to reach a wide audience, and individuals who have never been involved in protests now realize they can take action.

We can do a number of things to protest sexist and misogynist images of and behavior toward women. We can write letters, make phone calls, distribute newsletters, organize boycotts, present lectures, and conduct protest demonstrations. (For additional ideas and information on activism, see "Suggested Readings" at the end of this article.)

Writing letters is one of the easiest and quickest forms of protest. Some suggested guidelines include: (1) introduce yourself (for example, as a parent, customer, concerned citizen, business owner, teacher, or member of a particular organization); (2) describe the image or product, and if possible, include a photocopy; (3) make the company aware of its impact on society; use statistics from studies to strengthen your argument; (4) state that you want the company to reconsider its ad or product in terms of social responsibility; (5) note that you will use consumer leverage in the form of a boycott; (6) suggest positive alternatives; and (7) include a list of organizations to which you are sending a copy of your letter, i.e., newspaper and television editors and reporters, feminist and profeminist organizations, and appropriate local and state organizations.

Members of Challenging Media Images of Women have received positive results from their letter-writing campaigns. Sexist ads that have been discontinued or revised include some for Bain de Soleil suntan lotion, Dep shampoo, Caboodles makeup kit, and Reebok shoes for women. Protest letters educate people about the effects of sexist and misogynist imagery, make companies aware that we will not tolerate such imagery in the name of advertising or entertainment, and encourage others to take a stand with us.

Making *phone calls* requires even less time than writing letters, and the same format as the letter-writing outline can be used to get your point across. Many companies have 800 numbers so calling won't cost you a cent. In the summer of 1990, Melart Jewelers in Silver Spring, Maryland, pulled its "Hit Her with a Rock" diamond promotion from twenty buses after protestors pointed out that it trivialized violence against women. In February 1992, Brooks Pharmacy canceled a Valentine's Day ad on radio stations after one member of Challenging Media Images of Women called to protest. The ad featured an Arnold Schwarzenegger sound-alike going into Brooks to buy a gift and card for his valentine. The man behind the counter suggested that he also write a poem. In a heavy Germanic accent, the Schwarzenegger sound-alike recited, "Roses are red, violets are blue; you'd better be my valentine, or I'll pump you full of lead . . . or I'll shoot you in the head . . . or you're better off dead." The activist spoke to a public relations officer at Brooks and stressed that at best this ad trivialized violence against women, and at worst it condoned such violence. The ad was removed from all radio stations by noon the next day.

Producing a local *newsletter* allows you to network with area activists on direct action campaigns. By sending copies to your local news media, schools, and other organizations, you can recruit more members and obtain publicity to reach even more people. For example, the Action Committee to End Sexism and Violence Against Women in the Media produces a newsletter to keep members abreast of its local campaigns, meetings, and special events.

Boycotts are another way to challenge sexist and misogynist images of women in the media and elsewhere in the entertainment industry. While national boycotts require an incredible amount of organization and the support of powerful groups, and they can often take several years to get results, the threat of a boycott can be more powerful than the boycott itself.

Local boycotts can be effective in much less time. Get organizations to endorse your action. Inform the company that you are planning a boycott. You may be able to stop here, but be prepared to go ahead with the boycott. If you must proceed, send letters or press releases to editors at local and nearby newspapers and to managers at television and radio stations. Distribute flyers whenever and wherever possible, i.e., at work, meetings, and other events. Keep the boycott alive through the media.

Lectures at schools, community groups, and public forums are an excellent way to educate people about images of women in the media and pornography and to motivate people to take action. Call like-minded groups to find out who gives lectures in your area.

Demonstrations/pickets are excellent protest vehicles for many kinds of events, including comedy or music concerts; annual "swimsuit" magazine issues; openings of films, pornographic video stores and bookstores, breast-oriented restaurants, topless and strip clubs, etc. You can organize a demonstration/picket within a month or even less.

When you find out the date of the event, write a letter to the manager indicating that you plan to demonstrate; request that he/she reconsider the event. For example, in the case of an Andrew Dice Clay concert, cite statistics on the number of women who have been battered, raped, and murdered by men in your state. Stress the irresponsibility of inviting a comedian such as Clay, whose act is sexist and misogynist, degrades women, and trivializes violence against women. Send a similar letter to Clay's manager, Don Law. Realizing that most likely you won't receive a response, let alone a positive one, to this kind of request, begin planning the demonstration.

Having selected the date, place, and time for a demonstration/picket, invite other organizations to join you. Call local or nearby shelters for battered women, rape crisis centers, women's centers at colleges, feminist groups, antisexist men's groups, and other organizations. Let them know the media will be there. This will also be an opportunity for their members to speak out.

Prepare leaflets and posters. Show how Clay's act trivializes violence against women and contributes to sexist and misogynist attitudes and behaviors toward women; include quotes from Clay's act along with statistics on violence against women. Take the time to prepare effective (readable and well-written) posters. Most likely, they are the only thing that will appear in print and on television.

About a week prior to the event, send press releases to local media. If the concert is located near a major city, contact that city's media. Press releases should contain the date, time, location, names of groups sponsoring the demonstration, and reason you are demonstrating. Send releases to managing editors and/or reporters at newspapers and television and radio stations. Contact talk radio hosts as well as wire services such as the Associated Press and United Press International. The goal is to inform as many people as possible about your protest; newspapers around the country rely on AP and UPI for brief news reports. Follow up by phone with major media a couple of days after you mail (or fax) the press releases. Call editors of the arts section of major newspapers in your area. Find out who will be reviewing the concert; let the reviewer know that you will be demonstrating.

A few days before the demonstration, notify the community relations department at the local police station. Let them know you plan to hold a peaceful demonstration at the specified time and place. Get the name of the officer you spoke to; you may need to use it if you have difficulty at the demonstration.

Arrive at the site about an hour before the concert begins with plenty of posters and leaflets. It's a good idea for one or two spokespersons to let the manager know you are there. If the police are there, meet with them briefly. Remember to stay off private property (unless you want to risk arrest), and try to avoid arguing with hecklers. Meet with as many reporters as possible.

Don't be discouraged if your protest demonstration doesn't draw a large number of protestors; it's not always the numbers that count. Many veteran demonstrators stress the need to think beyond the demonstration itself. A protest demonstration is a public ritual—an opportunity to take back public space. It's important to cultivate the media before, during, and after such events. For example, after the demonstration, send a news release summarizing the event to local media, the names and faces section of newspapers, and AP and UPI. Even if only five protestors show up, the event is part of a continuum. You can refer back to the protest at lectures and during interviews, letting people know that some of us do not and will not accept a sexist and misogynist culture. When we take the time to get involved, we can play a role in reshaping our culture.

NOTES

1. David Bednarek, "Hooters Plans Site in Milwaukee," *Milwaukee Journal*, 3 February 1993, business section.
2. Eugene Carlson, "Restaurant Chain Tries to Cater to Two Types of Taste," *Wall Street Journal*, 20 March 1992, p. B2.
3. Seth Lubove, "How do you like our Hooters?" *Forbes*, 15 April 1991, p. 107.
4. Carlson, "Restaurant Chain Tries," p. B2.
5. Ibid.
6. Lubove, "How do you like," p. 107.
7. Ibid.
8. Carlson, "Restaurant Chain Tries," p. B2.
9. Ibid.
10. Lubove, "How do you like," p. 106.
11. Ibid.
12. Nick Ravo, " 'Quality' Topless Clubs Go for the Crowd in Pinstripes," *New York Times*, 15 April 1992, p. B1.

13. Ibid.
14. Advertisement, *Skyway News* (Minneapolis), 12 November 1991.
15. Dominic P. Papatola, "Like It or Not, Minneapolis vice entices some visitors," *City Business* (Minneapolis), 24 June 1992, p. 24.
16. On April 20, 1993, three former Hooters servers filed a suit against the restaurant in Bloomington, Minnesota. Charges include sexual harassment and discrimination, assault, and battery. The women are also asking as part of the settlement that Hooters change its name, stop requiring the skimpy uniforms, and implement and enforce a strict sexual harassment policy. Randy Furst, "Three Sue Hooters," *Star Tribune* (Minneapolis), 21 April 1993, p. 1B.
17. Ravo, " 'Quality' Topless Clubs," p. B4.
18. Ibid.
19. Letter, *Skyway News*, 20 October 1992.
20. Evelina Giobbe, "Why WHISPER Is Opposed to Strip Clubs," *WHISPER* (Women Hurt in Systems of Prostitution Engaged in Revolt) VI: 3–4 (Summer-Fall, 1992), p. 2.
21. Catherine Palczewski and the Solid Gold Core Committee, *Ibid.*, III:3 (Summer, 1989), pp. 1–2.
22. Giobbe, "Why WHISPER," pp. 1–2.
23. Ibid.
24. Ibid.
25. Ravo, " 'Quality' Topless Clubs," p. B1.
26. "Ruth Koscielak Show," WCCO, 10 September 1992. Data from Laura Kuhn, "Mega-Sexism at the Mall of America," unpublished paper, September, 1992.

SUGGESTED READINGS

Barry, Kathleen. *Female Sexual Slavery.* New York: New York University Press, 1979.
Bobo, Kim, Jackie Kendall, and Steve Max. *Organizing for Social Change: A Manual for Activists in the 1990s.* Washington, DC: Seven Locks Press, 1991.
Delacoste, Frederique and Felice Newman, eds. *Fight Back! Feminist Resistance to Male Violence.* Minneapolis: Cleis Press, 1981.
League of Women Voters of Minneapolis. *Breaking the Cycle of Violence: A Focus on Primary Prevention Efforts.* Minneapolis: April 1990.
Ryan, Charlotte. *Primetime Activism: Media Strategies for Grassroots Organizing.* Boston: South End Press, 1991.

SARAH CIRIELLO is the editor and a cofounder of the *Challenging Media Images of Women Newsletter,* established in 1988. CMIW is a feminist activist organization protesting sexism in the media, and its quarterly newsletter serves as both an educational tool and a protest vehicle. In her slide/lecture presentations on images of women in the media, Ciriello discusses many of the ways in which the mass media perpetuate and legitimize gender inequality, and encourages her audiences to read media images critically and to take an active role in the redesign of mass media to reflect the wholeness and diversity of women.

CIVIL RIGHTS ANTIPORNOGRAPHY LEGISLATION
Addressing the Harm to Women

by Steven Hill & Nina Silver

For men to give up what is culturally condoned—
pornography—means confronting not only
the violence in themselves but the male
privileges that go along with it.

I N FEBRUARY 1992, the movement to stop violence and discrimination against women won a remarkable victory when Canada's Supreme Court ruled 9–0 that obscenity is to be defined by the harm it does to women and not by what offends our values. "Materials portraying women as a class of objects for sexual exploitation and abuse have a negative impact on the individual's sense of self-worth and acceptance," read the court's landmark opinion, the first time a court has established the precedent that a threat to the equality and safety of women "is a substantial concern which justifies restricting the otherwise full exercise of the freedom of expression."

"In the United States, the obscenity laws are all about not liking to see naked bodies, or homosexual activity, in public," commented University of Michigan law professor Catharine MacKinnon, who helped write the law brief and, along with author Andrea Dworkin, has pioneered the "harm-to-women" approach to antipornography legislation. "Our laws in the United States don't consider the harm to women. But in Canada it will now be materials that subordinate, degrade, or dehumanize women that are obscene."

The Canadian Supreme Court's decision is the latest attempt in North America to enact civil rights antipornography legislation based on the "harm-to-women" approach. Previously several attempts had been made in the U.S. to pass such measures, most recently a Congressional bill called the Pornography Victims Compensation Act, which focuses on the harm done to women in both the production and use of pornography. In 1983 and 1984, the Minneapolis City Council passed the first civil rights antipornography ordinance written by MacKinnon and Dworkin, only to have it vetoed by the mayor both times. Then in Indianapolis the City Council passed, and the mayor signed, the first version of the Dworkin-MacKinnon ordinance to become law. In 1985 the law was struck down by the United States Court of Appeals for the Seventh Circuit as unconstitutional, a ruling later affirmed without comment by the U.S. Supreme Court. In 1988, a version of the Dworkin-MacKinnon ordinance was adopted in Bellingham, Washington, by voter initiative, garnering over sixty-two percent of the vote. It met a similar fate as the Indianapolis ordinance when it was struck down by a Federal District Court Judge.

In each case where the U.S. courts vetoed or revoked the civil rights

antipornography ordinance, pornographers, free speech fundamental-
ists, and civil libertarians (including some feminists) hailed the defeat as
a great triumph for First Amendment rights, decrying the censorship
and "chilling effects" they were certain would result had the ordinance
been passed. Some critics also claimed that pornography, rather than
being harmful, actually provides a cathartic outlet for antisocial attitudes
that otherwise might escalate into harmful behavior if the consumer did
not have access to the pornographic materials.

Are their claims true? And does the ordinance really equal censorship?
Or are the claims of the ordinance proponents true, that pornographic
images contribute toward violence and discrimination against women,
and that the ordinance is an evenhanded way to rectify such social, class-
based harm? Unfortunately, the debate has become a tangled mess of
accusations, errors, and outright lies, seemingly polarized to a point of
no return. After nine years of activism by ordinance proponents in the
United States that has yielded mixed results—followed by the triumph-
ant emergence of a "harm-to-women" antipornography obscenity law in
Canada—perhaps now is the time for us to calmly reassess the true
meaning of such civil rights antipornography legislation.

Two doubts seem crucial to resolve if any headway is to be made. The
first: is there in fact a need for this or similar kinds of legislation—or, put
another way, is any real harm caused by pornography that needs to be
addressed? And two: if it is decided that yes, there is harm and yes, we
need some legal redress, then is civil rights antipornography legislation the desired course, or will it lead to the censorship dreaded by its
opponents?

PORNOGRAPHY: HARMLESS OR HARMFUL?

In pornographic images and text, (usually) women are presented as
continually available sexually to (usually) men for the purpose of pleasing the male viewer. The dehumanization of women occurs because the
pornographic female images are not regarded as persons with feelings,
opinions, or needs of their own. This is what defines the women as commodities: they exist solely for the purpose of their consumers. The ambi-
ence is sexual, but the real setting is the marketplace. In hard-core porn,
not only are women presented as experiencing sexual pleasure in being

raped, they are also tied up, cut, mutilated, bruised, battered, and portrayed as enjoying this pain. They are also penetrated not only by men, but by objects and animals.

Opponents of the ordinance inevitably claim that there is no scientific evidence of the connection between "unreal" pornography and violence against women in the "real" world, but this claim is untrue. There have been hundreds of studies. The results of some of the most comprehensive of these studies have been published in books such as *Pornography and Sexual Aggression,* edited by Neil Malamuth and Edward Donnerstein (Academic Press, 1984); *Connections between Sex and Aggression* by Dolf Zillman (Lawrence Erlbaum Associates, 1984); and in the work of sociologist Diana Russell (see "Pornography and Rape: A Causal Model" in *Political Psychology* 9, no. 1, March 1988). Here are some of the findings:

• After exposure to pornography in a laboratory situation where women were depicted as enjoying rape, male college students ("average Joes" prescreened to select out "hostile" personalities) were more prone to accept commonly held conceptions such as "a woman really wants to be raped," and "*no* means *yes*." These men also denied the credibility of actual rape victims by viewing the victims as feeling less pain than they actually experienced, and by holding them responsible for their own rapes.

• Fifty-seven percent of these males indicated some likelihood that they would commit a rape if guaranteed that they would not be caught. They also claimed that thirty percent of the women they know would enjoy being aggressively forced into sexual intercourse.

• With a repeated exposure period of only two weeks, the subjects found violent pornography to be less and less violent, and they were increasingly less offended by the material. Most important, contrary to the cathartic benefits that some ordinance opponents mention, these men's sexual arousal did not decrease *but in some cases increased.*

• Finally, the researchers found that themes of violence and domination in pornography had very strong effects on adolescent boys and encouraged them to form stereotypes about human sexuality, rape, and violence.

Other social science research on media not limited to pornography found a direct link between people's attitudes toward sex and violence and what they see in the media. These studies confirmed that repetition played a significant factor in desensitizing men to women's experiences of being shamed, attacked, and punished. The more sensory input men received that promulgated sexual stereotypes about women, the less guilty and accountable they felt about replicating the behaviors they read about in books and viewed in images. Violence, humiliation, and eroticism became enmeshed in the same socially sanctioned matrix, so that sex was regarded as a situation of domination and power-over rather than reciprocity and love.

The scientific foundation of the "cathartic effect" has in recent years been refuted, yet anti-ordinance/pro-pornography supporters continue to promote this perspective as if mere repetition will wipe out the scientific record. The catharsis theory, which impressed the 1970 U.S. Presidential Commission on Pornography, is mostly based on research by Berl Kutchinsky. Kutchinsky had discovered that the relaxation of porn laws in Denmark and Sweden coincided with a decrease in reported sex crimes. But subsequent inspection of his study revealed that his correlation was poor, since he failed to account for other social factors, such as an abnormally high rape rate after the German occupation during World War II, which would have made any subsequent decrease of sex crimes seem statistically supportive of his original premise. Interestingly, Kutchinsky himself has since recanted his initial conclusions, noting that the rape rates of Denmark and Sweden have *increased* since he conducted his study. It should also be noted that Norway, which has a culture similar to Denmark and Sweden and far stricter laws against pornography, has had even greater success in combating sex crimes (34 percent decrease from 1970 to 1981, compared to a 14.2 percent decrease for Denmark).

In 1984, Dr. John Court examined changes in rape rates in several countries that had periods of greater or lesser legal control of pornography. He concluded that greater legal control of porn appears to hold down rape rates. Similarly, Baron and Straus (in studies published in 1984 and 1985) have shown a highly significant statistical correlation between state-by-state circulation rates for seven porn magazines (*Playboy, Oui, Hustler, Genesis, Gallery, Chic,* and *Club*) and state-by-state reported rape rates. Their study revealed that proliferation of pornographic magazines and the level of urbanization explained variance in rape rates more than did unemployment, economic inequality, sexual inequality, and social disorganization. In Mary Koss's 1986 national survey of over six thousand college students, she found that college men who reported behavior that meets the legal definition of rape were significantly more likely than men who did not report such behavior to be frequent readers of at least one of the following magazines: *Playboy*, *Penthouse*, *Chic*, *Club*, *Forum*, *Gallery*, *Genesis*, *Oui*, and *Hustler*.

Finally, the National Coalition on Television Violence has found over seven hundred fifty scientific studies and reports that show that TV and film violence are linked to increases in real-life violence and aggression in normal children and adult viewers. They have located only eighteen studies (some of which were funded by the entertainment industry) that show screen violence as having a cathartic effect on viewers. According to the NCTV, one out of eight Hollywood movies depicts a rape theme. By age eighteen, the average U.S. citizen will have seen 250,000 acts of violence and 40,000 attempted murders on television. A spokesperson for the American Psychological Association testified before Congress that "the relationship between televised violence and aggression is real, long lasting, and of practical as well as statistical significance."

Summing up the scientific evidence, Edward Donnerstein from the University of Wisconsin has testified:

> [If] you take a look at the research and really talk about hundreds and hundreds of studies . . . there is an incredible amount of consensus across populations and measures and studies. We are not talking about correlations where we get into chicken/egg problems of which came first; we are talking about *causality*.

Donnerstein affirmed the ability of his research to take certain types of pornographic images, expose people to those images, and make highly accurate predictions of potential aggressive behavior independent of the viewers' backgrounds, their past viewing habits, or their initial hostility. The scientific evidence, Donnerstein concluded, strongly advised that there are obvious relationships between pornographic material and subsequent assault.

> In fact, good colleagues of mine would argue that the relationship between particularly sexually violent images in the media and subsequent aggression and changes in callous attitudes toward women is much stronger statistically than the relationship

between smoking and cancer, mainly because most of that research is correlational. This is not.

But these are laboratory statistics, one might claim. What about real life? In one study conducted by Diana Russell, it was found that 14 percent of the 930 women interviewed reported that they had been asked to pose for pornographic pictures, and 10 percent reported that they had been upset by someone trying to get them to enact what had been seen in pornographic pictures, movies, or books. This study also established that only 7.8 percent of these women had *not* been sexually assaulted or harassed at some point in their lives. Additionally, the testimonies of law enforcement officials and sexual abuse counselors confirm that pornography plays an active role in the fantasies of both sexual offenders and mass murderers and in the acting out of their violence on their victims. Piles of pornography have been found in the homes of virtually every mass killer. In some cases, as with Ted Bundy, pornography has been used as an actual textbook that illustrated *how* to rape.

Undoubtedly the causes of rape are multi-etiological. Violent and sexist images, all by themselves, are not causing this epidemic of rape in our society. But the very proliferation of these images indicates the presence of this epidemic, as the images and the rapes reinforce each other. Why should social policy advocates—civil libertarian or otherwise—ignore such a well-documented body of scientific and anecdotal evidence about the contribution of these images toward violence against women and children?

PORN INDUSTRY PERFORMERS: STARS OR SCARS?

We now come to the issue of choice for a woman who takes part in the production of pornography. Is a performer in a pornographic film or photo a *willing* participant just because she has a smile on her face? At public hearings in 1983 before the Minneapolis City Council, when that council was considering the Dworkin-MacKinnon ordinance, woman after woman came forward and attested to the harm that pornography had personally caused her. Wives, women friends, and prostitutes testified about having been intimidated and physically coerced into performing in pornography by their husbands, partners, and pimps.

The testimony at the Minneapolis hearings was historic because it revealed to the world for the first time that pornography was not simply about "speech": it was, in fact, a *practice*, usually a business practice with a profitable bottom line, in which real things—dreadful things—happened to real people in its production. In subsequent years, runaway children have told their sad stories about running from sexually abusive parents and their ensuing lives on the streets, in which they were intimidated and coerced into performing in pornography by their "daddies" and pimps who had promised to protect them from danger. Rape victims of all ages, euphemistically called "models," have testified about being forced to perform sexual acts on film under threat of their very lives, with guns and knives off-camera. Women—coerced into having sex with animals or submitting to mass rapes by men (euphemistically called "gang bangs") on film—have related grotesque tales of being ordered to act as though they were enjoying themselves, despite the fact that they got cut from the ropes binding their genitals and the broken bottles and knives inserted into their vaginas in order to create the photographic images. This tendency toward the ugliest forms of exploitation and domination culminated in the appearance of "snuff films," in which women are actually raped and murdered, the atrocities are filmed and then distributed as movies for a viewing audience.

The most famous case of coercion into pornography is that of Linda Marchiano (a.k.a. Linda Lovelace), the "star" of *Deep Throat*, the largest-grossing porn film of all time. Marchiano has publicly stated and written in her book *Ordeal* how she was battered and terrorized during the making of that film. During the course of her life with her pimp/boyfriend Chuck Traynor, she was beaten repeatedly; her family was threatened with murder by Traynor if she tried to leave him; and on those occasions when she did try to escape, he brutally bludgeoned her within an inch of her life. Once, when she refused to make a film in which she was told to fornicate with a dog, a gun was pulled and she knew that if she did not comply she would be murdered. She made the film. When moviegoers view *Deep Throat* for their own "sexual liberation," what they are actually viewing is the cinematic recording of the rape and dehumanization of Linda Marchiano.

It is true that some women (and men) who act in pornographic films do so out of choice. However, gender-linked economic conditions often induce women to make that "choice." And an alarmingly high percentage of participants in the pornography industry have already been sexually abused at home and elsewhere before they ever make their "decision," thereby rendering them vulnerable to continuing the abusive cycle.

With such a mounting body of evidence that pornography harms—from the reams of scientific studies, the testimony of law enforcement and mental health officials, and the actual experiences of real, live women—the civil rights antipornography activists began to ask: *Whose* freedom, and *whose* speech, is being protected? When the American Civil Liberties Union defends the "freedom of speech" of the pornographers, an equally compelling argument can be made that they are denying the "freedom of speech" of all women. In Florida, when the ACLU filed an amicus brief defending the right of men to hang pornography in the workplace as a legitimate expression of their free speech, a counterargument was made that the ACLU was contributing toward the continued discrimination and harassment of working women.

Andrea Dworkin and Catharine MacKinnon, in *Pornography and Civil Rights* (Organizing Against Pornography, 1988), commented on the "free speech" controversy:

> Women screaming in pain in a pornography film is "speech." Women screaming in the audiences to express their pain and dissent is breach of the peace and interferes with "speech." "Snuff" is "speech." Demonstrators who use strong language to protest "snuff" are arrested for obscenity. When *Penthouse* hangs Asian women from trees, it is "speech." When antipornography activist Nikki Craft leaflets with the same photographs in protest, she is threatened with arrest for public lewdness. When B. Dalton sells pornography in a shopping mall displayed at a child's eye level, that is "speech." When Nikki Craft holds up the same pornography in the same shopping mall in protest, she is detained in a back room of B. Dalton's by the police for contributing to the delinquency of minors.

THE CIVIL RIGHTS ANTIPORNOGRAPHY ORDINANCE: FAIR OR FOUL?

With all this evidence, it seems difficult, even disingenuous, to argue that no harm results from the production or distribution of pornography. The larger point is: what, if anything, should be done about the harm? Is the civil rights antipornography approach a worthy attempt, or will it lead to the censorship and "chilling effect" that its detractors claim? To answer this question, it is necessary to examine the ordinance in some detail.

Like the Canadian counterpart that recently passed in that court, the United States version of the "harm to women" approach to antipornography legislation defines pornography as sex discrimination. Unlike the Canadian law, however, the U.S. version has not been framed in the context of a criminal obscenity law. Rather, it allows victims to bring civil lawsuits to seek monetary damages and injunctive relief from those who have harmed them. The ordinance spells out five unlawful practices:

• Coercion into performance in pornography;

• Forcing pornography on any person, including a child, in any place of employment or education, the home or public place;

• Assault or physical attack directly caused by specific pornography (there are many cases of sexual assault in which certain pieces of pornography were used as textbooks that illustrated *how* to assault);

• Defamation of any person through the unauthorized use in pornography of his or her name, image, or likeness;

• Trafficking in pornography—production, distribution, or sale of material that meets the definition of pornography in the legislation.

The law includes several safeguards to prevent censorship. One section states that "isolated passages or isolated parts shall not be actionable." This means that the isolated love scenes in a literary work, the occasional nude photo or sex scenes in a favorite book or film, or even the rape scenes in a romance novel or the erotic poetry of Yeats, could not make these books or films legally actionable. What *is* actionable are forms of expression that portray page after page, scene after scene of acts of violence, harm, and degradation against women. Another section of the law excludes from prosecution "city, state, and federally funded public libraries and public university and college libraries in which pornography is available for study."

In addition, civil suits can only be initiated by a victim who has been harmed in one of the five ways mentioned above by a specific piece of pornography, and the burden of proof is on the complainant. Unlike current obscenity laws, no criminal charges can result from the civil lawsuit, meaning that the ordinance could *never* be used by the government or law enforcement agencies to close a bookstore or jail someone as the result of producing or distributing pornography.

Despite these safeguards designed by the ordinance authors, anti-ordinance groups have not displayed a reciprocal sensitivity. Statements made by anti-ordinance spokespeople reveal a lack of concern or awareness about the social realities of pornography. "It is my position to defend my right to write. It's not my position to defend pornographers," states one romance novelist. Yet in joining a lawsuit filed against the Bellingham ordinance, the writer placed herself in the paradoxical position of doing just that. Furthermore, she conveyed the message that her privilege to write whatever she chooses—no matter how irresponsible, misleading, or inaccurate—is more important than the rights of women who are being forced into producing pornography, who are attacked and harassed due to pornography, and whose freedom of speech and rights to physical, economic, and political self-determination are harmed by the proliferation of pornography in our society.

"If people are willing to accept that books can have good influences, they must accept that some books may have negative influences on some people," says a librarian. The "free speech" argument, however, ignores the reality that pornography is not free speech per se but a $10 billion industry, and that real women and girls are coerced and abused in the actual production of porn. This argument also ignores the irony that when brutal or sexist acts become frozen in a media form, they are trans-mogrified into "art" and are then entitled to legal protection as "free speech."

Also—and this is very telling—the critics' claims that the ordinance would *automatically* lead to censorship are based on fears of "what ifs" and a distrust in the people who sit on juries to apply this legislation in a responsible fashion. Does the possibility exist for someone to abuse the law? Of course—just as someone might abuse sexual harassment or racial discrimination laws, or any other civil rights law. Undoubtedly, there have been civil suits that made unjust claims of discrimination of one sort of another. People motivated by money will try to abuse the system to "get rich quick." But does that mean we should eliminate all civil rights legislation pertaining to racial discrimination or sexual harassment? Of course not! Similarly with the civil rights antipornography approach: its potential benefits more than outweigh any harms. At least, the Canadian Supreme Court thinks so.

THE PSYCHOLOGY OF RESISTANCE

The volume of scientific studies and personal testimonies notwith-standing, most pro-pornography/anti-ordinance advocates still claim there is no proof that words and images have an effect on people's consciousness. But if words and images don't have power, what then is the basis for advertising? Reese's candy enjoyed a marked upsurge in sales after it made a brief appearance in the movie *E.T.* And daily we hear of the increase in various types of violence that mimic whatever was just in the news or in the latest crime movie. Clearly, there is more at stake here than just the presumed protection of "artistic expression." Why are otherwise educated people—even some feminists—refusing to educate themselves about the modern-day realities of the sex industry, about the scientific studies and women's testimony, and instead defending the pornographers? Why are they defending our *image* of freedom instead of perceiving the *real* lack of freedom behind the image?

Because women's bodies glut billboards, magazines, movies, and television—giving the message that women are less than human and enjoy such treatment—after a point we become callous to the sexual violence we see around us (whether real or Hollywood-created), and the violence ceases to have meaning. The misogyny and degradation become invisible—not because they aren't present, but because we have blocked them out. The constant becomes commonplace, commonplace becomes normal, normal becomes natural; and what seems natural can then only be regarded as right. Just as advertisers know to promote "bigger and better" in increasingly flamboyant ways because people become impervious to input over time, pornographers know to proliferate violence and degradation. The constant barrage of the mass media, then, desensitizing us to the routine and familiar existence of degrading images, becomes an a priori psychological inhibitor to antipornography measures such as the Dworkin-MacKinnon ordinance.

Most women would rather numb themselves to block out this horrifying input. To be aware of it daily may mean saying to themselves, "I live in a world where I am degraded, systematically humiliated, and considered worthless—and where all this is regarded as normal." How many women are willing to allow themselves to become this aware? It might mean living every single day with unbearable pain, especially if a woman's husband, lover, brother, friend, or father is an aficionado of pornography. How can she live with the contradiction?

Most men seem unwilling to admit and examine this contradiction inside themselves. To do so would mean that no matter how good a lover, provider, or parent a man thinks he is, his tacit approval of pornography makes him at best insensitive, at worst misogynistic, toward the very person he professes to care about. For men to give up what is culturally condoned—pornography—means confronting not only the violence in themselves but the male privileges that go along with it.

Part of male privilege is the control over money and power. And we fail to recognize that those with money and power control the image-making process. In fact, in the United States, it is possible for a wealthy person or institution to buy so much "free" speech in the form of magazines, radios, newspapers, and television stations that the freedom of speech of even a whole class of people—i.e. women—can be limited. The objective of power-mongers—whether they are pornographers, government officials, corporations, or special interest lobby groups—is to retain their position and power. And to do this they skillfully manipulate the images that deluge us every day.

CALL TO FREEDOM

After all the data are examined, we are left with the nagging question: what can be done about the women who are coerced into the making of pornography, and the rape, child abuse, and other forms of economic, political, and social discrimination that pornography fosters? The First Amendment must be balanced against Fourteenth Amendment rights, which guarantee each citizen "equal protection of the law."

This balancing is essentially what the Canadian Supreme Court did: it considered *both* the freedom of expression provisions and the equality provisions of the Canadian Charter of Rights and Freedom, and then rendered its decision. Kathleen Mahoney, law professor at the University of Calgary who argued the case for the Women's Legal Education and Action Fund, put it thus: "The court said that while the obscenity law does limit the charter's freedom of expression guarantee, it's justifiable because this type of expression harms women personally, harms their right to be equal, affects their security, and changes attitudes toward them so they become more subject to violence."

Despite the critics' claims of "chilling effects" and the specter of "government censorship" invading our lives to rip *The Color Purple* out of our hands and our libraries, the "harm-to-women"/civil rights approach to antipornography legislation is gaining acceptance precisely because it is a carefully conceived legal attempt to come to grips with the widespread availability of sexist and violent pornographic images in our society. There is a vast difference between the thought police—the censors that pro-ordinance activists are often accused of being—and the act of suing for damages resulting from pornography. The civil-rights approach of the Pornography Victims Compensation Act and the Dworkin-MacKinnon ordinance contrasts markedly with the moralistic approach of obscenity laws in the United States. "Obscenity laws [in the U.S.]," author John Stoltenberg writes in *Refusing to Be a Man,* "are inherently subjective and arbitrary in their application because they criminalize a notion of indecency that does no real harm. There's no evidence that obscenity causes any harm. But there's a lot of evidence that pornography—as defined in the civil-rights ordinance—is harmful."

To sum up: In the civil rights legislation, pornography is defined *according to harm,* and the claim is based *on injury to victim.* With the U.S. obscenity law, obscenity is defined by arousal and the crime is based on *offense to public morals,* which are arbitrary and fluctuate according to who is being offended. The reparation for a civil law breach consists of money damages or injunction, whereas the criminal redress for the obscenity law is imprisonment, fine, or censorship. The ordinance is intended to protect people from circumstances such as those that Linda Marchiano endured when she was kidnapped, forced at gunpoint to perform various demeaning acts, and raped off as well as on camera. Those women who "choose" to act in pornographic movies, or pose for centerfolds, will not be deprived of their right to do so. But the ordinance will allow those who wish to sue the distributors of the "art" they were subjected to or engaged in against their will to do this, *providing they can prove damage.*

What the "harm-to-women"/civil rights approach to antipornography legislation ultimately means is women believing in their human dignity and in their right to receive compensation through the justice system for brutal acts done to them. It's tempting for its critics to see the ordinance as other than it is, as somehow the same as U.S. obscenity laws, since demeaning printed and visual images—in advertising and other media as well as pornography—have so greatly saturated our lives and everyday consciousness that we tend to dismiss them as normal, as "the way things are." But "the way things are" has been proven to be devastating, not only by the scientific studies but also by the countless testimonies of women about the degradation, intimidation, and discrimination they suffered as a result of pornography. The theoretical realm of "just images and words" suffuses right into our daily lives.

With freedom of speech comes *responsibility* for that speech. The pornographer is not concerned about taking responsibility for the criminal acts involved in the production of pornography. Nor does the pornographer care about the responsibility of portraying people or sexuality in an ethical manner, or the damage that may result from a deceptive portrayal as evidenced by the weight of the sociological evidence and the heartbreaking testimony of many women and children. Pornography is about profits, pure and simple. And in this marketplace gone amok, anything is considered an exploitable and expendable resource, even women's bodies, even human sexual relations.

Federal Judge Frank Easterbrook of the Seventh Circuit, who penned the opinion that struck down the Indianapolis ordinance, nevertheless accepted the argument that pornography harms women: "Depictions of subordination tend to perpetuate subordination. The subordinate status of women, in turn, leads to affront and lower pay at work, insult and injury at home, battery and rape on the streets." Remarkably, Judge Easterbrook's opinion declared that "this simply demonstrates the power of pornography as speech" and that First Amendment rights take precedence over the harms done to women.

But the Canadian Supreme Court rejected this notion, for the first time acknowledging that women should not be forced to shoulder an unequal burden of harm. "If true equality between male and female persons is to be achieved," wrote Justice John Sopinka, "we cannot ignore the threat to equality resulting from exposure to audiences of certain types of violent and degrading material." The Canadian Supreme Court's decision gives hope and encouragement to those working to end violence and discrimination against women around the world.

STEVEN HILL is a writer, community organizer, youth counselor, and editor of the *Activist Men's Journal*. His articles, commentaries, poems, and poetry reviews have appeared in *Making Violence Sexy*, edited by Diana Russell, *The Humanist*, the *Seattle Times*, *Crossroads*, the *Madison (Wisconsin) Edge*, *Minnesota Review*, *Seattle Post-Intelligencer*, *Seattle Community Catalyst*, *La Voz*, *The Stranger*, *Written Arts*, *Prophetic Voices*, the *Peacemaker*, *San Fernando Poetry Journal*, *African Literature, Analysis and Critical Perspectives*, the anthologies *Grasp the Rainbow*, *Poets for a Liveable Planet*, and others.

NINA SILVER is a Reichian therapist and writer whose essays and poems on feminism, psychology, sexuality, and metaphysics have appeared in the *New Internationalist*, *off our backs*, *Central Park*, *Gnosis*, *Green Egg*, *Jewish Currents*, and the anthologies *Women's Glib*, *Call It Courage: Women Transcending Violence*, *Childless by Choice*, *Closer to Home: Bisexuality and Feminism*, and *Woman in the Window*. Her criticism of pornography and child abuse in the nudist movement was cited in the *Utne Reader* and the *New Yorker*, and her volume of poetry, *Birthing*, will be published in 1994 by Woman in the Moon Publications. She has just completed a book combining feminism, depth psychology, and the body/mind theories of Wilhelm Reich.

IN THE WAKE OF TAILHOOK:
A New Order for the Navy

by Barbara Spyridon Pope

After Tailhook, senior leadership was faced with a
fundamental dilemma. How could they prosecute,
sacrifice, young aviators for doing what some of them
had done ten or twenty years earlier? This is not unlike
the dilemma that Congress faces—how to censor
its members for behavior that others were guilty
of only a few years ago.

THE ANNUAL TAILHOOK Convention, named after the hook on carrier aircraft that catches the arresting cable on the deck of aircraft carriers, has taken place for more than twenty years as a celebration of the United States naval aviator, considered by many to be the best in the world. Naval fighter pilots have been the "fair-haired sons" of the Navy. Their aviation skills, dexterity, and technical competence are peerless. Daily, they live on the edge of danger, landing on and taking off from postage-stamp-sized airfields, often in the black of night and on pitching decks in rough seas. To do this takes nerves of steel. It also creates great tension and the necessity of having a release for this tension. Like parents who spoil their favorite child, the Navy "spoiled" these aviators and failed its responsibility to the junior officers to teach leadership and to create appropriate outlets for their stress and tensions. As a result, unruly behavior, heavy drinking, and wild shenanigans became an integral part of their tradition and, worse, became expected behavior among some. Each generation of aviators embraced the tradition of outdoing its predecessors, whether it was at sea in more advanced planes or ashore at the annual Tailhook Convention.

In 1985, convention attendees' behavior was so deplorable that the organization was investigated by the Navy Inspector General. As a result, written direction was disseminated to naval aviators to improve their behavior or jeopardize the convention's existence. The Navy thought leadership alone could change behavior and did not institute any training to assist in the changes. The behavior seemed to improve for a couple of years—until 1991, which was unique in several respects.

September 1991 was the first gathering of young, jubilant, Persian Gulf War experienced pilots. The A-12, naval aviation's expected next-generation aircraft, had just been cancelled. The competition with the Air Force for future roles and missions was not going well. When Congress proposed to open tactical aviation to women, many pilots felt threatened for two reasons: the community was facing substantial downsizing, and tactical aviation has historically been dominated by men. Thus, celebration, frustration, and fear of the future, fueled by excessive alcohol, created an explosive situation at the convention. This was a community well known for its raucous behavior, lack of tolerance for women, consumption of huge amounts of alcohol, and a mindset among some that fighter pilots were so special they were exempt from rules of good order and discipline. All of these factors culminated in the sexual assault of at least eighty-three women—twenty-two officers and sixty-one civilians—who were physically fondled, caressed, and had hands up their dresses and down their blouses; some were bitten on the buttock as they were physically picked up and passed down a gauntlet of drunken naval aviators. This was not the first year the gauntlet had occurred. Originally, it was with willing participants, some of whom were prostitutes and some who thought the gauntlet was "fun."

Unfortunately, in my opinion, the sexual assaults and the drunken parties were compounded by the failure of naval aviation leadership to respond and rectify the situation once the damage had occurred. Prior to the 1991 Tailhook Convention, the Secretary of the Navy released a sexual harassment policy that made explicit the commanders' responsibility and accountability for preventing sexual harassment in their commands, leaving little or no doubt that such behavior was prohibited conduct.

Unfortunately, the policy again was not followed by training to clearly explain the policy or to teach commanding officers how to change existing behaviors. They did not understand that sexist behavior in the workplace is inappropriate because it provides an atmosphere in which sexual harassment can flourish. Addressing attitudes and respect for human dignity are critical to eliminating sexual harassment from the workplace. Sexist behavior that creates a "hostile environment" for employees is prohibited by the Civil Rights Act of 1991.

After Tailhook, senior leadership was faced with a fundamental dilemma. How could they prosecute, sacrifice, young aviators for doing what some of them had done ten or twenty years earlier? This is not unlike the dilemma that Congress faces—how to censor its members for behavior that others had been guilty of only a few years ago. Not only did sexual assault take place as other officers stood by and watched, but officers sexually assaulted other officers, thereby destroying the sacred trust of honor among officers.

In addition, senior leadership was willing to believe that officers did not understand the difference between lying and self-incrimination. Protecting their fellow officers was more important than discovering who perpetrated the assault and restoring the good reputation of their service. It is astonishing that only a handful of the thousands of people interviewed by the Naval Investigative Service "saw" any misconduct. In light of these facts, it is deplorable that during the Navy's investigation no senior military leader had the moral courage to come forward and declare that the outrageous behavior at the 1991 Tailhook Convention were traditions no longer viable.

From my perspective, the lack of personal and professional outrage from aviation commanding officers at the behavior that took place both at and after Tailhook was as large an abrogation of peacetime leadership as any encountered in the history of the United States Navy. The honored and time-tested concept of accountability was suspended with regard to Tailhook. In the Navy, it is customary when a ship runs aground or an aircraft has a mishap that a complete and thorough investigation is conducted to include all regulations and policies. Upon completion of such investigations, the senior officer on the scene responsible for what transpired, along with the specific individuals who actually caused the situation, are held accountable. No such thorough investigation took place by the Navy with regard to Tailhook. Squadron commanders who were present in Las Vegas were not held accountable.

In the wake of Tailhook, former Secretary of the Navy Sean O'Keefe implemented an immediate mandatory one-day sexual harassment training for all employees, both military and civilian, in the Navy and in the Marine Corps. The training, which I was responsible for developing, was critical so every individual would have a clear understanding of the definitions, policies, responsibilities, and appropriate behaviors necessary for preventing sexual harassment. It was an important first step in defining sexual harassment and in giving supervisors and commanding officers tools for dealing with sexual harassment. The training sessions were conducted by technical experts in the fields of Human Relations and Equal Opportunity. The senior person at each session started the training by conveying his or her personal commitment as well as the Secretary of the Navy's commitment to eliminating sexual harassment from the workplace. A videotape from the Chief of Naval Operations or the Commandant of the Marine Corps articulating their personal commitment was also shown. Included in the training was a section on responsible alcohol use and a discussion about values, ethics, and human respect. This training is now required annually and is being included in all entry-level programs and leadership courses throughout the Navy and Marine Corps.

The next step was to create a Standing Committee on Military and Civilian Women in the Navy, which I chaired, to review the current combat exclusion rules, address the cultural climate, and make recommendations to the Secretary to eliminate sexual harassment. The Committee comprised five women and six men: myself, who was the Assistant Secretary of the Navy for Manpower and Reserve Affairs; an ambassador, who was also a decorated former naval officer and a member of the Board of Visitors to the Naval Academy; the Assistant Secretary of Labor for Policy; a Special Assistant to the President; the Vice Chief of the Navy; the Assistant Commandant of the Marine Corps; the Marine Lieutenant General responsible for training; a Rear Admiral, who was the deputy in charge of naval training; the Master Chief Petty Officer of the Navy; the Sergeant Major of the Marine Corps; and the Chair of the Department of Defense Advisory Committee of Women in the Military. It was also supported by a diverse, mixed-gender working group of about sixty people. While the committee did not take testimony on this subject, they reviewed all of the current studies and the testimony before the President's Commission on Women in Combat. This review culminated in over eighty recommendations being implemented to change the Navy's corporate culture, redefine combat exclusion, and implement an integrated systems approach to sexual harassment. As a result of these changes, the Department of the Navy became the first military department to open all ships, submarines and aircraft, and all career fields except direct hand-to-hand combat to women and assign all people based on requirement and readiness, not gender.

This review was a comprehensive analysis of Navy and Marine Corps professional development and sexual harassment policies and procedures, both formal and informal. From the onset of the review the focus was that of integration versus assimilation of women in the military. The members of the Standing Committee and its working groups were unanimous that discrimination of any type undermined the readiness of the military and was a waste of valuable resources—our people.

To begin changing the corporate culture, it was critical that we develop a definition that everyone could understand. With over a million people, military and civilian, active and reserve, from the ages of seventeen to sixty-five, we needed a commonsense definition that illustrated behavior. We adopted the green-yellow-red light definition, which groups behavior into categories or zones and gives examples:

Green Zone—These behaviors are not sexual harassment: performance counseling, touching that could not reasonably be perceived in a sexual way (such as touching someone on the elbow), counseling on military appearance, social interaction, showing concern, encouragement, a polite compliment, or friendly conversation.

Yellow Zone—Many people would find these behaviors sexist, inappropriate, and leading to sexual harassment: violating "personal space," whistling, gestures about personal life, lewd or sexually suggestive comments, suggestive posters or calendars, off-color jokes, leering, staring, repeated requests for dates, foul language, unwanted letters or poems, sexually suggestive touching, or sitting and gesturing sexually.

Red Zone—These behaviors are always considered sexual harassment: sexual favors in return for employment rewards, threats if sexual favors are not provided, sexually explicit pictures (including posters or calendars) or remarks, using status to requests dates, or obscene letters or comments. The most severe forms of sexual harassment constitute criminal conduct, e.g. sexual assault (ranging from forcefully grabbing to fondling, forced kissing, or rape).

We were careful to emphasize that the above examples are used as guidance only, that individuals believe they are being sexually harassed based on their perception, that each incident is judged on the totality of facts in that particular case, and that individuals' judgment may vary on the same facts. Therefore, caution in this area is advised. Any time sexual behavior is introduced into the work environment or among coworkers, the individuals involved are on notice that the behavior may constitute sexual harassment.

It was critical that we began to build trust into the system and truly encourage people to come forward to ask for help in understanding inappropriate behavior and in approaching an individual who might be guilty of sexist behavior or sexual harassment. To accomplish this and to preserve anonymity, to encourage resolution at the lowest possible level and to protect individuals, both recipients and those falsely accused, we instituted a toll-free line. This anonymous resource was an important step in convincing our work force that the Department of the Navy was serious about preventing inappropriate behavior and enforcing the policy.

After we conducted the sexual harassment training, we felt it was vital to develop a core values course that addressed values, ethics, and human decency to be integrated into all training. It was important that the Department clearly articulate what core values we felt were vital to individuals and to the organization in support of our overall organizational effectiveness. The Department of the Navy identified the values of integrity, honor, and commitment as the most important. It addressed expected behavior of all members of the naval service and used case studies to illustrate the impact of values on ethical behavior and to stimulate candid discussions.

We felt that we could control behavior through regulations and discipline, but to make a lasting impact on the individuals and to begin to change attitudes, we needed to invest time and energy reestablishing basic values. For military personnel who daily face life-threatening issues and must depend on their unit, squadron, company, and shipmates for survival, it was imperative not just that respect for women be emphasized but that respect for all human dignity be accentuated and tied to readiness. It was also important to have people understand their own ethics and what they were willing to compromise. One case study that effectively looked at core values and ethical behavior dealt with filing a travel voucher and how much an individual might be willing to compromise if no one was watching. It was also important to illustrate how once an individual begins to compromise ethics and values in one area, i.e. sexual harassment, the boundaries in other areas become blurred. This one-day course is being integrated into all training and leadership courses.

The last step was to develop a complaint resolution system that clearly delineated every individual's responsibility—recipient, alleged harasser, coworkers, and supervisors.

The legal definition of sexual harassment, the behavior zones, definitions of terms, individual responsibilities, accountability, and procedures were compiled in a succinct, easy-to-understand Secretary of the Navy Instruction 5300.26, which establishes a regulation to enforce the sexual harassment policy.

Had these changes been in place and integrated within the Navy ranks in 1991, the sexual harassment and assault that took place at that year's Tailhook would not have occurred. The challenge to the next administration will be to continue the momentum of change in the aftermath of Tailhook in the naval service and not let change be driven by such unfortunate incidents nor let change undermine the Navy's fundamental mission of national defense.

As the first female Assistant Secretary of the Navy in its history, I was in a unique position to observe many positive changes in the Department of the Navy. From my experience and observations over the last decade, I am convinced that women make a very valuable contribution to the naval service. Women have the commitment, dedication, intelligence, and leadership that is required of military service. I also believe that the opposition to full integration of women in the military comes from those who have never served alongside women, not from those who have worked and served with women. Like men, not all women are cut out for the sacrifices military service requires, but for those women who want to serve their country, the naval services are now committed to full integration.

Gender bias is certainly alive and well, but leadership in a specific organization is critical to whether it interferes with an individual's job. Most women join the military for the same reason men do: an opportunity to serve their country and to hold very responsible jobs at relatively young ages. The new integrated systems approach to sexual harassment will allow women to do their jobs effectively by getting at the attitudes that produce sexual harassment as well as the behavior.

BARBARA SPYRIDON POPE is the former Assistant Secretary of the Navy for Manpower and Reserve Affairs. She was the first female assistant secretary and senior female in the Navy's 217-year history. Ms. Pope was instrumental in developing training programs and implementing policies and procedures to begin the steps necessary to eliminate sexual harassment and to change the corporate culture of the Navy and Marine Corps. She was also a Deputy Assistant Secretary of Defense.

Ms. Pope is the founder and president of the nonprofit Foundation for the Prevention of Sexual Harassment and Workplace Discrimination. She is the president of the Pope Group, a management firm with expertise in downsizing, diversity, glass ceiling, and sexual harassment. She is the recipient of the 1993 Women Executives in State Government "Breaking the Glass Ceiling" Award.

NO LAUGHING MATTER:
Sexual Harassment in K-12 Schools

by Nan Stein

Listening to the stories of young women's experiences of
sexual harassment in schools has led me to see that schools
may in fact be training grounds for the insidious cycle
of domestic violence: girls learn that they are on their
own, that the adults and others around them will not
believe or help them when they report sexual
harassment or assault.

It came to the point where I was skipping almost all of my classes, therefore getting kicked out of the honors program. It was *very* painful for me. I dreaded school each morning, I started to wear clothes that wouldn't flatter my figure, and I kept to myself. I never had a boyfriend that year. I'd cry every night I got home, and I thought I was a total loser. . . . Sometimes the teachers were right there when it was going on. They did nothing. . . . I felt very angry that these arrogant, narrow-minded people never took the time to see who really was inside. . . . I'm also very angry that they took away my self-esteem, my social life, and kept me from getting a good education.

—sixteen-year-old from midsized city in Illinois

Being sexually harassed at school made me feel upset, angry, and violated. I mean, I shouldn't have to take this crap at school, should I? It's my right to go to school and not be harassed, isn't it? I feel confused because I wonder if *all guys* think those things about me! I feel insecure after this happens. I hate it. I shouldn't have to feel sexually intimidated by people who barely know me.

—sixteen-year-old from a midsized city in northern New England.

PEER-TO-PEER SEXUAL HARASSMENT is rampant in elementary and secondary schools. While sometimes identified and curtailed, more often than not it is tolerated, characterized as a normal stage in healthy American adolescent development. Frequently it is identified as "flirting" or dismissed as part of acceptable "initiation rites." "No harm done" and "no big deal" are the often-cited claims. Regardless of the ways school authorities rationalize its existence, sexual harassment interferes with a student's right to receive equal educational opportunities and is a violation of Title IX, the twenty-year-old federal law that outlaws sex discrimination in educational institutions receiving federal financial assistance.[1]

Sexual harassment in schools operates in full and plain view of others. Boys harass girls with impunity while people watch. Examples of sexual harassment that happen in public include attempts to snap bras, grope at girls' bodies, pull down gym shorts, or flip up skirts; circulating "summa cum slutty" or "piece of ass of the week" lists; designating special weeks for "grabbing the private parts of girls"; nasty, personalized graffiti written on bathroom walls; sexualized jokes, taunts, and skits that mock girls' bodies, performed at school-sponsored pep rallies, assemblies, or halftime performances during sporting events; and outright physical assault and even rape in schools.[2]

Sexual harassment is a form of sex discrimination and is illegal as defined by Title IX of the Educational Amendments of 1972, Title VII of the Civil Rights Act (1964 amended 1972)[3], the equal protection clause of the Fourteenth Amendment[4] of the U.S. Constitution, and numerous state criminal and civil statues[5]. The presence or absence of sexual harassment depends on the victim's perception of "unwelcomed" sexual behavior. Sexual harassment can range from touching, tickling, pinching, patting, or grabbing; to comments about one's body, to sexual remarks, innuendos, and jokes that cause discomfort; to obscene gestures, staring, or leering; to assault and rape.

Both students and employees are legally protected against sexual harassment, regardless of whether the perpetrator is an employee, a student, or an individual who is connected to the school district only by means of being part of an organization with which the school has a contractual agreement. Some forms of sexual harassment may also be actionable as child abuse, sexual assault, rape, pornography, criminal or civil libel, slander, or defamation of character. Victims, as well as educators or community members acting on the victim's behalf, may file sexual harassment complaints.[6] Sexual harassment contaminates the whole school environment, and its reach may embrace more than the immediate and intended target(s). Indeed, the school environment becomes poisoned for everyone—innocent witnesses and bystanders alike—in addition to the intended subject/victim of the sexual harassment.

The examples of peer-to-peer sexual harassment cited above are commonplace occurrences in elementary and secondary schools across the country, in small towns with homogeneous populations as well as in large cities with more culturally diverse populations.[7] The desperate dilemma facing victims of sexual harassment is how to avoid the upsetting and degrading incidents when they have become so acceptable, ordinary, and public. What happens in public, if not interrupted, becomes normalized and acceptable over time. Moreover, students have expectations that if something scary, unpleasant, or illegal is happening in school, especially if it occurs in public, someone with authority will intervene to stop it, help out, or at least believe the victim afterwards. Yet sexual harassment seems for the most part to proceed mostly without adult intervention, thereby exacerbating and broadening its reach and reign of terror. In schools sexual harassment is tenacious, pervasive, and operates as a kind of gendered terrorism.[8]

The following excerpts come from narratives written by young women about their experiences of sexual harassment in schools:

> The problem is, this is middle school, and they think it doesn't happen, but it does! He only gets a warning or, if I'm lucky, detention. It's so unfair! It's all over our school.
> —twelve-year-old, Atlanta area, Georgia

> He had a habit of trying to sneak up on girls and try(ing) to pull their shorts down. All the girls complained to the teacher —who yelled at him but did nothing. What made things harder was that some girls kidded with him, which may have encouraged him further. For about three months he continued. Some days were better than others; most people tried to avoid him. . . . What angers me is that even though I filed a formal complaint, the gym teacher didn't get in trouble. The boy was watched for a while until the principal had more evidence— then suspended for six days. The "big picture" is scarier than isolated incidents.
> —seventeen-year-old from New Jersey

> It was like fighting an invisible, invincible enemy alone. I didn't have a clue as to what to do to stop it, so I experimented [with] different approaches. Ignoring it only made it worse. It made it easier for them to do it, so they did it more. Laughing at the perpetrators during the assaults didn't dent the problem at all, and soon my friends became tired of doing this. They thought it was a game. Finally I wrote them threatening letters. This got me in trouble. But perhaps it did work. I told the school administrators what had been happening to me. They didn't seem to think it a big deal, but they did talk to the three

biggest perpetrators. The boys ignored the administrators and it
continued. And they were even worse.

—fifteen-year-old from a midsized city in Massachusetts

Of the times I was sexually harassed at school, one of them
made me feel really bad. I was in class and the teacher was
looking right at me when this guy grabbed my butt. The
teacher saw it happen. I slapped the guy and told him not to do
that. My teacher didn't say anything and looked away and
went on with the lesson like nothing out of the ordinary had
happened. It really confused me because I knew guys weren't
supposed to do that, but the teacher didn't do anything. I felt
like the teacher (who was a man) betrayed me and thought I
was making a big deal out of nothing. But most of all, I felt
really bad about myself because it made me feel slutty and
cheap. It made me feel mad too because we shouldn't have to
put up with that stuff, but no one will do anything to stop it.
Now sexual harassment doesn't bother me as much because it
happens so much it almost seems normal. I know that sounds
awful, but the longer it goes on without anyone doing anything, the more I think of it as just one of those things that I
have to put up with.

—fourteen-year-old from a midsized city in the Pacific
Northwest

The silences of adults in the school community represent negligence,
allowing and encouraging the sexual harassment to continue. The cyni-
cal, bitter lessons of silence and neglect affect not only the subjects of
sexual harassment, but also the witnesses. Boys as well as girls become
mistrustful of adults who fail to intervene, provide equal protection, and
safeguard the educational environment. Too many of our schools have
become unsafe, uncaring, and unjust.[9]

A HIDDEN CURRICULUM OF ABUSE AND POWERLESSNESS

Listening to the stories of young women's experiences of sexual
harassment in schools has led me to see that schools may in fact be

training grounds for the insidious cycle of domestic violence: girls learn that they are on their own, that the adults and others around them will not believe or help them when they report sexual harassment or assault. The school's hidden curriculum teaches young women to suffer abuse privately, that to resist is futile. When they witness harassment of others and fail to respond, they absorb a different kind of powerlessness—that they are incapable of standing up to injustice or acting in solidarity with their peers. Similarly, boys receive permission in schools, even training, to become batterers through the practice of sexual harassment. Indeed, if school authorities do not intervene and challenge the boys who sexually harass, the schools may be encouraging a continued pattern of violence in relationships. The larger societal problem of domestic violence may in fact be fueled in our schools as sexual harassment.[10] Moreover, the sorts of remedies school officials import into the school to resolve incidents of sexual harassment or teen-dating violence are often the same tactics found to be ineffective in diffusing domestic violence. In particular, restraining orders, often used by battered women in hopes of keeping their batterers away from them, are taken out by teenage couples when they sever their relationship. These measures, ineffectual in keeping batterers away from their targets,[11] may be even harder to enforce in a school community where students mingle in the cafeteria, hallways, and parking lot. Clearly, school officials cannot count on restraining orders to curb peer-to-peer sexual harassment in school and teen-dating violence.

"BULLYING" AS AN ANTECEDENT TO SEXUAL HARASSMENT

The antecedents to peer-to-peer sexual harassment in schools may be found in "bullying," behaviors children learn, practice, and/or experience beginning at a very young age. All boys know what a bully is, and many boys as well as girls have been victims of bullying. Teachers and parents know about bullying, and many accept it as an unfortunate stage that some children go through on their way to adolescence and adulthood. Left unchecked and unchallenged, bullying may in fact serve as fertile practice ground for sexual harassment.

Like its older cousin, sexual harassment, bullying deprives children of their rightful entitlement to be educated and secure in the knowledge

318 Nan Stein

that they will be safe and free from harm. While laws in many states outlaw the practice of "hazing" in educational institutions (defined as the organized practice of induction, usually into a fraternity or sports team, through degrading behaviors and/or physical assault), bullying floats free from legal restraint and adult intervention and is often not discussed as a deliberate part of the school curriculum.[12]

If educators and advocates pose and present the problem as "bullying" to young children, rather than labeling it immediately as "sexual harassment," we can engage children and universalize the phenomena as one that boys as well as girls will understand and accept as problematic. We will go a long way towards developing compassion and empathy in boys for girls and what it is that boys do to girls when they sexually harass them. Moreover, we can simultaneously avoid demonizing all little boys as potential "harassers" by initially presenting these hurtful and offensive behaviors as bullying. Activities that ask children to distinguish between "teasing" and "bullying" can help them focus on the boundaries between appropriate and inappropriate/hurtful behaviors. Gaining a conceptual framework and vocabulary that elementary school-age children can understand and apply will help them make the link and allow them to jump to discussions of sexual harassment.

Bullying and its links to sexual harassment in schools is of critical importance. Sexual harassment of girls by their male peers in school is more than the equivalent of the Tailhook scandal because, unlike Tailhook, the sexual harassment is not localized to one site during one week, but is a secret that happens in public every day in schools across the nation.

PROMOTING AWARENESS OF SEXUAL HARASSMENT IN SCHOOLS

We need to provoke a national awareness that sexual harassment exists in elementary and secondary schools. However, schools need to resist the temptation to treat sexual harassment symptomatically—a videotape here, a workshop there. Sexual harassment is a systemic problem; solutions must be systemic as well.

TRAINING PROGRAMS FOR STAFF AND STUDENTS

Everyone in the school's community, from custodians to bus drivers, classroom teachers, coaches, extracurricular advisors, the superintendent, and school board members, needs mandated professional development workshops and seminars on sexual harassment. Everyone must be trained to recognize sexual harassment, to know their responsibilities to report it to the proper individuals and agencies, and to create strategies to prevent and eliminate it. A cadre of both male and female staff members should receive intensive training and be designated to serve as "ombuds" available to the students.

Ongoing professional development for those who work or plan to work in any capacity in the schools must be offered and required in order to prevent and eliminate sexual harassment. Teacher preparation programs need to offer courses to preservice teachers that explain their responsibilities to intervene in order to discourage discrimination and harassment. Beyond this, such programs need to develop strategies for intervention and various models to resolve the problem.

The students as well must be included in ongoing conversations about sexual harassment and child sexual abuse in schools. Through orientation, assemblies, student handbooks, support/rap groups, peer advising, and activities and lessons infused into the classroom curriculum, the subject of sexual harassment must become a deliberate and frequent part of formal and informal curricula.

A NONLITIGIOUS INTERVENTION: "WRITE A LETTER TO THE HARASSER."

A top priority is the development of nonlitigious interventions that might remediate sexual harassment incidents before they escalate. One well-known activity is known as "Write a Letter to the Harasser." Developed by Dr. Mary Rowe, special assistant to the president at M.I.T. and first published in the *Harvard Business Review* (May/June 1981), this technique was adapted in 1983 by Dr. Rowe and me for application with high school students.[13]

Several assumptions underlie the tactic of sending a letter to the harasser:

1. It is an active response to the harassment by the subject/victim.
2. It changes the balance of power: the subject/victim becomes proactive and the harasser is placed in a "receiver" role.
3. It shows the harasser there are serious consequences to these behaviors that live beyond the time of the sexual harassment incident.
4. It catches the harasser alone. The letter should be given to the harasser by the victim (if she so chooses) in the presence of an adult staff member, preferably in the privacy of the adult staff member's office.

   Alternately, if the letter is sent to the harasser's home, the envelope should be marked "personal," and a carbon copy should be kept by both the subject/victim and by the adult advocate. It should be indicated in the letter that a carbon copy ("cc") has been sent to the adult advocate.
5. It forces the harasser to face up to behaviors in a different context from the one in which the harassment was committed. Sometimes the contrast between behaviors and values of the school setting and those of the home setting may give the harasser a new perspective on the harassing behaviors.
6. It allows the subject/victim to feel safe; the harasser is confronted, yet not in a face-to-face situation.
7. It protects the subject/victim legally by documenting the incident, behaviors, witnesses, and her feelings and serves to give the harasser "fair warning" to stop.
8. It helps the subject/victim realize that the harasser may not understand the effects of these behaviors, and that the harasser may not see these behaviors as the subject/victim does.
9. It helps to contain the incident of sexual harassment among a small group of people—the subject/victim, the adult advocate, and the alleged harasser.

Rowe suggests "a polite, low-key letter" in three parts. The first part should include a statement of the facts: "This is what I think happened . . ." with "a precise rendering of all the facts and dates relevant to the alleged harassment."

The second part "should describe the[ir] feelings, and what damage [they] think has been done." Appropriate statements in this section include opinions, feelings, anxieties, and worries, such as: "Your action made me feel terrible"; "I am scared that I'm going to be blamed for your behavior"; "You have caused me to ask for a transfer (drop out of class)." Finally, any perceived or actual costs and damage belong in this second section, according to Rowe.

The third and final part of the letter should contain "a short statement of what the accuser/victim would like to have happen next. Since most persons want the harassment to end, the letter might finish by saying so." Statements such as: "I want those behaviors of yours to stop because they make me feel awful, and they interfere with my concentration in class and with my homework . . . my grades have been falling" would be appropriate here. Finally, Rowe recommends that "if the letter writer believes [that] some remedy or recompense is in order, this is the place to say so."

In workplace settings among adults, Rowe reports that the alleged harassment nearly always stops: "The letter constitutes an attempt to settle the problem peaceably." In those cases where the harassment does not stop, the subject/victim "is always better off for having tried to stop the offense in a direct and unambiguous way."

This letter-writing tactic has proven to be transferable to peer-to-peer sexual harassment cases in schools.[14] With the collaboration of an adult trained in this technique, writing a letter to the harasser becomes a step toward taking some control over a situation that often causes depression, fear, bewilderment, anxiety, and anger in the subject/victim of the harassment. Thus, the act of letter writing is positive and even therapeutic because it is proactive. In fact, this letter-writing technique can become part of a larger "talk back" curriculum of activism and empowerment.[15]

Cooperation with a school staff member accomplishes other important goals: the subject/victim speaks to someone about the incident and her feelings; the incident is documented; and only a small group of people are involved in discussing the incident, thus maintaining the privacy rights of both the alleged harasser and the victim/subject. While the letter-writing technique is a proactive response for the victim/subject and one that respects the privacy rights of the accuser, unfortunately it does not mitigate the negative collective learning that has already occurred among the bystanders who witnessed or heard about the sexual harassment incident. The hidden curriculum of sexual harassment is still not addressed by this technique.

For that reason, letter writing should in no way be seen as a strategy to prevent or eliminate sexual harassment in general; it will not take the place of strategies such as training programs, support groups, discipline codes, and grievance procedures. Letter writing is a tactic and option for the subject/victim only, not for the school or administration. Additionally, in order to send a letter to the harasser, the subject/victim must know the perpetrator and/or be able to identify the harasser. It would obviously be difficult to implement this letter-writing tactic otherwise.

SAMPLE LETTER FOR STUDENT-TO-STUDENT HARASSMENT

Dear Richard,

I am writing to let you know how it's been to be in auto shop with you—some of the things that happened between us this year, how it felt to be in class with you, and what I want to happen from now on.

When I think back to the beginning of shop a few things are very clear in my memory.

1. The first week, when I started talking to you or someone else, you made cracks about me being pretty hard up if taking auto shop was the only way I could meet boys, or saying that maybe I was a "lezzie."
2. The next few weeks, I came into class and found my project wrecked or my tool box missing. You were always across the room watching and laughing.
3. The week of Halloween you started pinching me and daring the other guys to touch me or grab me.
4. Then you started pretending to slip and splash me with grease.
5. The Tuesday before Thanksgiving we were locked in the changing room together, and I'm sure it wasn't an accident. If Mr. Barnes hadn't heard me scream and unlocked the door, I don't know what would have happened.

Just to write these things down makes me remember how scared and lonely I always felt. So many days I would go home and cry for hours. I don't think you know how much it bothered me, and how rotten it made me feel. I'm like you Richard—I love cars and to tinker with things. I have to help out with family expenses, and after this shop I can get a good job. Being a girl doesn't make things all that different.

I'd like you to think about how you'd feel if your sister or your girlfriend told you that some guys did to her what you've done to me. I'm sure you wouldn't feel very good about this situation—I don't feel very good about it either. So, here's how I'd like you to change. First, I'd like you to treat me as a kid in the shop who likes work, is good at certain things, and just happens to be a girl. Second, stop daring the guys to tease me or touch me, since they do what you say. Third, I want you to stop teasing me, touching me, and interfering with my work.

I hope maybe things will change now that you know how I feel.

Susan

cc: J. Smith, Title IX Coordinator, Guidance Office.[16]

CURRICULUM MATERIALS

Another route to creating awareness about sexual harassment in schools is to use curriculum materials highlighting the problem head-on. The most engaging and useful kind of curriculum is one that uses prototypical case studies to illuminate all of the nuances, complexities, and subjective elements of sexual harassment. It is important to develop case studies that have relevance in the local context and thereby resist the temptation to succumb to a particular curriculum product as the be-all and end-all. The curricula described below each utilize case studies to some extent.

The first product created about sexual harassment in schools was *Who's Hurt and Who's Liable: Sexual Harassment in Massachusetts Schools*, developed and distributed by the Massachusetts Department of Education. First published in 1979, and currently in its fourth edition (1986), this curriculum and resource guide for school personnel contains classroom activities, guidelines for discussing sexual harassment with staff and students, sample policies and grievance procedures, and an extensive bibliography. Several case studies for classroom use are included. Several other state departments of education,[17] most notably

Minnesota (Kiscaden and Strauss, 1988), Washington (Northwest Women's Law Center, 1984; revised 1992), and New Jersey (Project TIDE, 1990), have produced derivative curriculum materials, relying heavily on the pioneering effort of the Massachusetts Department of Education. Each of these curriculum products contain some case studies, and is available to the general public at no cost or for a nominal price.

The highly original booklet *"Tune In to Your Rights: A Guide for Teenagers about Turning Off Sexual Harassment"* was created in 1985 by the Programs for Educational Opportunity at the University of Michigan. This readable and compelling text reads like a teenager's journal, with information on sexual harassment alternating with entries in a female student's diary. It is available in English, Spanish, and Arabic, and has sold over two hundred thousand copies. This booklet presents multiple points of view, including those of the young woman who is the victim/subject, her perpetrator, the other students who are bystanders and witnesses to the incidents, and those of the school's administration.

There are also four media productions on sexual harassment in schools. *No Laughing Matter: High School Students and Sexual Harassment*, produced and distributed by the Massachusetts Department of Education in 1982, uses docudrama vignettes about three young women's experiences with sexual harassment: the first young woman attends a traditionally male vocational school where she is subjected to teasing and demeaning behaviors by other students and teachers; the second young woman attends a regular, comprehensive high school and is harassed by a male student; and the third young woman experiences sexual harassment on the job. Interspersed throughout these vignettes are interviews with real teachers, administrators, and students, confirming the existence of sexual harassment in schools. The twenty-five-minute videotape has been sold to approximately three hundred school districts, colleges, state and federal agencies, and advocacy organizations. The Sex Equity Office of the California Department of Education developed a second media production in 1985. The two filmstrips, *It's Not Funny If It Hurts* and *Think About It—It Won't Go Away*, summarize the relevant laws geared to students and to school staff respectively. About two hundred copies have been sold to school districts both in and outside of California. A third videotape, produced in 1984 and distributed by the Northwest Women's Law Center in Seattle, discusses adult-to-student sexual harassment in schools and sexual harassment among employees in schools. It is particularly suitable as an introduction for adult audiences. The New Jersey Department of Education produced a fourth videotape in 1991, *Sending the Right Signals: A Training Program about Dealing with Sexual Harassment*, which focuses on students in vocational technical schools.

As the recognition of sexual harassment in schools has grown, more and spiffier media productions have become available. In 1992 alone, at least three new videotapes hit the market, including *Teen Awareness/Sexual Harassment: What It Is. What to Do*, (New Dimension Media, Eugene, Oregon); *Crossing the Line: Sexual Harassment Among Students* (Intermedia, Seattle); and *Sexual Harassment: What Is It and Why Should I Care?* (Quality Work Environments, Manhattan, Kansas). In general these more recent productions portray predominately white, middle-class students and schools, thereby reducing the usefulness of these videotapes since they do not reflect the true racial, ethnic, and linguistic diversity of America's children. Moreover, these more recent productions are far more costly (upwards of three hundred dollars) than the ones produced a decade earlier, which typically sell for under fifty dollars.

A fourth videotape series became available in 1993 from McGrath Systems (Santa Barbara, California) that sells for $1500 for a set of three (separate tapes for educators, for students, and for parents). While these productions portray multi-racial classrooms and use multi-racial hosts in sometimes lively and engaging formats (some segments are shot like music videos and include teenagers doing raps about sexual harassment), its price may be prohibitive for the educational market. No doubt other media productions will come into the educational market in the next year or so.

POLICIES AND PROCEDURES

An effective sexual harassment policy should begin with a clear statement that expresses disapproval of sexual harassment and a strong commitment to eliminating it. Victims should be encouraged to come forward, and all community members should be reminded of their responsibilities as bystanders and potential witnesses to report incidents of sexual harassment. Anything the school system writes should be in language accessible to all the students and community members. The policy should include definitions of sexual harassment that embrace peer-to-peer, adult-to-student, student-to-adult, and same-sex harassment. It is helpful to include examples of sexual harassment and child sexual abuse, indicating that these incidents and behaviors can happen both in public and in private.

An effective complaint procedure should include:

1. formal and informal procedures for complaining;
2. multiple points of entry, that is, different individuals to whom the complainant can go when initiating a complaint, including people of different races and both genders to serve as complaint managers or "ombuds";
3. a statement about no retaliation for complaining;
4. explicit procedures for maintaining confidentiality and privacy rights without promising absolute confidentiality;
5. a schedule for conducting and resolving the investigation and communicating with the complainant;
6. guarantees of due process, including specific disciplinary measures for dealing with sexual harassment;
7. a commitment to disseminate the policy and procedures widely and frequently;
8. a commitment to provide frequent informational and training sessions for the school staff, students, school board members, and parents; and
9. legal authority for the policy and procedures, citing the exact state and federal laws and regulations that govern sexual harassment and child sexual abuse.

STATE POLICY DEVELOPMENT

Concerned educators, parents, students, community members, and feminists must press policymakers to extend the new national awareness about sexual harassment in schools into the domain of legislation, regulation, and school board policy. First, policymakers must disentangle the jurisdictional confusion about which state agencies have authority to investigate complaints of sexual harassment and child sexual abuse in schools, and then publicize those lines of authority to the public and to students. In addition, they must design models for public policy, procedures, regulations, and delivery of services to ensure that children who experience sexual abuse and sexual harassment in school settings are heard and protected. Anti-hazing laws must be passed or strengthened to include those institutional/group acts of sexual harassment that sometimes pass for "initiation rites."

Moreover, state laws need to be created that require schools to offer training for students and staff as well as to formulate sexual harassment policies and grievance procedures. In 1989 Minnesota passed a comprehensive state law requiring both elements: training and policy development. Unfortunately a law California passed, effective January 1, 1993, contains only the requirement for policy development and dissemination. Other states, such as Massachusetts, have proposed bills that would emphasize the requirement to train staff and students. Passing comprehensive state laws will surely strengthen efforts at the local level.

CONCLUSION

Ultimately, a strategy to attack sexual harassment in schools needs to aim at a transformation of the broader school culture. Dealing effectively with sexual harassment is much easier if a school has committed itself to infuse a spirit of equity and a critique of injustice into its curriculum and pedagogy. On the other hand, harassment flourishes where children are practiced in the art of doing nothing in the face of unjust treatment by others. When teachers subject children to a "sit-down-shut-up-and-do-your-work" pedagogy, they don't learn to think of themselves as moral subjects, capable of speaking out when they witness bullying or other forms of harassment. If youngsters haven't been encouraged to critique the sexism of the curriculum, hidden and overt, then they are less likely to recognize it when they confront it in their midst. Too often, the entire school structure offers children no meaningful involvement in decision-making about school policy, climate, or other curriculum matters. Life in school rehearses children to be social spectators[18].

Sexual harassment in schools, a well-known social secret and national disgrace, must become a public concern in order for it to be obliterated

from educational settings. With sustained and multipronged educational efforts we can crack the denial and casualness surrounding the problem of sexual harassment in schools. Only in conjunction with efforts to
reduce other practices that promote and institutionalize inequalities in
schools, such as tracking/ability grouping, standardized testing, biased
curricula, and biased classroom practices and pedagogies, will our
schools become safe and conducive learning environments for all students, with equal educational opportunities and justice available for both
females and males. In order to live out the democracy, we need to practice it in our schools.

NOTES

The author would like to thank Bill Bigelow, teacher and author from Portland,
Oregon, for overall editorial suggestions and provocative, incisive comments about educational transformation, resistance, and activism.

1. Department of Health, Education, and Welfare, Title IX of Education
   Amendment of 1972, 20 U.S.C. sec. 1681 (P.L. 92–318), *Federal Register* vol. 40,
   no. 108, 4 June 1975, p. 24128:
   No person in the United States shall, on the basis of sex, be excluded from participation in, be denied the benefits of, or be subjected to discrimination under any
   education program or activity receiving Federal financial assistance.
2. Nan Stein, "School Harassment—An Update," *Education Week* 12:9, no. 37
   (4 November 1992).
3. Equal Employment Opportunity Commission, "Guidelines on Discrimination
   Because of Sex," 29 C.F.R. Section 1604.11, Part 1604, *Federal Register*,
   10 November 1980, p. 746676:
   Harassment on the basis of sex is a violation of Sec. 703 of Title VII. Unwelcome
   sexual advances, requests for sexual favors, and other verbal or physical conduct of
   a sexual nature constitute sexual harassment when (1) submission to or rejection of
   such conduct is made either explicitly or implicitly a term or condition of an individual's employment, (2) submission to or rejection of such conduct by an individual is used as the basis of an employment decision affecting such individual, or (3)
   such conduct has the purpose or effect of unreasonably interfering with an individual's work performance or creating an intimidating, hostile, or offensive working
   environment.
4. *Civil Rights Act of 1871, 42 U.S.C. sec. 1983*:
   Every person who, under color of any statute, ordinance, regulation, custom,
   usage, or any state or territory, subjects or causes to be subjected, any citizen of the

United States or any person within the jurisdiction thereof to the deprivation of any rights, privileges, or immunities secured by the Constitution and laws, shall be liable to the party injured in an action at law, suit in equity, or other proper proceeding for redress.

Section 1983, which is a federal statute, provides an avenue of redress for individuals who have been deprived of their federal constitutional or statutory rights at the behest of state authority. Section 1983 provides redress for violation of explicit constitutional rights (e.g., the right to due process) and also of federal statutory rights passed pursuant to constitutional authority.

5. Most states have laws and/or governors' executive orders prohibiting sexual harassment in employment, in the public sector, and in education. The agencies with oversight and jurisdiction are either the state's human rights commission or department (for example in Minnesota, Washington state, Montana) or a statewide equal opportunity office. For example, in Massachusetts, it is called the Massachusetts Commission Against Discrimination; in Rhode Island, it is called the State Equal Opportunity Office. In addition, in many states there are Executive Orders issued by the governors that address sexual harassment in all state agencies. Examples include:

   a) in Massachusetts, Executive Order No. 200 by (former) Governor Edward J. King on 20 August 1981, and reissued by his successor Michael S. Dukakis as Executive Order No. 240 in 1986;

   b) Rhode Island. Executive Order No. 91–39 issued on 28 October 1991 by Governor Bruce Sundhun.

6. Nan Stein, "It Happens Here, Too: Sexual Harassment and Child Abuse in Elementary and Secondary Education," in *Gender and Education*, ed. Sari Biklin and Diane Pollard, National Society for the Study of Education Yearbook, 1993.

7. Jane Gross, "Schools Are Newest Arena for Sex-Harassment Cases," *New York Times,* 11 March 1992, pp. 1, B8.

   Millicent Lawton, "Sexual Harassment of Students Target of District Policies," *Education Week* (10 February 1993), pp. 1, 15–16.

   Adrian N. LeBlanc, "Harrassment in the Halls," *Seventeen,* September 1992, pp. 162–65, 170.

   Elizabeth L. Spaid, "Schools Grapple with Peer Harrassment," *Christian Science Monitor,* 21 January 1993, p. 3.

   Nan Stein, "Sexual Harassment of High School Students: Preliminary Research Results," unpublished ms., Quincy: Massachusetts Dept. of Education.

   — "It Happens, Here, Too."

   — "School Harassment—An Update."

   — "Sexual Harassment in Elementary and Secondary Education."

   Nan Stein, Nancy L. Marshall, and Linda R. Tropp, "Secrets in Public: Sexual Harassment in Our Schools. A Report on the results of a *Seventeen* magazine survey," 1993, Center for Research on Women, Wellesley College, MA.

   — "Hostile Hallways: the AAUW Survey on Sexual Harassment in America's Schools," 1993.

   Susan Strauss, "Sexual Harassment in the Schools: Legal Implications for

Principals," *National Assoc. of Secondary School Principals Bulletin* (March, 1988), pp. 93–97.

8. Stein, "School Harassment—An Update."

9. Ibid.

10. Stein, "Secrets in Public: Sexual Harassment in Public (and Private) Schools," working paper 256, Center for Research on Women, Wellesley College, Wellesley, Massachusetts, December 1992.

11. Bob Hohler, "Court's Shield Can Draw a Bullet," *Boston Globe*, 7 October 1992, pp. 1, 26.
    Sonya Ross, "One Million Attacks on Women Reported," *Boston Globe*, 3 October 1992, p. 3.
    Adrian Walker, "Third of Court Orders Flouted, Officials Say," *Boston Globe*, 30 September 1992, p. 1.

12. Stein, "Secrets in Public."

13. Mary P. Rowe, "Dealing with Sexual Harassment," *Harvard Business Review* 59, no. 3 (May-June 1981), pp. 42–46.
    Nan Stein, ed., *Who's Hurt and Who's Liable: Sexual Harassment in Massachusetts Schools* (Qunicy: MA Dept. of Education, 4th ed., 1986).

14. Beverly W. Lydiard, "A Decade of Dealing with Sexual Harassment," *School Administrator* 1, no. 50 (January 1993), pp. 20–21.

15. Bill Bigelow, personal communications, February 1993.

16. Stein, *Who's Hurt and Who's Liable.*

17. *It's Not Fun—It's Illegal: The Identification and Prevention of Sexual Harassment to Teenageers, a curriculum.* St. Paul: Minnesota Dept. of Education, 1988.
    Sexual Harassment in Employment and Education, a manual. Seattle: Northwest Women's Law Center, 1992 (first edition 1984, distributed by the WA Office of Public Instruction).
    Sending The Right Signals: A Training Program About Dealing with Sexual Harassment. Trenton, NJ: New Jersey Dept. of Education, 1990.

18. Bigelow, personal communications, February 1993.

NAN STEIN is a research associate at the Center for Research on Women at Wellesley College, where she directs a national research project on sexual harassment and child sexual abuse in the schools. She was coprincipal investigator of the *Seventeen* magazine (September 1992) survey on sexual harassment in schools, which is the largest survey ever conducted on sexual harassment in schools and the first with a nationwide sample. In 1980–81, in her former capacity as the sex equity/civil rights coordinator with the Massachusetts Department of Education, Stein conducted the first survey in the country on peer-to-peer sexual harassment; in 1979, she developed the first curriculum on the subject, which is currently in its fourth edition (1986).

Stein frequently provides training to school personnel and students around the country on the problem of sexual harassment in schools and has published many articles in professional journals on the subject. She is a former middle-school social studies teacher. She is currently involved in a research project in fourth- and fifth-grade classrooms, looking at the links between bullying and sexual harassment. She has also served as an expert witness in school sexual harassment lawsuits.

VISIONS & POSSIBILITIES

Here are the voices of women and men who have glimpsed the
possibility of a transformed world and will share their visions of
personal as well as institutional change. Some of these visions
are hard to see; many veils must be lifted. We must learn
new language, new responses. As products of the rape
culture we all suffer deep interior divisions, but
we can learn to speak truth, resist seduction, and
come to terms. We can learn to hear the
voice of the not yet spoken in our desire
to change, to follow these promptings
of our best selves.

THE VEILS

by Louise Erdrich

We are all bound, we are all in tatters, we are all the
shining presence behind the net. We are all the face
we're not allowed to touch. We are all in need
of the ancient nourishment.

IT HAS DROPPED across my face again, the white net, the cloud that at one time or another obscures the features of every woman I have known. It is a snow falling, always, between my face and your face, the shocked expression of social chastity, the charged atoms of social courtesy. Oversimplified emotion, parenthetical dreams—the message is too acute. The veil speaks possession and possessed desire. A violent grace is required to lift the veil all on your own. By custom, the authority of touch is given to the priest, the husband. The woman's hands are always too heavy; the woman's hands are filled.

The veil is the symbol of the female hymen, and to lift it was once, and often still is, the husband's first marital privilege. The veil is the mist before the woman's face that limits her vision to the here, the now, the inch beyond her nose. It is an illusion of safety, a flimsy skin of privacy that encourages violation. The message behind the veil is touch me, I'm yours. The purity is fictional, coy. The veil is the invitation to tear it away.

Three Photographs:
In the first, my grandmother stands beside a fellow first communicant. Both are crowned with lilies and carnations, holding Christ's symbol erect. They are held, they are captured in the white shadow and the air of their substanceless caves, the veils they wear. Here is my grandmother at the age of twelve. In two more years, at only fourteen, too young, she will deliver her first child. Her face is beautiful, her ankles thick, her eyes too serious. It is as if, in this picture, she knows that she is just about to enter a room with many doors but no windows and no view.

Next photograph:
My mother on her wedding day, so beautiful with her veil thrown back that she clouds my father's shy face with happiness. She is adored, the ecstasy is on her, so plain to see. And there is something in her face of all that is to come—the healthy children, the long marriage, the love that is to bear the weight of conflict through so many decades—a durable look of pleasure.

Last picture:
Me at seven, with my mother's veil tacked onto a lacy headband. I might as well be holding my grandmother's candle, too. The nylon dress is small and scratches underneath my arms. My bangs are curled on rags,

my hair reaches down to my waist, and I have rehearsed over and over in
air and in the mirror the act of tipping my head back, eyes shut and
tongue out, receiving Christ.

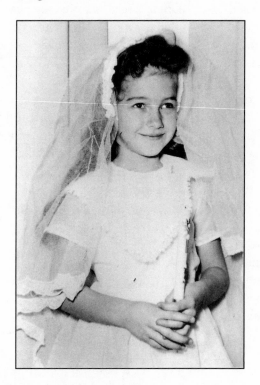

To keep my mouth shut. To turn away my face. To walk back down
the aisle. To slap the bishop back when he slapped me during confirmation. To hold the word *no* in my mouth like a gold coin, something valued, something possible. To teach the *no* to our daughters. To value
their *no* more than their compliant yes. To celebrate *no*. To hold the
word *no* in your fist and refuse to give it up. To support the boy who says
no to violence, the girl who will not be violated, the woman who says *no,
no, no. I will not.* To love the *no*, to cherish the *no*, which is so often our
first word. *No*—the means to transformation.

We are born in cauls and veils, and our lives as women are fierce and
individual dances of shedding them. We are stepping higher, higher
now, into the thinnest air. It takes about a decade of wild blue dancing to
shed just one. If we are lucky and if we dance hard enough, will we be

able to look each other in the eye, our faces clear, between us nothing but air?

And what do we do with the nets, the sails that luffed, that tangled around our feet? What do we do with the knowledge and the anger?

I see the veils twisted, knotted between us like sheets for escape. The taut material is strong when pulled and thinned to ropes between us. Primary cords. We can use the means and symbol of our long histories, as women, of emotional and intellectual incarceration. We can remove the flimsy shadows from before our faces and braid them into ropes. We can fasten the ropes between us so that if one of us slips, as we climb, as we live, there are others in the line to stand firm, to bear her up, to be her witnesses and anchors.

We are all bound, we are all in tatters, we are all the shining presence behind the net. We are all the face we're not allowed to touch. We are all in need of the ancient nourishment. And if we walk slowly without losing our connections to one another, if we wait, holding firm to the rock while our daughters approach hand over hand, if we can catch our mothers, if we hold our grandmothers, if we remember that the veil can also be the durable love between women. . . .

LOUISE ERDRICH is the author of two collections of poetry, *Jacklight* and *Baptism of Desire*, and four bestselling works of fiction: *Love Medicine* (winner of the 1984 National Book Critics Circle Award), *The Beet Queen, Tracks,* and, with her husband Michael Dorris, *The Crown of Columbus.* Her new novel, *The Bingo Palace,* will be published in January 1994 by HarperCollins. Her essays have recently appeared in *Harpers,* the *Georgia Review, Ladies' Home Journal,* and *Granta.*

THE LIE OF ENTITLEMENT

by Terrence Crowley

As a man, I accrue privilege simply by remaining silent,
accepting this legacy, and saying nothing about
its cost in terms of women's lives.

Lying is done with words, and also with silence.
—Adrienne Rich, *On Lies, Secrets, and Silence*

BECAUSE I WILL be using my personal experience as the vehicle for this essay, I want to start by saying a bit about who I am. I am a divorced white male in my early fifties. Reared in the southeast United States by working-class, Catholic parents, I earn my living as a self-employed furniture maker. I am university educated, middle-class, and straight. As such, I inherited all the privilege the rape culture provides.

The connection between my life and that culture was largely invisible to me until I began working with Men Stopping Violence, an organization dedicated to ending violence against women—specifically battering, rape, and incest. What I have learned through my associations with other men and in particular through my work with Men Stopping Violence is that, although my experience may differ from that of other men in some of its specifics, it is frighteningly similar at its core. In our childhood homes, on playgrounds, in locker rooms, in dormitories, and in fraternities of all kinds, men learned to define our masculinity in terms of our differentiation from what we felt was feminine as well as our ability to control women. The dichotomy was absolute: I was either in control or I was a pussy.

This said, what does my personal process have to do with transforming a rape culture? In particular, how do I support patriarchal values, making them seem almost "natural" when I choose not to reckon with them in my own movement through the world?

For me, a hint of an explanation came while experiencing the paradigm shift that took place when I began my training with Men Stopping Violence. I was certainly not a stereotypical villain when I came to the organization asking how I could help. In fact, I had a long history of politically correct and socially responsible behaviors. I spent ten years in a seminary where I learned empathy for the downtrodden and how to help them while pursuing my theological studies. I was outspoken against the Vietnam War even while in the military. In the late 1960s, I participated in civil rights marches and demonstrations in my native

Mississippi. I was the cofounder of a group working for environmental sanity in the panhandle of northern Florida. I studied and maintained a voluminous library of feminist writings. I was always careful to keep copies of *Z* magazine and the *Utne Reader* nearby. I worked for the passage of the ERA. I made it a point over the last fifteen years to choose strong, independent women as companions. For years, I participated in men's groups where I shared feelings and supported others in doing the same. Thirty years after the movement, I continued to ascribe to the hippie value that all men are brothers and conducted my business accordingly. A problem for me was finding other men who respected and shared such a liberal belief system; as a result, most of my friends were women. I worked and read to overcome my racist, classist, and sexist beliefs. In all honesty, I felt quite good about the job I'd done. I considered myself a politically concerned, sensitive, and principled person.

It was this man, immobilized by what I now recognize as my homophobia, who resistantly followed the wise and careful shepherding of a dear friend to the Men and Masculinity Conference held in Atlanta in 1990. There I became acquainted with Men Stopping Violence through the keynote address of its executive director, Kathleen Carlin. Through her I learned of the Principle of Intentions versus Effects; i.e., my intentions are not necessarily what gives my actions their moral value but rather their effects on others—specifically, those people who are disenfranchised by my privilege, those marginalized by my sense of entitlement. But Kathleen did not stop there. She went on to say that they, rather than I, were the ones to *name* those effects. What's more, they got to say what I needed to do to redress the damage.

Despite my liberal bent, these ideas caught me completely unawares. In that moment, my privilege was rendered visible to me in a way that was undeniable. With that epiphany came my first inkling of why my privilege remains largely invisible to me. So extreme and so complete was my privilege that to question it literally never entered my mind. My sense of entitlement insulated and isolated me from threats of any kind. I had no reason to be aware of my privilege.

The challenge to relinquish my privilege both chilled and excited me. However, the threat of that challenge made it very elusive to me. Trying to examine it made it invisible. Nonetheless, with a strange mixture of apprehension, confusion, and altruism, I called Men Stopping Violence the following week. I was ready to step into a position as an instructor in their batterer intervention program after an orientation to the organization. Hold up! There's a one-year training to be done? Well, after a review of my background, I will certainly be exempted from most of the internship.

I was hurt and angry to find that before I could work with the organization, I was to complete the entire year-long internship, a clear waste of my time and money. I thought these people were looking for help! I was incensed that my M.A. in psychology wasn't enough. I was confused that my work with prisoners while in the seminary wasn't enough. I was surprised that my former employment with vocational rehabilitation wasn't enough. I was indignant that my politics and environmental work weren't enough. I was outraged that my sagacity and righteousness weren't enough. What more did these people want?

My first class brought the answer. My internship began as a participant in a twenty-four-week class for batterers. The initial exercise was to check in with one's worst incident of abuse to women. After several days of struggle about whether to lie or not, it dawned on me that the training was not about helping "those guys"; it was about confronting my own abusive and controlling behaviors. My world quickly shifted 180 degrees: I was going to be held accountable in a very new way, accountable to women. I felt the Principle of Intentions versus Effects beginning to slowly recondense in my brain. I wanted out!

I wanted to be one of the good guys. I wanted to say what battering is about and who does it. I wanted to say what working on sexism looks like. I wanted to say what racism is and what to do about it. I wanted to be the one to say when homeless people, gays, people of color, and most especially women "go too far" in their self-expression. I wanted to define fair and just. I wanted to say what is appropriate and when. I wanted to say what is sensual and sexy. I wanted to say what "no" means. I wanted to say what is provocative or erotic for women. I wanted to say whether this sense of entitlement propagates and condones a rape culture. Last, if questioned, I wanted to deny this need for control.

It looked rough! I had twenty-three weeks of class and fifty-one weeks of training to go. Each week I struggled with the Principle of Intentions versus Effects while I identified my abusiveness and listed its effects on those I had silenced. Each week I sat with those intense feelings of vulnerability, fear, and confusion as the reality of women was brought into the room. Through this process, my acceptance of the Principle of

Intentions versus Effects grew. Yet, each week, I used my theological, psychological, social, and political training to concoct new ruses to allow me to jump outside that system of accountability.

The challenges for me surfaced in subtle attempts to control: Why do I shield my expectations from my partner, keeping her walking on eggshells, focused on my life rather than hers? How do I store disappointment for its ambush potential at a later date? Why, to feel safe, do I present myself as an emotional enigma that she must figure out? Why does being direct with women make me feel so vulnerable and out of control? Why is being sexual with a woman so important to me? What does it mean for me to be sexual with a woman? What am I trying to do when I pout and withdraw following a refusal of sex? What does it mean when a woman agrees to be sexual with me in the face of my sulking and moping around? What constitutes consent between someone of the subordinate and someone of the dominant caste? If I was unable to get control via psychological and verbal manipulation, would I take the next step—physical force? The "good guy/bad guy" model no longer made sense to me. I was simply another man moving across the continuum of controlling behaviors to get my way with women.

In retrospect, my training with Men Stopping Violence was needed to uproot my arrogance. To try to exempt myself was to lie about my involvement in a rape culture. I wanted to remain silent around my role in the perpetuation of a culture that condones violence against women.

I had not been exempted from the internship because my background and preparation had been carried out in an environment of disdain for the Principle of Intentions versus Effects. My previous training endowed me with the authority to take control, define solutions, and co-opt the "problem" people into carrying out my ideas. The two types of training are not the same, and it was critical that I have a clear understanding of that. For me to have received an exemption would have been to lie about women's reality—to say that I could in fact name it.

Most of what I brought to Men Stopping Violence was of enormous help to me as I assimilated the Principle of Intention versus Effects, but it was and sometimes continues to be an enormous burden to me while trying to negotiate the labyrinth of my sense of entitlement; my privilege always gives me permission to frame my perceptions as the Truth.

This lie of entitlement—my privilege to describe the reality of women—gives a rape culture its life. Patriarchy is predicated on this lie and our protective silence. It is the lie I wanted so badly to tell the class. It is the lie that allows me to describe myself as one of the "good guys." It is the lie not permitted in the classroom. When this lie is disallowed, the rape culture is challenged at its foundation. If I go on to name that lie, if I break ranks with the patriarchy by acknowledging that I cannot know the reality of those subordinated by the system of values that entitles me, that system is no longer seamless; its existence is endangered.

As a man, someone the rape culture has endowed with credibility, my schism has the potential to be all the more destructive. Of course I will be cast with the lot of women for this betrayal. Nonetheless, just as I was moved by the honesty of other men not to lie about my worst incident of abuse to a woman, so perhaps other men will be inspired by this truth-telling to break ranks. My vision is that this personal process moves logarithmically, reaching critical mass, and ultimately destroying the institutions that support and encourage rape.

I must confess I have difficulty holding this vision in focus, but I also know that I cannot work for something I cannot imagine. If I let my mind run wild, I can see men naming the lie of privilege in such numbers that this system of values begins to unravel. As it unravels, the rape culture begins to transform into one of respect and dignity for women.

What can keep this vision from being realized? Why is this vision so difficult for me to hold in focus? Because to stop lying means nothing less than changing what it means to be a man. Because my proclivity is to remain silent and to consolidate my power as a man—not to write this essay, not to blow the whistle on myself. Silence feels easy. I don't feel like a man when I'm not in control. I feel confused and vulnerable. It frightens me to say out loud: As long as men control women's bodies, a rape culture will continue. As long as men get to define the sexuality and eroticism of women, a rape culture will continue. As long as men link sexual excitement with control, domination, and violence, a rape culture will continue. Until the effects of men's behavior on women define the moral value of that behavior, a rape culture will thrive. Violence of all kinds can be seen as the refusal to accept the Principle of Intentions versus Effects. Privilege is always paid for by those it subjugates.

As a man, I accrue privilege simply by remaining silent, accepting this legacy, and saying nothing about its cost in terms of women's lives. Men can stop the lie of our inherent superiority in its tracks by simply not acting as if it were true. I do not mean to imply that what is simple will be easy. It is extremely difficult for me. But the process begins with the acknowledgment of privilege; the terms of my privilege are that I do not have to acknowledge it. The process begins with me saying aloud that the standards of gender identity are contrived to accommodate my privilege. The male/female dichotomy is based on relatively minor biological differences that are eroticized, fetishized, mythologized, and exploited to declare men and women "opposites." This social-political dichotomy is used to promote the idea of men as intelligent, rational, sagacious, and moral, while women are promoted as our opposites, as dense, emotive, obtuse, and evil. As I aggrandize myself, I demean my opposite. As I deify the masculine, I necessarily vilify women. The degradation not only makes attack permissible, it makes it a moral imperative.

When my privilege is laid out in all its ugliness, how can I remain silent? My hope is that what Gloria Steinem said of women's consciousness-raising groups in the 1970s is true for men today: "Personal truth-telling as a path to social change is the most important and enduring legacy." I am breaking my silence and trying to tell my truth, trusting social change will follow. If men break the silence in concert with one another, we can transform this rape culture. As the perpetrators, we can bring about the transformation today, if we so choose. If we maintain our silence, we doubtless will rape another six hundred thousand women in this country in the coming year and in each of the years to come.

My personal process has carried me to the place where I know that I am lying when I fail to acknowledge openly my privilege as a man, and that my failure to make that acknowledgment holds the rape culture in place. To transform the culture, I must transform what it means for me to be a man; I must relinquish my claim on women.

Acknowledgements: My thinking and writing is richly informed by the work of Kathleen Carlin, Andrea Dworkin, Kay Hagan, and the program staff of Men Stopping Violence.

TERRENCE CROWLEY was raised in Louisiana, Mississippi, and Alabama and has lived in Atlanta for the past eleven years. He is a self-employed furniture maker and for the past three years he has trained and worked with Men Stopping Violence. At MSV he is an instructor in the batterer's intervention program and has been part of MSV's workshop leadership team. Beginning with this piece, he is an essayist.

SEDUCED BY VIOLENCE NO MORE

by bell hooks

I was surprised by the number of young black women
who repudiated the notion of male domination but who
would then go on to insist that they could not desire a
brother who could not take charge, take care
of business, be in control.

WE LIVE IN a culture that condones and celebrates rape. Within a phallocentric patriarchal state the rape of women by men is a ritual that daily perpetuates and maintains sexist oppression and exploitation. We cannot hope to transform "rape culture" without committing ourselves fully to resisting and eradicating patriarchy. In his recent essay "Black America: Multicultural Democracy in the Age of Clarence Thomas and David Duke," Manning Marable writes: "Rape, spouse abuse, sexual harassment on the job, are all essential to the perpetuation of a sexist society. For the sexist, violence is the necessary and logical part of the unequal, exploitative relationship. To dominate and control, sexism requires violence. Rape and sexual harassment are therefore not accidental to the structure of gender relations within a sexist order." This is no new revelation. In all our work as thinkers and activists, committed feminist women have consistently made this same point. However, it is important to acknowledge that our movement to transform rape culture can only progress as men come to feminist thinking and actively challenge sexism and male violence against women. And it is even more significant that Manning speaks against a sexist order from his position as an African-American social critic.

Black males, who are utterly disenfranchised in most every arena of life in the United States, often find that the assertion of sexist domination is their only expressive access to that "patriarchal power" they are told all men should possess as their gendered birthright. Hence, it should not surprise or shock that many black men support and celebrate "rape culture." That celebration has found its most powerful contemporary voice in misogynist rap music. Significantly, there are powerful alternative voices. Mass media pays little attention to those black men who are opposing phallocentrism, misogyny, and sexism, who "rap" against rape, against patriarchy. The "It's a dick thing" version of masculinity that black male pop icons like Spike Lee and Eddie Murphy promote is a call for "real" black men to be sexist and proud of it, to rape and assault black women and brag about it. Alternative progressive black male voices in rap or cinema receive little attention, but they exist. There are even black males who do "rap against rape" (their slogan), but their voices are not celebrated in patriarchal culture.

Overall cultural celebration of black male phallocentrism takes the form of commodifying these expressions of "cool" in ways that glamorize and seduce. Hence, those heterosexual black males that the culture deems most desirable as mates and/or erotic partners tend to be pushing a "dick thing" masculinity. They can talk tough and get rough. They can brag about disciplinin' their woman, about making sure the "bitch" respects them.

Many black men have a profound investment in the perpetuation and maintenance of rape culture. So much of their sense of value and self-esteem is hooked into the patriarchal "macho" image; these brothers are not about to surrender their "dick thing" masculinity. This was most apparent during the case against Mike Tyson. Brothers all over the place were arguing that the black female plaintiff should not have gone to Tyson's hotel room in the wee hours of the morning if she had no intention of doing the wild thing. As one young brother told me last week, "I mean if a sister came to my room that late, I would think she got one thing on her mind." When I suggested to him and his partners that maybe a woman could visit the room of a man she likes in the wee hours of the night because she might like to talk, they shook their head, saying "no way." Theirs is a deeply engrained sexism, a profoundly serious commitment to rape culture.

Like many black men, they are enraged by any feminist call to re-think masculinity and oppose patriarchy. And the courageous brothers who do, who rethink masculinity, who reject patriarchy and "rape culture," often find that they cannot get any play—that the very same women who may critique macho male nonsense contradict themselves by making it clear that they find the "unconscious brothers" more appealing.

On college campuses all over the United States, I talk with these black males and hear their frustrations. They are trying to oppose patriarchy and yet are rejected by black females for not being masculine enough. This makes them feel like losers, like their lives are not enhanced when they make progressive changes, when they affirm the feminist movement. Their black female peers confirm that they do indeed hold contradictory desires. They desire men not to be "sexist," even as they say "but I want him to be masculine." When pushed to define masculine, they fall back on sexist representations. I was surprised by the number of young black women who repudiated the notion of male domination but who would then go on to insist that they could not desire a brother who could not take charge, take care of business, be in control.

Their responses suggest that one major obstacle preventing us from transforming "rape culture" is that heterosexual women have not unlearned a heterosexist-based "eroticism" that constructs desire in such a way that many of us can only respond erotically to male behavior that has already been coded as masculine within the sexist framework. Let me give an example of what I mean. For most of my heterosexual erotic life I have been involved with black males who are into a "dick thing" masculinity. I was in a nonmonogamous relationship of more than ten years with a black man committed to nonsexist behavior in most every aspect of daily life, the major exception being the bedroom. I accepted my partner's insistence that his sexual desires be met in any circumstance where I had made sexual overtures (kissing, caressing, etc.). Hence ours was not a relationship where I felt free to initiate sexual play without going forward and engaging in coitus. Often I felt compelled to engage in sexual intercourse when I did not want to.

In my fantasies I dreamed of being with a male who would fully respect my body rights, my right to say no, my freedom to not proceed in any sexual activity that I did not desire even if I initially felt that I wanted to be sexual. When I left this relationship, I was determined to choose male partners who would respect my body rights. For me this meant males who did not think that the most important expression of female love was satisfying male sexual desire. It meant males who could respect a woman's right to say no irrespective of the circumstance.

Years passed before I found a partner who respected those rights in a feminist manner, with whom I made a mutual covenant that neither of us would ever engage in any sexual act that we did not desire to participate in. I was elated. With this partner I felt free and safe. I felt that I could choose not to have sex without worrying that this choice would alienate or anger my partner. Braggin' about him to girlfriends and acquaintances, I was often told, "Girl, you betta be careful. Dude might be gay." Though most women were impressed that I had found such a partner, they doubted that this could be a chosen commitment to female freedom on any man's part and raised suspicious questions. I also began to feel doubts. Nothing about the way this dude behaved was familiar. His was not the usual "dick thing" masculinity that had aroused feelings of pleasure and danger in me for most of my erotic life. While I liked his alternative behavior I felt a loss of control—the kind that we experience when we are no longer acting within the socialized framework of both acceptable and familiar heterosexual behavior. I worried that he did not find me really desirable. Then I asked myself, would aggressive emphasis on his desire, on his need for "the pussy," have reassured me? It seemed to me then that I needed to rethink the nature of female heterosexual eroticism, particularly in relation to black culture.

Critically interrogating my responses, I confronted the reality that despite all my years of opposing patriarchy, I had not fully questioned or transformed the structure of my desire. By allowing my erotic desire to still be determined to *any extent* by conventional sexist constructions, I was acting in complicity with patriarchal thinking. Resisting patriarchy ultimately meant that I had to reconstruct myself as a heterosexual desiring subject in a manner that would make it possible for me to be fully aroused by male behavior that was not phallocentric. In basic terms, I had to learn how to be sexual with a man in a context where his pleasure and/or his hard-on is decentered and mutual pleasure is centered. That meant learning how to enjoy being with a male partner who could be sexual without viewing coitus as the ultimate expression of desire.

Talking with women of varying ages and ethnicities about this issue, I am more than ever convinced that women who engage in sexual acts with male partners must not only interrogate the nature of the masculinity we desire, we must actively construct radically new ways to think and feel as desiring subjects. By shaping our eroticism in ways that repudiate phallocentrism, we oppose rape culture. Whether this alters sexist male behavior is not the point. A woman who wants to engage in erotic acts with a man without re-inscribing sexism will be much more likely to avoid or reject situations where she might be victimized. By refusing to function within the heterosexist framework, which condones male erotic domination of women, females would be actively disempowering patriarchy.

Without a doubt, our collective conscious refusal to act in any way that would make us complicit in the perpetuation of rape culture within the sphere of sexual relations would undermine the structure. Concurrently, when heterosexual women are no longer attracted to "macho" men, the message sent to men would at least be consistent and clear. That would be a major intervention in the overall effort to transform rape culture.

BELL HOOKS is a writer, feminist theorist, and cultural critic. She is also the author of six books published by South End Press—the most recent being *Black Looks: Race and Representation*. She is currently completing a new work, *Sisters of the Yam: Black Women and Self-Recovery*.

RADICAL HETEROSEXUALITY
. . . or How to Love a Man and Save Your Feminist Soul

by Naomi Wolf

The radical heterosexual man must yield the automatic benefits conferred by gender. I had a lover once who did not want to give up playing sports in a club that had a separate door for women. It must be tempting to imagine you can have both—great squash courts *and* the bed of a liberated woman—but in the mess hall of gender relations, there is *no such thing as a free lunch*.

ALL OVER THE country, millions of feminists have a secret indulgence. By day they fight gender injustice; by night they sleep with men. Is this a dual life? A core contradiction? Is sleeping with a man "sleeping with the enemy"? And is razor burn from kissing inherently oppressive?

It's time to say you *can* hate sexism and love men. As the feminist movement grows more mature and our understanding of our enemies more nuanced, three terms assumed to be in contradiction—radical feminist heterosexuality—can and must be brought together.

RULES OF THE RELATIONSHIP

But how? Andrea Dworkin and Catharine MacKinnon have pointed out that sexism limits women to such a degree that it's questionable whether the decision to live with a man can ever truly be free. If you want to use their sound, if depressing, reasoning to a brighter end, turn the thesis around: radical heterosexuality demands substituting choice for dependency.

Radical heterosexuality requires that the woman be able to support herself. This is not to belittle women who must depend financially on men; it is to recognize that when our daughters are raised with the skills that would let them leave abusers, they need not call financial dependence love.

Radical heterosexuality needs alternative institutions. As the child of a good lifetime union, I believe in them. But when I think of pledging my heart and body to a man—even the best and kindest man—within the existing institution of marriage, I feel faint. The more you learn about its legal structures, the less likely you are to call the caterers.

In the nineteenth century, when a judge ruled that a husband could not imprison and rape his wife, the London *Times* bemoaned, "One fine morning last month, marriage in England was suddenly abolished." The phrase "rule of thumb" descends from English common law that said a man could legally beat his wife with a switch "no thicker than his thumb."

If these nightmarish echoes were confined to history, I might feel more nuptial; but look at our own time. Do I want the blessing of an institution that doesn't provide adequate protection from marital rape? That gives a woman less protection from assault by her husband than by a stranger? That assigns men seventy percent of contested child custodies?

Of course I do not fear any such brutality from the man I want to marry (no bride does). But marriage means that his respectful treatment of me and our children becomes, despite our intentions, a kindness rather than a legally grounded right.

We need a heterosexual vision of the marriage that gay and lesbian activists are seeking: a commitment untainted by centuries of inequality; a ritual that invites the community to rejoice in the making of a new, freely chosen family.

The radical heterosexual man must yield the automatic benefits conferred by gender. I had a lover once who did not want to give up playing sports in a club that had a separate door for women. It must be tempting to imagine you can have both—great squash courts *and* the bed of a liberated woman—but in the mess hall of gender relations, there is *no such thing as a free lunch.*

Radical heterosexual women too must give up gender benefits (such as they are). I know scores of women—independent, autonomous—who avoid assuming any of the risk for a romantic or sexual approach.

I have watched myself stand complacently by while my partner wrestles with a stuck window, an intractable computer printer, maps, or locks. Sisters, I am not proud of this, and I'm working on it. But people are lazy—or at least I am—and it's easy to rationalize that the person with the penis is the one who should get out of a warm bed to fix the snow on the TV screen. After all, it's the very least owed to me *personally* in compensation for centuries of virtual enslavement.

Radical heterosexuals must try to stay conscious—at all times, I'm afraid—of their gender imprinting and how it plays out in their erotic melodramas. My own psyche is a flagrant *son et lumière* of political incorrectness. Three of my boyfriends had motorcycles; I am easy pickings for the silent and dysfunctional. My roving eye is so taken by the oil-stained persona of the labor organizer that myopic intellectuals have gained access to my favors merely by sporting a Trotsky button.

We feminists are hard on each other for admitting to weakness. Gloria Steinem caught flak from her left-wing sisters for acknowledging in *Revolution from Within* that she was drawn to a man because he could do the things with money and power that we are taught men must do. And some were appalled when Simone de Beauvoir's letters revealed how she coddled Sartre.

But the anti-feminist erotic template is *in* us. We would not be citizens of this culture if swooning damsels and abandoned vixens had not been beamed at us from our first solid food to our first vote. We can't fight it until we admit to it. And we can't identify it until we drag it in, its taffeta billowing and its bosom heaving, to the light of day.

I have done embarrassing, reactionary, abject deeds out of love and sexual passion. So, no doubt, has Norman Schwarzkopf. Only when we reveal our conditioning can we tell how much of our self-abasement is neurotic femininity, and how much is the flawed but impressive human apparatus of love.

IN THE BEDROOM

Those are the conditions for the radical heterosexual couple. What might this new creation look like in bed? It will look like something we have no words or images for—eroticization of consent, the equal primacy of female and male desire.

We will need to tell some secrets—to map our desire for the male body and admit to our fascination with the rhythms and forces of male arousal, its uncanny counterintuitive spell.

We will also need to face our creature equalities. Animality has for so long been used against us—bitch, fox, *Penthouse* pet—that we struggle for the merit badges of higher rationality, ambivalent about our animal nature. The truth is that heterosexual women believe that men, on some level, are animals; as they believe that we are animals. But what does "animal" mean?

Racism and sexism have long used animal metaphors to distance and degrade the Other. Let us redefine "animal" to make room for that otherness between the genders, an otherness fierce and worthy of respect. Let us define animal as an inchoate kinship, a comradeship, that finds a language beyond our species.

I want the love of two unlikes: the look of astonishment a woman has at the sight of a male back bending. These manifestations of difference confirm in heterosexuals the beauty that similarity confirms in the lesbian or gay imagination. Difference and animality do not have to mean hierarchy.

MEN WE LOVE

What must the men be like? Obviously, they're not going to be just anyone. *Esquire* runs infantile disquisitions on "Women We Love" (suggesting, Lucky Girls!). Well, I think that the men who are loved by feminists are lucky. Here's how they qualify to join this fortunate club.

Men We Love understand that, no matter how similar our backgrounds, we are engaged in a cross-cultural (if not practically biracial) relationship. They know that we know much about their world and they but little of ours. They accept what white people must accept in relationships with people of other ethnicities: to know that they do not know.

Men We Love don't hold a baby as if it is a still-squirming, unidentifiable catch from the sea.

Men We Love don't tell women what to feel about sexism. (There's a postcard that shows a dashing young fellow, drawn Love-Comix style, saying to a woman, "Let me explicate to you the nature of your oppression.") They do not presume that there is a line in the sand called "enlightened male," and that all they need is a paperback copy of Djuna Barnes and good digital technique. They understand that unlearning gender oppressiveness means untying the very core of how we become female and male. They know this pursuit takes a lifetime at the minimum.

Sadly, men in our lives sometimes come through on personal feminism but balk at it intellectually. A year ago, I had a bruising debate with my father and brother about the patriarchal nature of traditional religious and literary canons. I almost seized them by their collars, howling "Read Mary Daly! Read Toni Morrison! Take Feminism 101. No, I *can't* explain it to you between the entrée and the dessert!"

By spring, my dad, bless his heart, had asked for a bibliography, and last week my brother sent me *Standing Again at Sinai*, a Jewish-feminist classic. Men We Love are willing, sooner or later, to read the Books We Love.

Men We Love accept that successful training in manhood makes them blind to phenomena that are fact to women. Recently, I walked down a New York City avenue with a woman friend, X, and a man friend, Y. I pointed out to Y the leers, hisses, and invitations to sit on faces. Each woman saw clearly what the other woman saw, but Y was baffled. Sexual harassers have superb timing. A passerby makes kissy-noises with his tongue while Y is scrutinizing the menu of the nearest bistro. "There, there! Look! Listen!" we cried. "What? Where? Who?" wailed poor Y, valiantly, uselessly spinning.

What if, hard as they try to see and hear, they cannot? Once I was at lunch with a renowned male crusader for the First Amendment. Another Alpha male was present, and the venue was the Supreme Court lunchroom—two power factors that automatically press the "mute" button on the male ability to detect a female voice on the audioscope. The two men began to rev their motors; soon they were off and racing in a policy-wonk grand prix. I tried, once or twice, to ask questions. But the free-speech champions couldn't hear me over the testosterone roar.

Men We Love undertake half the care and cost of contraception. They realize that it's not fair to wallow in the fun without sharing the responsibility. When stocking up for long weekends, they brave the amused glances when they ask, "Do you have this in unscented?"

Men We Love know that just because we can be irrational doesn't mean we're insane. When we burst into premenstrual tears—having just realized the cosmic fragility of creation—they comfort us. Not until we feel better do they dare remind us gently that we had this same revelation exactly twenty-eight days ago.

Men We Love must make a leap of imagination to believe in the female experience. They do not call women nags or paranoid when we embark on the arduous, often boring, nonnegotiable daily chore of drawing attention to sexism. They treat it like adults taking driving lessons: if irked in the short term at being treated like babies, they're grateful in the long term that someone is willing to teach them patiently how to move through the world without harming the pedestrians. Men We Love don't drive without their gender glasses on.

A PLACE FOR THEM

It's not simple gender that pits Us against Them. In the fight against sexism, it's those who are for us versus those who are against us—of either gender.

When I was sixteen, my boyfriend came with me to hear Andrea Dworkin speak. While hearing great feminist oratory in a sea of furious women changed my life, it nearly ended my boyfriend's: he barely escaped being drawn and quartered.

It is time to direct our anger more acutely at the Men We Hate—like Rush Limbaugh—and give the Men We Love something useful to do. Not to take over meetings, or to set agendas; not to whine, "Why can't feminists teach us how to be free?", but to add their bodies, their hearts, and their numbers, to support us.

I meet many young men who are brought to feminism by love for a woman who has been raped, or by watching their single mothers struggle against great odds, or by simple common sense. Their most frequent question is, "What can I do to help?"

Imagine a rear battalion of committed "Men Against Violence Against Women" (or "Men for Choice," or what have you) of all races, ages, and classes. Wouldn't that be a fine sight to fix in the eyes of a five-year-old boy?

Finally, the place to make room for radical feminist heterosexuality is within our heads. If the movement that I dearly love has a flaw, it is a tendency toward orthodoxies about other women's pleasures and needs. This impulse is historically understandable; in the past, we needed to define ourselves against men if we were to define ourselves at all. But today, the most revolutionary choice a woman can make is to affirm other women's choices, whether lesbian or straight, bisexual or celibate.

National Organization of Women President Patricia Ireland speaks for me even though our sexual lives are not identical. Simone de Beauvoir speaks for me even though our sexual lives are not identical. Audre Lorde speaks for me even though our sexual lives are not identical. Is it the chromosomes of your lovers that establish you as a feminist? Or is it the life you make out of the love you make?

"Radical Heterosexuality" appeared in the twentieth anniversary issue of *Ms.* magazine (Volume 3, Number 1, July/August 1992).

NAOMI WOLF was born in San Francisco in 1962. She was educated at Yale University and at New College, Oxford University, where she was a Rhodes Scholar. Her essays have appeared in various publications, including: the *New Republic, Wall Street Journal, Glamour, Ms., Esquire,* the *Washington Post,* and the *New York Times.* She speaks widely on college campuses. *The Beauty Myth* is her first book; *Fire With Fire* is a manifesto for a new wave of feminism (Random House, 1993). She lives in New York City.

COMIN TO TERMS

by Ntozake Shange

mandy fixed his dinner/ nothin special/ & left the door of
her room open so he cd see her givin herself pleasure/
from then on/ ezra always asked if he cd come visit her/
waz she in need of some company/ did she want a lil
lovin/ or wd she like to come visit him in his room/
there are no more assumptions in the house.

THEY HADNT SLEPT together for months/ the nite she pulled the two thinnest blankets from on top of him & gathered one pillow under her arm to march to the extra room/ now 'her' room/ had been jammed with minor but telling incidents/ at dinner she had asked him to make sure the asparagus didnt burn so he kept adding water & they, of course/ water-logged/ a friend of hers stopped over & he got jealous of her having so many friends/ so he sulked cuz no one came to visit him/ then she gotta call that she made the second round of interviews for the venceremos brigade/ he said he didnt see why that waz so important/ & with that she went to bed/ moments later this very masculine leg threw itself over her thighs/ she moved over/ then a long muscled arm wrapped round her chest/ she sat up/ he waz smiling/ the smile that said 'i wanna do it now.'

mandy's shoulders dropped/ her mouth wanted to pout or frown/ her fist waz lodged between her legs as a barrier or an alternative/ a cooing brown hand settled on her backside/ 'listen, mandy, i just wanna little'/ mandy looked down on the other side of the bed/ maybe the floor cd talk to him/ the hand roamed her back & bosom/ she started to make faces & blink a lot/ ezra waznt talkin anymore/ a wet mouth waz sittin on mandy's neck/ & teeth beginnin to nibble the curly hairs near her ears/ she started to shake her head/ & covered her mouth with her hand sayin/ 'i waz dreamin bout cuba & you wanna fuck'/ 'no, mandy, i dont wanna fuck/ i wanna make love to . . . love to you'/ & the hand became quite aggressive with mandy's titties/ 'i'm dreamin abt goin to cuba/ which isnt important/ i'm hungry cuz you ruined dinner/ i'm lonely cuz you embarrassed my friend: & you wanna fuck'/ 'i dont wanna fuck/ i told you that i wanna make love'/ 'well you got it/ you hear/ you got it to yr self/ cuz i'm goin to dream abt goin to cuba'/ & with that she climbed offa the hand pummelin her ass/ & pulled the two thinnest blankets & one pillow to the extra room.

the extra room waz really mandy's anyway/ that's where she read & crocheted & thot/ she cd watch the neighbors' children & hear miz nancy singin gospel/ & hear miz nancy give her sometimey lover who owned the steepin tavern/ a piece of her mind/ so the extra room/ felt full/ not as she had feared/ empty & knowin absence. in a corner under the window/ mandy settled every nite after the cuba dreams/ & watched the streetlights play thru the lace curtains to the wall/ she slept soundly the first few nites/ ezra didnt mention that she didnt sleep with him/ & they ate the breakfast she fixed & he went off to the studio/ while she went off to school he came home to find his dinner on the table & mandy in her room/ doing something that pleased her. mandy was very polite & gracious/ asked how his day waz/ did anything exciting happen/ but she never asked him to do anything for her/ like lift things or watch the stove/ or listen to her dreams/ she also never went in the room where they usedta sleep together/ tho she cleaned everywhere else as thoroughly as one of her mother's great-aunts cleaned the old house on rose tree lane in charleston/ but she never did any of this while ezra waz in the house/ if ezra waz home/ you cd be sure mandy waz out/ or in her room.

    one nite just fore it's time to get up & the sky is lightening up for sunrise/ mandy felt a chill & these wet things on her neck/ she started slappin the air/ & without openin her eyes/ cuz she cd/ feel now what waz goin on/ ezra pushed his hard dick up on her thigh/ his breath covered her face/ he waz movin her covers off/ mandy kept slappin him & he kept bumpin up & down on her legs & her ass/ 'what are you doin ezra'/ he just kept movin. mandy screamed/ 'ezra what in hell are you doin.' & pushed him off her. he fell on the floor/ cuz mandy's little bed waz right on the floor/ & she slept usually near the edge of her mattress/ ezra stood & his dick waz aimed at mandy's face/ at her right eye/ she looked away/ & ezra/ jumped up & down/ in the air this time/ 'what are you talkin abt what am i doin/ i'm doin what we always do/ i'm gettin ready to fuck/ awright so you were mad/ but this cant go on forever/ i'm goin crazy/ i cant live in a house with you & not fu . . . / not make love. i mean.' mandy still lookin at the pulsing penis/ jumpin around as ezra jumped around/ mandy sighed 'ezra let's not let this get ugly/ please, just go to sleep/ in yr bed & we'll talk abt this tomorrow.' 'what do you mean tomorrow i'm goin crazy' . . . mandy looked into ezra's scrotum/ & spoke softly 'you'll haveta be crazy then' & turned over to go back to sleep. ezra waz still for a moment/ then he pulled the covers off mandy & jerked her around some/ talkin bout 'we live together & we're gonna fuck now'/ mandy treated him as cruelly as she wd any stranger/ kicked & bit & slugged & finally ran to the kitchen/ leavin ezra holdin her torn nitegown in his hands.

    'how cd you want me/ if i dont want you/ i dont want you niggah/ i

dont want you' & she worked herself into a sobbin frigidaire-beatin fren-
zy . . . ezra looked thru the doorway mumblin. 'i didnt wanna upset you,
mandy. but you gotta understand. i'm a man & i just cant stay here like
this with you . . . not bein able to touch you or feel you'/ mandy
screamed back 'or fuck me/ go on, say it niggah/ fuck.' ezra threw her
gown on the floor & stamped off to his bed. we dont know what he did
in there.

mandy put her gown in the sink & scrubbed & scrubbed til she cd get
his hands off her. she changed the sheets & took a long bath & a douche.
she went back to bed & didnt go to school all day she lay in her bed.
thinkin of what ezra had done. i cd tell him to leave/ she thot/ but that's
half the rent/ i cd leave/ but i like it here/ i cd getta dog to guard me at
nite/ but ezra wd make friends with it/ i cd let him fuck me & not move/
that wd make him mad & i like to fuck ezra/ he's good/ but that's not
the point/ that's not the point/ & she came up with the idea that if they
were really friends like they always said/ they shd be able to enjoy each
other without fucking without having to sleep in the same room/ mandy
had grown to cherish waking up a solitary figure in her world/ she liked
the quiet of her own noises in the night & the sound of her own voice
soothin herself/ she liked to wake up in the middle of the nite & turn the
lights on & read or write letters/ she even liked the grain advisory show
on tv at 5:30 in the mornin/ she hadda lotta secret nurturin she had created for herself/ that ezra & his heavy gait/ ezra & his snorin/ ezra & his
goin-crazy hard-on wd/ do violence to . . . so she suggested to ezra that
they continue to live together as friends/ & see other people if they wanted to have a more sexual relationship than the one she waz offering . . .
ezra laughed. he thot she waz a little off/ till she shouted 'you cant imagine me without a wet pussy/ you cant imagine me without yr god-
damned dick stickin up in yr pants/ well yr gonna learn/ i dont start
comin to life cuz you feel like fuckin/ yr gonna learn i'm alive/ ya hear'
. . . ezra waz usually a gentle sorta man/ but he slapped mandy this time
& walked off . . . he came home two days later covered with hickeys &
quite satisfied with himself. mandy fixed his dinner/ nothin special/ &
left the door of her room open so he cd see her givin herself pleasure/
from then on/ ezra always asked if he cd come visit her/ waz she in need
of some company/ did she want a lil lovin/ or wd she like to come visit
him in his room/ there are no more assumptions in the house.

NTOZAKE SHANGE is a playwright, poet, and novelist who is best known for her play, *for colored girls who have considered suicide/when the rainbow is enuf,* for which she won an OBIE award. *for colored girls* has been produced on Broadway and in London and was featured on PBS's "American Playhouse Theater." Shange's other works for the stage include *Spell #7, a Photograph: Lovers in Motion* and her most recent performance piece, *The Love Space Demands.* She is the author of four collections of poetry and four novels, including *Betsey Brown,* which was adapted into a musical. Shange has received fellowships in playwriting from the National Endowment for the Arts and the Guggenheim Foundation.

IN PRAISE OF INSUBORDINATION, OR,
What Makes a Good Woman Go Bad?

by Inés Hernandez-Avila

There is an old Cheyenne saying, "A nation is not
conquered until the hearts of its women are on the
ground. Then it is done, no matter how strong the
weapons, or how brave the warriors." How do all of us as
women ensure that our hearts do not hit the ground?
What strategies might we as women use to remind
us to hold our heads and hearts high?

AN INDIAN[1] DANCER (who is gay) tells me laughingly how a group of Indian men "trained" (gang-raped) a young Indian woman dancer during a powwow weekend, and then the next day bragged about it while each man took credit for how well she was dancing.

Members of a multiethnic fraternity look on as one Chicano member drags his Chicana ex-girlfriend by her hair out of her car, throws her on the ground, and begins kicking her and beating her. None of the males moves to help her.

A distinguished senior Chicano scholar explains to me that his conflict with a younger and junior Chicana scholar is not personal, but strictly political. He tells me that he would "shoot" anyone, including his family, who gets in his way politically.

I read in a San Francisco newspaper how young, mostly undocumented, women immigrants from Mexico and Central America are being offered jobs as housekeepers and domestic servants, only to find once they begin working that their white male employers assume they are entitled to sexually harass and/or rape the women.

At a university awards banquet not too long ago, I found myself sitting near a white woman who informed me how much she and her husband have enjoyed traveling in Mexico. Unfortunately, I was not surprised when she proceeded to tell me (knowingly) how sorry she feels for Mexican women, having to contend as they do with "machismo." Instantly I heard my voice telling her, "Be careful." Somewhat startled, she answered, "What?!", to which I replied rather calmly, "You need to be careful about what you're saying—you see, that particular opinion is one that has marked a battleground between white feminists and feminists of color. A male chauvinist pig is a male chauvinist pig is a male chauvinist pig, in whatever culture he is from, and in whatever language you might use to name him." As Chicana scholar Emma Perez writes, "Many Anglos, particularly white feminists, insist that the men of our culture created machismo and they conveniently forget that the men of their race make the rules. This leads to problematic Chicana discourse within feminist constructs. When white feminists ardently insist upon discussing machismo, they impose phallocentric discourse. By 'centering' and 'focusing' upon the penis, they deflect from their racism. This evasion is both racist and heterosexist."[2] I need to say this because I do not want anyone to assume that if I am critiquing my own communities, I am placing the blame squarely on our "culture." I *am* assuming my right to question and to challenge what has come onto us *as* "culture" through the process of colonialism. On my dad's side, I am Tejana (which means a Chicana from Texas of Mexican descent; my Mexican ancestry is mixed blood Spanish and Indian, or mestizo). On my mom's side I am Nimipu (Nez Perce) from Washington state, of Hinmaton Yalatkit's (Chief Joseph's) band. I identify as a native woman of this hemisphere. I do not believe indigenous cultures before contact were perfect; however, they had not become so "civilized" that the cultures were completely self-destructive as today's "First World"[3] societies seem to be.

When Alice Walker wrote *The Color Purple*, she was criticized severely by many people for her supposed betrayal of the African-American community, because, they said, she made black men "look bad." That argument is an old line and an absurd critique. Alice Walker did not betray the African-American community. Those who condemned her betrayed her by wanting to silence her, just as they betrayed all those who knew of what she wrote. Walker's novel in one sense is an incisive internal critique of the dynamics of sexual and gender relations as she sees them in her community, contextualized in a blatantly racist/classist South, and grounded in a resurgent memory and a proud consciousness of African ancestry.[4] If I criticize the men or women of the Native American and Chicana/Chicano community who are perpetuating oppressive regimes of being, and sustaining "oligarchies of the spirit," that does not mean that I do not love my communities, or that I do not want to honor them or respect them. It is because I love them and care for them that I challenge them to unlearn the doctrine of subordination to which we have been subjected intentionally as colonized peoples, peoples who were supposed to have been "conquered" and so should know their place—which is a very tiny space indeed. For many indigenous peoples it is not even a closet; in many parts of this hemisphere it is often a *casa de cartón* (cardboard house).

I want to scream it out that we should know better, those of us who have endured diaspora and genocide. I want to make us look into the mirror to see how many of us have apparently accepted terrorism of ourselves and each other as a fact of life. My critique is also internal, contextualized in the historical experience of colonialism. By acknowledging the repressive and life-draining nature of the colonial experience, I do not mean to soften my critique in a way that might excuse the men who have exhibited violent behavior. I have no use for a political peace, for a false show of unity while our women and our children are being violated, battered, and abused or while our communities continue to suffer the effects of conquest. I cannot excuse the *patrón/patrona* politics that exists in both the Chicana/Chicano and Native American communities. I will not be silent when I feel that I am being intimidated, threatened, or harassed because I want to be an example of a woman who will not be brought down to the ground. I will not be a "good girl" and take whatever abuse is dished out to me (nor will I keep quiet when I see it happen to others) to make us all "look good." I have no interest in being a saint, a heroine, or a martyr. Maybe I get that from my Nimipu mother. She will not hang her head—she might look down because she does not want to watch as someone acts shamefully before her very eyes—but when she is ready she will look you straight in the eye. She is articulate both when she is silent and when she chooses to speak.

To the women of the communities I call my own, I want to ask, How can we be sure that we have divested ourselves of the imposed stereotypes of Native American women as submissive, passive squaws and drudges (or more recently, as mystical, unintellectual "bringers of good feelings"), and of Chicanas and Latinas as fiery, dumb, promiscuous sexpots? We must claim our power and give value to every aspect of ourselves, including our sexuality. Why can't more of us remember that we deserve to know pleasure and love? Why do so many of our women of all ages co-opt and succumb to mistreatment and degradation for the sake of having a partner, for the sake of having a spouse? How did so many of us become convinced that violence is eroticism? When did we come to feel worthless, undesirable, and crazy—as if something were dreadfully wrong with ourselves, as if the fault were ours—because we do not enjoy violent sex that is called by the name of *passion*, that is called by the name of *love*? What makes it so hard for us to say "I was raped"?

> Speechless women
> bartering *cuerpos*
> succumb
> for a touch
> for that closeness
> called love.
> —Inés Hernandez-Avila, "Cuernavaca—Pensavientos"[5]

To both the heterosexual and gay men of my communities I want to ask, Why do men argue that women really mean "yes" when they say "no"? Why do you try to justify your violence by insisting that the woman asked for it? Don't you see that this argument leaves you no defense when the victim of a rape or a beating is your mother, your sister, your lover, your wife, your daughter, or your granddaughter? Suddenly you will find yourself hearing someone say "She really asked for it," or, "She meant 'yes'"—and worse, you will find yourself believing it. I have been told by gay and lesbian sisters and brothers that the patterns of abuse apply to gay and lesbian relationships as well. How did all of us learn these patterns? Through whose eyes have we seen the dynamics of dating and courtship in, say, Hollywood movies? Through whose eyes have we seen intercultural "courtship" in movies and television?

As I watched a recent Seinfeld show with a Latina playing the part of a cleaning lady from Panama, my reading of this "comedy" revealed the blatant perpetuation and exploitation of racist, sexist, and classist stereotypes for the sake of "humor." In one scene Seinfeld's male sidekick confides that at work he has had sex on his desk with the cleaning lady. When this "buddy" admits that "he's always had a thing for cleaning ladies," Seinfeld responds that he's always had a thing for chambermaids. As the "reader" of this text, I understand white male entitlement when I see it, an entitlement that reeks of a colonialist as well as misogynistic mentality. Later, the sidekick tries to pass off a defective cashmere sweater to the Latina as a thinly veiled bribe to keep her quiet about the incident. She gushes over the sweater and recalls how in her native Panama, from the moment she first saw a cashmere coat, she was enthralled, and in a heavily sexual way, she says how much she has always "wanted" something cashmere.

The pseudoerotic nature of this scene, in which the Panamanian woman expresses "desire" towards Westernization, if you will, exemplifies the "right of conquest" being justified. In this white male capitalist (read colonialist/imperialist) fantasy, the woman of color, as well as the country she represents, "wants" to be subjugated, and the card that entices them both is consumerism, material culture. In the end the sidekick gets fired because of the sexual harassment, but the woman's boss gets to throw the sweater back at the jerk as a final message from the offended woman. The woman apparently protested only *after* she received the defective sweater, suggesting to us that the damaged goods she received upset her more than the rape. Had the goods not been defective, we are led to believe she would have been willing to continue "putting out" in exchange for the "benefits" of Western materialism (just as "Third World" countries are forced to "put out" because the power relations between them and "First World" countries is not equal). The woman's voice and her presence disappear, while the white male boss gets to deliver the blow to the errant sidekick, presumably as a way for the producers to safeguard against being seen as condoning sexual harassment. In effect, we are given the message, "Now, please understand, we don't want you to get the wrong idea about us. See, we're with it, the guy gets fired, what do you want?!" I was torn while watching this show between wishing the actress had refused the part (knowing that any parts for Latinas are extremely hard to get) and realizing that her choices, and the "space" that she is allowed to occupy, are indeed limited.

What is the difference between the colonization process here in the area that has come to be known as the United States and in the area that has come to be known as Mexico? What does this difference mean in terms of how "white America" sees mestizos, for instance, and other peoples from Mexico and Central and South America? Why is the guilt of much of white America (United Statesians) apparently so intense with respect to African-Americans, but not so with Native Americans, Mexicans, or other "Latin Americans"? Since we are the fewer in numbers, Native Americans, for the most part, have been rendered basically "invisible." We purportedly have "vanished" and are no longer an issue. Or, as one closed-minded young white male student told me in class about ten years ago, "How many of them are there left anyway?" With respect to Mexicans and other "Latin Americans," is this attitude prevalent because many EuroAmericans[6] clearly see the establishment of slavery as a product of British and then southern U.S. (and therefore their own) colonialism, but they do not see their complicity in the colonization of Mexico and Central and South America? Do white United Statesians see the Spanish and the Portuguese as responsible for those processes of subjugation via colonialism? Don't they see that just as "Manifest Destiny" justified U.S. imperialist expansion from East to West, as *God's will*, the Monroe Doctrine, the CIA, and Contragate have justified continued U.S. imperialist domination from North to South? Is it harder to recognize Native Americans (whether they are from the U.S.

or other parts of "Latin America," whether they are "full-bloods" or "mestizos") because this hemisphere is our land base? We have always been from here—we cannot go back where we came from.

How do patriarchy, misogyny, and imperialism contribute to the forming of a rape culture such as exists in the U.S.? Only recently, in light of the quincentenary celebrations (and Rigoberta Menchú's winning of the 1992 Nobel Peace Prize), has the "right of conquest"—the privilege of the "stronger" one to "discover," invade, violate, pillage, dispossess, and appropriate—been contested, by and on behalf of indigenous peoples, on a scale large enough to attract international attention. Paulo Freire's *Pedagogy of the Oppressed* still serves well to explain how a person who is oppressed internalizes the oppressor; the oppressor becomes a part of the person, so much so that the oppressed person adheres to the oppressor and only sees the world through the oppressor's eyes. Indeed, once the oppressed person becomes "liberated," even if only ostensibly, that person literally might not know how to act, except to follow in the footsteps of the one who has oppressed him or her. In this state of "false liberation," the dynamics of the power relations are interpreted simplistically; the oppressor has power, the oppressed does not. When the oppressed becomes "free," he or she must become like the oppressor in order to manifest the "power of freedom." "Freedom" in this context is defined as the "freedom to do as one pleases."

When "freedom" is not seen in terms of personal or social responsibility, nor defined with a mutuality that accords everyone the same rights, it becomes the freedom of privilege, the freedom of entitlement, authorized by "right of conquest" and enforced by notions of superiority. What are the manifestations of this "freedom" in contemporary society? Male entitlement. White skin entitlement. Class entitlement. Heterosexual entitlement. Youth entitlement. Ability entitlement. Adult entitlement. Employer entitlement. Senior worker entitlement. First World entitlement. Religious entitlement. And so on. In the United States today Native Americans still do not enjoy freedom of religion. Those settlers who came over here for "religious freedom" were as rigid in their prescriptions, once they got here, as those who had oppressed them and denied them freedom. Many of the descendants of these immigrants continue to adhere to the oppressor, as they persist in the need to impose their religious, cultural, and political wills on those who have been forced into a relationship with them that is unequal. The idea of indigenous peoples as "savage" and "primitive" also serves to enforce the internalized racism that mestizos and mestizas feel towards their own Indianness, allowing them to set themselves apart from the "real Indios and Indias," just as it continues to undermine native struggles for sovereignty. For native peoples, "sovereignty" is not what comes through "right of conquest" (that is, power over the ostensibly weaker, or the more vulnerable) but rather signifies empowerment through self-realization, self-representation and self-determination.

In a most profound way, when native peoples are prevented from practicing their ways of life (such as speaking their languages) and from sustaining their ancient belief systems, what is lost or endangered are those very principles that could help give direction to the transformation of a rape culture. Matriarchal, matrilineal cultures offer insights not only into tolerance (which to me is always begrudging) but also respect for difference, as in sexual orientation. Even in apparently patriarchal cultures, indigenous peoples acknowledge and honor their female principles, "women's culture," and women's teachings. As white feminist scholar Sally Roesch Wagner has testified, Iroquois women before European contact enjoyed rights that were unheard of for women in Europe at the time, including the right to divorce, the right to their children, property rights, the right to give birth or to abort, the right to birth control, the right to their sexuality, and the right to their say.[7] In the Iroquois tradition, women elders were (and are) the clan mothers; they had, and have, the power to name the sachems or the spokespersons for their people, and the power to depose them, should they not live up to their responsibilities. A man could not achieve a leadership position if he had ever committed a murder or a theft, or raped a woman. What Roesch Wagner suggests is that European women brought with them from Europe a "tradition of dissent"; what they found here in the "Americas" was the "practice of feminism," which gave them their own vision. It is not hard to understand why native women had to be cast later in the most demeaning roles as women and as Indians. It was (and is) critical to "Western civilization" and its sustainers to make Euro-American women feel that they are in a privileged position (socially, culturally and intellectually) with respect to all other women, and that they should be thankful that at least they are not "lowly women of color."

How long and why have sexuality and nationality been intertwined? For a very long time. But it has been my experience that people are uncomfortable talking about it, outside of their own communities anyway. I do know that many men of color still hate for women of color to date white men. These men of color see it as an affront to them personally, from a racial/ethnic viewpoint, as well as (often) a class viewpoint. They might not even know the woman of color in question! I understand, though, because many women of color have done this, too. In the Chicano/Chicana and Native American communities, when we used to criticize Chicanos and Native American men for wanting to date white women (in particular, white women "groupies" who just kind of "hung around" movement circles, waiting to be picked up by some dark-skinned man), the men would respond that they were "fucking the system," so we shouldn't worry. Interestingly enough, the men's argument postulated that white men had been "doing it" to women of color in this hemisphere ever since initial contact and imposition of colonial rule (witness the Spanish, the French, the British, and then the U.S. colonizing processes, including the institution of slavery), so why was it wrong for men of color to turn the tables on white men and "do it" to white women? As far as the men were concerned, "turnabout is fair play." War is war, and "the spoils of war are the spoils of war."

In Mexico, one of the most insulting things a man can say to another man is, "*Yo soy tu padre*" ["I am your father"]. For mestizos, the "conquistador" and the missionary (who is called "padre") figure into their collective memory as the "fathers," which is a cause for incredible shame in what might be called the Mexican psyche. The well-known Mexican intellectual Octavio Paz (in *Labyrinth of Solitude*) and many others have pointed this out. The men feel shame because they still feel helpless against the original devastation of the infamous and horrific "Conquest." The men (the native armies) were defeated overwhelmingly, even those who sought alliance with the invaders. They witnessed the end of a way of life, the rape of their women, the murder of their people, the destruction of their temples of worship, and the burning of their sacred histories. The women, on the other hand, witnessed the same extermination as they were being raped, as they saw their spouses go down in defeat, and as they watched their children slaughtered. They were made to go through an "ethnic cleansing" themselves by being forced to birth babies who were children of their own violators. As Susan Brownmiller so succinctly explains in a recent *Newsweek* essay, "Making Female Bodies the Battlefield":

Rape of a doubly dehumanized object—as women, as enemy—carries its own terrible logic. In one act of aggression, the collective spirit of women *and* of the nation is broken, leaving a reminder long after the troops depart. And if she survives the assault, what does the victim of wartime rape become to her people? Evidence of the enemy's bestiality. Symbol of her nation's defeat. A pariah. Damaged property. A pawn in the subtle wars of international propaganda.[8]

And an image engraved on the collective memory recalls the shame in a way that turns in on itself and becomes self-hatred.

Gloria Anzaldua says in her important work *Borderlands/La Frontera: The New Mestiza,* "The worst kind of betrayal lies in making us believe that the Indian woman in us is the betrayer. We, *indias y mestizas,* police the Indian in us, brutalize and condemn her. Male culture has done a good job on us. *Son los costumbres que traicionan. La india en mi es la sombra: La Chingada, Tlazolteotl, Coatlicue. Son ellas que oyemos lamentando a sus hijas perdidas.*"[9] Mexican "male culture," imposed through the "Conquest," has betrayed Indian women and mestizas, reducing the "India," Anzaldua says, to a shadow of herself, a shadow of the historical figure Malintzin, a shadow of the powerful manifestations of the highest female principle of the Aztecas, Tlazolteotl and Coatlicue, whose voices we hear lamenting their lost daughters. Tlazolteotl is the Great Mother Confessor, who hears all, who knows the extremes of love and lust, to whom nothing is a surprise, and who helps us to release our fears, our insecurities, our guilt, and our shame, to renew ourselves; she is the GodMother of Childbirth and Grand Governess of the Cycles of Women. Coatlicue is the Great EarthMother of the Serpent Skirts, the Tremendous Regulator of the Cycles of Life and Death (these are my names for these sacred beings).[10] And Malintzin is the native woman who became the unwilling consort of the invader Cortés, the only native woman who is remembered by name in the annals of the "Conquest," because she was brilliant and served as interpreter to Cortés. Malintzin, "La Malinche," "La Chingada" ("The Fucked Over One") is charged in the minds of many Mexican men with the infamy of surrendering herself to the enemy (she, too, is seen as "asking for it"; she, too, is seen as "wanting it"). And just as many women today identify with male interpretations of female behavior, many Mexican women have bought into the story of Malintzin's betrayal.

Ruega por nosotros	Pray for us
nuestra madre de las	our mother of tears
reinas lagrimas	
diosas mayas	like queens, Mayan goddesses
que en silencio tormentoso	who in tormented silence
con un grito callado	with a hushed cry
miran sus santas hijas	see their sacred daughters
relegadas a inferior posición	relegated to inferior positions
intoxicadas con la histeria	intoxicated with the silent
silenciosa	hysteria
de no poder aguantar	of not being able to bear [the pain]
mucho menos escapar	much less escape

—Inés Hernandez-Avila, "Rezo"[11]

In her early work *Woman Hating*, Andrea Dworkin says that "all women are not necessarily in a state of primary emergency as women. . . . As a Native American, I would be oppressed [she says] as a squaw, but hunted, slaughtered, as a Native American."[12] While I appreciate much of Dworkin's work, I object to her assumption about "squaws" (as well as her use of the term), and I disagree with her assessment that a Native American woman's "first identity" is as a Native American, rather than as a woman. The two are inseparable. It is *because* of a Native American woman's sex that she is hunted down and slaughtered, in fact, singled out, because she has the potential through childbirth to assure the continuance of the people. Since the invasion that began in 1492, indigenous women have been raped and forced to give birth to their violator's offspring. Some have had their own babies ripped out of their wombs, as has happened in recent years in places such as El Salvador, where even babies and children, if they are poor, are considered potentially subversive. In the U.S. many indigenous women have been sterilized, and their children have been taken from them to be placed in foster homes.

Five hundred years ago, in Mexico, native women themselves were put into boarding schools to be indoctrinated into Catholicism; the Spanish missionaries knew that the women were the teachers of culture, and so the collective memory of a Supreme Being that is a Dual Duality, MaleFemale/FemaleMale, as is the case with the Aztecas, had to be erased first from their minds and a male trinity put in its place. In the north, the boarding schools serve(d) much the same purpose. The spiritual traditions of native peoples in this hemisphere recognize(d) the centrality of the female principle, working in cooperation with the male principle. This reverence for the female principle, which manifests itself in a tremendous respect for women, is and has been one of the major targets of conversion. The Christian missionization campaign is still quite intense on Native American reservations. Institutionalized religion and capitalism both depend on patriarchal constructs for nourishment. As I said in an essay called "Open Letter to Chicanas: On the Power and Politics of Origin":

> Genocide is an instrument of imperialism, and both depend on cultural imperialism and the dialectic of terror to invade, violate, traumatize, exploit, and totally control human beings throughout the world.[13,14]

These are the intentional tools of conquest, meant to make us (as indigenous peoples) sick and keep us powerless and out of balance.

How can I speak of transformation without speaking of recovery? It has to do with how I see my own work as a scholar (and professor within the evolving disciplines), and the synergistic relationship (as Sau Ling-Wong and Patricia Riley might say) of ethnic studies, women's studies, gay and lesbian studies, cultural studies, and colonial discourse. What are we doing in these fields? Better yet, how do I see myself working within this vitalizing and revisionary context? The creative process for me *is* a critical process and vice versa—when I am writing and working, I am on a journey; I have a sense of where I am going and I am most comfortable when I let my intuition guide and protect me. I really believe that what we are doing in these "new" (relatively speaking) studies is contributing in a grand way to the healing of ourselves as a society, a global community in which humans one day will learn to coexist with each other and the rest of life, with the rest of our relations in the animal and plant worlds, the water worlds, the sky world. At least that is how I see my own work and the work of those individuals for whom I have a great respect. I am far from denying that these radical (root-digging) fields are not without their problems and contradictions. But I do feel that what many of us are doing is taking ourselves, and those who choose to go with us, through particular kinds of processes of self-realization in every sense of the word, especially when we recognize each other's work and are inclusive in our analyses of all the factors of difference that must be considered—race, ethnicity, class, gender, sexual orientation, age, and *history*, to name some of the most foregrounded ones.

For peoples who have been cast as "marginalized," this recovery process is a coming into consciousness that is dramatically realigning. Many Native American writers, for example, including myself, have voiced the stunning revelation, "Oh, I'm not crazy—I'm an Indian!" The field of Native American Studies has given indigenous peoples the tools and the techniques to be able to "doctor" ourselves, to be able to retrieve for ourselves, and shape, our faces and our hearts, which in the ancient Aztec tradition was the intent of education. Gloria Anzaldua knows this—that is why she named her most recent anthology *Haciendo Caras: Making Face/Making Soul.* And from an indigenous perspective, when you "doctor" someone, you must know what you are doctoring in its totality. For a holistic healing to occur, you (we) must take into account the whole of the body (politic), as well as the mind, the spirit, the heart, the will. You (we) must take into account the way energy is run, the way it is blocked, and the kind of energy being perpetuated, (self)destructive or creative. Are the forces of oppression or forces of liberation being served?

We must imagine a world without rape. But I cannot imagine a world without rape, a world without misogyny, without imagining a world without racism, classism, sexism, homophobia, ageism, historical amnesia and other forms and manifestations of violence directed against those communities that are seen to be "asking for it." Even the Earth is presumably "asking for it," as are all the endangered species. So are children, the disabled, anyone who is "different." Different from what? What is the scale we are using to determine who is "normal," who is "rational"? We are pitted against each other—why? Whose interests are being served by our mistrusting each other, fearing each other, despising each other, and even sometimes mounting "holy wars" against each other? And if we are to be in solidarity with each other as human beings and global citizens of our planet, how can we ask each other for support if we do not give our own?

How can my Native American brothers expect my support when they condone and/or participate in the hateful violation and degradation of Native American women (or any women)? How can my younger

Chicano brother dare to call himself committed to the people when he brutally beats up a woman for whatever reason? How can the ones who looked on and did nothing face themselves in the mirror? How can my older Chicano brother (who is a "leader") not see that the personal is indeed political, just as the political is personal, and that the causes he espouses and the factors of analyses that he considers crucial are intimately related to the issues of gender and sexuality, and to the right of women to be included in the struggle for their own sake (even, and perhaps especially, as dissenting voices) because "women's bodies are the battlefield." Why can't they see how hard it is for me to say to them "brother"? Until they change, I can barely spit the word out. And finally, I cannot imagine a world without rape without imagining a world that is not ruled by the logic of capitalism and imperialism which continues to justify subordination, dehumanization, and exploitation.

What do I imagine then? From my own Native American perspective, I see a world where sovereign indigenous peoples continue to plunge into our memories to come back to our *origin*ality, to live in dignity and carry on our resuscitated and ever-transforming "cultures" and traditions with liberty. I see a world where difference is respected rather than feared. Benito Juarez, the full-blood Zapotec Indian man who was the President of Mexico in the mid-1800s, put it succinctly: *"El respeto al derecho ajeno es la paz"* ["Respect for another's rights *is* peace"]. I see a world where Chicanos/Chicanas and other mestizos/mestizas take the radical step of getting to know the "Indian" side of their families in a way that is just and honorable. I see a world where native women find strength and continuance in the remembrance of who we really were and are (with all our attributes and all our faults!), a world where more and more native men find the courage to recognize and honor—that they and the women of their families and communities have the capacity to be profoundly vital and creative beings. It is hard for me to hold on to this vision, this waking dream, because the invasion, after all, continues. The waves of imposed terror are being felt here in the U.S., as well as from Mexico to the southernmost tip of South America, particularly in communities where indigenous people predominate, in Guatemala, El Salvador, Ecuador, Peru, Colombia, Bolivia, Brazil, Hawaii, Puerto Rico, and the reservations and rancherías within the U.S. As citizens (especially) of the U.S., and of a global society, we should be as conscious and committed to justice in this hemisphere as we are in this society and in other parts of the world. And this I know, and I have written about it in other places. According to the Aztec oral tradition (which yes, is very much alive), we are moving into the next sun, Coatonatiuh, the Sixth Sun of Consciousness and Wisdom. We are presently in the tumultuous transition period between the old sun and the new. In this period of transition, women are leading the way. Women are on the frontline, opening and clearing the paths. It is our turn.

There is an old Cheyenne saying, "A nation is not conquered until the hearts of its women are on the ground. Then it is done, no matter how strong the weapons, or how brave the warriors." How do all of us as women ensure that our hearts do not hit the ground? What strategies might we as women use to remind us to hold our heads and hearts high? We must stay as informed as we possibly can. I am thankful for the understanding and validation of Spirit as it manifests itself in the Native American community. I am thankful for each "text" which opens the way for me to go through and beyond, on my own path. I am grateful for each person who wins my heart with the example of her or his integrity. I realize that any collective is only as strong as each of its members, and that the Spider Grandmother of Many Names who sustains us all doesn't need for us to be throwing rocks at the very web or net(work) that we and she are trying to create. Every connection must be delicately woven, intricately and subtly connected, and strong. There must be individual growth for any collective to evolve. I give myself time to take care of myself. I learn how to cleanse myself and heal myself. I take care of my spirit, so that my spirit will help me take care of the rest of myself. I love and let myself be loved. I accept the responsibility of freedom that my *conciencia* offers me. I dance, I take my stands, and I choose with whom I will stand. I raise my voice in song, in prayer, in message, and yes, in protest and challenge. These are the things that are good for me. And if, by being good to myself in this way, I am called a "bad woman," a "traitor," a sellout, or a bitch, I don't care. I welcome my own delicious insubordination and savor its inspiration.

I want to thank Patricia Riley, Theresa Harlan, and Juan A. Avila Hernandez for their helpful comments in the preparation of this essay.

NOTES

1. While many native people here in the United States have begun to call themselves "Native American," some still refer to themselves as "American Indian" or "Indian." All three of these labels are problematic. Everyone in the "Indian" community knows that the term is a misnomer, but it is a word we have made our own. I will use "Native American" and "Indian" interchangeably in this essay.

2. Emma Perez, "Sexuality and Discourse: Notes from a Chicana Survivor," *Chicana Lesbians: The Girls Our Mothers Warned Us About,* ed. by Carla Trujillo (Berkeley: Third Woman, 1991), p. 163.

3. I realize that the terms "First World" and "Third World" are shifting and inexact, and so for the purposes of this essay I have put them initially within quotation marks.

4. I am also aware of the debate within the black community surrounding the terms "African-American" and "black American." "Africa" and "America" were not the original names of the continents we now know by those terms. I am certain that "Africa" had as many names as there were distinct indigenous peoples to name it, which is the case for "America" as well.

5. Inés Hernandez-Avila, "Cuernavaca—Pensavientos," *Frontiers: A Journal of Women's Studies* 2, no. 2 (Summer 1980), p. 52.

6. Again, the terms "white," "EuroAmerican," "Anglo-American," are approximations, and in and of themselves are contested terms. "Whiteness" is beginning to be interrogated in the same manner other "races" have been interrogating the terms that have been applied to them.

7. Sally Roesch Wagner, "The Iroquois Roots of Early Feminism." Lecture presented at the University of California, Davis, November 1989.

8. Susan Brownmiller, "Making Female Bodies the Battlefield," *Newsweek,* 4 January 1993, p. 37.

9. Gloria Anzaldua, *Borderlands/La Frontera: The New Mestiza* (San Francisco: spinsters/aunt lute, 1987), p. 22.

10. I do not agree with any analysis that rejects completely nor embraces wholeheartedly the "Aztec component" of contemporary Chicana/Chicano identity. The fact that Aztec cultural/philosophical foundations have figured into Mexican and Chicano/Chicana (cultural) nationalism cannot be ignored. The actual complexity of these foundations requires, I believe, careful consideration rather than uncritical acceptance or facile dismissal. In other essays I have urged the Chicana/Chicano community to come to tems with their actual indigenous ancestry, whatever that might be (and there are many possibilities). There are, however, useful (and by now familiar) concepts which Anzaldua and others have employed in their discussion of the "Indianness" of Chicanas and Chicanos. I myself have participated in the Mexico City based Conchero dance tradition since 1979, and so have had access to elders and to the dance community that carries on the Aztec dance and oral traditions. I do not pretend to be Aztec, however.

11. Inés Hernandez-Avila, "Rezo," *Con Razón, Corazón* (San Antonio: M & A Editions, 1987)
12. Andrea Dworkin, *Woman Hating* (New York: E.P. Dutton, 1974), p. 23.
13. Inés Hernandez-Avila, "Open Letter to Chicanas: On the Power and Politics of Origin," *Without Discovery: A Native Response to Columbus,* ed. by Ray Gonzalez (Seattle: Broken Moon, 1992), p. 155.
14. My emphasis here has been on the colonial experience as I see it affecting indigenous peoples of the Americas. By my use of the generic terms "capitalism" and "imperialism" I do not mean to excuse or espouse other forms of state repression, such as occurred in the former so-called socialist systems of Eastern Europe and the former Soviet Union.

INÉS HERNANDEZ-AVILA is Nimipu (a Nez Perce of Chief Joseph's band) on her mother's side and Tejana (Chicana) on her father's. An assistant professor of Native American Studies at the University of California/Davis, she has published one collection of poetry, *Con Razón, Corazón,* and is preparing a second for publication entitled *War Dance/Danza Guerrera: For All the Skins and All the Meskins.* She is also a widely published scholar and critic and has been a member of the Conchero dance community of Mexico City since 1979.

A WOMAN WITH A SWORD
Some Thoughts on Women, Feminism, and Violence

by D. A. Clarke

The man limps into the emergency room with one ear half torn off and multiple bruises. As he gasps out his story, the doctor shakes his head: "You mean you grabbed at her breasts and tried to pull her into your car? Well I mean, dummy, what did you expect?" And he gets no sympathy, not a shred, not from anyone.

JUSTICE IS A woman with a sword"—as slogans go, this one is strangely evocative. The sword, after all, is the weapon of chivalry and honor. Aristocratic criminals were privileged to meet their deaths by the sword rather than the disgraceful hempen rope; gentlemen settled their differences and answered insults at swords' point. Women and peasants, of course, did not learn swordplay. The weapon, like the concepts of honor and personal courage it represented, was reserved for men, and only those men of good birth; no one else was expected or permitted to have a sense of personal pride or honor. Offences against a woman were avenged by her chosen champion.

A woman with a sword, then, is a powerful emblem. She is no one's property. A crime against her will be answered by her own hand. She is armed with the traditional weapon of honor and vengeance, implying both that she has a sense of personal dignity and worth, and that affronts against that dignity will be hazardous to the offending party. This is hardly the woman of pornographic male fantasy.

In male fantasy, women are always powerless to defend themselves from hurt and humiliation. Worse, they enjoy them. Treatment that would drive the average self-respecting man to desperate violence makes these fantasy-women tremble, breathe heavily, and moan with desire: abuse and embarrassment are their secret needs. The "womanliness" invented by pornographers is a deep masochism, which renders women as powerless to defend self and others as the sweetness-and-light female patience and martyrdom of Christian romanticism. It's but a short step from the ladylike and therefore ineffectual face slaps of Nice Girls to the "hot and steamy surrender" in the dominant male's brawny embrace.

But a woman with a sword—*that* is a different matter.

The troublesome question of nonviolence haunts the women's movement and always has. We despise the brutality to which woman are subjected by men, the arrogance and casual destructiveness of male violence as embodied in domestic battery, gang skirmishes, and officially sanctioned wars. Feminists have traditionally opposed police brutality, the draft, warfare, rape, blood sports, and other manifestations of the masculine fascination with dominance and death.

Yet, like all oppressed peoples, women are divided on the essential question of violence as a tactic. When is it appropriate to become violent? Is the use of force ever justifiable? When is it time to take up arms?

to learn jujitsu? to carry a knife? Is violence just plain wrong, no matter who does it? Or can there be extenuating circumstances?

The flow of our debate is muddied by traditional ideas of womanliness with which feminists struggle. Are women really better than men? Are we inherently kinder, gentler, less aggressive? Certainly the world would be a better place if everyone manifested the virtues tradition assigns to Good Women. But will gentleness and kindness really win the hearts of nasty and violent people? Will reason, patience, and setting a good example make men see the error of their ways? Is "womanly" non-violence "naturally" the best and only course for feminists?

Historically, the prospect for peoples and cultures which avoid violence is not good. They tend to lose territory, property, freedom, and finally life itself as soon as less pleasant neighbors show up with better armaments and bigger ambitions. It's hard to survive as a pacifist when the folks next door are club-waving, rock-hurling imperialists: you end up enslaved or dead, or you learn to be like them in order to fight them. The greatest challenge to nonviolence is that to fulfill its promise it must be able to *prevent* violence. The image of the nonviolent activist righteously renouncing the use of force—while watching armed thugs drag away their struggling victims—is less than pleasing.

We have also the problem of effectiveness. Nonviolence is far more impressive when practiced by those who could easily resort to force if they chose. A really big, tough man in the prime of life who chooses to discipline himself to peace and gentleness is an impressive personality. A mob of thousands who choose to sit down peaceably and silently in the street, rather than smash windows and overrun police lines, is an unnerving sight. These kinds of nonviolence make a profound political point. But when women advocate nonviolence it may be much less effective.

Why? Because women are traditionally considered incapable of violence, particularly of violence against men. In the '40s the film beauty used to beat her little fists ineffectually on the strong man's chest before collapsing into passionate tears; in the '70s the ditzy female sidekick inevitably left the safety catch on when it was time to shoot the bad guy. Women are commonly held to be as incompetent at physical force as they are at mechanics, mathematics, and race-car driving. The only violence traditionally permitted to women is the sneaky kind: conspiracy, manipulation, deceit, poison, a stiletto in the back.

And when women do become violent, we perceive it as shocking and awful, far worse than the male violence which we take for granted. There is a self-serving myth among men that, given power, women would be "even worse" than the worst men—which, of course, justifies keeping women firmly in their place and making sure no power gets into their nasty little hands. Many of us believe that myth, to some extent: I can remember my mother (a strong and resourceful woman) retailing to me the common doctrine that the female camp guards of the Third Reich were worse than the men.

Of course, only a handful of women attained to power in Hitler's Germany; prison-guarding is an unfeminine occupation, also. So female camp guards, of high or low rank, were exceptional and therefore suspect. Their deeds are documented and unquestionably vile, but it's hard for me to say how they might be distinguished as measurably worse, more evil, than those of their male colleagues. What makes them worse in the eyes of Allied historians, I fear, is that in addition to their other crimes they *stepped out of women's place.*

This different perception of male and female violence, this double standard, afflicts women at the most elementary levels. When a man makes unwanted social advances to a woman in, let's say, a restaurant or theater, and she eventually has to tell him loudly and angrily to get lost—*she* is the one who will be perceived as rude, hostile, aggressive, and obnoxious. His verbal aggression and invasiveness are accepted and expected; her rudeness or mere curtness in getting rid of him is noticed and condemned. One of our great myths is that a "real lady" can and should handle any difficulty, defuse any assault, without ever raising her voice or losing her manners. Female rudeness or violence in resistance to male aggression has often been taken to prove that the woman was not a lady in the first place, and therefore deserved no respect from the aggressor or sympathy from others.

Until recently, violent women in fiction were always evil. Competence with guns, long blades, or martial arts automatically marked a female as "mannish," possibly lesbian, destined for stereotyping as a prison matron, pervert, man-hater, sadist, etc. On the other hand, cleverness with tiny silver-plated pistols, poison rings, or jeweled daggers identified the "snakelike" villainess whose cold and perfect beauty concealed a heart twisted by malice and frozen with selfishness. Heroines, predictably, fainted or screamed at moments of peril and then waited to be rescued in the penultimate chapter. By the 1920s the Good Girls might put up a brave struggle and kick the bad guy in the shins, but they certainly did not throw furniture, break necks, cut throats, or whip out a sword-cane and chase the villain through the abandoned warehouse.

Tougher females emerged for a while in the war years, but only in the last twenty years have fictional females arrived who are ready with fists, karate kicks, and small arms. A new genre of Amazon Fantasy has grown up where previously there were only one or two authors who dared to put a sword in a female character's hand. Warrior women have become protagonists, with books and even epics to themselves. Admittedly, most of them are required by the author (or editor) to Learn to Love a Man Again by the end of the plot, but at least they start out by avenging their own rapes and their family's wrongs. In commercial film (a conservative medium), fighting heroines and anti-heroines are beginning to surface: Sigourney Weaver in *Aliens*, Anne Parillaud in *La Femme Nikita*, Deborra-Lee Furness in *Shame*, and of course Geena Davis and Susan Sarandon in *Thelma & Louise*. Even in films with no pretense to social commentary or good intentions, fighting female sidekicks are popping up here and there (*Conan the Destroyer*, *The Golden Child*) who previously were restricted to the world of Marvel Comics.

Americans are beginning to be able to handle the idea of female rage and vengeance, or at least of serious female violence, in fiction. In much the same way, the reading public of the '20s and '30s began to accept the Career Woman long before women made real inroads into the professions. Does this mean something? Is the ability to be violent a prerequisite for equality—as the maintenance of army and arsenal is for nationhood? Are these fighting females a good sign?

Maybe. In a perfect world, no. In a perfect world we wouldn't lock our doors, and no one would know how to throw a punch or how to roll with one. In this world, alas, perhaps the price of full citizenship is the willingness and ability to defend oneself and one's dignity to the point of force.

We do respect people who "know their limits," who cannot be pushed past a certain point—just as we mistrust and disrespect those who have no give in them at all and overreact violently to every little frustration. We respect people who can take care of themselves, who inform us of their limits clearly and look prepared to enforce them. Women are traditionally denied these qualities—the "no means yes" of male mythology—and one reason for this is that we are denied the use of force. To put it very simply, little boys who get pushed around on the playground are usually told to "stand up to him, don't let him get away with it," whereas little girls are more usually advised to run to Teacher.

The bottom line in not being pushed around is our willingness and our capacity to resist. At some point resistance means defending ourselves with physical force. Women—kept out of contact sports, almost never trained in wrestling or boxing as boys often are, taught to flatter strong men by acting weak—are denied the skills and the emotional preparedness required to fight back.

Men commit the most outrageous harassments and insults against women simply *because they can get away with it.* They know they will not get hurt for saying and doing things that, between two men, would quickly lead to a fistfight or a stabbing. There are no consequences for abusing women.

There are several strategies for preventing crimes from happening. We start with education, reason, and our efforts to bring up children to be good adults. Then comes elementary preparedness and awareness on the part of the innocent. Then there is active resistance and self-defense when a crime is attempted. And as our last resort, there is the establishment of consequences for the perpetrator. Every time a man molests his daughter and still keeps his place in the family and community—every time a man sexually harasses a female employee and still keeps his job or his business reputation—every time a rapist or femicide gets a token sentence—there is a terrible lack of consequence for the commission of a crime.

We disagree as a society about the level of "punishment" or retribution or reparation which should be enforced. We can't agree whether murderers should themselves be killed. Most of us would agree that hanging is too severe a penalty for stealing a loaf of bread or a sheep, but is it too severe a penalty for hacking a woman to death? Some would say yes and some no. Others think we should abandon the concepts of punishment and reparation altogether, with their authoritarian implications, and concentrate on reeducating and reclaiming our errant brothers, turning them into better people.

While we argue about these things, women are steadily and consistently being insulted, molested, assaulted and murdered. And most of the men who are doing these things are suffering no consequences at all, or very slight consequences. The slighter the consequence of their offense, the more it seems to them (and to everyone) that there is really nothing so very wrong with what they have done.

When as a society we sanctimoniously clasp our hands and reject the death penalty, letting femicides and rapists free after token jail terms and "therapy," we merely make a callous value judgment. We judge that a man's life—even a rapist's or a murderer's—is more valuable than the life and happiness of the next woman or child he may attack. When a killer is released and kills again, those who signed his release were signing also the death warrant for his next victim, someone they did not know and could not identify. That person's life was the price of their squeamishness and reluctance to sign for the death (or life imprisonment) of a man they could name, whose face they knew.

If the State is not going to step in and enforce severe penalties for abusing and murdering women, then is it women's responsibility to do so? When a woman's dignity, honor, and physical person are assaulted or destroyed, how shall we get justice? How shall we prevent it from happening again?

If the courtroom and the law are owned by men (if a Clarence Thomas, for example, can be appointed to the Supreme Court regardless of the evidence that he routinely insulted and harassed women), at what point are women entitled to take the law into their own hands? At what point can we justify personal vendettas by angry survivors of male violence? What about violent action for political (rather than personal) agendas?

These are thorny questions for sure. Vigilantism is so very trendy in our fragmenting culture: in films and cheap novels by the dozen, angry protagonists (almost all male) go out and shoot up the bad guys in a series of solo crusades, for revenge and the justice that a corrupt and ineffectual System cannot provide. America's love affair with flashy violence and alpha-male bravado is so traditional and distressing that one does hesitate to suggest vigilantism as a feminist tactic.

Yet—but—on the other hand—sometimes a demonstration of violent rage accomplishes what years of prayers, petitions, and protests cannot: it gets you taken seriously. (On the other hand, it can also get you labeled crazy and put away.) Palestinian terrorists may have done more harm than good to their people's cause—or they may have been an essential part of a liberation struggle. It depends whom you ask.

When we consider violent political tactics such as terrorism and retribution, we have to remember that male implementation of these tactics is all mixed up with the traditions of male amusement and competition. Too often the political cause of the moment is no more than an excuse for a gang of rowdy boys to play about with high explosives and automatic weapons—just another form of blood sport. Often there is more violence, and more random violence, than is called for—simply because the terrorists are having so much fun frightening and killing people. Would women succumb to this temptation?

Another common belief about female violence is that it will only escalate male violence. I have heard from people of widely varying ages and politics the argument, "If women learn judo, then men will start using guns." This rather sidesteps the fact that a large number of men already own and use guns, knives, and other portable weapons; but it's a familiar argument from all liberation struggles. What if resistance to the occupier/oppressor leads only to increased brutality, repression, and suffering?

We can end up in a sadly familiar conflict: some women will hate and fear feminists and self-defense advocates because they anticipate that male anger, stirred up by these uppity females, will be vented on all women, including the "innocent." No liberation movement has ever escaped this bitter argument.

Will we make it worse by resisting? Feminists who demonstrated publicly and disruptively at the turn of the century were accused at the time of worsening women's prospects by their violent and provocative behavior; yet today we honor them as the instigators of changes that lifted women halfway out of serfdom. Certainly forceful and loud resistance to sexual assault tends to result more often in escape or reduced injury than "womanly" tactics such as tears, pleading, or cooperation.

If the risk involved in attacking a woman were greater, there might be fewer attacks. If women defended themselves violently, the amount of damage they were willing to do to would-be assailants would be the measure of their seriousness about the limits beyond which they would not be pushed. If more women killed husbands and boyfriends who abused them or their children, perhaps there would be less abuse. A large number of women refusing to be pushed any further would erode, however slowly, the myth of the masochistic female which threatens all our lives. Violent resistance to an attack has its advantages all round.

A backlash is always possible, whether women "behave" or not. The strength and viciousness of antifeminism, and its appeal, have a lot more to do with the prevailing economic and political weather than with anything women actually do. A subject population can be as polite, conciliatory, and assimilated as possible—and still wake up one morning to discriminatory laws, confiscation of property, and all the rest.

For these reasons the argument that female violence "will hurt only women" or "make things worse" seems irrelevant to me. In fact, female violence that hurts *only women* is perfectly acceptable. Women have always been given the dirty work of disciplining their daughters into women's place, whether this meant binding little girls' feet or blaming and beating them for being raped. Today, a "feminist community" which claims to find violence of all kinds distasteful is still able to find lesbian sadomasochism sexy and chic. Images of women hurting other women are widely accepted even where images of men hurting women are criticized.

Now, I am not particularly attracted to images of anyone being hurt, period. But I see potential value in fiction and film on the theme of women taking violent means of vengeance on rapists and femicides. One benefit is the assertion of female personal honor; another, quite frankly, is the shock value. Those who are appalled by the idea of vigilante women hunting down men should be asking themselves what they are doing about this world in which images of men hunting down, overpowering, and hurting women surround us. If violence is so terribly wrong when committed by women, then damn it, it is as terribly wrong when committed by men.

Let's face it, we still live in a world and a century in which a woman who walks (mistake) in the wrong part of town (oh dear) after dark (uh oh) alone (a big no-no) will be blamed by all and sundry if she is raped. People will ask what she expected, doing a fool thing like that.

It's interesting—amusing in a bitter kind of way—maybe even liberating—to envision a slightly different world. The man limps into the emergency room with one ear half torn off and multiple bruises. As he gasps out his story, the doctor shakes his head: "You mean you grabbed at her breasts and tried to pull her into your car? Well I mean, dummy, what did you expect?" And he gets no sympathy, not a shred, not from anyone.

If women become more violent, will the world be a more violent place? Perhaps, but it's not a simple equation of addition. We will have to subtract any violence that women *prevent*. So we will have to subtract a large number of rapes and daily humiliations suffered by women who today cannot or will not defend themselves. We might have to subtract six or seven murders that would have been committed by a latter-day Zodiac Killer, except that his first intended victim killed him instead. Suppose one of the women in the lecture hall in Montreal had been armed and skilled enough to take out Marc Lepine before he mowed down fourteen of her classmates. . . .

It's not as if we were suggesting that women introduce violence into the Garden of Eden. The war is already on. Women and children are steadily losing it.

And women are already violent. Women take out the anger and frustration of women's place, and the memory of their own humiliations and defeats, on each other, on their kids, and on their own bodies. Would we rather that incest survivors mutilate themselves, commit suicide, abuse their own children—or go and do something dreadful to Daddy? We don't know for sure that doing something dreadful to Daddy will heal a wounded soul, but it does seem more appropriate than doing dreadful things to oneself or any innocent bystander.

And one last great myth: "Violence never solves anything."

In the grand philosophical sense those words may ring true. Violence is like money: it can't make you happy, save your soul, make you a better person—but it certainly can solve things. When the winners exterminate the losers, historical conflicts are permanently solved. Many a high-ranking criminal has lived to a comfortable and respected old age only because a few pesky witnesses were no longer alive to testify. Many a dissatisfied husband has got rid of an unwanted wife. More women than we know have probably got rid of abusive husbands.

Violence definitely solves some things. A dead rapist will not commit any more rapes; he's been solved. Violence is a seductive solution because it seems easy and quick; violence is a glamorous commercial property in our time; violence is a tool, an addiction, a sin, a desperate resort, or a hobby, depending on where you look and whom you ask.

I am here to lay before you not a list of easy answers, but a tangle of difficult questions. Violence may be a tool and a tactic that feminists should use; certainly we ought to be putting some serious thought into it. If we refuse it, it should not be because it offends against our romantic notion of morally superior Womanhood, but for some better and more thoughtful reason. If we accept it, we had better figure out how to avoid becoming corrupted by it.

This piece was commissioned originally for the forthcoming anthology *Nemesis: Justice Is A Woman With A Sword*, edited by Nikki Craft, to be published by Always Causing Legal Unrest (ACLU)/Nemesis Publishing Concerns in 1994.

D. A. CLARKE is a feminist, lesbian, and technophile who has contributed irregularly to the literature of radical feminism over the last decade. She has written mostly about male violence against women and its marketability. Her most recent work will appear in the anthologies *Nemesis* (ACLU) and *Unleashing Feminism* (HerBooks, 1993). She finds patriarchy unacceptable.

TRANSFORMING THE RAPE CULTURE THAT LIVES IN MY SKULL

by Martha Roth

In the new world, women look eagerly for equal sexual
partners and participate fully in the rituals of courtship, love, and commitment. Men lose their
erections—and their desire—if their partners
aren't eager to make love.

IN PREPARATION FOR this book I had to read a lot of rape stories. They shocked and angered but also aroused me; my body responded to the ugly facts of rape as to the most delicate insinuations of erotica, and I fought my own response and felt ashamed.

I don't like pornography and don't use it, but sometimes in lovemaking my fantasies speak its language. I've tried to reprogram my erotic imagination, but the old hard-core fantasies swim back, and I have come to think of my sexuality as having been colonized by male-identified images. What Susan Griffin calls "the pornographic mind" has invaded and now occupies my most intimate space.[1] To the question of what lived in that space before, I have no answer, nor do I know whether the colonial invasion completely destroyed it.

I remember having an orgasm at the age of two. Wearing a starched frock, I lay across a wicker stool or ottoman on my tummy, rocking back and forth. A wonderful feeling flushed me with warmth, tightening my bottom, and I kept rocking. It happened again, many times, until I grew tired. My grandfather, who was supposed to be looking after me, snored in a chair.

During childhood I visited that sea of pleasure often. I lusted for little boys and thought of them while doing it. Dukey Larson had dark hair and pale, pale skin; I wanted to bite his white chest and carve my desire in his flesh.

As I grew older and learned to read, stories aroused me: the Snow Queen, who pierced Kay's heart with an icicle, or Dis, who carried Persephone off with gathered flowers falling from her arms. The full horror of the Nazi concentration camps became known when I was seven, and they filled the pages of *Life* magazine as they came into our house every Friday. Sometimes I imagined I was a naked victim interrogated by Gestapo agents in shiny leather coats. Sometimes I was a spy who had been captured and sent to a camp where prisoners were tormented for the amusement of their captors.

Throughout childhood I masturbated to these fantasies. It seemed "natural" that cruelty should excite me, and until the 1970s, when I read *Against Our Will*[2] and other feminist works and heard Robin Morgan say, "Pornography is the theory, rape is the practice," it never occurred to me to wonder why I connected cruelty with sensual pleasure.

The common association of orgasmic release with fantasies of pain—either given or received—has led many writers to conclude that the connection is hard-wired into our brains, part of the same reflex. Discussions of rape often begin at this point, with the assumption that it's "natural" for men to experience arousal at a partner's real or fantasized pain.

This assumption certainly underpins the "rape is more fun" position of such anxious wannabe primitives as Camille Paglia, and it's implicit in sociobiologists' description of rape as "an adaptive evolutionary strategy" for sprinkling an individual male's semen as widely as possible within a population of breeding females.[3] Yet virtually every other aspect of human sexuality has been shown to be a learned response, including how to procreate.[4] If human arousal is labile, in the sense that it can attach to different stimuli (body parts, music, plastic raincoats), then why has the human species persisted over many millennia in keying to images of violence and pain? Why haven't we chosen tenderness?

Perhaps the answer lies in psychosexual development, in the individual histories of many millions of young humans. Perhaps most young children experience early genital pleasure in a context of guilt, coercion, or outright abuse. Perhaps this happens to so many of us that it amounts almost to a cultural constant. Young children touch their genitals casually at first, then for comfort. When caregivers discourage this touching for pleasure or reassurance, children quickly learn shame and concealment. Shame is so specifically bonded to feelings of genital pleasure that many people can't feel one without the other; hidden things become sexualized and all pleasure is guilty pleasure.

Male children, as Ruth Herschberger wrote fifty years ago in her wonderful, ovular book, *Adam's Rib*, get a double message.[5] They may have their hands slapped for masturbating, but there is one socially approved reason for them to touch their penises—they must learn to aim a urine stream, and they're praised for doing it well. Female children never have a "good" reason to touch their vulvas.

My grandfather snored in a chair. I know he was there, but I don't remember his speaking to or touching me. I remember being careful to do my rocking quietly, while he slept. What had gone on while he was awake?

Years later I told two friends about this memory. "My God," said one, her cheeks flaring crimson. "He diddled you." "Yup," said the second. "That's what it sounds like."

I can't put together what I remember about this grandpa—bald, hawklike, smelling of bourbon—and child molestation, but if someone else had told me this story that's what I would conclude: someone, probably grandpa, had stimulated her.

What if the secret of sexual arousal to cruelty slumbers in most children's early experiences? What if, in many cases, our first sensual responses are drawn from us by adults we depend on for care, and we hold within us forever the association of pleasure with abuse of power? Even when the sex play is gentle and loving, even when the intention is to give pleasure to the child, the imbalance of power between child and guardian guarantees that pleasure will be experienced as abuse.

I'm guessing, of course, at things I can never know for sure. Perhaps the scene as I remember it wouldn't be enough to cement the connection of pleasure with cruelty, sex with violence. I also had a nursemaid with Germanic ideas of early toilet training who may have stimulated me in the course of vigorous cleaning; a working mother whom I seldom saw; and an affectionate but preoccupied father. Grandpa might get a little drunk on a Sunday afternoon and amuse himself by fondling a child who couldn't tell on him. Little girls' vulvas are exquisite miniatures, with their perfect frills of flesh. Add these up and you might get a girl-child who fetishizes certain kinds of cruelty and who masturbates compulsively to ease her anxiety.

Toilet training frequently involves violence of various kinds, from the suppressed rage of the frustrated trainer to punishments for "soiling" to threats of castration. I used to work with a woman who complained about her two-year-old twin boys. "They wet all the time. I tell 'em I'm going to cut it off if they can't keep it dry." "You shouldn't do that," we told her. "It's really bad for them to scare them like that."

She would shrug and the next day tell us about "whacking" one of her sons on his penis when he wet.

Girls experiencing sexual abuse from their mothers often report a connection to toilet training, washing, or "intestinal cleansing."[6] Most parents and caregivers are more sensible and sympathetic, I hope, but I suspect many still discourage little boys and girls from handling their genitals for pleasure or reassurance. Children generally receive praise and approval for disciplining other primitive pleasures such as urinating, defecating, and eating, but years, decades must pass before genital pleasure can come out into the light, and by then it's too late. The only sexual pleasure for which most people ever reward their daughters comes after a marriage ceremony, in connection with producing new children. Many young girls either deafen themselves to the insistent calls of their flesh or they sneak pleasure, often surrounding it with an elaborate barricade of concealment, guilt, and (at least fantasized) punishment.

In *Pornography and Silence*, Griffin theorizes that sexual arousal in response to cruelty stems from a need to punish the "vulnerable feeling self," the child-self that first experienced pleasure and opened itself to feelings of love and trust. When these feelings are hurt or betrayed, as they almost universally are, the child-self takes the betrayer's part, turns its pain inward, and punishes its own vulnerability. Fantasies of punishment or revenge bond to the longings for pleasure, defending them from further injury.

Many little boys are circumcised, of course, and thus carry almost from birth a memory of pain in the part of their bodies that also yields the greatest pleasure. Uncircumcised boys sometimes experience irritation or infections under the foreskin. (I know many millions of women worldwide also experience genital mutilation, but I'm writing about contemporary American culture, where reported incidents of rapes are highest and where my own consciousness was colonized.)

Little boys have a narrower compass of approved behavior than little girls. Girls can wear skirts or trousers, play with trucks or dolls, paint their faces, hammer nails, dance, run races, wear nail polish, beat drums, build blocks, cook, play ball, solve puzzles, and cuddle stuffed toys. Active play, passive listening, and creative exploration are all seen as healthy and "natural" for little girls, while parents worry about a boy who draws and paints, dresses up, and prefers playing house to playing ball.

We send boys the message that we expect them to grow into men who like hard, heavy things, who compete and play to win, who armor their bodies against touch, and who secrete androgens when anxious. We train little boys to mistrust each other and to defend themselves physically against aggression.

Teenage boys have high levels of testosterone, and testosterone correlates with aggression throughout the primate world. But when you watch very young boys, from three to six, you can see that their aggression is mainly a response to frustration or anxiety. It seems to me that we also train little boys to make testosterone by introducing anxiety into their lives, for example, by channeling them into competitive play. If this is so, then high levels of androgen secretion in teenage boys might partly result from anxiety induced by pressures to perform their approved masculine roles, and by internal contradictions in those roles. We expect them to excel in competition while maintaining friendships with their competitors; we expect them to exercise independent judgment while submitting to authority.

Testosterone secretion, stimulated by these binds, disposes them to violent behavior. When they react violently to the internal contradictions, we label them as having "poor impulse control." If they succeed in channeling their violence into sport, warfare, or intellectual endeavor, we praise them. *Of course* they will use violence in expressing their sexuality; sexual arousal evokes unacceptable longings for tenderness and intimacy and threatens them with vulnerability and loss of control.

We have understood for a long time that young males learn rapist behavior before they desire sexual relations, and when they do, their model for lovemaking features domination and submission. I'm suggesting that culture encourages both men and women to associate sexuality with violence because of the haphazard, abusive ways we learn about our sexual capacities. Many children first experience genital pleasure in a context of subordination to a dominant figure, and that pleasure reinforces the lesson so that every repetition forges a stronger link. Others repress the knowledge of genital pleasure, and when culture expects them to deploy it, they find they cannot scale the barricade of guilt and punishment.

Much of the literature of sexual violence has shown that men who rape—men who are caught—are men who have experienced physical and emotional abuse as children, including sexual abuse. Women who sexually molest children are almost invariably survivors of early sexual abuse. But I'm not concerned here with criminal acts as the law defines them. I want to understand something about the rape culture that has crept into my skull and peopled my earliest erotic fantasies with torturers and murderers—because I had a safe, "normal," "happy" childhood.

Behavioral biology, as mentioned, suggests that all human sexual behavior is learned. Sexual energies may be inborn, but the range and the specific forms of their expression are determined by multiple factors, mostly unknown. Culture does its damnedest to turn us all into heterosexuals with high anxiety levels who fetishize each other's bodies and consume goods as a substitute for sexual activity, but the margin of "failure"—gays and lesbians, nonconsumers, celibates, and others who don't buy in—should clue us to possibilities of resistance.

Following the clue, we might recognize that human sexual response, though sturdy, is unpredictable and that it is affected (like the human feeding response) by many other pressures and currents. Anorexia and bulimia, for example, are intractable medical problems. For people with these disorders, factors beyond biology have twisted a life-sustaining response into a life-threatening one. That's an extreme example, but I believe it's something like what happens to women's sexuality when our arousal becomes keyed to cruel and violent images.

This twisting of women's sexual response is socially encouraged—as anorexia is encouraged by the presentation of progressively thinner women as "beautiful"—so we can become at least partly willing victims of men whose arousal has also become keyed to cruelty and violence, sometimes referred to as *conquest*. I remember my shock at a lover who asked plaintively, "Couldn't you just fight me a little?"

In her essay "Seduced by Violence No More" [see pp. 353–359], bell hooks speaks of the need for a woman to "reconstruct [her]self as a heterosexual desiring subject" so that she can "be fully aroused by male behavior that is not phallocentric." For me, this means male behavior that does not center on fantasies of the phallus as weapon and lovemaking as abuse. Too many women share the fantasies of abuse because, I'm guessing, too many of us have been abused.

Defenders of consensual sadomasochism claim that bondage, spanking, and varieties of metal and rubber toys allow men and women to explore their fantasies of domination and subordination "safely," that is, with partners who won't murder them. But where is the sexual variation that lets us explore fantasies of equality? How can we liberate our senses so that we are *not* aroused by pain?

If, in raising boys, we emphasize achievement more than exploration and competition more than cooperation, we will train them in competitive, goal-directed behavior, including sexual behavior, and we will give them bodies–or body images–that are dominating rather than receptive or playful. After our early freedom to be androgynous and to explore multiple roles, girls enter a cultural corral at puberty where we are stigmatized if our bodies aren't soft and pliant and if we don't please males.

Human brains developed civilization, with its accompanying discontents. We don't know exactly what reciprocal effects these discontents have on our brains, although we now blame "stress" for conditions that range from baldness to stomach ulcers and heart disease. With the many miraculous interventions that doctors and scientists can perform, we're still ignorant about a wide range of interactions between physiology and behavior. We know that in young mammals the learning process, including the acquisition of language in humans, physically changes the brain. Each increment of learning makes others possible. We don't know what other reciprocal influences shape our bodies/selves; we haven't a clue to how language or other developmental learning affects the endocrine system.

Human sexual arousal, in the words of Ann Snitow, is a seriously undertheorized topic.[7] Many investigators, from Kinsey and his colleagues to Robert Stoller, accept the kinship of sex and violence as a fact of human psychology.[8] For reasons I've tried to set out here, I believe this kinship is learned and not innate, and that my shamed arousal at reading about violence is an artifact of my upbringing. I believe that humans can learn to raise our children without molesting them, and that if we succeed in doing this we have the ability to end sexual violence. If young children could learn the uses of pleasure on their own terms, they might grow into adolescents and then adults for whom sexual desire accompanies feelings of fondness and sympathy.

It looks like an impossible task: the history of art, the world's literature, and a multibillion-dollar global enterprise of pornography and prostitution block our path. Yet I can envision it.

If our social priorities truly were human—if we placed the true welfare of our species above everything—we would find cooperative endeavor the most effective mode of organizing social life. We would figure out how to share the world's resources in an equitable, sustainable manner, and we would teach our children that the making of children is potentially the most important act of their lives. People would train themselves for parenthood, physically and emotionally, and they would contribute as best they could to cooperative nurseries, child-care centers, and schools.

In my new world, everyone cares for young children. Everyone learns that human babies come into the world as primitive as monkeys but with enormously greater capacities. Everyone knows children's genital play is healthy and good, and we give young children as much freedom as we safely can, confident that they will learn civilized behavior—including toilet training—because we who love them model it for them. We don't produce anxiety by encouraging children to compete or to perform before they're ready, and when young boys and girls meet a relaxed acceptance toward everything they do, they show less aggression. Everyone understands that children want to learn—that it's hard to *keep* children from learning—and that learning is a great pleasure.

We teach children reverence for their bodies and sympathy for other species, both plants and animals; until they are taught to trash it, young children feel kinship with the world. As they come to express physical love for one another (and who knows when that might be?), children are taught to make love tenderly and mutually. Little girls and boys learn human anatomy and physiology all their lives; they understand their minds and bodies are expressions of their single human selves and not separate terrains ruled by warring spirits.

Since I don't believe in the devil, nor in evil except as a terrible defect in human learning, this is a world without demons. A few centuries of changed culture could root the demons out of human psyches, turning off the appetite for cruelty. In the new world, women look eagerly for equal sexual partners and participate fully in the rituals of courtship, love, and commitment. Men lose their erections—and their desire—if their partners aren't eager to make love. Because the need to dominate is no longer part of their gender socialization, men are able to accept tenderness as fully as women and to experience pleasure unhooked from fantasies of pain. Some people express their sexuality loosely, casually; some confine their lovemaking to a single partner, finding the subtle deepening of long intimacy more than makes up for lack of variety. Some people choose not to express themselves sexually at all.

Sexual violence gradually becomes a memory, a story that crones and codgers tell late at night around the fire (we still make fires). Younger people can't believe the stories.

"Why would anyone want to do that?" they ask. "Didn't they understand pleasure?"

Soon the young people don't even want to hear the old stories. Rape has become alien to human experience; worse, it sounds unattractive.

I'm sure we can do this. We can do anything.

NOTES

1. Susan Griffin, *Pornography and Silence: Culture's Revenge against Nature* (New York: Harper Colophon Books, 1982).
2. Susan Brownmiller, *Against Our Will: Men, Women, and Rape* (New York: Simon & Schuster, 1975).
3. R. Thornhill and N.W. Thornhill, "The Evolutionary Psychology of Men's Coercive Sexuality," *J. Behavioral & Brain Sciences 15*, no. 2 (June 1992), pp. 363–75.
4. Harry F. Harlow, *Learning to Love* (New York: Jason Aronson, 1974).
   William H. Masters with Virginia Johnson, *Human Sexual Response* (Boston: Little, Brown & Co., 1966).
   Shere Hite, *The Hite Report: A Nationwide Study on Female Sexuality* (New York: Macmillan, 1976).
5. Ruth Herschberger, *Adam's Rib* (New York: Harper & Row, 1970).
6. Flora Rheta Schreiber, *Sybil* (New York: Warner, 1973).
   Toni A.H. McNaron and Yarrow Morgan, *Voices in the Night: Women Write about Incest* (Cleis Press, 1982).
7. Ann Snitow, personal communication, 1992.
8. Alfred C. Kinsey et al., *Sexual Behavior in the Human Male* (Philadelphia: W.B. Saunders Co., 1948).
   Robert J. Stoller, *Sexual Excitement: Dynamics of Erotic Life* (Washington, DC: American Psychiatric Press, 1986).

A native midwesterner, **MARTHA ROTH** is a writer and coexecutive editor of *Hurricane Alice: A Feminist Quarterly*. Raised by working parents, she absorbed a practical feminism, and coming of age in the fifties, she was part of the upheavals that prepared the sixties: obscenity trials, Beat literature, McCarthyism, and struggles for abortion rights. As "Martha Vanceburg" she has cowritten two books of daily meditations, *The Promise of a New Day* with Karen Casey (Hazelden, 1983) and *Family Feelings* with her late mother, Sylvia Silverman (Bantam, 1989), and written a daybook for expectant mothers, *A New Life* (Bantam, 1990). Her short stories, essays, and criticism have been widely published, and she has traveled and lectured in Europe and North America. She has been married to Marty Roth since 1957, and they have three children: Molly, Jennifer, and David.

UP FROM BRUTALITY
Freeing Black Communities from Sexual Violence

by W. J. Musa Moore-Foster

An assault upon a woman's sexuality is the bedrock
symbol of male supremacy. Those men who exult in this
kind of violation are not necessarily out of touch with
their feelings. To the contrary, they may be tapping
into feelings of control and dominance, and yet
may see in the suffering of their victims a
mirror image of their own degradation.

BLACK-ON-**B**LACK CRIME attracts public commentary like no other issue in contemporary America. Urban news broadcasts are awash with images of drug-dealing, gang violence, and the self-destruction of a generation of African-American youth. While these images tend to have a singularly male character, violence against women in Black communities persists and is on the increase. Yet our awareness of such violence is too often dependent on sensationalistic reporting that focuses on personalities rather than exploring the underlying social relationships that have created an increasingly predatory climate for women where they live, work, or even worship with men. Cases as far apart in context as Hill-Thomas and Washington-Tyson reflect the celebrity-driven nature of media coverage as much as they do the ambiguity of the public's response.

Generally, the issue gets squeezed to the margins of public policy debate or sabotaged by persons unwilling to face the reality of the perilous existence of African-American women in their own country. Nevertheless a few women and men (unfortunately, far fewer men) persist in raising the question of the unconscionable maltreatment of Black women by Black men and the nearly casual way it has come to be accepted as a condition of modern living. Without fail, they are regularly assailed for "airing dirty laundry," "perpetuating negative stereotypes," or "being co-opted by the man-hating feminist agenda," quite often by men who assert they care for and about "the Sisters." One reason for this contradiction is that African-American men encounter multilayered obstacles in understanding rape and other forms of gender-directed violence. Among them are an inadequate knowledge of history, confusion over the meaning and use of power, a corroded sense of personal accountability, and a debilitating "phallocentric" social education. I fervently believe that it is vital for Black men to grasp both the facts and the feelings surrounding sexual victimization if we are to do our part in the creation of a culture that does not nurture rape in any of its physical or metaphysical manifestations.

For some of us the pathway to a deeper understanding of rape may not lie merely in a straightforward presentation of the evidence but rather in our subconscious memory. That is where I rediscovered Johnson Square.

Johnson Square was a park in the Baltimore neighborhood of my childhood and the most imposing landmark on this well-traveled stretch of Biddle Street, an avenue connecting downtown to the far East Side. It was both bridge and border, Lovers' Lane and sports field. Within its arbored pathways, the younger and older generations of Black folks gathered to rest, to talk, and to escape the yardless confines of our row houses with their famous marble steps. The park proper was situated several yards back from the sidewalk in all directions. It was perched atop a plateau so steep and wonderful that every kid on our block found no greater delight from May through November than rolling down its grassy hills, spinning like barrels over a green waterfall, screaming and laughing with the hysteria that accompanied our planned abandon. The square belonged to the Black community in the waning years of segregation, when neighborhood boundaries were tinged with the blood of racial conflict. I never envisioned a time when I could not go to the park, for any reason.

I can remember when that notion left me. My family was seated around the dinner table when the news of a young woman's violent assault and murder in Johnson Square came over the radio. She had been found that morning behind one of the rows of hedges lining the paved walkways of the park. I have always felt that from the precise moment of this deed, the life of Johnson Square was utterly subverted. It was not merely that it became an unsafe place to be after dark, but it began to symbolize the accelerated decay of our community.

Once the square had beckoned us like an emerald oasis in the center of an urban desert. Now it loomed in our consciousness as a mecca of terror. It rose up out of fear, mocking the line between civil authority and "the 'hood." The city government responded by flooding the neighborhood with German shepherds and white policemen. The dogs were trained to attack, and the men were trained to let them chew on whomever crossed their path. After sundown, Johnson Square took on the appearance of a perverse Sherwood Forest, a nocturnal, atavistic reminder of our primordial origins. The park, which once teemed with more diversity of life than a coral reef, became a meeting place for antisocial bandits, a magnet for predatory activity, a site of gun battles, and a refuge for those fleeing the police. The final desecration occurred when the hills of the park were sealed over with concrete aggregate and high-intensity, "anticrime" lights were installed at strategic points. To me Johnson Square sank beneath the burden of wrongdoing and reemerged as an ultramodern, truncated pyramid, sheared off at the top and choked off at its roots—completely. It had been transformed by neglect and civic efficiency into a stark, fortress-like monument to the living dead.

The experiences of my childhood pale in comparison to the collective history of African-Americans in our society, but each person's experience is useful in its own way. Although our history does not begin with our bondage in America, the role of slavery in shaping a framework for race and gender relations is critical to an understanding of the oppression of women. However, to connect the contemporary victimization of Black women by Black men to the exploitation of our ancestors is not as fruitful an exercise as it was during the 1960s, when African-American family life was being popularly characterized as a matriarchal, dysfunctional subversion of the patriarchal family, a misguided viewpoint still widely held. It is also a commonly held belief that gender roles were reversed within the slave household and, by extension, within the slave community. Yet, it was during the antebellum period that African-American women were singled out to be victimized and objectified through sexual violence and manipulation at the hands of the slaveholders or through their authority. Ironically, the historical image of the Black man is that he was less than a man because he could not, and therefore did not, protect the women of his community. Certain male slaves, in fact, accepted the master's "gift" of access to women as a reward and as recognition of their own elevated status within the community of slaves. It is just as ironic, then, as Angela Davis has argued, that "when working-class men of color accept the invitation to rape extended by the ideology of male supremacy, they are accepting a bribe, an illusory compensation for their powerlessness."

Sexual violence in African-American communities is indeed connected to the objectification of women facilitated by capitalism. But it is also derived from historical inequalities rooted in and expressed through various ideologies of male supremacy, ideologies which are not entirely dependent upon a specific economic regime. Black women struggled against male domination in precapitalist societies before the slave era, as well in the aftermath of its demise. Through the division of labor, the allocation of scarce resources, and the appropriation of political power, men of African descent have maintained a discernible, if tenuous, upper hand.

The image of the Black man as rapist was concocted in the crucible of

American slavery, but it was generations later, after Emancipation, when the stereotype was most broadly perpetuated, as Logan, Hernton, and others have pointed out. It has served as a twofold barrier to dialogue about both the nature of race and gender relations outside the Black community and the quality of gender relations within it.

The horrific symbol of the Black man as the vehicle of a "fate worse than death" has been exploited by the dominant culture as a means of arguing for its moral superiority and as a way of perpetuating its monopoly over the means of violence. This, among other factors, has unfortunately produced in many African-American men a defensive knee-jerk reaction to the mention of rape. Nevertheless, Black women have not been spared the sexual violence of Black men. The hostile reception of *The Color Purple* provides an interesting example of how deeply resistant some African-American men are to discussing the problem outside the parameters of entrenched, gender-based ideological combat. However, there are a number of us who have not only intervened in acts of sexual violence against women but who also feel that we must bear witness to women's strength and courage.

My closest encounter with an active rapist occurred nearly twenty-five years ago. As a college student in Washington, D.C., I enjoyed a fictive kinship with a small group of women with whom I was intimately but not sexually involved. We loved each other. I felt honored to be regarded as their brother, friend, and confidant. We lived less than a block from each other, but our buildings could not have been more different. My home was in a towering gray tenement whose bloom had wilted before I was born.

My "play sisters" lived in the Windamere, a haven for middle-class professionals and civil servants, with a sprinkling of college students, all dutifully screened by a resident manager, the formidable Mrs. Tilly.

One fall evening, the entire building was alerted to the presence in the neighborhood of a young rapist armed with a steak knife. After being identified as a "family member" to Mrs. Tilly, I joined my friends in a grim vigil, although my fear very nearly matched their own. They had asked me to join other residents in patrolling the building, to accompany them to the basement laundry room, and to camp out in their apartments if need be. I felt they had asked me because I was big and kind. I was undeniably large but not particularly aggressive. I was known as a bookworm, not a "thumper." In addition, I was reluctant to arm myself for fear of being injured out of mistaken identity by vigilantes or the police. The D.C. police were known for their propensity for shooting first and not quite getting around to asking questions. I went along with the plan to patrol the building every evening, out of loyalty more than confidence that I could intimidate a slashing psychopath. I felt I had to do something other than try to comfort my friends with words. As things turned out, I was actually able to intervene in one assault and contribute to the apprehension of its pathetic perpetrator. Yet my feelings were closer to the grief of the victims than to anything vaguely heroic.

One evening I showed up early to surprise my "sisters" by cooking dinner. I had no sooner gotten the pots going when I heard terrifying screams for help accompanied by a strange, flat series of thuds coming from the hallway. I ran out to find a young, slightly built Black man straddling a middle-aged Black woman whom I recognized as a Caribbean neighbor, Mrs. Brown. She was physically winning the struggle by holding onto her assailant with one hand while beating him soundly about the head with a large, square purse in the other. I saw an expression of grateful relief on his face before he fled through the fire exit. Mrs. Brown's crying persisted through the arrival of the police and the reporting process and did not stop when I left her in the hands of her adult children. The "Steak Knife Rapist" was apprehended later that night, but a sound sleep eluded me. I had seen the face of a man's cowardice, and at the same time I had witnessed the kind of courage it takes for women to go about their daily lives. I was filled simultaneously with loathing and awe. Mrs. Brown had fought valiantly for her life and lived to tell others. I had come to her assistance but not to her rescue. She was safe for the moment, but her situation was unchanged.

The radically romanticized myth I had been nurturing about the supreme sovereignty of the masses of Black people had crumbled in front of my eyes. My classmates and I had been reading Cleaver's *Soul on Ice*, and I remembered his crowing about "practicing" sexual assaults on Black women before "moving up" to rape White women. I felt disturbed and ashamed by his notions that the politics of race could provide an ideological rationale for violence against all women. I also felt humbled by the fact that I had been allowed to learn why he was so insanely wrong.

Few African-American men will have the opportunity or the motivation to confront their assumptions about aggression before those assumptions merge as codified behavior. For those of us who came to adulthood in the 1960s, aggression was politicized as a rite of passage into manhood. Our fantasies of righteous, purifying violence, fueled by rather literal readings of Sorel, Fanon, and Mao, not to mention Huey, Bobby, and Malcolm, have been fairly well recorded for posterity. For all the hell we raised and all the White people we rattled, we had not turned our scrutinizing intellects toward gender relations. Despite our familiarity with the example of powerful, visionary women, from Fannie Lou Hamer to Elaine Brown, we did not learn nearly as much from their lives or work as we needed.

If we African-Americans are to survive as a people, fundamental change in men's attitudes about women must begin and persist. A major effort to reeducate youth about respect and the unacceptability of sexual violence must be a priority of the highest order whenever we meet to discuss our future. Before we can initiate the groundwork for this effort, we who would be teachers must open ourselves to a critical rethinking of gender roles that goes beyond the current lip service our society pays to equity.

We need compassionate teachers—women and men—from many walks of life to join us in this work. They must be prepared to demonstrate that strength has many ways of being expressed and that coercion has no place in intimate relations, not to mention its diminishing value in our global community.

Each of us must speak out against the depiction of violence against women and against all forms of shaming addressed to them. This will undoubtedly mean taking on the White pimps who run major record companies, the misguided young Black men who are "prostituting" for them, and if need be, the American Civil Liberties Union, which defends their right to "free" speech.

We must courageously address the issue of accountability for the words and deeds that are destroying us every day. We are a race that is self-destructing before our very eyes and the eyes of our children. In my brief lifetime we have gone from a people who would greet each other as brother and sister to folks who salute one another as "gangsta" and "ho." Until we can commit to the overthrow of the regime of commonplace and terroristic violence under which Black women and children live within our own communities, any discussion of political power and economic rejuvenation is moot.

Our ancestors struggled for human dignity under the most brutal form of slavery known to humankind. Yet we are witnessing the reenslavement of future generations to ideas and practices that perpetrate violence against females of all ages. There is cause for great alarm, but there is a greater need for thoughtful action. As men, one of the things we ought to be thinking about is how we came to inherit such rage and alienation. In a related manner, we should examine how we perceive the natural world and the life processes within it. We are likely to find that there is little precedent in the animal kingdom for the way we treat each other.

Young men, at the earliest feasible age, must be taught how to interact with women in ways that are not exploitative. They must learn that sharing is a process more profound than a simple division of goods, services, money, or labor. It must come to mean something more intimate, more mutually gratifying, involving both surrender and elevation on a spiritual level.

At the core of these vital lessons is a redefinition of power as something other than domination or control. Our current thinking associates power with the ability to shut down choices for other people. We need to demonstrate that power can also mean the ability to open up possibilities for the fulfillment of ourselves and of others. Applied in a social sense, this is the type of power that rebuilds and resurrects, that energizes hope, that heals wounds rather than creates them. Ideally this power does not corrupt but purifies; it augments rather than diminishes human potential.

We need a new vocabulary for intimacy. What we hear on a daily basis in public places is hurtful, vicious, and utterly unrelated to joy. The Top Ten music videos notwithstanding, we must not be afraid to assert that love is more than passion and that passion is a great deal more than genital friction. Sexuality begins with knowing that we matter and deserve to be cared about. Similarly, hurt, shame, and low self-esteem result when we are convinced that we are undeserving of anything else.

An assault upon a woman's sexuality is the bedrock symbol of male supremacy. Those men who exult in this kind of violation are not necessarily out of touch with their feelings. To the contrary, they may be tapping into feelings of control and dominance, however perverse. On the other hand they may see in the suffering of their victims a mirror image of their own childhood degradation. Sadly enough, it is perhaps only in a culture supportive of such degradation that men can continue to boast about their misdeeds in the company of other men without fear of retaliation or ostracism.

To men of African descent everywhere, I offer this last challenge: Let us strive to be loved rather than feared in our homes, where we work, and with each other. To make this choice and to work diligently toward it as a goal would be the benchmark for a kind of freedom our world has rarely seen but now needs in abundance.

W.J. MUSA MOORE-FOSTER is a multicultural educator and consultant whose areas of concentration are history, literature, women's studies and public policy. He has had over twenty years experience in post-secondary instruction and has conducted primary research on major projects on the family life of African American males. A human rights activist since the age of fifteen, he has worked with the National Welfare Rights Organization, the Black Land Movement and the Poor People's Campaign. Moore-Foster is a board member of Black, Indian, Hispanic and Asian Women in Action (BIHA) and dedicates this essay to Alice Lynch, its Executive Director. He currently coordinates diversity resources related to student services and staff development for school districts and for other clients through his consulting firm, the tertius group, inc. He lives with his wife and two daughters in Maplewood, Minnesota, where he is completing a doctoral program in the History of African Peoples at the University of Minnesota.

WHOSE BODY IS IT, ANYWAY?
Transforming Ourselves to Change a Rape Culture

by Pamela R. Fletcher

Being in this intimate relationship with my young body,
I grew to understand and confirm three things: my body
belongs exclusively to me, my soul is not at rest when
my body is detached, and we (body and soul)
must take good care of each other.

RAPE

I never heard the word while growing up. Or, if I had, I blocked it out because its meaning was too horrific for my young mind: a stranger, a weapon, a dark place, blood, pain, even death. But I do remember other people's responses to it, especially those of women. I specifically remember hearing about Rachel when I was in high school in the '70s. The story was that she "let" a group of boys "pull a train" on her in the football field one night. I remember the snickers and the looks of disgust of both the girls and the boys around campus. It was common knowledge that nobody with eyes would want to fuck Rachel; she had a face marred by acne and glasses. But, she had *some* body.

While I am writing this essay, I remember the stark sadness and confusion I felt then. This same sadness returns to me now, but I am no longer confused. Then I wondered how she could "do" so many guys and actually like it (!). Then I thought maybe she didn't like it after all, and maybe, just maybe, they made her do it. But the word rape never entered my mind. After all, she knew them, didn't she? There was no weapon, no blood. She survived, didn't she? And, just what was she doing there all by herself, anyway? Now, I know what "pulling a train" is. Now I know they committed a violent crime against her body and her soul. Now I know why she walked around campus with that wounded face, a face that none of us girls wanted to look into because we knew intuitively that we would see a reflection of our own wounded selves. So the other girls did not look into her eyes. They avoided her and talked about her like she was "a bitch in heat." Why else would such a thing have happened to her?

I tried to look into Rachel's eyes because I wanted to know something—what, I didn't know. But she looked down or looked away or laughed like a lunatic, you know, in that eerie, loud, nervous manner that irritated and frightened me because it didn't ring true. Now I wonder if she thought such laughter would mask her pain. It didn't.

PAINFUL SILENCE AND DEEP-SEATED RAGE

I remember another story I heard while I was in college. Larry told me that his close friend, Brenda, let Danny stay over one night in her summer apartment after they had smoked some dope, and he raped her. Larry actually said that word.

"Don't tell anyone," Brenda begged him. "I never should have let him spend the night. I thought he was my friend."

Larry told me not to ever repeat it to anyone else. And, trying to be a loyal girlfriend to him and a loyal friend to Brenda, I didn't say anything. When we saw Danny later at another friend's place, we neither confronted nor ignored him. *We acted as though everything was normal.* I felt agitated and angry. I wondered why Larry didn't say anything to Danny, you know, man-to-man, like: "That shit was not cool, man. Why you go and do somethin' like that to the sista?"

It never occurred to me to say anything to Brenda, because I wasn't supposed to know, or I was supposed to act as though I didn't know, stupid stuff like that. I sat there, disconnected from her, watching her interact with people, Danny among them, acting as though everything was normal.

DENIAL

Since I began writing this essay two months ago, I have had such difficulty thinking about my own related experiences. I hadn't experienced rape. Or, had I? For months, in the hard drive of my subconscious mind, I searched for files that would yield any incidence of sexual violence or sexual terrorism. When certain memories surfaced, I questioned whether those experiences were "real rapes."

I have some very early recollections that challenge me. Max, my first boyfriend, my childhood sweetheart, tried to pressure me into having sex with him when we were in junior high. Two of my friends, who were the girlfriends of his two closest friends, also tried to pressure me because they were already "doing it" for their "men."

"Don't be a baby," they teased. "Everybody's doing it."

But I wouldn't cave in, and I broke up with Max because he wasn't a decent boy.

A year later, when we reached high school, I went crawling back to Max because I "loved" him and couldn't stand his ignoring me. He stopped ignoring me long enough to pin me up against the locker to kiss me roughly and to suck on my neck long and hard until he produced sore, purple bruises, what we called hickies. I had to hide those hideous marks from my parents by wearing turtleneck sweaters. Those hickies marked me as his property and gave his friends the impression that he had "done" me, even though we hadn't gotten that far yet. We still had to work out the logistics.

I hated when he gave me hickies, and I didn't like his exploring my private places as he emotionally and verbally abused me, telling me I wasn't pretty like Susan: "Why can't you look like her?" And I remember saying something like, "Why don't you go be with her, if that's what you want?" He answered me with a piercing "don't-you-ever-talk-to-me-like-that-again" look, and I never asked again. He continued, however, to ask me the same question.

In my heart, I realized that the way he treated me was wrong because I felt violated; I felt separated from my body, as if it did not belong to me. But at sixteen I didn't know how or what to feel, except that I felt confused and desperately wanted to make sense out of what it meant to be a girl trapped inside a woman's body. Yes, I felt trapped, because I understood that we girls had so much to lose now that we could get pregnant. Life sagged with seriousness. Now everybody kept an eye on us: our parents, the churches, the schools, and the boys. Confusion prevailed. While we were encouraged to have a slight interest in boys (lest we turn out "funny") so that ultimately we could be trained to become good wives, we were instructed directly and indirectly to keep a safe distance away from them.

We liked boys and we thought we wanted love, but what we really wanted as youth was to have some fun, some clean, innocent fun until we got married and gave our virtuous selves to our husbands just as our mothers had done. We female children had inherited this lovely vision from our mothers and from fairy tales. Yet now we know that those visions were not so much what our mothers had experienced, but what they wished they had experienced, and what they wanted for us.

We thought "going with a boy" in the early '70s would be romance-filled fun that involved holding hands, stealing kisses, exchanging class rings, and wearing big lettered sweaters. Maybe it was, for some of us. But I know that many of us suffered at the hands of love.

I soon learned in high school that it was normal to be mistreated by our boyfriends. Why else would none of us admit to each other the abuse we tolerated? These boys "loved" us, so we believed that they were entitled to treat us in any way they chose. We believed that somehow we belonged to them, body and soul. Isn't that what many of the songs on the radio said? And we just knew somehow that if we did give in to them, we deserved whatever happened, and if we didn't give in, we still deserved whatever happened. Such abuse was rampant because we became and remained isolated from each other by hoisting our romances above our friendships.

We didn't define what they did to us as rape, molestation, or sexual abuse. We called it love. We called it love if it happened with our boyfriends, and we called other girls whores and sluts if it happened with someone else's boyfriend or boyfriends, as in the case of Rachel and "the train."

We called it love because we had tasted that sweet taste of pain. Weren't they one and the same?

REALIZATION

One sharp slap from Max one day delivered the good sense I had somehow lost when I got to high school. After that point I refused to be his woman, his property. When I left home for college, I left with the keen awareness that I had better take good care of myself. In my involvement with Max, I had allowed a split to occur between my body and my soul, and I had to work on becoming whole again.

I knew that I was growing stronger (though in silent isolation from other young women and through intense struggle) when I was able to successfully resist being seduced (read: molested) by several college classmates and when I successfully fought off the violent advances and the verbal abuse (what I now recognize as an attempted rape) of someone with whom I had once been sexually intimate.

But how does a woman become strong and whole in a society in which women are not permitted (as if we need permission!) to possess ourselves, to own our very bodies? We females often think we are not entitled to ourselves, and many times we give ourselves away for less than a song. The sad truth of the matter is that this is how we have managed to survive in our male-dominated culture. Yet, in the wise words of the late Audre Lorde, "the Master's tools will never dismantle the Master's house." In other words, as long as we remain disconnected from ourselves and each other and dependent on abusive males, we will remain weak, powerless, and fragmented.

A NOT-SO-AMBIGUOUS BEGINNING

I am cute and three years old. My mother has braided my hair and decorated it with red barrettes. I sit on the edge of the couch dressed in a red checkered jumper that ties in the back. I swing my legs back and forth, back and forth. I lift and spread them in the air. I am making a discovery. I am in awe of my long legs and the way they move. My body tingles with pleasure. This is how a sparrow must feel while soaring freely in the sky.

"Don't ever do that again," my father says. "Always sit with your legs closed."

Suddenly my joy is squelched by the strange tone of his voice, and I crash.

This is a recurring and haunting memory.

Had I been my brother, I would not have been scolded for exploring my physical prowess. I would not have been commanded to stop my arousing behavior. My father was only doing his duty to control me and to train me to be his proper, feminine little girl. But what is so wrong about a girl knowing and appreciating her body? Whose body is it, anyway? My tender, indomitable spirit would not surrender.

In discovering quite early that there is a strong and essential connection between body and soul, I could not stop loving and moving my legs. I simply moved my body out of my father's sight whenever my soul wanted to enter into the purely physical world that liberated me from my constrictive surroundings. In that other world I ran races, climbed trees, roller-skated, hopscotched, and tusseled with the neighborhood boys while wearing dresses with shorts underneath. And don't ask me why, but I never ever thought that the boys were stronger and faster and braver than I. Many of them could not even compete against me, especially in races. Fortunately, I had yet to encounter the myth that boys are inherently better athletes than girls. It never occurred to me to be worried about my being a girl who was really acting like a boy. I only did what was natural. I was in love with my body, so if it enjoyed doing wild things, I had to make it happy.

Being in this intimate relationship with my young body, I grew to understand and confirm three things: my body belongs exclusively to me, my soul is not at rest when my body is detached, and we (body and soul) must take good care of each other. As a black woman-child living in a predominantly white, suburban world, I had to find ways to invent an affirmative reality, and I used my body to help me cement the cracks in my soul split by the daily onslaught of the racism that prevailed outside my home and the sexism that permeated the air inside it. In elementary and junior high school I became an athlete, specifically a runner. I sprinted the fifty-yard dash to keep from dying inside and leaped the broad jump to forget momentarily what I had to remember: I am constantly at odds with the white and male world.

Ironically, my father was quite pleased with my first-place accomplishments in the fifty- and one hundred-yard dashes and the 440 relay race in which I always held the anchor position.

"You could win gold metals just like Wilma Rudolph," he said one day. He rarely missed my practices and never missed my races.

"We're going to go to the Olympics," he announced on another day with a smile. He was quite serious and began to coach me on the side.

My mother, on the other hand, would have nothing to do with my athletic ability or activity. It embarrassed her. "I don't know why you want to do something that's going to make your legs look muscular and ugly like a boy's."

I longed for her approval. Since she had enrolled me in ballet and tap dance lessons when I was a child, I assumed that she would be supportive of my joining a dance troupe in high school. One day I came home with my costume, ready to demonstrate the dance I had choreographed for an upcoming performance. I put on the gold leotard and the leopard-print wraparound skirt and began to move like a sultry big cat.

"Look how skinny you are!" she laughed.

I evaporated into a wisp. Up to that moment I was quite proud of my body because it was strong and supple, so I was confused by her outburst. At the time I didn't know what she meant by it. I just knew that somehow I felt ashamed. Later, during my dance performance, my mother's laughter and words resounded in my head, and I wished she and my shame would disappear from the auditorium.

I now know that I suffered the same bewilderment I had encountered as that three-year-old child with her legs sticking straight up in the air.

Just like that child, I was doing something natural and liberating, and she, just like my father, focused solely on my body and ignored my soul. Now I know that they were distracted and troubled by the freedom I granted my body and the joy I took in connecting to myself. After all, as a female I was supposed to be bashful, restrained, and disconnected. They felt uncomfortable with my love for my body and for physical pleasure; they associated the body with *shame.*

Both times my soul parried their attempts to subjugate my body. I would not allow them to constrict me because I could not allow them to split me in half, taking away my selfhood, diluting my power.

I stopped running in high school and began to dance seriously, later joining a dance troupe in college. After college I continued to dance, run, and do whatever I felt I needed to do to free myself from the trap that society had set for women like me.

THE MORE THINGS CHANGE . . . OR, A 1990s TALE

What I did not realize then as a woman-child and what I know now is that the body and soul connection I derived from my physical activity built a strong sense of self that I now exude. This self-contained, self-assured image is what others see, especially those men who are prone to victimize and rape women. This is not an image I can see so readily, but my friends and colleagues see it: "You walk in like you own the place," or "You move around with that 'don't-you-dare-mess-with-me' look." I've often heard, "You don't look like a victim." This "attitude" that I convey is rarely staged intentionally. It must be my soul guarding my body from anyone's attempt to split me in half.

I am not naive nor arrogant enough to think that, because of this image, I could never or will never be raped or molested. I know all too well that I cannot control everything—or anything, for that matter. For instance, if the conditions are just right and if someone considers you vulnerable, he will strike.

Let me illustrate. In September 1992, I was granted a six-week residency at a Wyoming arts program to work on a novel-in-progress. During that six-week retreat, I wrote and took the necessary time to recuperate from the recent and tragic death of my partner, with whom I had had a six-year relationship. Five of those years we had shared a home. Wyoming's desolate but serene landscape calmed me, and each day I grew spiritually stronger as I healed.

The evening before my departure, the evening before I was to venture out into the real world again, my new friends, the other residents, and I sat together at the dining table for a special going-away meal for the three of us who were leaving the next day. During our wonderfully prepared meal, we were bothered by the thick, strong smell of smoke, but we didn't see any sign of fire. As the sun set, we discovered a gray, ominous cloud of smoke and the glorious blaze of a brush fire. I had never witnessed such a sight in person before. I was both mesmerized and frightened by it. It seemed so close. In fact, it was rapidly approaching our ranch. Volunteer fire fighters soon lined their pickup trucks along the dirt road next to the ranch. We were instructed to go to a neighboring town located twenty miles away.

The group, seven women and one man, decided to seek refuge in a bar until further notice. I had an immediate gut reaction about going to a bar because 1) I don't drink, and 2) I don't trust drunk white males. I was the only black person and I felt unsafe. I determined, however, that I would be safer with the group than I would be staying somewhere else alone. Against my better judgment, I went to this white bar in a white town, and I held my breath.

I was in that bar for about fifteen minutes when I encountered a large, drunk white cowboy who asked me to dance. I politely declined his invitation. Before I knew it, he put down his beer bottle and began to fidget with the fanny bag that hung around my waist. I had everything of value that I could fit inside that small pouch: cash, traveler's checks, credit cards, airline tickets, and my medicine bag.

Alarmed, I asked him, "What are you doing?"

"I'm turning this around so we can dance."

"ButIsaidIdon'twannadance."

He ignored me and then seized me by my waist, lifting me up from my stool. Then he began to carry me to the dance floor with his arms wrapped tightly around my torso. The right side of my face smashed against his chest. My feet dangled below me. Realizing that my legs could not touch the ground, I suddenly became unglued. I felt shocked and afraid. How could I get away if my legs were immobilized? I repeated as calmly and slowly as possible, "I told you I don't want to dance with you. Leave me alone." I also felt stupid and wondered how I could have allowed myself to be in this white bar surrounded by virtual strangers.

When I told him that there was no music playing, he said, "Who needs music?" He continued to carry me toward the bandstand. Nearby was a pool table. Scenes of *The Accused,* a movie based on a true story in which a woman gets raped on a pool table in a bar in Bedford, Massachusetts, played in my head in accelerated motion. I thought, "I'm going to be raped. This is how it happens. I'm going to be raped." I could not believe this situation was happening to me; I felt utterly alone and terrified. Would anyone help me? Would anyone care?

Although I did and said all I could to resist, this man, who held me so tightly I felt as if he were crushing my bones, would not hear my voice. Finally John, the lone man in my group, jumped up.

"Leave her alone; she's with me," he said, rushing up to him.

John had to say it several times before the drunk man acknowledged his male voice and released me.

"All right, buddy, she's all yours," the cowboy said, jovially slapping John on his back. Actually, I was bracing myself for a barroom brawl.

What struck me at that point was that it was not safe for me to be there without a man to claim me; it took a man to save me from another man. Crudely speaking, it was a transfer of property. My body did not belong to me. It belonged to one of them. And I could not help but wonder how much my color played a part in this madness. After all, when the cowboy entered the bar with two of his friends, they immediately walked up to me, and one of them announced, "We saw you walking around today." One frightening thing about this announcement was that when they saw me that afternoon, I was twenty miles away from that bar, strolling along the dirt road near the residency ranch, and I had not noticed them driving by.

The other frightening thing is that they paid little or no attention to the white women in my group. As John so astutely observed, "You were prey, Pamela. I've never seen anything like it. It was like watching *Thelma and Louise.*" John also said that he could vividly imagine what fantasies went through their minds earlier when they spied me, an attractive African-American woman wandering around the countryside (an odd sight, indeed), and when they saw me later as they walked through the door of that bar. I, too, can imagine what they saw: a hot, wild, and wanton dark body for their pleasure.

Lord knows I was fortunate to escape that place physically unscathed. But, days later, I could still feel his rough grasp around my waist. My body felt so sore, I wondered if I was only imagining that the hurt was there when it was really in my soul; I felt like such a fool. That night, unlike any other time, my soul suffered a deep wound that has yet to heal. I'm certain that other such incidences pierced my soul, but this time was different somehow. This time it happened in the presence of other people, other women, who felt no affinity with me, who could not or would not identify with my precarious condition. As a result, it is difficult not to blame myself or not to feel ashamed, especially when the women in my group told me, "It wasn't personal, Pamela. They were only trying to be friendly, but they didn't know how to be," and "It's because you look so exotic, you know." And the final blow delivered with sharp laughter: "Do you always get hit on like this?" Their insensitivity stabbed me. I wonder just how impassive they would have been had the situation been reversed, had one of them found herself molested by a large, drunk black man in a black bar in a black town. I found it ironic and painful that John realized and admitted what they dared not acknowledge. He was the courageous and compassionate one. Those women epitomized the mark of female oppression: they entered into a conspiracy with the white patriarchy for a false sense of security. Did they forsake their femaleness to reap the benefits of their white skin privilege? If I had been white, would they have had a similar response? Whatever influenced them consciously or unconsciously, they merely reaffirmed and reinforced a sexist and racist white male-dominated culture. I fear that I could have been raped, and these women would have done nothing to help me.

Despite how alone and frightened I felt, I knew that I was not going to yield to that man under any circumstances. My body is mine, and I had a right to refuse to give it to him, even in a dance. Somehow I remained calm, even when another man, who walked into the bar immediately following the incident, approached only me for a dance. I wanted to scream: "Do I have a goddamn open season sign on my forehead, you crazy jerks?" I felt so angry and violated, I wanted to blast all of them, both the men and women. My friends tell me that I managed to get out of there safely because I didn't break under the man's pressure. I am uncertain and full of rage.

A CALL FOR SELF-EXAMINATION AND TRUE CHANGE

I am certain, however, that while today we females cannot control the violent world in which we live, we must take control over our bodies. To me, it is at least one step we can take to challenge this rape culture in which we live. In protecting ourselves, we must realize that we cannot afford to continue to dissociate our bodies from our souls. We must claim ourselves as whole human beings. When we are empowered physically, we are both spiritually and physically strong. Being in tune with our bodies helps us to trust our instincts. We are aware of what is going on around us and are able to guard ourselves against danger. When and if we are in danger, we are able to rely on our physical selves as much as possible to free ourselves from harm because we know and trust our strength. When our souls are connected to our bodies, we do not allow our bodies to be taken for granted or to be taken away from us—at least not without a struggle.

I envision a world in which all girls are free to experience and move our bodies as we grow into ourselves. I hope for a time when females are no longer afraid to move and push our bodies because we no longer believe the myths that competition is not feminine, that we are less competitive and aggressive than males, that we cannot attain peak athletic performance during menstruation, that weight lifting builds large muscles in females, that contact sports harm our reproductive organs and breasts, and that we cannot regain physical prowess after childbirth. I envision a world in which it is just as common and natural for females as it is for males to be physically active in any sport or activity we choose.

This new world is only possible when we women take control over our body imagery. As long as we believe that we are weak and dependent on men for our self/body definitions and for our safety, we will continue to be paralyzed by our fears and controlled by our sense of inferiority.

Moreover, we must realize how much we, ourselves, perpetuate our rape culture when we abandon, reject, and alienate our selves and each other. Yes, it is quite difficult to admit, but we must be honest with ourselves and each other if we are ever to heal. Just imagine how different our lives would be today if we were not injured by internalized misogyny and sexism. Imagine how different our lives would be if we would only open our mouths wide and collectively and loudly confront males and *really* hold them accountable for the violent crimes they perpetrate against females. Imagine how our lives would be if all mothers tell their daughters the truth about romantic love and teach them to love themselves as females, to value and claim their bodies, and to protect themselves against violent and disrespectful males.

What if we girls in junior high and high school believed we deserve respect rather than verbal and sexual abuse from our male classmates? What if we girls in my high school had confronted the gang of boys who raped Rachel that night in the football field twenty years ago, rather than perpetuated that cycle of abuse and shame she suffered? What if Larry and I had confronted Danny for raping Brenda that summer night in her apartment? What if Brenda had felt safe enough to tell Larry, me, and the police? What if the women in Wyoming had confronted that man while he terrorized me rather than defended him? What if they had protected, comforted, and supported me? What if we females believed ourselves and each other to be as important and deserving of our selfhood as we believe males to be? Just imagine.

Envision a time when we women are connected to ourselves and each other, when we no longer feel the need and desire to conspire with men against each other in order to survive in a misogynist, violent culture. We must alter our destructive thinking about being female so that we can begin to accept, love, and cherish our femaleness. It is the essence of our lives.

Readjusting our lens so we can begin to see ourselves and each other as full, capable, and mighty human beings will take as much work as reconstructing our violent society. Neither job is easy, but the conditions and the tasks go hand in hand. Two ways to begin our own transformation are to become physically active in whatever manner we choose so we can take pleasure in fully connecting to ourselves and in growing physically stronger, and to respect, protect, support, and comfort each other. Once we stop denying that our very lives are endangered, we will soon discover that these steps are not only necessary but viable in empowering ourselves and claiming our right to exist as whole human beings in a peaceful, humane world.

PAMELA R. FLETCHER is a writer who teaches writing, literature, and women's studies courses. She has taught at the University of Minnesota, Carleton College, and the Loft: A Place for Writing and Literature. Currently she teaches at North Hennepin Community College in Brooklyn Park, Minnesota.

THE NOT YET SPOKEN

by Susan Griffin

The erotic life no longer defined by conquest and
dominion or submission seems endless in its own
surprises. New solar systems, whole galaxies,
appear just on the surface of the skin.

ACULTURE WITHOUT RAPE. What would it be? This is a daunting question. Rape is not an isolated event. So much surrounds it, preceding and following, as cause and effect. Not only social structure, the father as head of the household, but theology, God in the image of man, not woman. Not only gender, the idea of masculinity as aggressive, but an unspoken quality of mind born of an atmosphere of assumed, often invisible violence.

And the absence of this violence? The thought perhaps is too terrifying to imagine. Such tenderness when one has learned so well to survive in a more brutal environment.

I am thinking now of my own writing. Years of exploring who we are now, this wounded state, the history of our suffering. What, then, do I write in this New World?

The very medium of my work is threatened. Language, the shape of the sentence, words, the sound of speech, even thought itself, or at least the shape of thought, possibly consciousness, and certainly, literary form.

Blank as a white page for a moment, I am silent.

And then in the silence, I begin to sense some other being. Out there at the edge of the circle of my focus, is something barely visible, hardly heard, felt more than anything, but delicately. Though this peripheral consciousness is neither delicate nor frail. For look, it persists, and as I listen more closely, I realize this oddity has some familiarity, has in fact been with me for years. Surviving all skepticism, all warnings to disappear, this stubborn chrysalis of an existence is as old as I am.

And how would I describe It? Existing at the edge of my awareness, this phenomenon seems both inside and outside my own existence. As I write I experience it as longing, despair, frustration. My inclination is to take my sentences and my words and shake them loose. Because just underneath or inextricably mixed with the old syntax, there is a whisper. A hint of another voice, with so much more in it.

I might say to you that this nascent voice, just now brushing against my ears, is rich with complexity. But then again, it is not at all dense. Rather, the opposite is true. This is a voice containing much more space than I had imagined a voice could have. Not a hemming and hawing kind of space. But that species of space that exists in music. The resonance of the air, even in silence, is somehow affected.

Which makes sense of course because, as I am just beginning to grasp now, this voice is the sound of the Not Yet Spoken.

Similar to yet also distinct from the sound of those secrets told in the back rooms of a house.

Were they not the first words I ever learned about sex? That triangle I liked to put my hand to as a child. My grandmother taking me to the back of the house. Telling me I mustn't put my hand there. The men look. And we must not let them see.

No, this is a different unspoken. Although I wonder now if the Not Yet Spoken is in part a legacy of years of forced silence. Pushed out of language, the wordless world becomes more vibrant to us.

I am thinking of that wonderful film *Daughters of the Dust*, the way this work portrays the effects of history and social systems on language. There is an unwritten law that the master enforces on the slave requiring the repression of a whole range of thought and feeling. Yet that which is forbidden persists, goes on, develops in other forms. There are two languages in the film. One spoken, a rich evocative dialogue laden with different levels of meaning. But the camera records another language too, what Julie Dash, the maker of the film, calls "the nonverbal means of communicating" which has been in the process of creation "since the time of slavery."

What would such a language be if released from the imprisoning circumstance of its birth?

A language that does not buttonhole, pinion, make a conquest of and a privileged claim on being.

Two hundred years into the future when It has taken Its rightful place in our mouths, I picture my grandmother speaking gently, with a slant metaphor (shaped like an open door), of the magic of triangles. *Oh, triangles! Triangles!* she will nearly sing. *What magic in triangles.*

She will not be more explicit. Is this modesty or coyness or fear? No, merely that, in some contexts, the explicit is considered reductive because it robs us of the many dimensions, the largeness of experience.

But what about precision?

Might not new words be required for us to speak to each other? Because this new consciousness has ushered in such a vast perceptual field: what was there all along except that we were too crude to see it. Those old plots: boy gets girl; boy overtakes and forces girl; boy sweeps girl off her feet; girl lies under boy glad to be taken; girl twines around boy like vine to rod; girl stands still, waiting for boy to chase her; etc., etc., etc., those old plots have faded away; they are no longer interesting, they seem archaic. And in their place, a multitude of stories spring up revealing nuances, moods, glances, conversations, qualities of touch, moments of meeting, exchanges that two centuries ago escaped us entirely.

It is what long ago opened up between two women, beyond the roles of gender, a psychological terrain infinitely more variegated, subtle, even startling.

And could it be that the old violence with its ability to shock and startle filled a void made by the too predictable plot?

The rigid roles we once played as men and women robbed us of our birthright, an infinitely more complex range of being belonging to us all. To repeat and repeat the old stories, so automatically, bending our thoughts and feelings like trees into the straightened lines of railway tracks going nowhere new, sent us into a despairing boredom. The inner coherence having been lost, there seemed no use to these efforts. So violence seemed in those days like life returning, blood red, primary and intense, unfettered.

It was of course the same with sensation. In those who were numbed by trauma, the infliction or suffering of pain was used to enliven feeling. But that is the old culture.

Now, two hundred years hence, there is no question of that void. The erotic life no longer defined by conquest and dominion or submission seems endless in its own surprises. New solar systems, whole galaxies, appear just on the surface of the skin. And just as the Inuit people need many words for snow, our erotic lexicon has expanded too. Cascades of words drop off the tongue. And the geography of language, the sounding and hearing board of grammar, allows for a more sensitively calibrated movement of mind than one would have imagined before. It is no longer (subject) white knight (verb) sweeps (object) lady off her (indirect object) feet. Grammar has become more supple, like a strong but not overdeveloped muscle, able to shift with sudden grace, wash like a wave of sensation through consciousness.

But now I am pausing. My breath is momentarily taken away. Yet I am not certain how to proceed. Some consideration is making me uncomfortable. What about the old, I wonder. I am thinking of the foghorns in San Francisco Bay. Some practical engineers replaced them with newer, more efficient models. But the sound was thin, tinny, false. Everyone rebelled against them. We wanted back the old sound. Slightly forlorn, bass tones swelling mournfully as the gray mist enshrouded us.

And now I am slightly indignant. Is It a merciless revolutionary, a Robespierre or Stalin of language calling for the destruction of age-old traditions, sounds that over time have acquired a certain patina, have in them histories that go back centuries, structures, words, usages, rhymes, forms with which I know as a writer I can evoke whole worlds in an instant?

With the dispensing of certain Tragic plots, will It be foolishly attempting to eradicate the dark altogether, instituting a Brave New World of Hallmark Card sentiments, insipid, boring, and in some terrible way, a lie?

But no, as I catch another glimpse of the Not Yet Spoken shrinking at the borders of my imagination, I see I have mistaken Its nature altogether. It is not without revolutionary fervor, but It has a more organic nature in the manner It chooses to come into being. It prefers play to slash-and-burn. Turns cliché inside out. Makes use of the familiar to surprise. The old tune (as in a rendition by Thelonious Monk) contains a very new phrasing, which, one feels, must have been there all along. In the old world and its associations, many others are discovered.

I am reminded then that we do not heal from the past by forgetting it. The dark does not disappear. There is memory. There are aftershocks. And even as the aftereffects unto many generations begin to disappear, there is the dark within us. That old plot in which the heroine or hero must conquer an enemy, slay a dragon, or return with a prize has been refigured. The enemy is not outside us but in us.

And is this terrifying? Yes. But also thrilling, provoking another kind of courage that gives us more than death. Indeed perhaps that old grammar—subject, verb, object—can be continued. But now object and subject are seen to partake of each other, and so the sentence is no longer simply linear; it is a circle, and all pronouns are reflexive.

But does this imply a monolithic sameness? The end to all difference, conflict, variety, or even perspective? No. In this yet-to-be-born rhetoric, debate and disagreement, discernment, disputation, and argument remain, even flourish. It is simply that lines are not drawn so rigidly. The greatest dialogues are noted for certain qualities of ambiguity, for transformations occurring in the midst of exchange. An orator is never humiliated for being proven wrong. The standard aims more toward grace and flexibility, for a desire to know so fervent that the speaker is swept away from the realm of ego and becomes by passionate embrace a lover of what is.

For existence, as we understand It in this future time, is not something to be possessed or dominated, controlled or violated. It is the greatness and largeness inside and outside of ourselves, a mystery and yet known, seeking to be spoken. And if we always fail somehow in our efforts to capture it, how could it be otherwise? The Not Yet Spoken is always changing. And we know this. The very word "rape" with its terrible history has come also to signify "the resistance to change in all Its manifestations." And the word "rapist": "one who is afraid of his or her own nature; therefore, dangerous."

SUSAN GRIFFIN is a writer, poet, and playwright whose work is known for innovation both in literary form and social thought. She is the author of several ground-breaking books, each of which has helped to shape movements for social change, including *Woman and Nature, Pornography and Silence,* and *Rape, the Politics of Consciousness.* Her latest book, *A Chorus of Stones: The Private Life of War,* brings the question of gender to bear on war and the history of nuclear weapons. This work was nominated for a National Book Critics Award, was a jury nominee for a Pulitzer Prize, and won the Bay Area Book Reviewer's Association Award for Non-Fiction. Her play *Voices* won an Emmy Award, and her most recent collection of poetry, *Unremembered Country* received a Silver Medal from the California Commonwealth Club. She has also been awarded an NEA grant and a MacArthur Fellowship for Peace and International Cooperation.

ORGANIZATIONS TO CONTACT

There are hundreds of organizations working on issues related to *Transforming a Rape Culture*. The following list includes just a few of the national organizations and resources, many of which have state or local chapters as well.

Center for the Prevention of Sexual and Domestic Violence
1914 N. 34th St., Suite 105
Seattle, WA 98103
(206) 634–1903

Challenging Media Images of Women
P.O. Box 902
Framingham, MA 01701
(508) 879-8504

Clearinghouse on Child Abuse and Neglect Information
P.O. Box 1182
Washington, D.C. 20013
(703) 821–2086

Committee for Children
172 20th Ave.
Seattle, WA 98122
(206) 322–5050

The Feminist Institute Clearinghouse
P.O. Box 30563
Bethesda, MD 20814
(301) 951–9040

Foundation for the Prevention of Sexual Harassment
and Workplace Discrimination
601 13th St. N.W., Suite 1150
Washington, DC 20005
(202) 393-0091

Men Overcoming Violence (MOVE)
54 Mint St., Suite 300
San Francisco, CA 94103
(415) 777-4496

Men's Anti-Rape Resource Center
P.O. Box 73559
Washington, DC 20056
(202) 529-7239

National Assault Prevention Center
P.O. Box 02005
Columbus, OH 43202
(614) 291–2540

National Clearinghouse on Marital and Date Rape
2325 Oak St.
Berkeley, CA 94708
(510) 524-1582

National Coalition Against Domestic Violence
P.O. Box 15127
Washington, D.C. 20003
(202) 638-6388

National Coalition Against Sexual Assault
2428 Ontario Rd. NW
Washington, D.C. 20009
(202) 483–7165

National Organization for Men Against Sexism (NOMAS)
54 Mint St., Suite 300
San Francisco, CA 94103
(415) 546-6627

National Organization for Women
1000 16th St. NW, Suite 920
Washington, D.C. 20036
(202) 331–0066

National Victim Center
309 W. 7th St., Suite 705
Fort Worth, TX 76102
(817) 877–3355

Women Against Pornography
P.O. Box 845, Times Square Station
New York, NY 10036
(212) 307–5055

ADDITIONAL READING

Assiter, Alison. *Pornography, Feminism and the Individual.* Concord, MA: Pluto Press, 1989.

Bart, Pauline B., and Patricia H. O'Brien. *Stopping Rape: Successful Survival Strategies.* New York: Pergamon Press Inc., 1985.

Bode, Janet. *Voices of Rape.* New York: Franklin Watts, 1990.

Brittan, Arthur. *Masculinity and Power.* New York: Basil Blackwell, Inc., 1989.

Brownmiller, Susan. *Against Our Will: Men, Women and Rape.* New York: Bantam Books, 1975.

Dworkin, Andrea. *Pornography: Men Possessing Women.* New York: GP Putnam's Sons, 1979.

————. *Intercourse.* New York: The Free Press, 1987.

Eisler, Riane. *The Chalice and the Blade: Our History, Our Future.* New York: HarperCollins, 1987.

Faust, Beatrice. *Women, Sex and Pornography: A Controversial Study.* New York: Macmillan, 1980.

Gilligan, Carol, Nona P. Lyons, and Trudy J. Hanmer, eds. *Making Connections: The Relational Worlds of Adolescent Girls at Emma Willard School.* Cambridge, MA: Harvard Univ. Press, 1989.

Gilman, Charlotte Perkins. *Herland and Other Stories.* Edited by Barbara H. Soloman. New York: Signet Classic, 1992.

Gorman, Carol. *Pornography.* New York: Franklin Watts, 1980.

Griffin, Susan. *Pornography and Silence.* New York: Harper and Row Publishers, 1981.

Gubar, Susan, and Joan Hoff. *For Adult Users Only: The Dilemma of Violent Pornography.* Bloomington: Indiana Univ. Press, 1989.

Guberman, Connie, and Margie Wolfe, eds. *No Safe Place: Violence Against Women and Children.* Toronto: The Women's Press, 1985.

Guernsey, JoAnn Bren. *The Facts About Rape.* New York: Crestwood House, 1990.

Hagan, Kay Leigh, ed. *Women Respond to the Men's Movement.* San Francisco: Harper-SanFrancisco, 1992.

Hazen, Helen. *Endless Rapture: Rape, Romance and the Female Imagination.* New York: Charles Scribner's Sons, 1983.

Heilbrun, Carolyn G. *Reinventing Womanhood.* New York: W. W. Norton and Co., 1979.

Jackson, Donna. *How to Make the World a Better Place for Women in Five Minutes a Day.* Los Angeles: Hyperion, 1992.

Kappeler, Susanne. *The Pornography of Representation.* Minneapolis: Univ. of Minnesota Press, 1986.

Kimmel, Michael S., ed. *Men Confront Pornography.* New York: Crown Publishers, Inc., 1990.

Kivel, Paul. *Men's Work: How to Stop the Violence That Tears Our Lives Apart.* Center City, MN: Hazelden Educational Materials, 1992.

Leghorn, Lisa, and Katherine Parker. *Woman's Worth: Sexual Economics and the World of Women.* Boston: Routledge and Kegan Paul, 1981.

Le Guin, Ursula K. *Always Coming Home*. New York: Bantam Books, 1985.

Levy, Barrie, ed. *Dating Violence: Young Women in Danger*. Seattle: Seal Press, 1990.

MacKinnon, Catharine A. *Feminism Unmodified: Discourses in Life and Law*. Cambridge, MA: Harvard Univ. Press, 1987.

Madigan, Lee, and Nancy Gamble. *The Second Rape: Society's Continual Betrayal of the Victim*. New York: Lexington Books, 1991.

Mamonova, Tatyana. *Women and Russia: Feminist Writings from the Soviet Union*. Boston: Beacon Press, 1984.

Medea, Andrea, and Kathleen Thompson. *Against Rape: A Survival Manual for Women: How to Avoid Entrapment and How to Cope with Rape Physically and Emotionally*. New York: Farrar, Straus and Giroux, 1974.

Miedzian, Myriam. *Boys Will Be Boys: Breaking the Link Between Masculinity and Violence*. New York: Doubleday, 1988.

Miles, Rosalind. *Love, Sex, Death, and the Making of the Male*. New York: Summit Books, 1991.

Minnesota Women's Fund Report. *Reflections of Risk. Growing Up Female in Minnesota*. Patrice Tetlin, February 1990.

Parrot, Andrea. *Coping With Date Rape and Acquaintance Rape*. New York: The Rosen Publishing Group, Inc., 1988.

Plaskow, Judith, and Carol P. Christ, eds. *Weaving the Visions: New Patterns in Feminist Spirituality*. San Francisco: HarperSanFrancisco, 1989.

Provenzo, Eugene F., Jr. *Video Kids: Making Sense of Nintendo*. Cambridge, MA: Harvard Univ. Press, 1990.

Ranke-Heinemann, Uta. *Eunuchs for the Kingdom of Heaven: Women, Sexuality, and the Catholic Church*. New York: Penguin Books, 1988.

Rape in America. A Report to the Nation. Prepared by National Victim Center and Crime Victims Research and Treatment Center, 1992.

Reiss, Albert J., Jr., and Jeffrey A. Roth, eds. *Understanding and Preventing Violence*. National Research Council Panel on the Understanding and Control of Violent Behavior. Washington, DC: National Academy Press, 1993.

Ruether, Rosemary Radford, ed. *Religion and Sexism*. New York: Simon and Schuster, 1974.

Russell, Diana E. H. *The Politics of Rape: The Victim's Perspective*. New York: Stein and Day Publishers, 1975.

————. *Rape in Marriage*. Bloomington: Indiana Univ. Press, 1982.

————. *Sexual Exploitation: Rape, Child Sexual Abuse and Workplace Harassment*. Beverly Hills: Sage Publications, 1984.

Sanday, Peggy Reeves. *Fraternity Gang Rape: Sex, Brotherhood, and Privilege on Campus*. New York: New York Univ. Press, 1990.

Sanday, Peggy Reeves, and Ruth Gallagher Goodenough. *Beyond the Second Sex: New Directions in the Anthropology of Gender*. Philadelphia: Univ. of Pennsylvania Press, 1990.

Schuler, Margaret, ed. *Freedom From Violence: A Study of Convicted Rapists*. Cambridge, MA: Unwin Hyman, Inc., 1990.

Senate Judiciary Committee, Majority Staff Report. "The Response to Rape: Detours on the Road to Equal Justice." May 1993.

Shuker-Haines, Frances. *Everything You Need to Know About Date Rape*. New York: The Rosen Publishing Group, Inc., 1990.

Smith, Joan. *Misogynies: Reflections on Myths and Malice*. New York: Fawcett Columbine, 1989.

Snodgrass, Jon, ed. *For Men Against Sexism*. Albion, CA: Times Change Press, 1977.

Stoltenberg, John. *Refusing to Be a Man: Essays on Sex and Justice*. New York: Meridian, 1990.

Tavris, Carol. *The Mismeasure of Woman.* New York: Simon and Schuster, 1992.

Thorne, Barrie. *Gender Play. Girls and Boys in School.* Rutgers, NJ: Rutgers University Press, 1993.

Tomaselli, Sylvana, and Roy Porter, ed. *Rape: An Historical and Social Enquiry.* New York: Basil Blackwell, Inc., 1986.

Tong, Rosemarie. *Women, Sex, and the Law.* New Jersey: Roman and Allanheld, 1984.

U.S. Department of Justice. *Criminal Victimization in the United States.* A National Crime Victimization Survey Report, Bureau of Justice Statistics. December 1992, NCJ-139563.

U.S. Department of Justice. *Female Victims Of Violent Crime.* Prepared by Carolyn Wolf Harlow. Bureau of Justice Statistics. January 1991, NCJ-126826.

Vanderbilt, Heidi. "Incest: A Chilling Report." *Lear's,* February 1992.

WAC STATS. The Facts about Women. The Women's Action Coalition. New York: The New Press, 1993.

Warshaw, Robin. *I Never Called It Rape.* New York: Harper and Row Publishers, 1988.

Wisechild, Louise M., ed. *She Who Was Lost Is Remembered: Healing From Incest Through Creativity.* Seattle: The Seal Press, 1991.

Wolf, Naomi. *The Beauty Myth: How Images of Beauty Are Used Against Women.* New York: Anchor Books, 1991.

INDEX OF CONTRIBUTORS

SUBJECT INDEX

MISSION STATEMENT

Milkweed Editions publishes with the intention of making a humane impact on society, in the belief that literature is a transformative art uniquely able to convey the essential experiences of the human heart and spirit.

To that end, Milkweed Editions publishes distinctive voices of literary merit in handsomely designed, visually dynamic books, exploring the ethical, cultural, and esthetic issues that free societies need continually to address. Milkweed Editions is a not-for-profit press.

.